The common writer in modern history

Manchester University Press

The common writer in modern history

Edited by
Martyn Lyons

MANCHESTER UNIVERSITY PRESS

Copyright © Manchester University Press 2023

While copyright in the volume as a whole is vested in Manchester University Press, copyright in individual chapters belongs to their respective authors, and no chapter may be reproduced wholly or in part without the express permission in writing of both author and publisher.

Published by Manchester University Press
Oxford Road, Manchester M13 9PL

www.manchesteruniversitypress.co.uk

British Library Cataloguing-in-Publication Data
A catalogue record for this book is available from the British Library

ISBN 978 1 5261 7075 0 hardback
ISBN 978 1 5261 9479 4 paperback

First published 2023
Paperback published 2026

The publisher has no responsibility for the persistence or accuracy of URLs for any external or third-party internet websites referred to in this book, and does not guarantee that any content on such websites is, or will remain, accurate or appropriate.

EU authorised representative for GPSR:
Easy Access System Europe – Mustamäe tee 50,
10621 Tallinn, Estonia
gpsr.requests@easproject.com

Typeset by Newgen Publishing UK

Contents

List of figures — vii
List of tables — ix
Notes on contributors — x

1 The common writer in history – Martyn Lyons — 1
2 Writings on the walls: approaches to graffiti in the early modern Hispanic world – Antonio Castillo Gómez — 21
3 'No more for Now or Praps Never': the meaning and function of pauper writing in Britain, 1750s to early 1900s – Steven King — 45
4 Common writers in German-speaking countries from the eighteenth century to the twentieth century as agents of a language history from below – Stephan Elspaß — 65
5 Narrating injuries and injustices: life stories in the struggle for working-class rights in Britain, 1820–1945 – T. G. Ashplant — 82
6 Music and affective signalling in an immigrant letter from 1844 – David A. Gerber — 103
7 Pen, paper and peasants: the rise of vernacular literacy practices in nineteenth-century Iceland – Sigurður Gylfi Magnússon and Davíð Ólafsson — 121
8 Questioning 'the common writer': ordinary writings from the Emagusheni trading station in Pondoland, 1880–84 – Liz Stanley — 140
9 Madlands: Vincenzo Rabito as a writer – David Moss — 159
10 Copying, citing and creative rewriting: the transmission of texts and ideas in Finnish handwritten newspapers – Kirsti Salmi-Niklander and Risto Turunen — 176
11 Choreographing correspondences: how the state shaped soldiers' mail in the US Army and the Red Army during the Second World War – Brandon M. Schechter — 195

12 'Dear Prime Minister': the rhetoric of apology and affiliation in letters to Robert Menzies, Australian Prime Minister, 1949–66 – Martyn Lyons   217

Select bibliography   235
Index   245

Figures

2.1 *Vítores* in the Colegio Mayor de San Ildefonso, office of the Rector of the University of Alcalá (circa sixteenth century to seventeenth century) (by permission of the Universidad de Alcalá, photo Antonio Castillo Gómez) — 27

2.2 [Left] Devils encouraging a couple to have sex, in the upper cloister of the old convent of St Francis of Assisi in Tepeapulco (Hidalgo, Mexico). Two horned figures can be made out, standing to the right and left of a prone couple having sex. [Right] Tracing of photograph on the left (by permission of the Instituto Nacional de Antropología e Historia, Secretaria de Cultura-INAH-Mex) — 31

2.3 *Descent into Hell*, in the prison of the Inquisition in Palermo, seventeenth century (by permission of David Sebastiani) — 33

2.4 Detail of a battle scene in the ancient convent of St Nicholas of Tolentino in Actopán (Mexico), circa 1629 (by permission of the Instituto Nacional de Antropología e Historia, Secretaria de Cultura-INAH-Mex) — 35

2.5 Graffiti saying 'fueresse luego oliveros' or 'fueresse oliveros', at the entrance gate to the old hospital of Santa Creu in Barcelona, 1640–52 (photo Antonio Castillo Gómez) — 37

3.1 Chelsea workhouse petition, 1871 (UK National Archives, MH 12/6996/12662/1871) — 50

6.1 The transcription of music tentatively identified as *Caledonian March*, found in Thomas Steel's letter to his sister Lilly, 5 November 1844 (by permission of the Wisconsin State Historical Society, WHI 38821) — 104

9.1 Vincenzo Rabito's autobiography, p. 1 (by permission of Giovanni Rabito) — 165

10.1 *Kuritus*, 21 August 1910 (Työväen Arkisto – Finnish Labour Archives – photo Risto Turunen) 178
10.2 *Valistaja*, 10 March 1916 (Työväen Arkisto – Finnish Labour Archives – photo Risto Turunen) 179
11.1 V-mail Valentine drawing from Sgt Jed Ryley, of 397th Infantry regiment in France, to Miss Lee Leahy in Noroton, CT, with army censor's stamp in top left corner, circa 1945 (US Postal Museum, Floyd S. Leach collection 0.260305.50.17.2, via Creative Commons) 198
11.2 Triangle letter from Solomon Kantsedikas, probably in Latvia, to his wife Elisheva in Vilnius, 11 June 1945 (by permission of Blavatnik Archive, New York MISC 095.584) 201

Tables

3.1 Models of the writing culture of the poor 59
10.1 Text circulation in two Finnish handwritten newspapers 181

Notes on contributors

T. G. Ashplant is Visiting Professor at the Centre for Life-Writing Research, King's College, London. His research interests lie in life writings as a source for exploring the construction and transformation of class and gender subjectivities, and their relationship to political identities. He recently edited a special issue of the *European Journal of Life-Writing* on 'Life writing "from below" in Europe' (2018) and co-edited, with Ann-Catrine Edlund and Anna Kuismin, *Reading and Writing from Below: Exploring the Margins of Modernity* (2016). He is author of *Fractured Loyalties: Masculinity, Class and Politics in Britain, 1900–30* (2007). Email: t.g.ashplant@kcl.ac.uk.

Antonio Castillo Gómez is Professor in the History of Scribal Culture at the University of Alcalá, where he directs SIECE (the Interdisciplinary Seminar in the Study of Written Culture). He is a specialist in the history of written culture in the Hispanic world in the early modern period and the author of *Leggere nella Spagna moderna: erudizione, religiosità, svago* (Reading in modern Spain: scholarship, religion and entertainment) (2013). Together with Verónica Sierra Blas, he has edited a substantial series of works on reading and writing, including *Cinco Siglos de Cartas: Historia y prácticas epistolares en las épocas moderna y contemporánea* (Five centuries of letters: epistolary practices in modern and contemporary history) (2014). Email: antonio.castillo@uah.es.

Stephan Elspaß is Professor of German Linguistics at the German Department of the University of Salzburg. His research focusses on language variation and change and the history of New High German. He is the author of *Sprachgeschichte von unten* (Language history from below) (2005) and several articles on historical sociolinguistics and the role of common writers in language standardisation processes. Email: Stephan.Elspass@plus.ac.at.

David A. Gerber is Distinguished Professor of History Emeritus at the University of Buffalo. In addition to numerous published essays on immigrant personal correspondence, he is co-editor, with Bruce S. Elliott and Suzanne M. Sinke, of *Letters across Borders: The Epistolary Practices of International Migrants* (2006) and the author of *Authors of Their Lives: The Personal Correspondence of British Immigrants to North America in the Nineteenth Century* (2006). Email: dagerber@buffalo.edu.

Steven King is Professor of Economic and Social History at Nottingham Trent University. He has wide-ranging interests across the fields of historical demography, courtships, women's suffrage and welfare history. In recent years he has been exploring the nature and meaning of working-class writing, with a particular focus on the epistolary relationships between claimants and welfare officials between the 1750s and early 1900s. His book *Writing the Lives of the English Poor* (2019) won the British Academy Peter Townsend Prize in 2019 and the British Records Association Janette Harley Prize in 2020. Email: steven.king@ntu.ac.uk.

Martyn Lyons is Emeritus Professor in History and European Studies at the University of New South Wales in Sydney. He has published several studies on ordinary writings and on the history of reading and writing practices in Australia and Europe, including most recently, co-edited with Rita Marquilhas, *Approaches to the History of Written Culture: A World Inscribed* (2017) and *The Typewriter Century: A Cultural History of Writing Practices* (2021). He was foundation co-editor of *Lingua Franca: The History of the Book in Translation*, 2015–21. Email: M.Lyons@unsw.edu.au.

Sigurður Gylfi Magnússon is Professor of Cultural History at the Department of History and Philosophy, University of Iceland. He is the author of twenty-five books. His latest in English are: *Wasteland with Words: A Social History of Iceland* (2010); *What is Microhistory?* (2013), co-authored with István M. Szijártó; *Minor Knowledge and Microhistory* (2017), co-authored with Davíð Ólafsson; and *Emotional Experience and Microhistory* (2020). He is co-editor, with István M. Szijártó, of a new book series, *Microhistories*, published by Routledge. Email: sgm@hi.is.

David Moss has taught social anthropology and Italian Studies at Griffith University, Brisbane and the University of Milan. He has been a visiting fellow at the Luigi Einaudi Foundation, Turin, and at All Souls College, Oxford. He has published widely on Italy: on banditry in Sardinia, left-wing political violence, the response to HIV/AIDS, patronage, how appointments to Italian universities are made and the evolution of Italian Studies in Australia. His most recent publications examine Vincenzo Rabito's autobiography, *Terra matta* (Madlands). Email: dmoss26@gmail.com.

Davíð Ólafsson is Assistant Professor of Cultural Studies at the Faculty of Icelandic and Comparative Cultural Studies, University of Iceland. His main research fields are post-medieval manuscript studies, literacy studies and contemporary popular culture. Among his publications are, co-authored with Sigurður Gylfi Magnússon, *Minor Knowledge and Microhistory: Manuscript Culture in the Nineteenth Century* (2017) and *Frá degi til dags: Dagbækur, almanök og veðurbækur 1720–1920* (Day by day: diaries, almanacs and weather journals in Iceland 1720–1920) (2021). Email: do@hi.is.

Kirsti Salmi-Niklander is University Lecturer in Folklore Studies at the Department of Cultures, University of Helsinki. Her research interests include oral literary traditions, book history, oral history and working-class and immigrant cultures. One of her most recent publications, co-edited with Heiko Droste, is *Handwritten Newspapers: An Alternative Medium during the Early Modern and Modern Periods* (2019). Email: Kirsti.salmi-niklander@helsinki.fi.

Brandon M. Schechter was awarded his Ph.D. from the University of California (Berkeley) in 2015. He was Elihu Rose Scholar in Modern Military History at New York University and Visiting Assistant Professor at NYU Shanghai. His book, *The Stuff of Soldiers: A History of the Red Army in World War II through Objects* (2019), was awarded the Paul Birdsall Prize by the American Historical Association. Email: bmschechter@gmail.com.

Liz Stanley holds the established Chair of Sociology at the University of Edinburgh and is a Fellow of the Academy of Social Sciences. A feminist sociologist, her work has focussed on historical topics and methodological issues, and in recent years has concerned letters and related writing practices. She has explored the settler colonial presence in South Africa over three decades of research and ensuing publications. For more information, go to www.sociology.ed.ac.uk/people/staff/stanley_liz. Email: Liz.stanley@ed.ac.uk.

Risto Turunen is a doctoral candidate in history at Tampere University. He defended his thesis, *Shades of Red: Evolution of the Political Language of Finnish Socialism*, in spring 2021. Turunen has published articles on labour history, conceptual history and digital humanities based on his dissertation project. Email: Risto.turunen@tuni.fi.

1

The common writer in history

Martyn Lyons

The history of scribal culture as a field of study

In 1880, Joachim Martin, a carpenter from the village of Crots in the French department of the Hautes-Alpes, was laying new floorboards in the nearby Château de Picomtal. As he worked, he took a black crayon and, on the underside of the parquet bricks he was assembling, wrote a text, part journal part autobiography.[1] Altogether, seventy-two pieces of his hidden autobiography were discovered when new owners of the chateau started renovations in 2000. Although his work is legible, it is now impossible to reconstitute the sequence in which the textual fragments were composed. Martin wrote of his work, his employers, local political figures, the harvest from his fields (for he was a smallholding peasant as well as a craftsman), and he also commented on sexual behaviour in his village. He directly addressed his unknown future reader, assuming that he would be a fellow carpenter and that he, Joachim Martin, would be long dead when his writing was read. Apart from constituting a good example of 'writing from below' in a literal as well as a metaphorical sense, Martin's inscribed parquet floors illustrate the unexpected ways in which people of modest social origins left written traces of their otherwise obscure existences. French anthropologist Daniel Fabre usefully labelled such texts 'ordinary writings', and they form the subject of this book.[2] Writings like those of Joachim Martin enable us to rescue forgotten lives from anonymity and give them some shape and substance.

Martin's floorboards are of potential interest to several kinds of scholars: regional historians of the Hautes-Alpes and the Embrunnais area, political historians interested in popular attitudes during the early years of the French Third Republic and possibly social historians investigating sexual mores in this period. Most importantly, Martin's inscribed parquet floor is material for the historian of scribal (or, if you prefer, written) culture. This book is intended as a contribution both to the history of scribal culture and to the new history from below. It does not aim to be comprehensive, nor does it aim to showcase a representative sample of work in the field. It brings together some leading practitioners from different disciplines to give a clearer idea of the broad scope and concerns of the history of scribal culture, with particular reference to the 'common writer'.

It contributes to a 'new history from below', which attempts to give voice and agency to members of the subordinate classes. This is a new history in the sense that it does not view the subordinate classes, as the Annales school tended to do, as an anonymous mass described in terms of impersonal statistics. It is a history from below which parts company with François Furet when he asserted in 1963 that 'number and anonymity' were the only ways to include the masses in a broader historical narrative.[3] It is a new history, too, in that it is not primarily focussed, as Marxists have been, on the growth of working-class consciousness and militancy and it is not driven forward by the history of political struggles.[4] Instead, whether we consider ego-documents, life writing of different kinds, correspondence, or graffiti in streets and prisons, we place value on the subjective experience of the individual in a given historical environment. We consider such writings as significant sources for mental beliefs, the influence or lack of influence of writing models emanating 'from above', intimate lives, patriotic sentiments or their absence, a sense of identity and so on.

Considering the past from the viewpoint of non-elites opens up the possibility of an alternative history which contrasts with conventional top-down political narratives. It changes the perspective, focussing on the assumptions and concerns of the so-called silent masses and finding them to have been not so silent after all. It provides an insight into the cultural universe of the poor, the mental world of the soldier and the personal struggles of the young emigrant or pauper. The aim, according to one Italian historian, is 'to give a voice, a personal identity, a subjectivity, a presence and dignity back to the ordinary protagonists of history'.[5] In practice, whenever historians invest value in ordinary lives, they invariably discover that the individuals they study are not at all 'ordinary'. The new history from below is making great efforts to unearth more direct evidence of the writings of the poor and the marginal – the writings of those who in the past have not always been credited with the ability to write competently at all. Ordinary writers can only be fully understood if we listen to their own voices, however inarticulate they may seem, and regard them as active agents in their own history rather than passive receptacles for official ideologies. Our world, according to French historian Arlette Farge, has been inhabited by so many invisible beings, who remain isolated in their own poverty or swallowed up by wars or powerful waves of migration, that historians are now under an obligation to treat them as living, feeling subjects.[6]

In his landmark study, *The English Common Reader* (1957), Richard Altick mapped out the new historical field of working-class reading for the first time, and his pioneering work led in direct descent to scholarly masterpieces on British working-class autodidacts by David Vincent and Jonathan Rose.[7] By entitling this collection of studies *The Common Writer*, I pay indirect and implicit homage to Altick's initiative. The history of the book, however, together with its offspring, the history of reading, have tended to marginalise the history of writing practices. Of the fifty-five chapters that make up Wiley-Blackwell's *Companion to the History of the Book*, only four can be clearly identified as referring to the history of writing practices.[8] The rest are primarily concerned with the history of book manufacture and of the book trade. The world of print usually dominates scholarly study in modern history to the extent that it eclipses the rich and varied world of manuscript culture. As Francesco Ascoli has recently insisted, however, handwriting has never ceased to be of great importance, notwithstanding the invention of printing. The histories of manuscript and print intersect and influence each other, but each one served a different purpose; it is time to jettison conventional histories of written communication presented in three consecutive phases, in which manuscript came first, then print, then the digital age.[9] They all overlapped, and continue to do so.

At some point the history of writing seems to have drifted free from book studies and from the history of reading, like a melting ice floe, until the 'new literacy studies' invited us to fit these disparate pieces of the literacy jigsaw back together again. For scholars of the new literacy studies, the different ways in which we engage with literary culture, from reading a newspaper to writing a personal letter, can all be categorised as 'literacy events', elements of vernacular, everyday forms of literacy, whether they involve reading, writing or a combination of both.[10] The study of ego-documents, argued Shanti Graheli, shows us that 'the history of reading is deeply entwined with the history of writing practices'.[11]

It would be misleading, however, to give the impression that the history of scribal culture came into being solely as the poor relation of its elder sibling, the history of reading. In practice, many different disciplines come together under its banner, as the variety of the backgrounds of contributors to this volume demonstrates. Archaeologists and anthropologists have worked in this territory for decades, pursuing their own distinctive priorities. Their fieldwork has been the basis for an exploration of the complex relationships between the oral and the literate which has illuminated writing practices in ancient societies as well as in more modern contexts in Africa, South America and the Asia-Pacific region. We can equally turn the lens inward, to explore literacy and orality among the 'white tribes' of the western world, just as the British Mass Observation Project, established in 1937, attempted to construct an 'ethnography of ourselves'.[12] Palaeographers, in their turn, help us decipher ancient and medieval manuscripts and explain the history of handwriting systems. Specialists in literary studies have a long-standing interest in autobiographical writing, which they have now broadened to embrace non-canonical and often inexpert writers. In the Nordic countries, the key discipline of folklore studies has played an important role in the study of peasant writings, as Kirsti Salmi-Niklander's trajectory illustrates. Historical sociolinguists, too, have recently grasped the potential of 'ordinary writings' to provide valuable insights into language change, as demonstrated by Stephan Elspaß's contribution in this volume (Chapter 4). The cultural historian is only one of several travellers in this motley caravan of scholars.

There are tentative signs that ordinary writings are coming increasingly into scholarly focus, at least in continental Europe. In 2022, the *Revista de historiografía* devoted a special dossier, edited by Patrizia Gabrielli, to the popular writings of war and emigration in Italy. In the same year, the *Revue d'histoire du dix-neuvième siècle* produced a thematic issue on 'Ecrits et écritures populaires'.[13] This volume goes further towards clarifying where the history of scribal culture stands and what it stands for. Its scope is broad in terms of writing genres. It includes life writing of different kinds, including the autobiographies of criminals, narratives of religious conversion or of political engagement, as well as extraordinary creations like the enormous typescript produced by the Sicilian roadmender Vincenzo Rabito (see Chapter 9). These are not literary autobiographies, but they represent the life experiences of ordinary and sometimes marginal people. Correspondence, too, is a focus of the history of scribal culture, including letters from soldiers, prisoners, emigrants, and paupers seeking welfare benefits. The exchange of letters is one genre of ordinary writings which inevitably brings together the study of both literacies: reading and writing. This collection includes the genre of 'writing upwards', in which employees, subjects and citizens petition their boss or their political leader. Manuscript culture is a phenomenon sometimes considered in relation to print, but much less often treated in its own right. Graffiti and handwritten newspapers are examples discussed in this collection. Whatever the writing genre under discussion, we seek to understand the importance of writing and the reasons why, in given historical situations, people chose this medium to protest, communicate or demand a favour from a superior. Written texts are not simply evidence of something beyond themselves, as when a soldier's letter home gives us information about the morale of the army. Writing is examined here for what it says about itself – its purpose and function, its social grammar and norms of composition, the materials and the technology which enable it to happen and at the same time define its possibilities.

Some writers familiar with the act of writing formed their characters evenly and accurately. They had mastered the use of margins and blank spaces on the page. Those for whom writing was a rare activity experienced difficulty in holding a straight line and following the conventions of epistolary literacy concerning margins, indentation, spelling and grammar. In Parma in 1870, Eufrosina Serventi congratulated her fiancé Pietro on his writing skill, telling him in one letter: 'Your writing looks like it's printed, mine on the other hand really looks like chicken feet.'[14] She knew she could not match Pietro's greater facility and accuracy with the pen, but, chicken feet or not, she commands as much of our attention as her more polished lover. Here she gave us a good example of the ways in which correspondence often contains a metalanguage, in which writers reflect on their own practices and expectations of each other. Letters, in other words, speak about themselves.

The intellectual heritage

One way in which historians of scribal culture collectively assert their disciplinary identity is in recognising common ancestors. A few notable scholars provide a common intellectual heritage and thus help to define the historical study of writing practices. The foremost of these was Armando Petrucci, in his published work on epistolary culture, manuscript culture, public inscriptions and monuments to the dead, mainly in the period stretching from late antiquity to the Renaissance.[15] Petrucci was first and foremost a palaeographer, one who regarded a close description of the formal characteristics of any text as the fundamental starting point for historians of the book. But he went further, to consider the social and cultural status of the writer, the social distribution of literary competence and the sociocultural context in which a given text was produced.[16] Petrucci argued that writing, along with the social distribution of writing skills, gives us an indispensable key to unlock the workings of any given society. The uses of writing lay bare the inequalities and power structures on which past societies rested. According to Petrucci: 'Every age and every society can be better understood and appreciated through studying the uses it makes of writing as an instrument, the ways in which writing and reading competence is distributed throughout society, and the functions that it attributes to scribal production and its various typologies.'[17] Petrucci's statement could stand as a foundation text for the history of scribal culture.

Petrucci did more than anyone to bridge the gap between the erudite but dry examination of manuscripts and the broader concerns of the sociocultural historian. The important work of Antonio Castillo Gómez and his colleagues at the very active centre for the study of written culture at the University of Alcalá[18] is in direct line of descent from Petrucci's initiatives.

It has succeeded, better than Petrucci himself, in applying to writings in the modern world some of the expertise first acquired in the study of ancient and medieval manuscripts. Significantly, this centre's website takes Petrucci's text cited above as its masthead.

Petrucci is not the only guru who has shaped this field of study. As far as the burgeoning study of prison writings is concerned, for instance, Michel Foucault has been a common point of reference. In France, Philippe Artières's studies of nineteenth-century criminal autobiographies take something from Foucault's interest in *anormaux* (deviant lives) as well as from his interest in prisons and his analysis of medical knowledge as a *savoir-pouvoir*, an instrument of power.[19] For other scholars, Jack Goody has also been extremely influential, especially for his analysis of writing as a 'technology of the intellect' with the potential to transform the thinking processes of the writer as well as of the reader.[20] His arguments about how a new graphic mentality came to be formed have attracted plenty of favourable attention, especially in France.[21] For students of ego-documents, which embrace various forms of life writing, Jacob (or Jacques) Presser is an obligatory starting point.[22] In the study of autobiographies of non-literary writers, the work and reflections of Philippe Lejeune have become almost legendary.[23]

This book is indebted most of all to the ethnologist Daniel Fabre, who coined the phrase 'ordinary writings' in his studies of the uses of writing in the rural south-west of France.[24] As noted earlier, our title, *The Common Writer*, acknowledges Altick's initiative in studying 'the common reader', but in this book we refer equally to 'ordinary writings' and 'ordinary writers', regarding the ordinary writer and the common writer as synonymous. The phrase 'ordinary writings' has several dimensions. On one level, it refers to a range of non-literary writings, the kind of personal and often ephemeral texts that we rely on to organise our lives, such as household budgets, shopping lists and reminders of all sorts. These are vernacular and ordinary writings, the kind which the sociologist Bernard Lahire calls 'domestic writings' and the Mass Observation Project calls hidden or 'invisible writings'.[25] We may also include here the intense copying activities of the Rouennais school students studied by Marie-Claude Penloup.[26] She did not focus on their in-school activities, but instead revealed a rich world of leisure time copying of poems, songs, jokes, mottoes and even entire novels by adolescents who had experienced 'the literary temptation'.

'Ordinary writings' also has another meaning: it refers to the authors themselves and their modest social origins. This book understands the phrase principally from this perspective, denoting the textual practices of subordinate classes and marginalised groups. The focus in what follows is on the everyday cultural practices and self-representation of people of low social status and perhaps imperfect literacy competence.

Writing from below

Until recently, the history of popular (i.e. lower-class) writing has revolved around a handful of well-known but exceptional cases, frequently cited for their extraordinary achievements. Angela Veronese, a gardener's daughter born near Treviso in 1779, is one, brought to scholarly attention by Marina Roggero.[27] Because Veronese wrote an autobiography, we are well-informed about her early reading of romances, fables and lives of the saints.[28] We discover peasants reading Tasso and Ariosto aloud on winter evenings, since she herself joined them. We know of her keen desire to read and later to write, although her education was typically piecemeal, and that she concealed her youthful writing from her disapproving parents.

Clelia Marchi is another well-known case, and a much more recent one, having written her autobiography on a *matrimoniale* (double bedsheet) after the death of her husband in 1972. Her 'Libro-Lenzuolo' (sheet book) is preserved today in the Archivio Diaristico Nazionale in Pieve Santo Stefano, where it is exhibited once a year like the ostension of a saintly relic.[29]

The First World War autobiography of Louis Barthas, a cooper from the Aude department in south-west France, has become another emblematic case of popular writing.[30] Barthas was an insubordinate soldier, and his writing reflected his regional loyalties and Occitan roots – all reasons why French scholars might be interested in him. Most importantly, the publication of his autobiography in 1978 balanced historians' customary reliance on the war memoirs of well-educated and highly articulate army officers and started a trend to expand the common stock of reference texts to include the writings and experiences of ordinary soldiers.

Another candidate is the Barcelona tanner Miquel Parets, born in 1610, who wrote a much-cited historical chronicle with an eyewitness account of the plague of 1651.[31] Parets copied official documents into his account, including the entire text of the Treaty of the Pyrenees between Spain and France in 1659. His anonymous translator compared Parets to the mythical Icarus, who had flown too near the sun, burned his wings and fallen to earth: he was an over-adventurous writer with ambitions beyond his proper station. Perhaps the Sicilian peasant Vincenzo Rabito, discussed in this book by David Moss and the subject of a film, has also joined this 'anti-Pantheon' of once obscure but now eminent peasant and worker-autobiographers.

The point here is that behind these individual stars, who all undoubtedly deserve their place in the limelight, there lie hundreds of thousands, if not millions, of other ordinary writers whose existence remains shadowy and whose engagement with the written word is rarely appreciated. The astronomical statistics on postal items sent from the fronts during the First World War suggest the writing 'bulimia' which swept through Europe's peasant armies in the trenches:[32] four million items issued daily from the French army in 1915;[33] the Italian army produced four thousand million items in three and a half years of war, in spite of the fact that 35 per cent of Italians were officially illiterate on the eve of the conflict; Germany produced at least thirty thousand million items.[34] For many, the act of writing was unfamiliar and laborious, but absolutely essential to keep in contact with families and let them know that one was still alive. Laurent Pouchet, a thirty-year-old vigneron from the Hérault, forced himself into the writing habit. He wrote home in 1915 looking forward to the day when 'lon pourra finir toutes çes comédi decriture cela sera une joie un bonheur pour nous [sic]' (we will be able to finish with all this writing farce, it will be a joy and happiness for us).[35] Writing was often a chore, and drafting a letter often required the help of a friendly comrade, but it had become an absolute daily necessity for millions of untutored correspondents like Pouchet.

Historians are accustomed to interrogating soldiers' correspondence about their experience of warfare and, more recently in France, about the degree to which they were patriotically committed to fighting for their country in 1914–18. But historians of scribal culture are in search of additional information from this outpouring of popular writing. They see it as evidence of literacy and of writing practices, and as an indication of the purpose and function of writing itself. Many peasant writers, after all, wrote very little at the time about their combat experience, and an unprepared reader may be surprised by the laconic tone of their letters and by the banalities which filled them. Their laconism and banality, however, were significant. The main purpose of writing home from the trenches was consolatory, to reassure parents and loved ones that everything was alright, no matter how horrific the reality of soldiers' lives may have been. The primary function of the soldier's letter was to show that he was still alive; the content of what he wrote was incidental to this fundamental message.

The age of mass trans-oceanic migrations generated another enormous corpus of letter writing from below. Besides the work of Laura Martínez Martín in this field, we can also consult book-length studies of Irish emigrants' letters from Australia and British emigrants' correspondence from North America.[36] Emigrants' letters can be very productively mined for information about the experience of emigration itself and about the process by which men and women who began life in a new country gradually acquired a double identity. They provide an alternative to the economic history of mass migration, inviting us to see emigrants not simply as a mass of anonymous particles magnetised by push-and-pull factors, but as individual agents determining their own future, usually as part of an overall family strategy for survival. Studying letter writing from below has the effect of giving a voice to individuals who are otherwise subsumed within a global mass of labour market statistics.

As with soldiers' letters from the front, however, emigrants' letters can tell us more if we pause our data mining for a moment and consider them as letters per se. They are precious documents about the practice of writing itself, about the rules and tacit conventions governing all epistolary exchanges, about the history of language usage and about the importance of literacy. For Spanish and Italian emigrants to the Americas, literacy was of vital importance, not just for gaining employment in warehouses, shops and small businesses but also for maintaining contact with their families and the social networks from which they had uprooted themselves. Many of them left Spain as no more than teenage boys, with a very incomplete grasp of how to read and write. Nothing illustrates the value they placed on literacy better than the investment made by successful Asturian migrants in the local schools of their province of origin. They were determined that the next generation of emigrants should be better equipped than they had been.

Whether the focus is on letters, autobiographies, graffiti or other genres, the new history from below is potentially a political project. The writings of ordinary people form the materials for a counter-history, and several nineteenth-century British worker-autobiographers intended that their own writing should serve exactly that subversive purpose. No one else, they knew, would provide the kind of working-class history they wanted to leave behind them, and a few were well aware that no adequate history of the radical Chartist movement had appeared in their lifetimes. William Adams, son of a Cheltenham plasterer, a former Chartist and republican, set out to put the record straight. 'It is extremely unlikely,' he wrote at the beginning of the twentieth century, 'that any competent and satisfactory narrative of a stupendous national crisis [i.e. Chartism] will ever now be given to the world.' His account, he promised, 'will relate the commonplace experiences of a humble worker in a humble sphere of life'.[37] Radicals like Adams wanted to balance the public record, giving their own versions of their role in British radicalism. At their best, they offered a kind of alternative political history of the nineteenth century.

The successors of those radical working-class writers can be found among the correspondents of the Mass Observation Project, based at the University of Sussex, invited at regular intervals to write their observations of British daily life. They too contributed, as they themselves saw it, to an alternative history of the 1980s and 1990s which would balance and rectify versions published by the rich and powerful, and which would contradict the distortions and stereotypes peddled by the mass media. One fifty-three-year-old male contributor, invited in 1991 to reflect on his own written efforts for the

Mass Observation Project, participated in this democratic writing enterprise with enthusiasm, in these words:

> The words of the peasants of the Middle Ages are lost to us, swallowed up in the silence of an enforced illiteracy. What did they think, when they trooped in for Mass under the censorious eyes of a fat priest or burned a greedy lord's castle? [...] I remember the faintly opprobrious label 'history from below' was placed on the kind of work Sussex [University] was instrumental in making happen. Fucking right on, I'd say. I'd rather have that sort of history than history written by eminent ass-lickers, honours-junkies and apologists for state crimes.[38]

Whatever the genre, the new history from below aims to make visible the writings of ordinary people, neglected and disqualified by a dominant culture, but capable of enriching our understanding of the many meanings of literacy. 'Can the subaltern speak?', asked Gayatri Spivak in an essay now celebrated in post-colonial studies; even if subalterns could speak, they were likely to remain subalterns until they could also write.[39]

Common features of ordinary writings

What common characteristics do the various genres of ordinary writings share? Seven defining elements are usually present.

Firstly, they are normally written by authors of modest social origins. In the European context, this leads us into the cultural world of peasants, artisans and workers. Historians of ordinary writing have been vague about the sociology of the authors they study. To some extent, this has been a deliberate strategy to allow for some social mobility, as peasants become teachers and artisans become merchants and so on. Sometimes, too rigid a classification can create more problems than it appears to solve. In Chapter 8, however, Liz Stanley asks pertinent questions about the general applicability of the European model and about the assumptions we make about social status. The ways in which we think of the subordinate classes in western Europe in the 1880s may need some modification if our model is to carry weight in the colonial context, where sociological categories were intersected and undermined by a racial divide.

Secondly, ordinary writers write in unorthodox genres: not merely diaries and autobiographies which follow recognisable literary models, but also songbooks, recipe books, historical chronicles, home-made encyclopaedias, hymnbooks, sketchbooks and combinations of all of these. Originating in thirteenth-century Italy, the *libri di ricordanze* recorded family genealogies, baptisms, marriages and deaths, and historical chronicles in which the authors recorded major events, especially disasters like great floods or earthquakes. Peasants listed harvest yields and each year wrote down a summary of income and expenses. These 'memory books' (to give a generic title to a phenomenon which has had several labels) were a hybrid genre, part history, part genealogy, part business accounts. They do not fit any canonical literary genre and constitute a distinct form of popular writing. These ordinary writers were not literary writers; they used their own vernacular style, and their literacy practices were rooted in everyday life.

Thirdly, the materials they used may be improvised, as in the case of Joachim Martin and his parquet flooring with which this chapter began. Spanish emigrants, after a long day at work, wrote home on pages torn from accounting ledgers; soldiers in the trenches scribbled postcards home by the light of a lantern dangling from a bayonet. They appropriated whatever was available to satisfy their urgent need to write. When Australian Aboriginal peoples petitioned their government, they sometimes presented their requests as traditional bark paintings, in a proud statement about the independence and longevity of their culture.[40] The material aspects of writings from below are sometimes unexpected but frequently significant.

Fourthly, if ordinary writers had received only a partial or interrupted formal education, they did not always apply all the standard protocols of grammar and orthography. Their letters were often devoid of punctuation, as their sentences ran into each other without a break. Occasionally, on the other hand, the opposite was true: their punctuation was overzealous, as in the case of Vincenzo Rabito. Their capitalisation was irregular, and their grammar and spelling tended to follow spoken usage rather than standard written practice. Australians wrote prolifically but not always accurately to their Prime Minister Robert Menzies during the 1950s and 1960s. Those with a grievance wanted to be 'compessated', or they complained that the attitudes of 'offissialdom' were far from 'addiquett'. They wrote 'leased' for least, 'sincear' for sincere, 'ledgeslation' for legislation or 'hole' for whole. They were frustrated if a request was 'refewsed', and they expressed their general detestation for 'polatishons'.[41] Ordinary writers' word separation was random, as sometimes they combined several words together into one (hypo-segmentation), and at other times went to the opposite extreme, dissecting words into neatly autonomous syllables (hyper-segmentation).

Ordinary writings are distinguished, fifthly, by the presence of orality and gesture in the text. Just as the spelling and punctuation of ordinary writers were inconsistent, so too were their lexical choices and their use of language in general. One consistent characteristic of ordinary writing, whatever its national context, was the presence within it of oral speech and dialectal forms. The writers used dialect for many different reasons: sometimes it was a source of humour; at other times it was an expression of local solidarity with one's readers; and sometimes it came naturally, as when the writer was mentally struggling to translate from a local into a national language. Leo Spitzer, as a censor reading the correspondence of Italian prisoners-of-war in Austria during the First World War, decided that 'the letter doesn't give a picture of dialect but rather of a struggle between dialect and the written word'.[42]

This is why language historians like Stephan Elspaß question the traditional linguistic emphasis on the development and legitimation of standard national norms (see Chapter 4); instead of this teleological exercise, they propose a history of language change from below. Such a history parts company with the study of canonical texts, manuals and school grammar books to concentrate instead on spoken language and more informal linguistic registers. Historico-linguists have not always been generous in their estimates of the ordinary writer's achievements. They have categorised the unorthodox use of language as deviance, *défaillance*, substandard or nonstandard in relation to a national norm. Historians of scribal culture seek less derogatory ways to label the object of their investigation.

The ordinary writer is not only close to the world of oral communication but also part of a culture which embraces gesture and symbol. Letters by ordinary writers do not always show a mastery of blank spaces on the page; in fact, they may try to cover every millimetre with writing, saturating all the graphic space available. But they nevertheless have a keen sense of the theatre of letter writing, and gestures of love, deference or obedience are inherent in their letters home. This is best illustrated by the so-called 'bowing letters' of Polish emigrants writing home from North and South America. Their greetings were highly ritualised, and as they wrote they imagined arriving home after a long absence, thus: 'We step across your threshold and we greet you and we kiss your hand and feet.'[43] After this, the writer would perform a ritual of 'bowing' to absent members of the family. The letter home was not just an intermingling of writing and the spoken word, but also a ceremonial act with multiple dimensions.

The sixth characteristic is that correspondence of ordinary writers tends to be formulaic. So often do they repeat themselves that one ambitious language specialist has reduced their common structure to six key elements.[44] First came the formal greeting (*salutatio*), to be followed in every letter from an emigrant or a soldier by two important steps. These were a report on letters sent and received (*confirmatio receptionis*) or the expression of anxiety because some had *not* been received, followed by a reassuring discourse about the writer's health (*dissertatio valetudinis*). All this was the prelude to the body of the letter, containing whatever news the writer wished to relate (*narratio*). This might be combined with a simple request (*petitio*), as when soldiers asked for a food parcel or warmer clothing. Then came the farewell (*nuntiatio parentum*), in which the writer said goodbye to a number of family members, addressing them all carefully in turn and in order of seniority, obeying an important ritual aiming to resituate the writer within the social network from which he or she was temporarily or permanently absent. The farewell closed this highly structured sequence. In such letters, the narration, or the argument of the letter, might take up a very small part of the whole, whereas discussions of health and of mail either received or on the way, together with long lists of relatives acknowledged by the writer, consumed the overwhelming bulk of the text. In the past, this dismayed some editors of letter collections, who decided to delete long opening and closing sections of correspondence for publication. In so doing, they eliminated parts of the text which were of high importance to the letter writer.

The seventh characteristic of ordinary writing is its inherent gender bias, although the preponderance of male writers is perhaps not as dominant as might be assumed from my previous focus on soldiers' letters. Letters from the front can be supplemented by letters *to* the front, from wives, lovers and mothers, as well as by letters from female nurses. In addition, we have letters from the period of the First World War from women who were forcibly evacuated from war zones. So the epistolary landscape of war was not exclusively masculine. More variety is found in letters of emigration. Laura Martínez Martín estimates that about 60 per cent of emigrants' letters from America were written by men.[45] A precise gender breakdown, however, is problematic, since many letters did not have a single author, but were collectively drafted by different family members. The male majority in any corpus of letter writing perpetuates an imbalance which probably goes back to the beginnings of written communication. It reflects the historically dominant role of men in politics, business and administration, as well as the more widespread distribution of writing literacy skills among men than women.

The plan of the book

The contributions to this book are presented in a roughly chronological order. They illuminate several different genres of popular writing. As well as correspondence of various sorts and life writing, they also examine graffiti and handwritten newspapers. In some studies, as we shall see, there is no exclusive focus on a single genre. The collection ebbs and flows between detailed studies of a small number of documents (or even of just one letter) and broader overviews of large bodies of data.

The next chapter belongs to the latter category, and it takes us back to the early modern period with the study of graffiti as a historical source. Writing on walls, Antonio Castillo Gómez has written, may be the most prevalent form of writing in history, but its existence is often ephemeral and the historian has difficulty in attributing authorship.[46] The graffiti of the Inquisitorial prisons of the Spanish Empire, which archaeologists are nowadays eager to preserve, represent cries of survival, holy images, prayers and poems – one-sided written conversations which broke the solitude and isolation of incarceration.

Correspondence is the focus of Steven King's work in Chapter 3, which analyses an enormous corpus of British pauper letters written both before and after the New Poor Law of 1834. King has argued that pauper writers seeking welfare exercised some degree of agency, understood what administrators wanted to hear and influenced the workings of government legislation. He is sensitive to the linguistic registers of the letters and what he calls the 'anchoring rhetorics' which govern them.[47] In a previous work, I situated the explosion of popular writing in the late nineteenth century for France, Spain and Italy;[48] King's analysis implies that in Britain the process may have happened at least half a century earlier. He reflects on the literary competence of the British poor and stresses the value invested in writing by poor supplicants.

Stephan Elspaß is concerned with linguistic variations in ordinary writing, using a selection of texts by common writers in German-speaking Europe (Chapter 4). Elspaß represents the important linguistic dimension of the discipline of scribal culture and writing from below. He is interested in how and why language changes and how far change is driven by vernacular usage rather than 'from above'. The presence of oral speech in texts is a recurring theme here.

The collection discusses life writing in different countries and from different angles of vision. T. G. Ashplant's survey of British working-class life writing discusses manifestations of the genre in the nineteenth and early twentieth centuries (Chapter 5). He shows that government inquiries into social problems in this period gave workers an unprecedented opportunity to present their own narratives of their grievances, working conditions and injuries at work. There were limits to the scope of their testimonies, as they depended on intermediaries for the amplification of their accounts and they feared reprisals from employers at work. Ashplant is concerned throughout to consider the publishing avenues open to ordinary autobiographers.

David A. Gerber takes us into the world of emigrants' letters home by dissecting the correspondence of one Scotsman in Wisconsin with his sister in London in 1844 (Chapter 6). Strictly speaking, the letter writer, Thomas Steel, does not fit our usual categorisation of the ordinary writer, as he was an educated physician, albeit an impoverished one. But he adopted an unorthodox genre when he transcribed a musical extract in one of his letters. Gerber attempts to identify the music and explain what it may have meant to both writer and recipient.

Chapter 7 introduces us to the exceptionally vigorous manuscript culture of the Nordic countries, focussing again on the late nineteenth century. 'Vernacular literacy', as understood by Icelandic scholars Sigurður Gylfi Magnússon and Davíð Ólafsson, has often been undervalued.[49] The concept refers to forms of literacy rooted in the home and in everyday life, as opposed to dominant forms of literacy taught by educational institutions. The sociologists and anthropologists of the new literacy studies cited by the authors have rejuvenated the study of literacy, but they have their limitations. They emphasised the ways in which acts of reading and writing have ideological underpinnings and are embedded in an immediate social and political context; but they rarely paid much attention to the ways that reading and writing take place within a *historical* context. Magnússon and Ólafsson provide an antidote.

Liz Stanley's approach in Chapter 8 is to investigate not one genre, but the whole written production of a trading station in Pondoland, in the Eastern Cape area of South Africa. Here she is able to include letters, accounts, ledgers and transaction records. They emanate from a variety of writers: white storekeepers and missionaries, and the black chiefs and advisors of King Mqikela. Her analysis of the records of the Emagusheni trading station in the 1880s shows that notions of hierarchy and status, intersected by race categories, were complex, changing and contingent on the context. In the records, writers of limited literary ability are found among both members of the black elite and the white traders who supplied them. This raises questions about our European categorisations of the common writer and ordinary writings. In the settler colonial situation, our familiar terms of analysis may be inadequate.

In Chapter 9, David Moss then changes the focus and the location. In contrast to Ashplant's broad overview of life writing, he presents some issues surrounding a single author: the Sicilian peasant and roadmender (in fact he had many different jobs) Vincenzo Rabito, born in 1899. Rabito's prize-winning work was over a thousand pages long, typed on his old Olivetti in a single, continuous flow, without margins or paragraphs. As a result, his book *Terra matta* (Madlands) was an editor's nightmare.[50] He put a semicolon between every word. Rabito had never been to school, and his text was full of Sicilianisms. Moss elucidates the success of Rabito's enterprise, and the implications of transposing it to the stage and the cinema.

In the case of Finnish handwritten newspapers, discussed in Chapter 10, Kirsti Salmi-Niklander and Risto Turunen draw on two samples from literally hundreds of possibilities. They show the importance of such newspapers for the labour movement, but their main concern here is the relation between print and manuscript. Digital methods have enabled them to trace the printed sources of many texts transformed into manuscripts for local consumption. The authors turn normal expectations on their head by illustrating the significance of hand-copying from printed sources.

In Chapter 11, Brandon M. Schechter builds on and extends his previous work on the letters of soldiers in the Red Army to offer comparisons with the correspondence of American soldiers during the Second World War. He describes the physical properties of the letters and their generic qualities before discussing the ways in which the chaplaincy of the US Army and the Political Directorate of the Red Army shaped and utilised these missives in an attempt to improve morale. Schechter examines the constraints of censorship in each setting, suggesting that a distinct genre emerged, with remarkably similar writing from within the ranks of both a liberal and an authoritarian regime.

In the final chapter, Martyn Lyons introduces 'writing upwards', in which humble subjects throughout history have petitioned rulers, workers have written to their bosses and impoverished refugees have sought help from aid relief committees. The writers often sought some personal gain, but sometimes their object was not self-interest but simply reassurance. They put their faith in letter writing to cut through bureaucratic obstacles and reach out to a higher source of power. Letters received by Australian Prime Minister Robert Menzies during his long second term of office (1949–66) could be abusive or deferential, hostile or supplicatory. This chapter discusses two common rhetorical strategies adopted by ordinary writers approaching Menzies: the technique of apology and the rhetoric of a claimed affiliation.

In conclusion, the study of historical literacy no longer focusses as it once did on statistical studies of literary ability. Instead, it probes access to reading and writing, and the uses to which literate people put their skills. In considering the uses and functions of writing in different historical contexts, we must henceforth include writers who lacked formal education and who did not enjoy full mastery of literacy skills. We question the pervasive assumption that the lower classes, the poorly educated, or *peu-lettrés* or *analfabetizados*, have left little trace of their existence because they never mastered the pen or the pencil. Their allegedly poor level of literacy competence has sometimes been offered as an excuse for the marginalisation of the illiterate or semi-literate in dominant historical narratives. This book argues that it is time to include their writing and that, in order to interpret it, a flexible disciplinary matrix is required.

Notes

1 Jacques-Olivier Boudon, 'Sous les parquets du château de Picomtal. Les écrits posthumes d'un menuisier des Hautes-Alpes (1880–1881)', *Histoire, économie et société*, 33:1 (2014), 72–86.
2 Daniel Fabre (ed.), *Écritures ordinaires* (Paris: P.O.L/Centre Georges Pompidou, 1993).
3 Cited in Antonio Gibelli, 'Scritture popolari e Grande Guerra: una rivoluzione copernicana', *Revista de historiografía*, 37 (2022), 39–57, p. 47.
4 Harvey J. Kaye, *The British Marxist Historians: An Introductory Analysis*, (Cambridge, UK: Polity, 1984).
5 Quinto Antonelli, 'La Grande Guerra: l'ora dei testimoni', in Fabio Caffarena and Nancy Murzilli (eds), *In Guerra con le parole: il primo conflitto mondiale dalle testimonianze scritte alla memoria multimediale* (Trento: Fondazione Museo Storico di Trento, 2018), pp. 35–52, p. 35.
6 Arlette Farge, *Instants de vie* (Paris: École des Hautes Études en Sciences Sociales, 2021), p. 22.
7 Richard D. Altick, *The English Common Reader: A Social History of the Mass Reading Public, 1800–1900* (Chicago: Chicago University Press, 1957); David Vincent, *Bread, Knowledge and Freedom: A Study of Nineteenth-Century Working-Class Autobiography* (London: Europa, 1981); Jonathan Rose, *The Intellectual Life of the British Working Classes* (New Haven, CT: Yale University Press, 2001); Martyn Lyons, 'La culture littéraire des travailleurs. Autobiographies ouvrières dans l'Europe du XIXe siècle', *Annales: histoire, sciences sociales*, 56:4–5 (2001), 927–46.
8 Simon Eliot and Jonathan Rose (eds), *A Companion to the History of the Book*, 2 vols (Oxford: Wiley-Blackwell, 2nd edition, 2019). I refer to the following chapters: 'Palaeography and Codicology', 'Parchment and Paper: Manuscript Culture 1100–1500', 'The Common Writer since 1500' and 'The New Textual Technologies'.
9 Francesco Ascoli, *La penna in mano: per una storia della cultura manoscritta in età moderna* (Florence: Leo S. Olschki, 2020), p. 10.
10 David Barton and Mary Hamilton, *Local Literacies: Reading and Writing in One Community* (London and New York: Routledge, 1998), pp. 1–12 and Chapter 14.
11 Shanti Graheli, 'Readers and consumers of popular print', *Quaerendo*, 51 (2021), 61–94, p. 65.
12 Dorothy Sheridan, Brian Street and David Bloome, *Writing Ourselves: Mass-Observation and Literacy Practice* (Cresskill, NJ: Hampton Press, 2000), Introduction.
13 Patrizia Gabrielli (ed.) 'La storia e i soggetti. La "gente comune", il dibattito storiografico e gli archivi in Italia', *Revista de historiografía*, 37 (2022), 8–126; Alexandre Frondizi and Emmanuel Fureix (eds) 'Ecrits et écritures populaires', *Revue d'histoire du dix-neuvième siècle*, 65 (2022).
14 ADN (Pieve Santo Stefano) E-89, Eufrosina Serventi, 27 December 1870.

15 Armando Petrucci, *La Scrittura: ideologia e rappresentazione* (Turin: Einaudi, 1986); Armando Petrucci, *Writing the Dead: Death and Writing Strategies in the Western Tradition*, trans. Michael Sullivan (Stanford, CA: Stanford University Press, 1998); Armando Petrucci, *Scrivere Lettere: una storia plurimillenaria* (Rome: Laterza, 2008), and many other studies.
16 Armando Petrucci, *Prima lezione di paleografia* (Rome and Bari: Laterza, 2002), Introduction.
17 Armando Petrucci, *Scrittura e popolo nella Roma Barocca, 1585–1721* (Rome: Qasar, 1982), p. 9.
18 Seminario Interdisciplinar de Estudios sobre Cultura Escrita (SIECE): www.siece.es/, accessed 16 January 2023.
19 Philippe Artières, *Le livre des vies coupables: Autobiographies de criminels (1896–1909)* (Paris: Albin Michel, 2000); Philippe Artières, *Un séminariste assassin: L'affaire Bladier, 1905* (Paris: Centre National de la Recherche Scientifique, 2020).
20 Jack Goody, *The Domestication of the Savage Mind* (Cambridge, UK: Cambridge University Press, 1977) and *The Logic of Writing and the Organisation of Society* (Cambridge, UK: Cambridge University Press, 1986).
21 Nicolas Adell, 'Writing one's life: The French school of the anthropology of writing', in Martyn Lyons and Rita Marquilhas (eds), *Approaches to the History of Written Culture: A World Inscribed* (Cham, Switzerland: Palgrave Macmillan, 2017), pp. 97–116.
22 Rudolf Dekker, 'Jacques Presser's heritage: Egodocuments in the study of history', *Memoria y civilización*, 5 (2002), 13–37.
23 Philippe Lejeune, *Le pacte autobiographique* (Paris: Seuil, 1975); Philippe Lejeune, *Le moi des demoiselles: enquête sur le journal de jeune fille* (Paris: Seuil, 1993), among many other titles; '"Cher Philippe": A *Festschrift* for Philippe Lejeune', special issue of *European Journal of Life Writing*, 7 (2018).
24 Fabre (ed.), *Écritures ordinaires*; Daniel Fabre (ed.), *Par écrit. Ethnologie des écritures quotidiennes* (Paris: Maison des Sciences de l'Homme, 1997).
25 Bernard Lahire, *La Raison des plus faibles* (Lille: Presses universitaires de Lille, 1993); Sheridan *et al.*, *Writing Ourselves*, pp. 14 and 283.
26 Marie-Claude Penloup, 'Literary temptations and leisure-time copying: Spontaneous adolescent writing in contemporary France', in Martyn Lyons (ed.), *Ordinary Writings, Personal Narratives: Writing Practices in Nineteenth and Twentieth-Century Europe* (Bern: Peter Lang, 2007), pp. 191–206.
27 Marina Roggero and Maria-Novella Borghetti, 'L'alphabétisation en Italie: une conquête féminine?', *Annales: histoire, sciences sociales*, 56:4–5 (2001), 919–24.
28 Angela Veronese, *Notizie della sua vita scritte da lei medesima* (Florence: Le Monnier, 1973), first published 1826.
29 Clelia Marchi, *Gnanca na Busia, 1912–1985* (Pieve Santo Stefano: Mondadori, 1992); Martyn Lyons, *The Writing Culture of Ordinary People in Europe, c. 1860–1920* (Cambridge, UK: Cambridge University Press, 2013), pp. 3–8 and 28–32.
30 Louis Barthas, *Les Carnets de Guerre de Louis Barthas, Tonnelier, 1914–19* (Paris: Maspéro, 1978).

31 James Amelang, *The Flight of Icarus: Artisan Autobiography in Early Modern Europe* (Stanford, CA: Stanford University Press, 1998).
32 Gérard Bacconnier, André Minet and Louis Soler (eds), *La plume au fusil: les poilus du Midi à travers leur correspondance* (Toulouse: Privat, 1985), p. 17 for 'bulimia'.
33 *Ibid.*, p. 29.
34 Antonio Gibelli, 'Emigrantes y Soldados. La escritura como práctica de masas en los siglos XIX y XX', in Antonio Castillo Gómez (ed.), *La conquista del alfabeto: Escritura y clases populares* (Gijón: Trea, 2002), pp. 189–203, p. 197.
35 Agnès Steuckardt, 'L'avvenire nelle lettere dei *poilus* comuni', in Caffarena and Murzilli (eds), *In Guerra con le parole*, pp. 203–20, p. 218.
36 Laura Martínez Martín, *Voces de la ausencia. Las cartas privadas de los emigrantes Asturianos a América (1856–1936)* (Gijón: Trea, 2019); David Fitzpatrick, *Oceans of Consolation: Personal Accounts of Irish Migration to Australia* (Melbourne: Melbourne University Press, 1995); David A. Gerber, *Authors of their Lives: The Personal Correspondence of British Immigrants to North America in the Nineteenth Century* (New York: New York University Press, 2006). I have not forgotten the literature on Italian emigration; for example, Antonio Gibelli and Fabio Caffarena, 'Le Lettere degli Emigranti', in Piero Bevilacqua, Andreina de Clementi and Emilio Franzina (eds), *Storia dell'emigrazione Italiana* (Rome: Donzelli, 2002), pp. 563–74.
37 William Edwin Adams, *Memoirs of a Social Atom*, 2 vols (London: Hutchinson, 1903), 1: pp. xvi and 154.
38 Sheridan *et al.*, *Writing Ourselves*, p. 196.
39 Gayatri Chakravorty Spivak, 'Can the subaltern speak?', in Cary Nelson and Lawrence Grossberg (eds), *Marxism and the Interpretation of Culture* (Chicago: University of Illinois Press, 1988), pp. 271–316.
40 For the Yirrala bark petitions (1963), see www.foundingdocs.gov.au/scan-sid-57.html, accessed 2 March 2021.
41 Martyn Lyons, *Dear Prime Minister: Letters to Robert Menzies, 1949–1966* (Sydney: University of New South Wales Press, 2021), pp. 31–4.
42 Antonelli, 'La grande guerra', pp. 42–3, citing Spitzer, *Lettere di Prigionieri*.
43 Witold Kula and Josephine Wtulich, *Writing Home: Immigrants in Brazil and the United States, 1890–1891* (New York: Columbia University Press, 1986), pp. 104 and 535.
44 Joachim Steffen, 'Les lettres des poilus et de leurs prédécesseurs; l'ars dictaminis populaire en France dans la diachronie', in Joachim Steffen, Harald Thun and Rainer Zaiser (eds), *Classes populaires, scripturalité et histoire de la langue: un bilan interdisciplinaire* (Kiel: Westensee, 2018), pp. 171–95.
45 Martínez, *Voces de la ausencia*, pp. 21–2.
46 Antonio Castillo Gómez, 'Secret voices: Prison graffiti in the Spanish Empire (16th–18th Century)', *Quaderni storici*, 157:1 (2018), 137–64, pp. 137–8.
47 Steven King, *Writing the Lives of the English Poor, 1750s–1830s* (London: McGill-Queen's University Press, 2019).
48 Lyons, *The Writing Culture of Ordinary People in Europe*.

49 Sigurður Gylfi Magnússon and Dávíð Ólafsson, *Minor Knowledge and Microhistory: Manuscript Culture in the Nineteenth Century* (London: Routledge, 2017).
50 Vincenzo Rabito, *Terra Matta*, ed. Evelina Santangelo and Luca Ricci (Turin: Einaudi, 2014); 'The story of *Terra matta*', special issue of *Journal of Modern Italian Studies*, 19:3 (2014), ed. David Moss.

2

Writings on the walls: approaches to graffiti in the early modern Hispanic world

Antonio Castillo Gómez

The common writer, ordinary writings and graffiti

Ever since Neanderthals started scribbling and painting in rock caves thousands of years ago, walls have been used for communication in general, and writing in particular. An infinite number of texts, scribbles and sketches have been affixed to, painted or inscribed on them – some elaborate and others more crude, some well-prepared and others more spontaneous, some issuing from the authorities regulating or protecting the use of those spaces and others clearly illegal and unauthorised.

Graffiti are extremely diverse in terms of the circumstances in which they were created and the many purposes for which people wrote messages or ordered them to be written. In this chapter, I will discuss various forms of mural graffiti, setting aside for the moment other wider applications of the term 'graffiti' to incisions on pottery and other objects, and marginal annotations and drawings in manuscripts and printed books.[1]

However hard the authorities tried (and still try) to prohibit writing on walls, the immediacy of walls makes them a space available to all. In the past, and specifically in the early modern Hispanic world with which this chapter is concerned, walls carried many written and visual traces of ordinary (or 'common') writers – that is to say, writers who did not belong to the social, political or religious elite. We can call those involved in this everyday gesture 'ordinary writers' in the sense that they did not aim for any literary merit. Their works exhibit the features which Daniel Fabre ascribed to 'ordinary writings': 'They aspire neither to the scrupulous exercise of correct usage nor to the consecration which, for more or less two centuries, has accompanied literary distancing.'[2] Here I consider ordinary writers as more or less similar to those identified by Samuel Johnson (1709–84) in his comments on Thomas Gray's *Elegy Written in a Country Churchyard* (1751): 'In the character of his *Elegy* I rejoice to concur with the common reader; for by the common sense of readers uncorrupted with literary prejudices, after all the refinements of subtility and the dogmatism of learning, must be finally decided all claim to poetical honours.'[3]

I focus therefore on a form of inscription (including drawing and painting), which in many cases was spontaneous and in others premeditated, sometimes done casually and at other times produced with the clear intention of enduring over time. In some cases graffiti took on a transgressive character when they appeared on walls where it was not permitted to write, but in other cases this was not so, because the authors were themselves the owners of the spaces where graffiti appeared or because graffiti were written in places where they were tolerated; for example, in prisons or shrines. From a historical perspective, graffiti are not always marginal, and they do not always fulfil the three criteria for transgressive communication listed by Francisco M. Gimeno Blay: 'Whoever writes on walls is, consciously or consciously, violating society's standard of conduct for communication, in various ways: 1) by illegally appropriating the space, 2) by using non-standard language and 3) in the contents of the texts communicated.'[4]

The Italian word 'graffiti' was not used until the discovery of the graffiti at Pompeii in the eighteenth century, and early modern Castilian adopted various terms to refer to the practice. Thus, in the *Tesoro de la lengua castellana o española* (1611) by Sebastián de Covarrubias (1539–1613), 'writing on the wall' (*escribir en la pared*) is documented as one form of 'writing'.[5] In one graffito in the Castle of Alaquàs, one could read 'whoever did the lettering (*letrero*) was drunk',[6] though the word *letrero* could equally refer to inscriptions on stone, coats of arms and coinage. If we turn to the *Corpus diacrónico del español*, limiting our search to the period 1500–1799, this polysemy is confirmed, and it also applies to the word *rótulo* (a sign or lettering).[7] Lastly, when French historian and politician Antoine de Brunel (1622–96) visited Madrid, he noted some graffiti in the street 'insulting women and well-born ladies' ('femmes de bien') and wrote: 'They are far from respectable and it is said that one woman, seeing their shameful parts painted on a wall with this inscription, *Sin hundo*, immediately took some charcoal and added *falta de corda*.'[8]

Historiography and sources

Historical graffiti have only recently qualified as a subject of scholarly research, largely because of persistent prejudices – which have not been entirely overcome – against their legitimacy as a historical source.[9] One landmark can nevertheless be identified in the recognition and analysis of a series of Florentine remains by the painter Carlo Lasinio at the end of the eighteenth century.[10] At almost the same time as Lasinio's book was published, the Danish scholar Frederik Münter travelled to Italy, where he took the opportunity to view the graffiti in the Inquisitorial prison in Palermo, as he noted in his diary.[11] Leaving aside various works in the mid-nineteenth century on headstones and outdoor engravings, another important moment came with the publication of Raphael Garrucci's work on the graffiti at Pompeii,[12] followed by the fourth volume of the *Corpus Inscriptionum Latinarum*, devoted to writings on the walls at Pompeii and Herculaneum,[13] as well as other contemporary studies on graffiti on historical monuments.[14]

The Palermo graffiti were rediscovered a little later, in 1906, by the anthropologist Giuseppe Pitré, although his work only appeared posthumously.[15] The first Spanish studies of historical graffiti appeared at about the same time, and they made a valuable contribution to the accurate dating of ancient remains, as was the case with the medieval graffiti found on the wall running from the San Miguel hermitage to the path to the sacred mount in Granada, and other discoveries in the castle of Alcalá de Guadaira (Seville).[16] More systematic investigations were carried out in Catalonia in the early 1930s, including those on the graffiti discovered on the romanesque murals of Sant Miguel de Cruïlles (province of Gerona).[17]

Under Franco's dictatorship, Spanish university research entered a period of deprivation and intellectual decline from which it only began to emerge at the end of the 1960s. The dominant approach, however, was a far cry from the historical focus then being developed by Violet Pritchard in her study of medieval graffiti carved into the walls and pillars of many British churches.[18] Her work staked a claim for the importance of writings and drawings on walls for our knowledge of the economy, social structure and way of life of a given place and time, and she treated them as historical sources.

This new perspective was enriched in subsequent publications, some of which expressly concerned the modern era. For example, Juliet Fleming's monographs examined graffiti and other written phenomena like tattoos and ceramics in early modern England,[19] Raffaella Sarti's work analysed the extensive corpus in the ducal palace of Urbino,[20] Charlotte Guichard studied the signatures and messages written on Roman frescoes by visitors to the city from the sixteenth to the nineteenth centuries[21] and, more recently, there is Giovanna Fiume's work on the impressive collection in the ancient Inquisitorial prison in Palermo.[22] We can add to these the various studies on graffiti in the Hispanic world referred to in the course of this chapter, together with compendia of historical graffiti in different periods which illustrate the vitality currently enjoyed by this field of research.[23]

As this academic work highlights, the first impulse has been to ensure the preservation and study of the surviving sources and of those which have surfaced as a result of archaeological intervention. For several decades archaeology has confronted new challenges, at a time when cultural heritage has consolidated its importance as a research field attracting public interest. As a result, what once was covered in plaster is now revealed, recovered, documented, studied and preserved in museums. Of course some evidence will always be permanently lost, because of: (1) its material fragility, caused by the techniques employed in its creation and the places where it is written or painted; (2) the changes and renovations which the buildings and sites of inscription have undergone; and (3) some heritage restoration policies followed in the past, which took little care to preserve them and regarded them as insignificant and little more than vandalism.

As well as preserving graffiti, preferably in situ, and establishing a full description, researchers must take account of all those sources which help to explain them and identify their space-time co-ordinates, which may include, for example, literary and visual sources from which we can document the place of graffiti in daily life and in the social imaginary of the past. Archival documentation is indispensable, whether for information about the buildings where graffiti are found or to interpret them from as many angles as possible, from establishing the identity of the authors or artists to deducing their motives for writing. Political and ecclesiastical regulations, ordinances and edicts, moral treatises and legal literature are fundamental for elucidating the legality or illegality of the practice, even if this is not always clear cut, and for understanding the ethical and criminal status of some graffiti.

References to graffiti can be traced in autobiographical texts, biographies, travel diaries, chronicles and historical works. Authors of such texts often note messages written on the walls. Bernal Díaz del Castillo (1496–1584), who participated in the conquest of Mexico and wrote the monumental *Historia verdadera de la Conquista de Nueva España*, finished in 1568 and published for the first time in 1632, referred in this work to graffiti which appeared daily on the walls of the palace where Hernán Cortés lived: 'While Cortes was at Coyoacan, he lodged in a palace with whitewashed walls on which it was easy to write with charcoal and ink; and every morning malicious remarks appeared, some in verse and some in prose, in the manner of lampoons.' After giving a detailed account of their contents, he added that Cortés himself joined the mural conversation, writing that 'a blank wall is a fool's writing paper'. By next morning, someone had added: 'a wise man's too, who knows the truth, as His Majesty will do very soon!' According to Diaz, this was enough for Cortés to identify the authors as his enemies Diego Velázquez, Gregorio de Villalobos and Juan de Mansilla, and he 'flew into a rage and publicly proclaimed that they must write no more libels or he would punish the shameless villains'.[24]

The wall and the hand

As Roland Barthes remarked about the contemporary age, 'what constitutes graffiti is in fact neither the inscription nor its message, but the wall'.[25] Writing or sketching on a wall is not comparable to doing so on paper. The smooth or rough quality of the surface governs the movement of the hand so that the writer's meagre level of graphic competence is not always to blame for the poor execution of the work. On a wall, it is harder to keep a straight line, maintain even spacing between letters or produce an accurate sketch, which does not mean these will not sometimes be achieved.

The careful execution of certain graffiti throws doubt on the spontaneity often attributed to them. No doubt many scribbles, incomplete drawings or calligraphic exercises are spontaneously produced, but others are preliminary sketches of what the writer sought to write or represent, and many reflect a desire for permanence or a premeditated idea, even if the final outcome is affected by the technique adopted or the inconsistency of the surface of the wall. Some graffiti on the walls of the Inquisitorial prison in Palermo not only demonstrate the level of graphic and linguistic competence of their authors, probably clerics, but also suggest some planning and preparation, and they resemble the format Armando Petrucci called *scrittura d'apparato* (formal or monumental writing).[26] In Fiume's opinion, we should not consider them as part of a graphic exhibition – another idea of Petrucci – mounted by the Inquisition; rather, they were produced by prisoners in order to take control of the space and give their cell a sacred significance, just as drawing figures of saints also did.[27] This would also apply to the sentence daubed in regular, black capital letters which runs like a frieze around several walls of the episcopal prison in Tarazona (Zaragoza province). Finding inspiration in confessional handbooks and moralising literature, the text encouraged prisoners to ready themselves for death and place their hopes in divine justice.[28]

The technique employed by the prisoners might have been: making an incision on the wall with a punch, a key or some instrument that would leave a mark; painting or writing with charcoal or ochre or rust from their chains, brick dust, soot from candles or some other pigment; or chipping out the wall with a spike, chisel and mallet. It would have depended on the type of surface, the instruments at hand and the time available. Prisoners, for example, could take all day to produce graffiti, while graffiti produced by masons and craftsmen building ramparts, palaces, churches and personal residences had to be written in a moment of leisure or during a celebration at the end of their work.

On a purely graphic level, walls document the daily uses of writing and, allowing for the problems of any given surface, they reflect the literacy competence of the authors. At one end of the scale, there were those who wrote fairly correctly and imitated the formal techniques of monumental inscription,[29] while at the other end, there were those who showed lesser writing skills or a more fragile control of literacy, or both. The walls illustrate the graphic evolution of the early modern era: in graffiti from the late fifteenth and the early sixteenth centuries, gothic script is still present or else it coexists with humanist script which is becoming more widespread, as we see in other areas of scribal production – all products of the diverse scriptural world of the territories of the Hispanic monarchy. As the sixteenth century advanced, the role of humanist script grew more dominant, and it is very visible in the Palermo graffiti, which mainly date from the seventeenth century. In the Iberian Peninsula and in the American viceroyalties, humanist script dominates in capitals, whereas bastard script is preferred for lower case, and this preference persists in eighteenth-century examples.

The languages of graffiti represent a broad geographical spread and considerable cultural diversity. Graffiti in Spanish, Italian, French and English have been recorded in the Inquisitorial prison of the El Trovador tower in the Aljafería Palace in Zaragoza.[30] In the Palermo prison, the cultural mix of the Mediterranean left its mark in graffiti: in a total of 264 items of text, the languages most represented were Latin (121, 46 per cent), Italian (59, 22 per cent) and Sicilian (46, 16 per cent), with small numbers (making up less than 1 per cent each) in English (6), Hebrew (2) and Spanish (1) as well as a few that were bilingual (Latin and Italian, Latin and English). The language could not be identified for 33 items (13 per cent) because of their illegibility and poor state of preservation. Of the total number of texts, 80 per cent are in prose, including verses and psalms from the Bible, and the rest in verse, mainly in Sicilian.[31] In some houses in Granada, where some areas were devoted to semi-public use (e.g. as a workplace), different inscriptions have been found in Arabic, providing certain confirmation of the use of this language in the sixteenth century in spite of the Christianisation of the city.[32] Similarly, in New Spain, we find some inscriptions in Náhua and Tarasco (Indigenous languages of central Mexico).[33]

Although it is often impossible to match graffiti inscriptions with their authors, the authors, usually male but sometimes female, came from a wide range of social groups. Their identity largely depends on the moment when they wrote, and on the site and the purpose of the building. Just as members of the nobility left their marks on the walls in the Castle of Alaquàs,[34] so people of modest social status from the countryside wrote graffiti in the military prison at Broto (Huesca province) as well as in other town jails in south-east Aragon.[35] The names scratched on a building as construction progressed belonged to the workers and artisans who worked on it.[36] In fortresses, it is no surprise to find graffiti written by soldiers, including foreign soldiers like the British ones in the War of the Spanish Succession (1701–15), who left written traces in Villena castle.[37] In the belfry of Mallorca cathedral, along with the graffiti of bandits and various artisans, a certain Antoni Casnoves (probably Casanoves) explained that he was a bugler, Sebastià Sbert was a haberdasher and trimmer and Joan García a turner.[38] In the Palermo prison, we find graffiti of many clerics, not surprisingly because ecclesiastics constituted one third of the Inquisition's prisoners in this region.[39] Religious themes, however, were not particularly prominent in their graffiti, but they were in the old episcopal prison in Tarazona.[40] Students and professors were responsible for graffiti in the form of *vítores*, many of them simply testing new pens, like those on the interior window sills of the Colegio Mayor de San Ildefonso in Alcalá de Henares (*vítores* are signs painted in black or ochre marking the public celebration of a graduation with a university degree or some other personal achievement; see Figure 2.1).[41]

One prisoner in the Inquisitorial prison in Palermo invited others to continue the map of Sicily which he had begun;[42] additions were made to works by later writers; writers imitated components written or drawn earlier; or graffiti replied to other graffiti in a kind of mural conversation – all of which suggest interaction and a sense of community. This is most evident in graffiti in prisons, where the inmates shared the same isolation and loss of freedom, but it also appears in messages left by pilgrims in various shrines. There is nothing

Figure 2.1 *Vítores* in the Colegio Mayor de San Ildefonso, office of the Rector of the University of Alcalá (circa sixteenth century to seventeenth century). Photo Antonio Castillo Gómez. All rights reserved and permission to use the figure must be obtained from the copyright holder, Universidad de Alcalá.

in the Hispanic world to compare with the Italian shrines of Sebastiano in Arborio and the sacred mount of Varallo, both in Vercelli province. According however to Joris Hoefnagel, one of the collaborators on the *Civitates Orbis Terrarum*, there was a hermitage in the mid-sixteenth century on the hill of St Helena in Granada, which was a former mosque, and 'nearly all' visitors to the city wrote their names on its walls: 'ad quod fere omnes, qui Granatam visere cupiunt, ascendunt, ut eius templi muro, suum, et patriae nomen inscribant' (which nearly all those who desired to see Granada climbed, and on the wall of the shrine, inscribed their names and country).[43]

Is writing graffiti, authorised or unauthorised, a legal or illegal practice? The answer is not as straightforward as it seems, especially in past societies. As far as graffiti in domestic interiors is concerned, aside from the permissiveness described by Juliet Fleming in Elizabethan England,[44] the use of such spaces depended on the owners, who held 'lordship over graphic space'.[45] According to Joseph Hall (1574–1656), author of the dystopian *Fooliana* (1605), it was in bad taste that 'the houses are all passinglie well painted within, especially with the names of their ancestry, their guests, and acquaintance, gracefully delineate with coale and candle', which led him to add the marginal note: 'muro bianco carta di matto: a white wall is a foole's book'.[46]

While some graffiti were tolerated and even well regarded, others were rejected and even persecuted for different reasons. Hence, an edict of the rector of the Roman Studium Urbis, issued in 1689, severely forbade 'anyone to paint and write with charcoal, pencil, chalk or other instruments on walls, doors, chapiters, windows, columns, cornices, chairs or benches'. Aside from the fact that this pointed out the many ways of writing or painting graffiti on a variety of surfaces, this mandate was expressly aimed at 'any indecent figure or expression, letters, signs, characters, verses, mottos, portraits, arms, emblems', and warned all not 'to soil them in any way, even when agreeable things are painted or written'.[47] Mainly for aesthetic reasons, the city of Arezzo prohibited the drawing of 'signs, scribbles or other things with coal or something similar' in the Loggia della Misericordia, decorated by Giorgio Vasari.[48]

The graffiti of the sacred mount of Varallo, founded in 1491 by the Franciscan friar Bernardino Caimi (1425–99), were expressly banned by several bishops, and the ban was reinforced by an order of the Counter-Reformation bishop Carlo Bascapè (1550–1615), who ordered a notice to this effect to be placed on the door to the shrine and in the chapels. But the decree failed to have the desired effect, because not even the Franciscans who looked after the shrine supported it, knowing full well that the future maintenance of the sanctuary largely depended on donations from pilgrims.[49] At San Sebastiano in Arborio, where about 150 graffiti were carved into the mural paintings between the sixteenth and the nineteenth centuries, it appears there was no prohibition against it.[50] These two cases were treated quite differently, although the graffiti in both testified to the devotion of visitors.

In early modern prisons, with their own penitentiary regime and dark and insanitary cells, a certain tolerance prevailed, at least in the Inquisitorial prisons.[51] On the other hand, the exchange of messages between prisoners and the outside world was more strictly controlled – at least the regulations suggest this – and probably more so in the prisons of the Holy Office.[52]

Nowhere in the early modern Hispanic world do we encounter any prohibition resembling the Barcelona ordinances of 1302, which stated: 'It is forbidden to paint or write on the enclosures or walls of the streets or thoroughfares, and anyone who has painted or written on their walls and enclosures is to erase all of them.'[53] Nevertheless, when graffiti defamed living people or divinities, or attacked Catholic faith and morality, it is reasonable to assume that the same censure and punishment applied to them as it did to libellous pamphlets.[54] The Jesuit Gerónimo López raised definite moral objections to the graffiti he encountered in Valencia and Salamanca when he went there to preach in 1651 and 1653, respectively. As soon as he arrived in each city, he warned that 'the walls, doors and hallways of many houses, streets and squares' had been defaced by obscene and blasphemous messages. Outraged, he devoted occasional sermons to the topic and, from the pulpit, exhorted the people to erase them. He even threatened to do so himself, 'going through the streets with a pot of lime, mixed with water, erasing these abominable and ugly things with a brush'. But it did not go any further. The faithful obeyed and a group of people, led by nobles and priests, immediately got down to work.[55]

Reading graffiti

In *El lazarillo de ciegos caminantes*, a sort of travel guide to Buenos Aires and Lima, probably printed between 1775 and 1776, the author Alonso Carrió de la Vandera provided this notice about the practice of writing names and indecencies on the walls of Peruvian inns (*tambos*):

> In addition to the obscenities that they print on the walls with coals, there is no table or bench where the surname and first name are not carved in the iron hand of these fools. This last usage is very old among pilgrims from distant lands, to give news of their routes to those who seek them along the royal road, putting dates on the walls of hospitals, which custom became so common in America that there is no *tambo* or cave that is not adorned with names, surnames and obscene words.[56]

This is one of those literary references which we cannot match with any recorded graffiti, but without it we would not know of their existence.

Similarly Bernal Díaz del Castillo, mentioned earlier, quoted one inscription written in charcoal on marble in a house in Texcoco, in which some Spaniards had been detained, saying: 'Here was imprisoned the unfortunate Juan Yuste with many others who followed in his company.'[57]

Graffiti 'convey a message in the form of writing, but at the same time they cannot exist without the material support and the context in which they are found';[58] in other words, 'the support is part of the message'.[59] Interpreting graffiti, however, is often risky and may yield uncertain results, given the fragmentary nature of the surviving evidence. Most of it comes from interiors: churches, palaces, convents, residences, prisons, fortresses, etc. On exterior walls, on the other hand, all that has survived apart from inscriptions of monuments are the *vítores* of university students.[60]

On a figurative level, what stands out in these corpuses is the repetition of certain themes, whether geometrical (grills, cruciforms, steles, circles, triangles or lines), vegetable, zoomorphic, anthropomorphic, architectural, nautical, military, religious or connected to clothing, celebrations, etc. – that is to say, everything that used to be part of the artist's life or which might evoke certain memories, especially if he remained in the same place for some time, which might have been the case with prison graffiti. Thus we find sketches with religious and naval themes everywhere, although there are many variations in the kind of ship portrayed, depending on where the graffiti were written.[61] In former Mexican convents, as one might expect, we find Indigenous themes and images, like the *tamenes* (porters) painted in the convent of St Francis of Assisi in Tepeapulco (Hidalgo state). Here we also find graffiti expressing a coarse sense of humour, creatures like the *tarasca* (a kind of snake), large heads, giants, dancers, devils and a witch, as well as sirens or bulls. In one scene, some devils can be observed inciting a couple of lovers to fornicate (see Figure 2.2).[62]

As for textual graffiti, it is often difficult to make out the precise content because they are not completely legible, or because the text has been written over or obscured by adjacent inscriptions. We frequently find numerical marks to record the passing of time (for instance, in prison) together with the dates when the graffiti were created and the status of the authors or some other information which helps us to contextualise them. This is obvious in registers of births in baptisteries and deaths in crypts. One example stands out in the graffiti preserved in Ibiza's cathedral, which we might call 'professional', in the sense that they were created by the priest and the secretary responsible for ecclesiastical documentation. Because so many graffiti were recorded here, they constitute a sort of book of the dead on the wall. The text is often very concise and confined to no more than a name and a date, but sometimes it notes the act of burial and the profession of the deceased: 'D(i)a 20 de Abr(i)l de (17)66 sen(terro) (Ys)abet Briones'

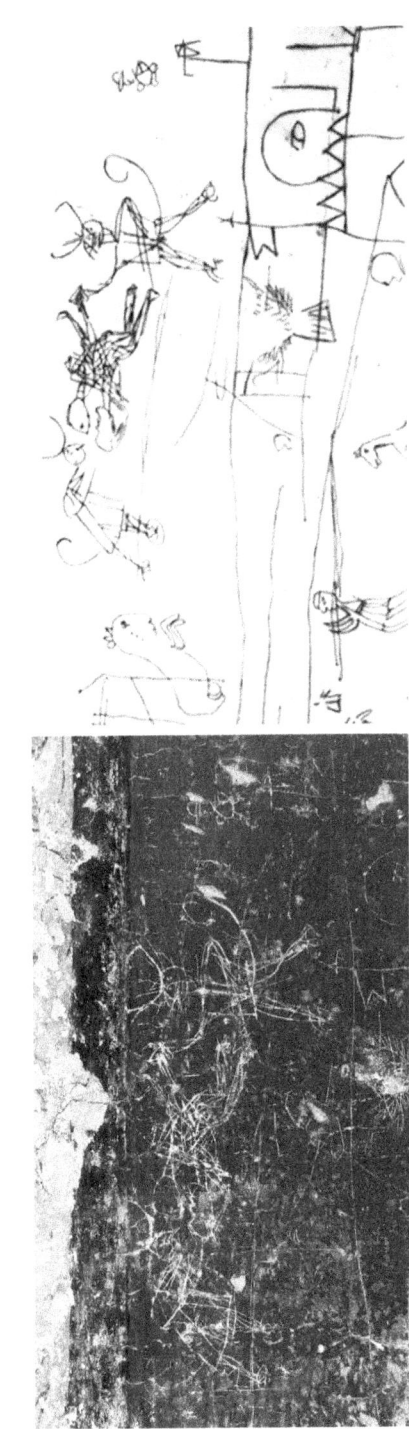

Figure 2.2 [Left] Devils encouraging a couple to have sex, in the upper cloister of the old convent of St Francis of Assisi in Tepeapulco (Hidalgo, Mexico). Two horned figures can be made out, standing to the right and left of a prone couple having sex. [Right] Tracing of photograph on the left. All rights reserved and permission to use the figure must be obtained from the copyright holder, Instituto Nacional de Antropología e Historia, Secretaría de Cultura-INAH-Mex.

(On 20 April 1766 Ysabet Briones was buried) or 'Dia 18 octubre de (17)86 se enterro D(o)n Domingo Rosello P(res)b(ite)ro' (On 18 October 1786 Don Domingo Rosello, priest, was buried).'[63]

Writers in prisons scratched their names on the walls, and Ruth Ahnert has remarked that 'writing one's name inside a prison means asserting the existence of the writer, even if he was about to die'.[64] In such circumstances, their assertive and testimonial function is incontrovertible; but this is not confined to prisons. Thus, in the Yuso monastery of San Millán de la Cogolla (La Rioja municipality), a residence for novices, the walls recorded their dates of arrival, the days they took holy orders and other details of monastic life.[65] Writing one's name on a wall was a way of leaving a trace of one's existence and presence. When an author added references to their profession, with dates and short remarks, they were composing a sort of 'minimal autobiography', free of 'any useless or impossible extra narrative'.[66]

Names and other marks repeated several times suggest the writers were practising how to write. Writers wrote about almost anything on the walls – songs, prayers, proverbs and poems, and some coded political criticism, which is probably how we should interpret this text: 'Aragon ne tiene justicia ni guardahazón (*sic*) (There is no justice or security in Aragon)', written in capitals in a cell in Tarazona jail.[67] There are two graffiti in the Castle of Alaquàs containing literary references. One is the work of somebody clearly familiar with Ariosto, as they wrote: 'Long live the house of Mongrana and Chiaramonte and may the Maganzas die', indicating leading protagonists in *Orlando furioso*. Below this phrase, he sketched a disembarkation scene reminiscent of engravings in the first Castilian translation of the poem (published in Antwerp, 1549) and in the Venetian edition of 1584.[68] The second example dates from the mid-sixteenth century and contains ten complete stanzas, with a few variations, of a poem by Alonso Pérez de Vivero (1458–1508), Viscount of Altamira.[69]

Between heaven and earth

The prisoner's uncertain destiny, the need for divine counsel in difficult situations and the religious tenor of the period influenced the prolific Christian symbolism evident in graffiti. In Broto jail, Christian symbols coexisted with pagan elements typical of the rural communities of the Ara valley in Huesca.[70] Alongside prayers, quotations from the Bible, psalms and sacred names, the rich iconography of the graffiti in the Inquisitorial prison in Palermo, executed with extraordinary skill, constitutes 'a true inventory of early modern religious observance'.[71] The *Crucifixion* painted in one cell and the *Descent into Hell* in another (see Figure 2.3), together with numerous effigies of saints, are enough to persuade us that these were the work

Figure 2.3 *Descent into Hell*, in the prison of the Inquisition in Palermo, seventeenth century. Photo David Sebastiani. All rights reserved and permission to use the figure must be obtained from the copyright holder, David Sebastiani.

of professionals. The artists, moreover, had a pictural culture and memory drawn from the interplay between the repertoire of reputed Italian painters and the imagery of *edicole sacre* (local shrines), popular engravings and secular art.[72] This is not only true of prisons – although these paintings could take on a special significance in that context – as drawings of crosses, calvaries, crucifixions, monograms or representations of Christ, and images of the Virgin and saints appear in every site.

Religious graffiti in prisons can be interpreted as way of appropriating a space of oppression in order to create a more friendly environment and to convert it into a place of worship. Prayers and images painted on the walls could stimulate the prisoner's memory and support him in his devotions.[73] Of course, images that in one context expressed religious devotion and provided spiritual consolation might in another context provoke quite a different response. They might go as far as the 'small rebellion' that Giovanna Fiume detected in the figures of the halberdiers accompanying Christ on the road to Golgotha painted in Palermo prison; their clothing betrays them – they are dressed as officers of the Inquisition instead of Roman soldiers.[74] Graffiti might also be part of a declaration of heterodoxy, like that of the apostate Gabriel Tudesco, imprisoned in 1630 in the same Palermo prison after refusing to abjure Islam. On the wall of his cell, he sketched an image of Our Lady of Itria, 'which was complete and very fine', and then defaced the crucifixes and saints surrounding it with his own excrement.[75]

Among the themes and stories immortalised in graffiti, we also find frescos about historical events. In Palermo prison, there is a sketch of the Battle of Lepanto attributed to the fisherman Francesco Mannarino, imprisoned for apostasy. According Fiume, he may have been inspired by Paolo Veronese's allegories painted in the 1570s (*Allegory of the Battle of Lepanto*, 1572–73, and *Allegory of Lepanto*, 1578), which Mannarino may have seen in Venice, where he was pardoned by the Holy Office.[76] Another prisoner, this time a military man, Andreo Bernat, used the walls of Bellver castle to represent the siege of that fortress during the War of the Spanish Succession. Imprisoned in 1714 according to one inscription, he produced a scene composed of a series of galleons with identifiable flags (English, the fleur-de-lis or a cross), castles, doves, a two-headed eagle (the emblem of the Habsburg dynasty) and firing cannons.[77]

These images were produced in prison, but we can find examples of visual graffiti with historical meaning elsewhere too. In the ancient Augustine convent and college of St Nicholas of Tolentino in Actopán (Mexico), a series of graffiti forms a narrative cycle. Completed in the old cells of the upper cloister, probably at the beginning of 1629 (a date taken from one of the graffiti), the graffiti represents the fall of Viceroy Diego Carrillo de Mendoza y Pimentel (d. 1636), Marquis of Gelves, following the rebellion of 1624, and it served as a warning to his successor, Rodrigo Pacheco y Osorio (1580–1652). On the northern wall, a scene represents a welcoming feast for a powerful personage, but it is accompanied by swords and monsters, underlining the many-sided interpretations suggested by these graffiti (see Figure 2.4). The interaction of European elements like the Habsburg coat

Figure 2.4 Detail of a battle scene in the ancient convent of St Nicholas of Tolentino in Actopán (Mexico), circa 1629. All rights reserved and permission to use the figure must be obtained from the copyright holder, Instituto Nacional de Antropología e Historia, Secretaria de Cultura-INAH-Mex.

of arms with Mexican themes like the eagle devouring the serpent, recalling the foundation myth of the city of Tenochtitlán, illustrates the hybrid culture which developed in the american territories and invites multiple readings. There is a parallel between some of the figures and other paintings in the convent that were completed by Indigenous artists, and also with some Indigenous codices, pointing to the Otomi people as possible authors of these unusual visual graffiti.[78]

We find a similar cultural hybridity in the figurative panel on three levels drawn in the prison of the Holy Office in Llerena (Badajoz province), dated before 1570, when the Inquisitorial court changed location. According to Francisco Ascacibar, these graffiti tell a story in images about cultural encounters in New Spain during the early years of conquest. Various figures and symbols portray the destruction of Mayan and Aztec traditions, while others represent the new social and spiritual order established by the Spanish conquistadors.[79]

This kind of testimony illustrates the interpretive complexity of some graffiti, especially paintings, in a period when the wall clearly played a significant role as a barometer of the historical realities and political and religious problems of the Hispanic monarchy. This also gives us the key to interpret the succinct phrase 'fueresse luego oliveros' or 'furesse oliveros' (the word 'luego' is partially unclear), which can still be read in the Calle del Carme in Barcelona, at the entrance to the old hospital of Santa Creu (see Figure 2.5). It is only a hypothesis, but it is a reasonable guess that 'oliveros' refers to the Count-Duke Olivares, minister of King Philip IV. The message would then make sense in the context of the Reapers' War (1640–52), the Catalan uprising against the King, which the royal favourite played a great part in suppressing.[80]

Colophon

In spite of the scepticism which has been voiced for some time in some academic circles, it is clear that historical graffiti constitute a dynamic and expanding area of research, attracting various approaches and analytical points of view: historical, artistic, linguistic and, of course, all those concerned with the history of written culture. As we have seen, all ranks of people wrote about any manner of things, and they did so inside churches, convents, prisons, castles or private residences. In graffiti within their own walls and in the streets, as well as in graffiti which have only left a record in chronicles, biographies and other kinds of literature, the prosperous classes have left traces of their presence, as in the graffiti found in aristocratic palaces. So too have the educated classes, as shown by some of the poems and

Figure 2.5 Graffiti saying 'fueresse luego oliveros' or 'fueresse oliveros', at the entrance gate to the old hospital of Santa Creu in Barcelona, 1640–52. Photo Antonio Castillo Gómez. All rights reserved and permission to use the figure must be obtained from the copyright holder, Antonio Castillo Gómez.

prayers on walls. But many ordinary people are also represented, some sufficiently literate and others who handled their writing instruments a little more awkwardly. Ordinary writers recorded words and drawings on whatever walls were available (e.g. in prisons), either because they had no paper to hand or perhaps because 'paper was not necessarily the most obvious, or suitable, medium for writing', as Juliet Fleming wrote about the graffiti in private English homes in the early modern period.[81]

The functions of graffiti were as varied as the urges to write or draw which drove their authors. Many wished to leave a trace of themselves; hence the proliferation of names which we encounter everywhere. Other graffiti, like prayers and devotional mottos, demonstrate the religiosity of the period both in their orthodoxy and heterodoxy. Some perform an explicatory function almost in the style of a notary or a chronicler, as in the case of graffiti by friar Severino Roures, who wrote in one of the confessionals in the eastern gallery of the gothic cloister in the old Carmen convent in Valencia – these were closed up definitively on 4 July 1670 when the cloister was renovated.[82] He even noted the cost of the renovations – 1,050 pounds – and the prior responsible. Others, like those graffiti which express the blend of cultures and religions in some territories of the early modern Hispanic empire, require us to consider multifaceted interpretations. Lastly, we must not overlook graffiti reflecting the political moment, even if these are not the most plentiful, whether they are critical, like the ones in Barcelona already mentioned, or in praise of a king, as in the effigies of Philip IV or slogans like 'long live the King', with all his titles, that somebody wrote in the belfry of the church of San Salvador in Cocentaina, Alicante, where surely not many people could have seen it.[83]

In conclusion, picking up a piece of chalk or charcoal to write or draw implied a desire for self-expression, communication and leaving a memorial which we should not overlook. Graffiti are not banal writings, but rather they constitute a rich source of historical information, even if they remain hostage to the fragility of preservation and all the problems inherent in their contextualisation, and above all when we are dealing with names with no dates, freestanding phrases or unspecified drawings. Graffiti challenge us as historians because they often register the voices of ordinary people unaccustomed to the act of writing.

Translated by Martyn Lyons

Notes

This work was supported by the Spanish government's Research Agency project '*Vox populi*. Spaces, practices and strategies of visibility of marginal writing in the early modern and modern periods' (PID2019-107881GB-I00AEI/10.13039/501100011033).

1. Jason Scott-Warren, 'Reading graffiti in the early modern book', *Huntington Library Quarterly*, 73:3 (2010), 363–81; Janine Roger, 'Graffiti and the medieval margin', in Chloé Ragazzoli, Ömür Harmansah, Chiara Salvador and Elizabeth Frood (eds), *Scribbling through History: Graffiti, Places and Peoples from Antiquity to Modernity* (London: Bloomsbury, 2017), pp. 175–88.
2. Daniel Fabre, 'Introduction', in D. Fabre (ed.), *Écritures ordinaires* (Paris: P.O.L/ Centre Georges Pompidou, 1993), pp. 11–19, p. 11.
3. Samuel Johnson, 'The life of Gray', in S. Johnson, *The Lives of the Poets (1779–81)*, ed. G. B. Hill (Oxford: Clarendon, 1905), https://jacklynch.net/Texts/gray.html, accessed 29 April 2022.
4. Francisco M. Gimeno Blay, '*Défense d'afficher*. Cuando escribir es transgredir', in F. M. Gimeno Blay and María Luz Mandingorra Llavata (eds), '*Los muros tienen la palabra*'. *Materiales para una historia de los graffiti* (Valencia: Publicacions Universitat de València, 1997), pp. 11–26, p. 14.
5. Sebastián de Covarrubias, *Tesoro de la lengua castellana o española* (1611), ed. Martín de Riquer (Barcelona: Altafulla, 5th edition, 2003), p. 541.

6 Víctor Manuel Algarra Pardo and Paloma Berrocal Ruiz, *Los grafitis históricos del castel de Alaquàs* (Alaquàs: Ayuntamiento, 2016), p. 11.
7 Real Academia Española, *Corpus diacrónico del español*, www.rae.es/banco-de-datos/corde, accessed 14 April 2022.
8 Antoine de Brunel, *Voyage d'Espagne, curieux, historique et politique, fait en l'année 1655* (Paris: Robert de Ninville, 1666), p. 47. '*Sin hundo*' perhaps means *sin fondo*, a bottomless pit, alluding to a woman with an insatiable sexual appetite. '*Falta de corda*' perhaps should read '*falta de cuerda*', because *corda* is Catalan, meaning 'without a rope'. One woman at least is here accused of being a prostitute, hence the drawing of the female genitalia.
9 Carlo Tedeschi, 'I graffiti, una fonte scritta trascurata', in Daniele Bianconi (ed.), *Storia della scrittura ed altre storie* (Rome: Accademia Nazionale dei Lincei, 2014), pp. 363–81.
10 Carlo Lasinio, *Ornati pressi da graffiti e pitture antiche esistenti in Firenze, Pagni e Bardi* (Florence, 1789).
11 Øjvind Andreasen (ed.), *Frederik Münter et Mindeskrift, vol. III: Aus den Tagebüchern Friedrich Münters, Wander-und Lehrjahre eines dänischen Gelehrten. 2 Teil, 1785–1787* (Copenhagen: Haase, 1937), pp. 50–2.
12 Raphael Garrucci, *Graffiti di Pompei* (Paris: Benjamin Duprat, 1856).
13 Karl Zangemeister and Richard Schöne (eds), *Inscriptiones parietariae Pompeianae, Herculanenses, Stabianae* (Berlin: Akademie der Wissenschaften, 1879).
14 Charles Reed Peers, 'Greek graffiti from Der el Baharí and El Kab', *Journal of Hellenic Studies*, 19 (1899), 13–18.
15 Giuseppe Pitré, *Del Sant'Uffizio di Palermo e di un carcere di esso* (Rome: Società editrice del libro italiano, 1940).
16 Tijnófilo [Diego Marín López], 'Crónica del Centro', *Boletín del Centro Artístico de Granada*, 1:6 (1886), 1–3; Claudio Sanz Arizmendi, 'Grafitos antiguos del castillo de Alcalá de Guadaira', *Revista de Archivos, Bibliotecas y Museos*, X:7–8 (1906), 101–5.
17 Joaquim Folch i Torres, 'Les pintures murals de Sant Miquel de Cruïlles i els grafits de les pintures murals catalanes', *Butlletí dels Museus d'Art de Barcelona*, 12:11 (1932), 146–50.
18 Violet Pritchard, *English Medieval Graffiti* (Cambridge, UK: Cambridge University Press, 1967).
19 Juliet Fleming, *Graffiti and the Writing Arts of Early Modern England* (Philadelphia: University of Pennsylvania Press, 2001).
20 Raffaella Sarti, 'La pietra racconta. Un palazzo da leggere', in R. Sarti (ed.), *La pietra racconta. Un palazzo da leggere* (Casinina: Arte Grafiche della Torre, 2017), pp. 14–183, and by the same author in English, 'Renaissance graffiti: The case of the Ducal Palace of Urbino', in Sandra Cavallo and Silvia Evangelisti (eds), *Domestic Institutional Interiors in Early Modern Europe* (Farnham, UK: Ashgate, 2009), pp. 51–81.
21 Charlotte Guichard, *Graffitis. Inscrire son nom à Rome (XVIe-XIXe siècle)* (Paris: Seuil, 2014).

22 Giovanna Fiume, *Del Santo Uffizio in Sicilia e delle sue carceri* (Rome: Viella, 2021).
23 Pablo Ozcáriz Gil (ed.), *La memoria en la piedra. Estudios sobre grafitos históricos* (Pamplona: Gobierno de Navarra, 2012); Francisco Reyes Téllez and Gonzalo Viñuales Ferreiro (eds), *Grafitos históricos hispánicos I. Homenaje a Félix Palomero* (Madrid: Universidad Rey Juan Carlos, 2016); Francisco Reyes and Gonzalo Viñuales (eds), *Grafitos históricos hispánicos II* (Madrid: Asociación para la Investigación y la Difusión de la Arqueología Pública, JAS Arqueología, 2020).
24 Bernal Díaz, *The Conquest of New Spain*, trans. J. M. Cohen (London: Penguin, 1963), pp. 411–2.
25 Roland Barthes, *L'Obvie et l'obtus* (Paris: Seuil, 1992), p. 154, first published 1982.
26 Armando Petrucci, *La scrittura. Ideologia e rappresentazione*, ed. Antonio Ciaralli with Attilio Bartoli Langeli and Marco Palma (Rome: Luiss University Press, 2021), p. 20, first published 1986.
27 Giovanna Fiume, 'Justice, expiation and forgiveness in the graffiti and drawings of Palermo's secret prisons', *Quaderni storici*, 157:1 (2018), 95–7; Fiume, *Del Santo Uffizio in Sicilia*, pp. 268–73.
28 José Ángel García Serrano, *Tiempo de Graffiti. Los calabozos del Palacio Episcopal de Tarazona (s. XVIII-XIX)* (Zaragoza: Institución Fernando el Católico, 2013), pp. 124–7.
29 'QVID MAGNVM PRODEST ARgeNTI PONDVS ET AVRI / SOLA MANES VIRTVS CETERA MORTe CAduNT' (What will be the use of all the gold and silver / in the end when death comes, only virtue remains) – declared a graffito in the Castle of Alaquàs. Cf. Algarra Pardo and Berrocal Ruiz, *Los grafitis históricos del castel de Alaquàs*, p. 7. The authors point out that the inscription was completed in humanist capitals, although in the reproduction a few lower case letters are visible.
30 Carmen Fernández Cuervo, 'Los grabados de la torre del Trovador', *Cuadernos de Historia 'Jerónimo Zurita'*, 19–20 (1967), 201–28.
31 Rita Foti, 'Dal palinsesto al corpus', in R. Foti, *I graffiti delle carceri del Santo Uffizio di Palermo* (Palermo: Palermo University Press, 2002), pp. 8–9.
32 Barrera Maturana, *Grafitos históricos en la arquitectura doméstica granadina, siglos XVI-XVIII: documentación, estudio y catalogación*, unpublished Ph.D. thesis, University of Granada, 2017, pp. 871–84.
33 Alessandra Russo, 'Activar el monumento. La narración figurativa de los graffiti novohispanos', *Nuevo Mundo Mundos Nuevos*, Virtual exhibitions, astronomy section, published 10 February 2005, http://journals.openedition.org/nuevomundo/641, accessed 30 April 2022; Igor Cerdá Farías, *Grafitos coloniales. Imágenes sacras y seculares en el exconvento de San Juan Bautista Tiripetío, Michoacán* (Morelia: Universidad Michoacana de San Nicolás de Hidalgo, 2009), p. 137.
34 Algarra Pardo and Berrocal Ruiz, *Los grafitis históricos del castel de Alaquàs*, pp. 8–10.

35 José Luis Acín Fanlo, Elena Aquilué Pérez and Rosa Abadía Abadías, *Los grabados de la torre de la cárcel de Broto* (Broto: Ayuntamiento, 2005); José Antonio Benavente Serrano, Angels Casanovas, Jordi Rovira and Maria Teresa Thompson, 'Les graffiti des prisons du Bas-Aragon (Espagne): un cas exemplaire de patrimonialisation', *Le Monde alpin et rhodanien*, 1–2 (2004), 131–44.

36 María Luz Mandingorra Llavata and Elisa Varela Rodríguez, 'Escribir en el Palacio Real. Los graffiti del mirador del rey Martí', in Gimeno Blay and Mandingorra Llavata (eds), *'Los muros tienen la palabra'*, pp. 115–19; Felipe Mejías López, 'Entre bóvedas y grafitis. Intervención arqueológica en la Sala del Órgano de la Basílica de Ntra. Sra. del Socorro de Aspe', *La serranica* (2020), 132–42, p. 141.

37 Laura Hernández Alcaraz, *Grafitis medievales y postmedievales de Villena (Alicante). Documentos gráficos para la historia*, Ph.D. thesis, University of Alicante, 2015, p. 53, http://rua.ua.es/dspace/handle/10045/53124, accessed 29 April 2022.

38 Margalida Bernat i Roca, Elvira González Gozalo and Jaume Serra i Barceló, 'Els graffiti del campanar de la Seu de Mallorca', *Estudis Baleàrics*, IV:23 (1986), 7–46, pp. 31 and 37, illustrations pp. 10, 12 and 95.

39 Francesco Renda, *L'Inquisizione in Sicilia. I fatti. Le persone* (Palermo: Sellerio, 1997), p. 244.

40 José Ángel García Serrano, *Graffiti de otro tiempo. Los calabozos del Palacio Episcopal de Tarazona (s. XVI-XVIII)* (Tarazona: Centro de Estudios Turionenses, 2019), p. 137. Inmates of episcopal prisons included not just clerics but all those who failed to comply with some doctrinal requirement.

41 Rosa Serrano Pozuelo, 'Primeros "grafitis" estudiantiles en el Rectorado de la Universidad de Alcalá (ss. XVI–XVII)', https://uam.academia.edu/RosaSerranoPozuelo, accessed 30 April 2022.

42 Fiume, *Del Santo Uffizio in Sicilia*, pp. 256–7.

43 'Amoenissimum castri granatensis, vulgo Alhambre dicti, ab Oriente prospectum' (The most attractive view of the walled city of Granada, commonly known as the Alhambra, seen from the east) – description of Granada by Joris Hoefnagel, 1564, in Georg Braun and Frans Hogenberg, *Civitates Orbis Terrarum* (1598), Vol. V, p. 14. Cf. Joaquín Gil Sanjuán and Juan Antonio Sánchez López, 'Iconografía y visión histórico-literaria de Granada a mediados del Quinientos', *Chronica Nova*, 23 (1996), 73–133, p. 132.

44 Fleming, *Graffiti and the Writing Arts of Early Modern England*.

45 Petrucci, *La scrittura*, pp. 20–1.

46 Cited in Fleming, *Graffiti and the Writing Arts*, pp. 40 and 49.

47 Armando Petrucci, *Public Lettering: Script, Power and Culture* (Chicago: University of Chicago Press, 1993), pp. 92–3.

48 Evelyn Welch, *Shopping in the Renaissance: Consumer Cultures in Italy, 1400–1600* (New Haven, CT: Yale University Press, 2005), p. 121.

49 Guido Gentile, 'Gli interventi di Carlo Bascapè nella regia del Sacro Monte di Varallo', in *Carlo Bascapè sulle orme del Borromeo. Coscienza e azione pastorale in un vescovo di fine Cinquecento* (Novara: Interlinea, 1994), pp. 444–5; Marianne Ritsema van Eck, 'Graffiti in medieval and early modern religious

spaces: Illicit or accepted practice? The case of the *sacro monte* at Varallo', *Tijdschrift voor Geschiedenis*, 131:1 (2018), 59–64.
50 Véronique Plesch, 'Memory on the wall: Graffiti on religious wall paintings', *Journal of Medieval and Early Modern Studies*, 32:1 (2002), 167–98; Véronique Plesch, 'Graffiti and Ritualization: San Sebastiano at Arborio', in Joëlle Rollo-Koster (ed.), *Medieval and Early Modern Rituals: Formalized Behavior in Europe, China and Japan* (Leiden: Brill, 2002), pp. 127–46.
51 Gianclaudio Civale, '"Animo carcerato". Inquisizione, detenzione e graffiti a Palermo nel secolo XVII', *Mediterranea*, XIV:40 (2017), 249–94, p. 265.
52 Antonio Castillo Gómez, *Entre la pluma y la pared. Una historia social de la escritura en los Siglos de Oro* (Madrid: Akal, 2006), pp. 95–120.
53 Carmen Batlle i Gallart and Teresa-María Vinyoles i Vidal, *Mirada a la Barcelona medieval desde les finestres gòtiques* (Barcelona: Rafael Dalmau, 2002), p. 17.
54 Antonio Castillo Gómez, '"Être non seulement libellé mais aussi exposé au public". Les inscriptions censurées au Siècle d'Or', in Alexandra Merle and Araceli Guillaume-Alonso (eds), *Les voies du silence dans l'Espagne des Habsbourg* (Paris: Presses universitaires de Paris-Sorbonne, 2013), pp. 309–28.
55 Martín de la Naja, *El misionero perfecto: deducido de la vida, virtudes, predicación y missiones del venerable y apostólico predicador padre Gerónimo López, de la Compañía de Jesús* (Zaragoza: Pascual Bueno, 1678), pp. 276–7 and 299.
56 Alonso Carrió de la Vandera (1715–83), *El lazarillo de ciegos caminantes* (Caracas: Biblioteca Ayacucho, 1965), p. 113.
57 Bernal Díaz del Castillo, *Historia verdadera de la conquista de la Nueva España*, ed. Guillermo Seres (Madrid: Real Academia Española, 2011), p. 551.
58 Mia Gaia Trentin, *I graffiti come fonte per la storia delle pratiche religiose medievali*, unpublished Ph.D. thesis, University of Venice, 2011, p. 141.
59 Véronique Plesch, 'Destruction or preservation? The meaning of graffiti on paintings in religious sites', in Virginia Chieffo Raguin (ed.), *Art, Piety, and Destruction in the Christian West, 1500–1700* (Farnham, UK: Ashgate, 2010), pp. 137–72, p. 153.
60 Luis Enrique Rodríguez-San Pedro Bezares, 'Vítores académicos en el mundo hispánico', in José Manuel Calderón Ortega, Manuel Casado Arboniés and Alejandro Díez Torre (eds), *Historia universitaria de España y América* (Alcalá de Henares: Universidad de Alcalá, 2016), pp. 661–73.
61 Elvira González Gonzalo and Bernat Oliver Font, *Los barcos de piedra. La arquitectura náutica balear a través de los grafitis murales. Siglos XIV-XVII* (Palma de Mallorca: Institut d'Innovació Empresarial de les Illes Balears, 2007).
62 Elías Rodríguez Vázquez and Pascual Tinoco Quesnel, *Graffitis novohispanos de Tepeapulco, siglo XVI* (Mexico City: INAH, 2006), p. 104.
63 Víctor M. Algarra Pardo, 'Efímero recuerdo de la muerte. Los graffiti de la Catedral de Ibiza. Siglo XVIII', in Gimeno Blay and Mandingorra Llavata (eds), *'Los muros tienen la palabra'*, p. 169. And see baptisms registered in the baptistery of Parma, in Marzio Dall'Acqua, *Voci segrete dai muri. Controstoria Parmigiana* (Parma: Artegrafica Silva, 1976), p. 74.

64 Ruth Ahnert, 'Writing in the Tower during the Reformation', *Huntington Library Quarterly*, 72:2 (2009), 168–92, p. 177; Ruth Ahnert, *The Rise of Prison Literature in the Sixteenth Century* (Cambridge, UK: Cambridge University Press, 2013).
65 Maria Begoña Arrúe Ugarte, 'Los grafítos históricos del antiguo noviciado benedictino y torre del monasterio de Yuso', in M. B. Begoña Ugarte, Álvaro Rodríguez Miranda and José Manuel Valle Melón (eds), *Trazados de arquitectura y grafítos históricos en el Monasterio de San Millán de la Cogolla, de Yuso (La Rioja): una historia constructiva y conventual marcada en los muros* (Logroño: Fundación San Millán de la Cogolla, 2022), pp. 201–5.
66 Massimo Miglio, 'Il Castello graffiato', in Bruno Contardi and Henrik Lilius, *Quando gli dei si spogliano. Il bagno di Clemente VII a Castel Sant'Angelo e le altre stufe romane del primo Cinquecento* (Rome: Società romana editrice, 1984), pp. 101–14, p. 110.
67 García Serrano, *Graffiti de otro tiempo*, pp. 125 and 138.
68 Algarra Pardo and Berrocal Ruiz, *Los grafitis históricos del castel de Alaquàs*, p. 6.
69 Víctor M. Algarra, Rafael Beltrán and Paloma Berrocal, 'Un *graffiti* con versos del vizconde de Altamira en la pared del Castell d'Alaquàs (c. 1550)', *Revista de Literatura Medieval*, XXVI (2014), 77–96.
70 Acín Fanlo *et al.*, *Los grabados de la torre de la cárcel de Broto*, pp. 24–9.
71 Fiume, *Del Santo Uffizio in Sicilia*, p. 251.
72 *Ibid.*, pp. 254, 261–4 and 277–92.
73 Civale, '"Animo carcerato"', p. 272.
74 Giovanna Fiume, 'Soundless screams: Graffiti and drawings in the prisons of the Holy Office in Palermo', *Journal of Early Modern History*, 21:3 (2017), 188–215.
75 Archivo Histórico Nacional, Madrid, *Inquisición*, L. 1744, expediente (exp. – dossier) 24, carpeta (carp. – file) 2, 2° proceso (trial), ff. 10v–16v. On this affair and the trials of Tudesco, see Civale, '"Animo carcerato"', pp. 291–3.
76 Maria Sofia Messana, *Il Santo Ufficio dell'Inquisizione. Sicilia, 1500–1782* (Palermo: Istituto Poligrafico Europeo, 2017), first published 2012, pp. 52–5; Civale, '"Animo carcerato"', p. 275; Fiume, 'Soundless screams', p. 206. Mannarino had been taken prisoner on a Barbary pirate ship and organised a successful mutiny of Christian slaves who took control of the vessel. In Venice, they sold it and shared the profits. Mannarino, accused of Islamic sympathies, persuaded the Inquisition that this had been a pretence to deceive his captors.
77 Elvira González Gozalo, 'Nuevos grafitos descubiertos en la torre del homenaje del Castillo de Bellver', in *Actes du XVe Colloque International de Glyptographie de Cordoue* (Braine-le-Château: Centre international de recherches glyptographiques, 2006), pp. 161–78, see pp. 161 and 168.
78 Alessandra Russo, 'Atravesando la zona de silencio: graffiti coloniales en las letrinas del convento de Actopan', in Magdalena Garrido Caballero and Gabriela Vallejo Cervantes (eds), *De la Monarquía Hispánica a la Unión*

Europea: relaciones internacionales, comercio e imaginarios colectivos (Murcia: Universidad de Murcia, 2013), pp. 41–77.

79 Francisco J. Mateos Ascacibar, 'Rescate de un cómic del siglo XVI: crónica de un judío en la conquista de México', in Felipe Lorenzana de la Puente and F. J. Mateos Ascacibar (eds), *La España del Quijote: IV Centenario Cervantes* (Llerena: Sociedad Extremeña de Historia, 2017), pp. 258–67.

80 See newspaper reports: Xavier Teros, 'Fuérese Oliveros', *El País*, 23 March 2013.; Xavi Casino, 'El grafiti de la Guerra del Segadors', *La Vanguardia*, 4 March 2015, www.lavanguardia.com/local/barcelona/20150304/54427845253/grafiti-guerra-segadors.html, accessed 18 April 2022. On the Catalan revolt, see John E. Elliott, *The Revolt of the Catalans: A Study in the Decline of Spain (1598–1640)* (Cambridge, UK: Cambridge University Press, 1984), first published 1963.

81 Fleming, *Graffiti and the Writing Arts*, p. 10.

82 For an incomplete transcription, see Dolores García Hinarejos, *Historia y arquitectura del Convento del Carmen de Valencia* (València: Generalitat Valenciana, 2009), p. 22. See also Carmelo Pérez, 'Sale a la luz la "vida oculta" del Centre del Carme', *El Mundo.es Comunidad Valenciana*, www.elmundo.es/elmundo/2009/09/14/valencia/1252927414.html, accessed 29 April 2022.

83 Pere Ferrer Marset and Amparo Martí Soler, 'Iglesia del Salvador', in Mauro S. Hernández Pérez and Pere Ferrer Marset (eds), *Graffiti. Arte espontáneo en Alicante* (Alicante: Museo Arqueológico, 2009), pp. 101–65, pp. 108 and 111.

3

'No more for Now or Praps Never': the meaning and function of pauper writing in Britain, 1750s to early 1900s

Steven King

Introduction

The 1601 Old Poor Law was framed on the basis that parish officials and people falling into dependence on poor relief would know and see each other. In essence, the relief transaction was assumed to be one in which orality dominated and the written record would stem from disputes (legal records) or spending (overseers' accounts). We now know that by the 1750s and more strongly from the early 1800s, such oral encounters were increasingly supplemented or replaced by epistolary negotiation. This was inevitable when migration took larger and larger numbers of people away from places where they 'belonged' under the law and, thus, from the sites where they had a right to apply for poor relief.[1] Until recently, it was less well-known that the poor, paupers and their advocates continued this epistolary activity after the advent of what is widely known as the New Poor Law in 1834. They wrote locally (little of which survives) and to the variously constituted central authorities and to third parties such as newspapers (much of which survives).[2] Indeed, they wrote with such frequency, intensity and purchase that the central authorities even considered imposing a blanket 'no reply' policy.[3] The poor's grasp of literacy may have been fragile in many cases and places, but the existence of a substantial set of letters with little evidence of the presence and activity of scribes points to an important seam of attainment well before the familiar benchmarks for improving literacy from the mid-nineteenth century.[4] In turn, such material has been used to argue that the poor could exert agency in shaping the scale, duration and form of relief even though neither the Old nor the New Poor Law gave them any rights to welfare.[5]

My primary purpose in this chapter is not to continue and deepen the discussion of agency, though in practice a consideration of pauper writing is inextricably entwined with this issue, as we shall see. Nor am I particularly interested here in the way that the poor laws worked, the function of letters in negotiating welfare or the detailed rhetorical tropes deployed.

Rather, I want to look at the meaning and function of writing for the poor correspondent, asking questions such as: Where did the poor gain their literacy and how did they maintain it? Why did the poor write as opposed to adopting some other means of communicating with those who held power? How did the poor understand the act and process of writing? What value and meaning did they ascribe to the written word? And how did poor writers learn and unlearn the linguistic registers that ebbed and flowed in this long period of societal and cultural change? Ultimately, a corpus of the size and reach of that deployed here allows us to understand and trace different models of writing circulating among the poor: writing as habit; writing as last resort; writing as painful necessity (literally in some cases); writing as investment; writing as precaution; writing as a symbol of respectability and honesty; and writing as an expression of self.

A letter corpus

This chapter brings together, for the first time in publication, the pauper and advocate letters located and transcribed as part of two consecutive Arts and Humanities Research Council grants: one (Pauper letters in Britain and Germany, 1780–1929) covering the Old Poor Law from the 1780s until 1834; and the other (In their own write) covering 102 poor law unions under the New Poor Law from 1834 until the early 1900s.[6] Amounting to some five million transcribed words in total, the corpus contains material from communities in every county in England and Wales and also several Scottish counties.[7] The quality of literacy varies across a wide spectrum. At one end lies Richard Garlick of Kirkby Lonsdale (Westmorland), who on 2 May 1820 wrote to say:

> my Rint is Due on the 11th of May and I ham not Hable to pay it my self my Famley is so large for it is verey hard work to get meat for them let a lone aney thinges whitch I hope you will have the gudness to send my Rint and a trifell be sides for we are most nacked for Cloathing and wear all of want of shirting we have non casley [i.e. no coats] of aney sort and I hame not habel to get them aney for the times is so verey bad for ther is nothing to be haded with weving with Children at present but I hame Hired with my Hould Master a gane for the sumer Cesan that is ould Martlemess so I hope you will have the Goodness to send It by the Beare for I hame in Great nessitey at present and I am not hable to get out of it with out the help of you you If I could I schud think it verey gret shame to send to you[8]

The other end of the spectrum is embodied in the perfect hand of James Richards of Kilmington (Devon), who opened his 963-word letter of 7 October 1846 in the following way:

Gentleman

> I have presumed the liberty to lay before you the following Case for your immediate Adjudication and Attention. I Married my present Wife the proprietor of a small Freehold in Axminster parish in April 1844, on the conditions of a Deed, settling it on her, as her own during her life, giving me my life interest in the Property conveying the after Freehold on her Son (not born under Wedlock) if he survived me, but if I survived him for the Freehold to my Heirs &c. This Property was Mortgaged in 50£ to Mr le Bond Attorney, Axminster, which I knew of when I married my Second Wife in 1844 she proved to be labouring with the Cancer in the left Breast which was cut off in October 1844.[9]

He went on to ask for help in realising the value of the property so that he might pay for further treatment.

Broadly, the quality of literacy among the poor, advocates and officials improved over time, but even by the 1890s it is possible to find instances of remarkably tenuous writing skills. There is more continuity to other aspects of the dataset. Thus, while both the pre- and post-1834 samples include formalised petitions, almost all letters from poor writers and their advocates took the form of familiar letters.[10] We find by accident (changes in handwriting style and literacy quality in a letter series) or statement (someone acknowledges authorial help) some 600 instances of the use of scribes in the corpus. In terms of wordage or author numbers, however, this pales into insignificance given the dimensions of the wider sample, and we can be relatively certain those who signed pauper letters also generally wrote them. Women and children are under-represented as writers throughout the period covered, while men, the aged and sick are over-represented in almost all places. Under both poor law systems, advocates and poor writers who sent just one or two letters dominate a count of the number of writers. Equally, however, those who wrote multiple letters and entered into sustained correspondence account for a much larger share of the letters sent and the wordage of those letters than their numerical importance might allow. These biases mean that we have to beware of simply reconstructing the meaning and significance of writing on the basis of letters from sick and aged men. One further contextual variable is also important: the pre-1834 material contains just a handful of letters written from inside workhouses, whereas for the New Poor Law this rises to more than 37 per cent of the letters. These disparities reflect the very different roles and longevity of workhouses under the Old Poor Law versus the New, but also the fact that post 1834 paupers understood that they had an unobstructed right to send and receive letters in the workhouse context. The right was affirmed by the central authorities in disputes over missing mail or that which had been opened by workhouse staff prior to its being given to the pauper.[11] This is an important observation of the data, not least because New Poor Law workhouses tended to cater not only for the perennially poor but also the shamefaced poor who had once 'been' somebody.[12] We find little evidence of these people becoming de facto workhouse scribes, but there is evidence (often from their own pens) that they percolated knowledge of how to confront the Poor Law authorities through the workhouse hierarchies.[13]

Finding written words

The question of where ordinary people learned whatever literacy skills they had is now well-trodden ground for Britain.[14] In the letter corpus, however, surprisingly little reference was made to personal histories of schooling, apprenticeship, Sunday schools or work-related literacy. Nor do we find a single reference to learning obtained via the variously constituted workhouse schools in the post-1834 period. Even young people writing in the three decades after the 1870 Education Act, or Catholics and others with a Nonconformist background who were often given specific additional instruction by Nonconformist ministers while living in institutions, failed to mention learning to read or write. This may be a reflection of the immediacy of the sources and their function as mechanisms of reportage, embellishment and contestation. Certainly, poor people and paupers/pauper children who went on to write autobiographies tended to reflect on this issue at least in passing.[15] We can also deduce more from the letters than is boldly stated. In particular, and as noted earlier, both the pre- and post-1834 letter sets contain texts from the shamefaced poor, who would have been used to reading and writing as part of their jobs and professions. We encounter everyone from ex-poor law officials, clerks and authors through to master sailmakers, inventors and printers. This sort of writer is found more often after the 1850s and more frequently in larger urban areas, but they are nonetheless a core feature of Old Poor Law writing too. Still, the presence or absence of this group and related mechanisms of transference does not explain the origin of most literacy, and without further record linkage work at scale, it is impossible to speculate confidently.

Two further things are, however, important. When John Hennis wrote to the parish of St Clement Danes (London) on Friday 4 March 1814 and worried in a postscript 'I fear you cannot read this Scrawl', he was one of only a handful of pre-1834 authors who was self-aware enough to reference the quality of his letter writing.[16] In part, this absence reflects the fact that the poor knew they were corresponding with officials and vestry members whose grasp of grammar, capitalisation, spelling, punctuation and spacing were not in general better than their own. Exactly the same palette of mistakes, and exactly the same broad spectrum of handwriting quality, is to be found across the advocate, pauper and official substrata of the corpus.[17] For the New Poor Law sample, self-knowledge of handwriting was much more frequent and sustained, with 198 references to poor writing or expression, either direct or indirect (as in blaming the quality of pen, ink or paper). This is typified by James Barnett, writing from Sheffield workhouse on 28 August 1882, who apologised for his letter and explained that 'Having no ink for that purpose, and having been forbidden to borrow any, I am compelled to use a substitute', clearly signalling that the central authorities could and should expect a better hand; that is, that there was an acceptable quality of writing.[18] The second observation about the data is that multiple signatory letters increased over time. Under the Old Poor Law, we see husbands and wives both signing letters, but only in the letters of advocates do we see multiple unconnected people signing a single letter. For the post-1834 period, the frequency of husband-and-wife letters increased, but we begin to see a new genre of text in the sense of grievance letters signed by multiple paupers and poor writers. Sometimes these took the form of a petition, but mostly they were familiar letters which took up a collective issue to do with the workhouse, local policy or the actions and reputations of a particular member of staff. Figure 3.1 shows the ending of one such letter, where the writers signed in a circular form so as to ensure that no one was identified as the original author. Instances such as this provide a hint at how authors found their linguistic registers, but they also perhaps tell us about how partial literacies were fused together to be more than the sum of the contributing parts.[19]

It is easier to see how literacy levels were maintained and linguistic registers developed by poor writers than how they were attained in the first place. Inevitably, the process of sustained reading, writing and correspondence about relief created a circularity in which we might expect improvement. Given the sheer variety of orthographic text and the ebb and flow of writing quality according to the health and momentary circumstances of the individual, it is impossible to conceive of an index of literacy that would capture changes over time and the duration of correspondence, at least at the corpus level. Poor writers sometimes explicitly noted impediments to writing, as, for instance, did Mary Forde, writing from Caversham (Berkshire) on 5 June 1788 to explain that her handwriting was different to prior letters because 'the bones in my hand is broke', or John Watson of Sheffield who noted on 7 December 1878 that 'I have had to write this upon my knee amid the noises that are so common in this place'.[20] Nonetheless, writers in both the pre- and post-1834 samples also explicitly noted, or more often implied, that sustained correspondence had led to better and more extensive expression. David and Martha Clark, for instance,

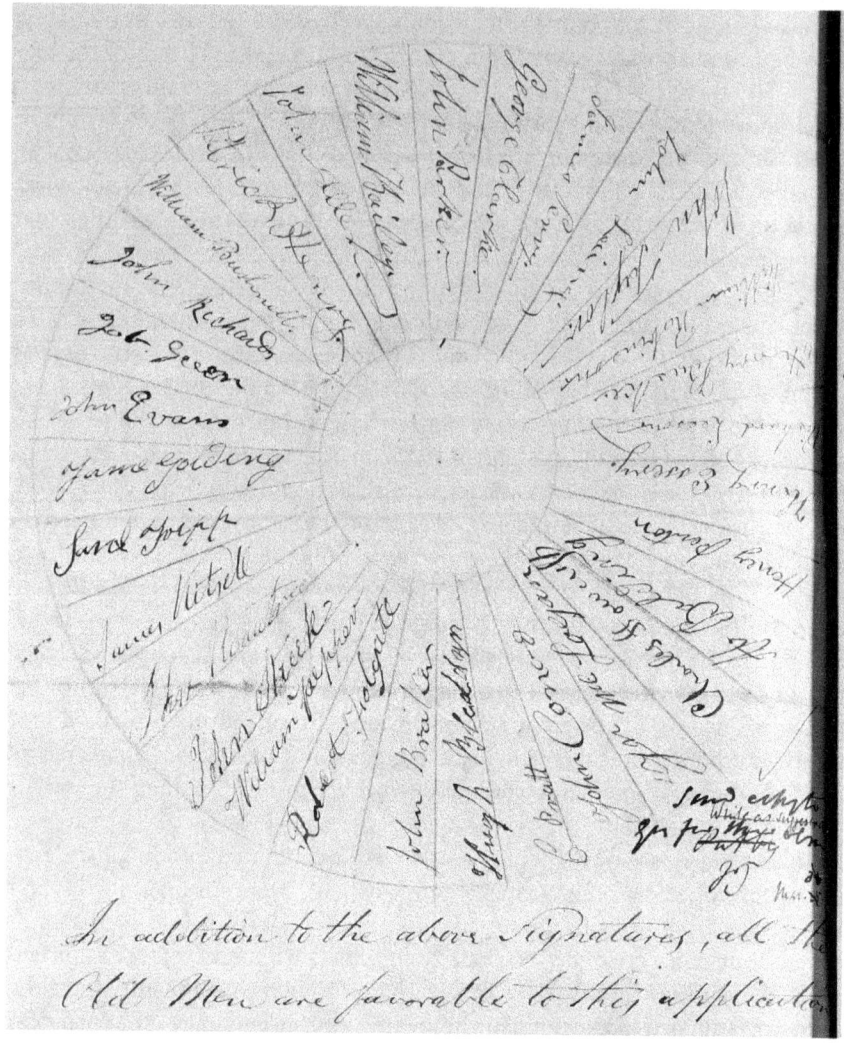

Figure 3.1 Chelsea workhouse petition, 1871 (UK National Archives, MH 12/6996/12662/1871). All rights reserved and permission to use the figure must be obtained from the copyright holder.

wrote from Norwich (Norfolk) to Peterborough (then Northamptonshire) in February 1801 after a period of sustained correspondence and were confident enough to be 'flattering myself [the hand was David Clark, though both husband and wife signed] I write to gentlemen well aquainted with every circumstance'.[21] Literacy for those on or negotiating to get poor relief was also maintained and improved by interaction with advocates. Under the Old Poor Law, King and Jones have shown that few extended letter series relating to a single individual or family did *not* also contain advocate letters, and we too easily assume that turning to an advocate reflected lack of literacy as opposed to other strategic reasons.[22] It is much less often appreciated that advocates were also a prominent group of writers to the central authorities under the New Poor Law. The single advocate Joseph Rowntree, for instance, wrote more than a hundred thousand words of the corpus, and there are many reasons to think that poor people had input into both what was written on their behalf and how it was written, with more than two hundred instances where it was stated or implied that the subject of the letter had read and approved it. In turn, such advocates often wrote on behalf of those who they assumed would be able to regain their independence. Many did, even if they then returned episodically to request relief or to have a sojourn in the New Poor Law workhouse. How literacy levels were maintained in the newly joined public domain is unclear, though we know that at least some of the formerly dependent poor followed the example of Thomas Robinson of Preston (Lancashire), who left the relief lists to take up a factory job that would have required him to maintain and even improve his literacy levels.[23] Certainly there is little evidence for any part of our period that those who moved between dependence and independence and back again were any less literate when they took up the pen to write once more.

The fact is, then, that literacy levels were maintained and that many paupers and claimants were much more literate than we could ever have expected from long-standing research on the continuance of oral traditions, limited schooling capacity, the place of children as earners in the household economy and the transience of writing as opposed to reading skills.[24] In turn, they used linguistic registers which demonstrated both very significant continuity *and* change over the period from 1750 to 1900. There is not the space here to survey the intricate detail of these registers. Some are obvious given the earlier discussion. Joseph Rowntree provoked poor people and paupers to write and even admitted to telling them what to write or what models of writing would be successful.[25] In similar fashion, it is a short speculative step to suggest that the letter in Figure 3.1 was written by one of the clerks who had fallen down the social scale to become an inmate of Chelsea workhouse, and that those who signed the letter also learned from its writing.[26] And of course the serial letter writers, whose words do so much to bring the whole corpus to life, inevitably conveyed their own knowledge of letter structure, rhetoric and linguistic register to other claimants, recipients and institutional inmates who wished to author their own texts, as I have already suggested. Indeed, many of them were like Frank Burge in the Poplar workhouse, who explicitly acknowledged helping other people plan what to write even if he did not write the letters himself.[27] In short, there can be no doubt whatsoever that a common pot of linguistic knowledge on which the poor could draw existed and grew organically. Part of that growth was the emergence of completely new registers, including languages of disability, rights associated with trade union membership, necessary and proper relief, and registers rooted in the changing popular knowledge of medicine and science. We also see from the 1820s an increasingly important seam of language related to the sense that the conditions and experiences described in letters should, must and would be brought to the attention of the general public. The frequency with which writers under the New Poor Law sent in press cuttings with their correspondence to the central authorities suggests that this was not mere rhetoric. On the other hand, there are also startling absences. Luddism, the Swing Riots, Chartism, Radicalism and their associated registers have the smallest footprint in the sample. More detailed consideration of 'networks of textual transmission' is clearly required.[28]

For the purposes of this chapter, however, it is the continuities in registers that are most striking. Three were of particular reach. Thus, under both the Old and New Poor Laws, our writers used the words of (and sometimes directly quoted) the responses they received from officials and the laws and public debates that framed their decisions.[29] In the pre-1834 system, this sort of linguistic acquisition was common but not systematic. Thus, Elizabeth Lang wrote from London on 3 December 1812 to tell her parish that she had got 'the Last 2 pounds you sent Me which I Recd with Every Insult that Cold possable be offered' and went on to give a rebuttal of the doubts about her honesty in the letter that had accompanied that relief.[30] Sartory Gray likewise wrote from London on 13 March 1796 to say that his hopes of becoming independent by putting two of his children to work in a starch warehouse had been 'Disapointed' because 'just after I got to Town their was a Bill pass in the House of Commons' which blocked the use of wheat for the making of starch until 1797.[31] In the post-1834 period, the establishment of centralised processes, central–local referencing systems, formal rules and regulations for the remit of workhouse and union employees, and massive publicity of the law and codified regulations of poor relief meant that the poor and their advocates systematically appropriated the linguistic registers of officialdom.[32] By way of example, William Leeson wrote to the central authorities from Chelsea workhouse on 16 August 1866 and his 473-word letter was precisely wrapped in this sort of language. Complaining that he had been assaulted by the master and a pauper servant, Leeson wrote:

don't know whether it is contrary to your rules, and regulations, to allow one pauper to <u>domineer,</u> over <u>another,</u> Gentlemen. I am 61 years of age, and I believe according to your Rules, I am entitled, to an aged diet and having applied to the master, which he refuses to transfer me without I Produce my Register of Birth. which does not lay in my power of doing.[33]

Leeson had not read the codified regulations of the Poor Law Board (*I believe*), but his outline knowledge of their intent suggests that both knowledge and the associated linguistic register were in common circulation.

A second continuity is the use of registers rooted in the symbolism of religion and associated Christian philosophies including philanthropy. These were not static registers. The Christian opposition to slavery and the conditions of slavery wherever they might be found was a fleeting reference point in the pre-1834 letters but attained real purchase in the post-1840s as the poor were likened, and likened themselves, to black 'slaves', in un-Christian thraldom to employers, ratepayers and the state.[34] However it was constellated, the linguistic motif of Christian values was a constant, exemplified in the phrasing of the title for this chapter. Here John Cuthbertson wrote from Daventry (Northamptonshire) on 12 January 1755 to say that the overseer would likely hear from him 'No more for Now or Praps Never' given that he was about to enter the 'Vale of Tears and Shadow'.[35] Towards the end of our period, John Price, writing from Aberystwyth (Cardiganshire) on 6 May 1869, was even more explicit. Noting that he did not want to produce a text in the 'nature of the long winded-epistle more especially so as my penmanship is at times not *now* above legible', he nonetheless went on to write a 1,244-word excoriation of the Aberystwyth Board of Guardians.[36] This was framed at either end with Christian theology, philosophy and linguistic registers. Price warned the officials to 'take warning & not provoke the Lord to vengeance he has no pleasure in the Death of the wicked in proof of which he offers forgivness upon very easy terms – Belief or Faith Reformation or Repentance so why will you perish by doing the Devil's work'. Recalling God's will, the Christian logic of forgiveness, false prophets and the importance of Christian philanthropy, he reminded the central authorities that

> It will not do for your Board or myself to go to war with Heaven for it is useless kicking against the Pricks _ God has commanded all to be kind & compassionate towards the poor _ What does your concience say does it answer in the affirmative or the negative does it ^{say} yes or no to you that you are or are not kind to them _ I hope Gentlemen as men & brethren that have hereafter to stand before that Judgement Act of Christ & that your conscience is not drunk[37]

Finally, and very importantly for this chapter, Price wrote, 'I am taught that the English Tongue is not confined to any particular class but is common property' and noted that they had 'no power to muzzle a British Subject'.[38] He had a right to write as a citizen of the state and a subject of God, but more than this he had an obligation to write in order to prevent tyranny. Lest we think that Price was unusual in knowing and employing these linguistic registers, almost every one of the 102 poor law unions dealt with here was home to a writer like him. Given the well-rehearsed decline in Anglicanism in the nineteenth century, this long-term persistence of religious registers is notable and important.[39]

A third continuity can be observed in registers that signal the inevitability of dependence and a corresponding obligation to offer welfare. Historians of the later nineteenth century have understood such registers as intimately connected to the development of poverty lines[40] and the changing location of fault for poverty, arguing that we see the emergence of a language of 'honest poverty' and universal citizenship.[41] We certainly see this in the corpus, as for instance in the case of Benjamin Handcock of Great Yarmouth (Norfolk), who on 15 June 1864 wrote to the central authorities asking that they

> please condescend to make an order that when the aged or afflicted cannot go in person for what guardians allow which is not enough to feed a dog that the person insult not honest & afflicted poverty its no use complaining against jack in office his is sure to injure the person complaining not with truth but by base insinuation[42]

In practice, however, even poor writers under the Old Poor Law framed in their writing a notion of honest poverty. They pointed in sustained fashion to prior contribution, the raising of independent children, the inevitability of declining labour power with age and the pervasiveness of disabling sickness or spousal death. Some even lectured or hectored the officials to whom they wrote, as did George Hales, writing from the Isle of Man to Brimpton (Berkshire) on 16 October 1827. He had been struggling for sixteen months 'in Consequence of the Death of my Wife who Died in Child Bed of her Twenty Second Child and left me with A large Family with out Any Employment to suport them Sir I Now Apply for Mentaineince for five out of Seven the youngest'. Hales assumed relief would be inevitable, but ended with a strong assertion of the consequences of inaction, stating: 'Now Sir I hope you will be so Good to Let me have An Answer by Return of Post that I may Know how to Act in my Present State if I Receive No Answer in three Posts I shall Embark my Family for Liverpool and Proceed Direct to my Parish'.[43] Well before the development of poverty lines, then, poor writers could elaborate a model of respectable citizenship (in this case raising twenty-two children) which deserved, indeed required in natural justice, a favourable response. It was part of what we might understand as the 'writing knowledge' or discourse community of every pauper and poor applicant.

Valuing written words

It would be easy to continue the analysis of where the poor found words, but there is a more important question that should tax us: why did the poor write as opposed to adopting some other means of communicating with the powerful? The answer is obvious if the writer lived many miles or counties away from those making decisions. Yet, under the Old Poor Law, some 75 per cent of all writers lived within walking distance of the place to which they wrote.[44] The dynamics changed under the New Poor Law, since what the sample captures is that many (but not all) letters were written to London after other letters had been exchanged by the parties at the level of the poor law union. Nonetheless, it would have been possible for the poor to systematically seek advocates, speak to journalists or send collective petitions, as did ordinary people seeking redress for a variety of other reasons.[45] Yet the personal familiar letter remained the dominant form across our period. How did poor writers understand the act and process of writing? What value and meaning did they ascribe to the written word? The corpus provides a remarkably comprehensive answer to these questions.

Thus, and in line with much research on other forums of epistolary exchange, poor writers across the temporal and spatial dimensions of the letter sets associated writing with authenticity and honesty. When Mary Life of Clitheroe (Lancashire) wrote on 13 January 1830, she provided information on the condition of another pauper and ended her last sentence with the assertion that for 'the truth of this you may refer to Mr Grundys as he Know I shoud not write false'.[46] The sense that writing was conceived simultaneously as a signal of truth and that it also imposed an obligation to *tell* the truth is intriguing but by no means unique in the sample. If we turn back to the eighteenth century, George Bradford also provides a similar exposition. He wrote a series of letters from London to Oxford in the 1750s and 1760s. His letter of 15 August 1754 apologised for giving 'you So Much Trouble'. Nonetheless, he hoped that Mr Brown the overseer would

> be So Good as to Excuse Me for if I was not in the Condition I Mention'd I should not have Been so Earnest In My Request But as I Told you In My Last that my Few Goods that I Have are Liable to be taken every Day for Rent that I owe and I Have made away with Every thing that Possible I can Spare to Subsist with.[47]

The earnest request of Bradford's prior letter was meant to convey desperation and precariousness and he assumed that the circumstances would speak for themselves both in that letter and in the one he now conveyed. As a postscript, he invited the overseer to visit him if the written word was insufficient.[48] Poor writers in the post-1834 sample also persistently implied or stated that the fact of their writing should convey honesty over and above the exact contents of the letter. Some, like William Josh Davies of Aberystwyth, added further embellishment to convey honesty. His letter of 7 January 1869 offering a comprehensive list of charges (and supporting evidence) against Mr Griffiths, the workhouse master, noted that he provided this information out of integrity and honesty. To give the letter extra weight, he signed himself 'formerly Magd. Coll Cambridge' (once again giving a sense in which workhouses could contain highly literate members of the shamefaced poor) and told the Poor Law Board:

> I have tried to remedy matters locally without troubling your honourable board but to no purpose I have therefore no alternative but a public Expose sense of shame alone will act upon some bad constitutions and habits & caustic [alone] will suit some cases – how I have been insulted & snubed I will not trouble you with my motives have been pure & I appeal to my God for the truth[49]

Here, then, God was the ultimate arbiter of the truth of the written form, an elegant elision of the linguistic registers and functions of writing already encountered in this chapter.

These claims to what we might style 'honest writing' overlapped with a second consistent motif: the claim to respectability as evidenced by the act of writing. This is subtly different from the familiar sense that literacy and respectability were linked in the popular imagination. Many writers knew that their literacy was what John Swales called 'shabby' in his letter of 18 March 1798.[50] Rather, poor people and paupers tried to suggest that their struggle to write in an unfamiliar or at least episodic medium or under particularly trying circumstances should be taken as a sign of that respectability.[51] Struggle codified character, and character moved seamlessly into the respectable self. Thus, on 23 March 1888, Hannah Berry Pearson began a remarkable series of letters to the Local Government Board about her experiences in the Dorking (Surrey) workhouse. Here she 'do hereby humbley ask your protection and aid', melding together the opening of a petition with the content of a familiar letter. This spoke to her uneasiness with the medium (at least in terms of how to approach the central authorities), but she noted:

> My age is fifty nine years I am an honest sober and respectable woman having no home or friends to assist me, and as the law demands that I should find

shelter I am compeled from time to time to seek a home in Dorking Union where if I dare to utter a complaint I am in danger of having a Magistrate and a doctor brought to me to try to catch me in my words in private in order to intimidate me with a threat to send me to a lunatic asylum (where I may be kept for years at an unnecessary expence to the country.[52]

Deploying familiar rhetorical tropes of feminine dependency and a knowledge of the law (she was in danger of being classed as a vagrant), Pearson claimed to be the subject of persecution in a determined attempt to drive her mad. Ultimately, though, she was respectable, and the letter contrasts the competing authority of her private oral words and the now public written transcript.

Most writers also assumed or (sometimes) stated that they wrote because the written word carried weight and reach, something we see clearly in Pearson's story. Post 1834, it mattered that a poor writer knew the correct form of address for the Poor Law Commissioners in London, that they knew to quote reference numbers in their replies to central authorities and that they could quote or paraphrase the regulations, orders and processes that governed local poor relief. Whether the central authorities or the local Poor Law guardians thought in the same way is doubtful, but this is not the point. A letter to the central authorities was more than words; it carried some sense of formality and expectation.[53] Thus, Robert Hawkins wrote to the Poor Law Board from Faversham (Kent) on 8 May 1851 to say: 'Kind sirs I have been persuaded to right these few lines to you hoping to receive your kind advice upon a very important buseness as concerns myself'.[54] He then outlined a separation from his wife and asked under what circumstances he might avoid prison for not supporting her. His friends (he was persuaded) and Hawkins himself invested the central authorities with ultimate authority and expected a written and authoritative judgement from them which would provide a waymarker in his turbulent relationship. It is a short step from cases such as this to a sense that even episodic or intermittent 'wins' for poor writers were enough to sustain a view that letter writing gave the poor a formal place in the business of poor relief. In the pre-1834 Old Poor Law, there was not of course a central authority, but this did not lessen the belief of the poor in the authority bestowed by writing. These authors quoted precedent, imposed time limits for replies (as we saw earlier) and asserted that the written record should act as a warning in the case that inaction resulted in spiralling parish bills or untimely deaths.

Some of these themes are familiar from the epistolarity of other social groups. Rather less obvious is that the struggle for literacy we plainly see in many written texts masks the fact that some poor people *enjoyed* writing. They valued the act in and of itself and interpreted the ability and opportunity to write as a protection of selfhood at a time when they found themselves under the authority of poor law officials, confined to workhouses or managing on what were always residual welfare payments. Writing was, in other words, understood as a creative act. We see these emotional infusions on a number of levels, including constructing the inability to write or the inability to get writing materials as 'torture',[55] adding literary and personal flourishes to letters, setting an agenda for reform, rehearsing a personal story at length or recounting a history of written engagement with the public sphere.[56] These observations apply across the whole period covered here but are wonderfully captured in the 5,459 words of John Watson, encountered earlier, writing from Sheffield in the late 1870s. His opening letter of 4 December 1878 noted that he had initially been admitted to the vagrant ward but 'had no opportunity of testifying to the correctness of Mr Greenwood's general observations', a literary reference to the sensational exposé of life in a vagrant ward by a Victorian journalist.[57] He then went on, across several letters, to set out his personal history as an inventor of numerous devices, to illustrate a wide awareness of public debate and, above all, to embellish texts with his own poetry, which he claimed had been subject to wide perusal and approval by the public elite, starting with these lines:

> "Big things have little things upon their backs that bite 'em
> "But little things have lesser things and so ad infinitum
> "The rats came in nor wanted stairs
> "Yes they came to act as preyers.[58]

In every sense, then, his writing was a creative act, one which embodied, captured and maintained a public selfhood in uncertain times.

Constructing and concluding

Thus far, this chapter has dealt in the currency of individual stories drawn from a vast dataset, which embody or emblematise core approaches to the act and understanding of writing. It is, however, possible to go further and through close and persistent reading identify several models which locate and crystallise the wider culture of writing by the dependent and marginal poor. These are set out in Table 3.1. Of course elements of the different categories could appear in the same letter and repeatedly over a whole letter set. Nonetheless, almost all Old and New Poor Law letters can be said to have a dominant approach. This is perhaps exemplified by the letter of sixteen-year-old Charles Smith, written from Newbury (Berkshire) on 28 April 1866. He outlined a series of abuses by the master of the workhouse and noted that he had begun to draft a letter, in pencil, to the Chair of the Board

Table 3.1 Models of the writing culture of the poor

Model	Expression
Writing as habit	Carrying paper; acting as delegated writer; advice to others; apologies for something other than a 'normal' hand; references to prior authorship; lack of apology for writing
Writing as last resort	Registers of exhausted possibility; constructing officials as the last hope; apologies for writing quality; being advised to write; calls for rescue[63]
Writing as emotional act	Literary references and flourishes; personal story at length; direct or implied registers of emotion to frame the letter or the act of writing; notions of selfhood; demands for justice; fear; sadness
Writing as painful necessity	Lack of choice; the physical and emotional turmoil of writing or completing a letter; submission; shame
Writing as precaution/ investment	Desire to have written judgements or decisions; forewarning of future problems; written word as authoritative; requirement to enter into correspondence; the value of writing versus other forms of communication and in terms of time, work or postage foregone
Writing as a symbol	Text embodying selfhood, identity, respectability, honesty, rationality and knowledge
Writing as defence	Defence of self against local authority; defence against tyranny; defence of others; the singularity of the writers and her/his circumstances; outlining costs of inaction

of Guardians, Mr Eyre. He explained that the Master and Porter had seen him writing:

> I was going to bed and the Master asked me what I had in my pockets I told him I had some Paper – he told the Porter to see what I had – they were both together. The Porter pulled out all I had and took them away from me. No one told me to write this Letter I meant to send it to Mr. Eyres I thought it was best to write first before I spoke to the Guardians about the Master's conduct. I did not sign the Letter as I had not quite finished it. I bought the Paper to write on. I bought 4 sheets and gave three of them away to some of the Men in the Workhouse.[59]

Smith's story contains elements of writing as habit, last resort and emotional act, but it is primarily an example of writing for defence against tyranny.

There is not the space here to explore these models further – though the examples encountered already in this chapter can slot neatly into the schema – but we do need to reflect on the wider context. Thus, it goes without saying that for our understanding of the Old and the New Poor Law, the fact that the poor wrote or encoded[60] – that is, had an understanding of the meaning and purpose of writing and invested real significance in the act and record of writing – mattered. But their activity also has wider implications. The cultures of writing outlined in Table 3.1, encourage us to think of the dependent poor as active citizens well before the later nineteenth century, when many historians have come to see citizenship as concept and practice extended to the poorer sorts. Equally, we can see that the dependent and marginal poor framed multilevel expectations of the state and that as the information state expanded, our writers were able to extend, codify and rationalise those expectations and duties. And of course we can see that even in the eighteenth and early nineteenth centuries the poor were often surprisingly literate and able to experience epistolary culture in emotional and creative, as well as simply functional, terms. Above all, these letters encourage us to look again at the way in which dependence affected the sense of self for those who had been independent and would mostly go on to independence again.[61] Quietly, if not altogether expertly, the poor created what Martyn Lyons styles a 'rich subterranean world of ordinary writings' with the intent of locating and challenging their place in wider matrices of cultural and social power.[62]

Notes

1 Steven King, *Writing the Lives of the English Poor, 1750s–1830s* (London: McGill-Queen's University Press, 2019).
2 From 1834 to 1847, the central authority was styled the Poor Law Commission, from 1848 to August 1871 the Poor Law Board, and from 1871 to 1919 the Poor Law Department within the Local Government Board. For clarity, I use 'central authorities' unless it is essential to refer to one of the specific authorities.
3 Natalie Carter and Steven King, '"I think we ought not to acknowledge them [paupers] as that encourages them to write": the administrative state, power and the Victorian pauper', *Social History*, 46:2 (2021), 117–44.
4 On this benchmark, see Martyn Lyons, *The Writing Culture of Ordinary People in Europe c. 1860–1920* (Cambridge, UK: Cambridge University Press, 2013), p. 10.
5 King, *Writing the Lives*; Steven King, Paul Carter, Natalie Carter, Peter Jones and Carol Beardmore, *'In Their Own Write': A New Poor Law History from Below* (London: McGill-Queen's University Press, 2022).

6 Held respectively with Andreas Gestrich of the German Historical Institute London, and Paul Carter of The National Archives (henceforth TNA).
7 England and Wales constituted legally and structurally a single welfare system. Scotland was partially aligned in 1845 and only fully in 1905.
8 Cumbria Archive Service (henceforth CAS), WPR 19-7-6-13-9. On qualities of literacy, see Martyn Lyons, *A History of Reading and Writing in the Western World* (Basingstoke, UK: Palgrave, 2010), p. 179.
9 TNA MH 12/2098, 12526/A/1846.
10 See Thomas Sokoll, *Essex Pauper Letters 1731–1837* (Oxford: Oxford University Press, 2001), pp. 1–52.
11 Carter and King, '"I think we ought not to acknowledge them"', pp. 119–20.
12 The shamefaced poor were individuals who had once held a much higher social position but now found themselves to be dependent paupers. Thus, the corpus contains letters from former poor law guardians, inventors, authors, ships' captains, 'gentlemen', local politicians and shopkeepers.
13 On this process, see Lyons, *The Writing Culture of Ordinary People in Europe*, p. 48.
14 Elaine Brown, 'Gender, occupation, illiteracy and the urban economic environment: Leicester 1760–1890', *Urban History*, 31:2 (2004), 191–209; Ros Crone, 'Educating the labouring poor in nineteenth-century Suffolk', *Social History*, 43:2 (2018), 161–85; David Vincent, *Literacy and Popular Culture: England 1750–1914* (Cambridge, UK: Cambridge University Press, 1989).
15 See most recently Alannah Tomkins, 'Poor law institutions through working-class eyes: autobiography, emotion, and family context, 1834–1914', *Journal of British Studies*, 60:2 (2021), 285–309.
16 City of Westminster Archive Centre B1350-9.
17 This issue carries on post 1834. The magistrate Edward Coke wrote to the central authorities from Mansfield on 5 March 1846 and noted that 'I marked my letter "Private" because it was, like this, a mere hurried scrawl and quite unfit for an office file' (TNA MH 12/9361/238, 3296/B/1846). The observation that class, status or role did not always correlate with literacy is consistently made in other European contexts. See, for instance, Kaisa Kauranen, 'Did writing lead to social mobility? Case studies of ordinary writers in nineteenth-century Finland', in Martyn Lyons (ed.), *Ordinary Writings, Personal Narratives: Writing Practices in Nineteenth and Early Twentieth-Century Europe* (Bern: Peter Lang, 2007), pp. 51–68, p. 61. An anonymous referee for this volume suggests that poor-quality handwriting might signify confidence in writing rather than the opposite. There is support for this view in the post-1834 corpus, but even here other signals of a struggle with literacy – random capitalisation, poor grammar, lack of punctuation, random misspelling – are still often shared by paupers, advocates and officials until well into the 1880s.
18 TNA MH 12/15488, 84988/1882. Patrick Joyce, 'The people's English: language and class in England 1840–1920', in Peter Burke and Roy Porter (eds), *Language, Self and Society: A Social History of Language* (Cambridge, UK: Polity, 1991), pp. 154–90, p. 169, argues that writing was used as a tool to construct deservingness.

19 On delegated writing, see Emily Pyle, 'Peasant strategies for obtaining state aid: a study of petitions during World War 1', *Russian History*, 24:1 (1997), 41–64, p. 43, and Martyn Lyons, 'The power of the scribe: delegated writing in Modern Europe', *European History Quarterly*, 44:2 (2014), 244–62.

20 Rothersthorpe Parish Chest (Northamptonshire); TNA MH 12/15485, 83044/1878. Both writers draw attention to the fact that writing required concentration, something which is now well established more widely. See Ivor Timmis, *The Discourse of Desperation: Late Eighteenth and Early Nineteenth-Century Letters by Paupers, Prisoners and Rogues* (London: Routledge, 2020).

21 Northamptonshire Record Office, 261p, Overseers' Correspondence of Peterborough St John Parish.

22 Steven King and Peter Jones, 'Testifying for the poor: epistolary advocates for the poor in nineteenth-century England and Wales', *Journal of Social History*, 49:4 (2016), 784–807.

23 CAS, WPR 19–7–6–21–25.

24 The full range of this foundational literature is considered in King et al, *In Their Own Write*, Chapter 1.

25 Peter Jones and Steven King, *Pauper Voices, Public Opinion and Workhouse Reform in Mid-Victorian England – Bearing Witness* (Basingstoke, UK: Palgrave, 2020), Chapter 3.

26 This seems a universal observation. See, for instance, Arun Kumar, 'Letters of the labouring poor: the art of letter writing in colonial India', *Past and Present*, 246:1 (2020), 149–90.

27 Jones and King, *Pauper Voices*, Chapter 4.

28 Matylda Włodarczyk and Irma Taavitsainen, 'Introduction: Historical (socio) pragmatics at present', *Journal of Historical Pragmatics*, 18:2 (2017), 159–74, p. 165. Contrast these absences with Bart De Sutter and Maarten Van Ginderachter, 'Working-class voices from the late nineteenth century: "propaganda pence" in a socialist paper in Ghent', *History Workshop Journal*, 69:1 (2010), 133–45.

29 As ordinary people did in other contexts. See Ian McNeely, *The Emancipation of Writing: German Civil Society in the Making, 1790s–1820s* (Berkeley CA: University of California Press, 2003), pp. 13–128.

30 West Sussex Record Office, Par 206–37-8-35, Westbourne Overseers' Correspondence.

31 *Ibid*. This was because of widespread famine in the 1790s.

32 On borrowed language, see Lyons, *A History of Reading and Writing*, pp. 75–82.

33 TNA MH 12/6994, 34141/1866. The emphasis here was added in a different ink *after* the letter had been completed or sent.

34 As, for instance, did John Smith, writing to the Poor Law Board about the things he had seen as a resident of the Liverpool workhouse in November 1865. TNA MH 12/5978, 41230/1865. We also see references to monastic slavery.

35 Rothersthorpe Parish Chest.

36 My italics. The sense that he was increasingly unable to write is clearly conveyed. On apologies for writing more generally, see Lyons, *The Writing Culture of Ordinary People in Europe*, p. 35.
37 Spaces are underlined in the original; superscript indicates an insertion above the line.
38 TNA MH 12/15801, 28020/E/1869, 6 May 1869. This evidence sits well with that of Joyce, 'The people's English'.
39 For an overview, see Keith Snell and Paul Ell, *Rival Jerusalems: The Geography of Victorian Religion* (Cambridge, UK: Cambridge University Press, 2000).
40 There were by this time at least five competing methodologies for calculating the 'poverty line', resulting in very different proportions of the population being counted as poor.
41 Marjorie Levine-Clark, *Unemployment, Welfare and Masculine Citizenship: So Much Honest Poverty in Britain 1870–1930* (Basingstoke, UK: Palgrave, 2015).
42 TNA MH 12/8640, 24531/1864. Superscript indicates an insertion above the line.
43 Berkshire Record Office, D/P 26/18/1, Brimpton Overseers' Correspondence.
44 Peter Jones and Steven King, *Navigating the Old English Poor Law: The Kirkby Lonsdale Letters, 1809–1836* (Oxford: Oxford University Press, 2020), pp. 1–27.
45 See Mike Sanders, 'From "technical" to "cultural" literacy: reading and writing within the British Chartist movement', in Ann-Catrine Edlund, T. G. Ashplant and Anna Kuismin (eds), *Reading and Writing from Below: Exploring the Margins of Modernity* (Umeå: Royal Skyttean Society, 2016), pp. 285–300.
46 CAS, WPR 19-7-6-13-9.
47 Oxfordshire Record Office, PAR 207/5/A7/6, Oxford St Martin Overseers' Correspondence.
48 Martyn Lyons, 'Writing upwards: how the weak wrote to the powerful', *Journal of Social History*, 49:2 (2015), 317–30. Although Lyons here suggests that attending in person or being seen 'was a way of validating' the written word of the weak (p. 324), in our sample the poor clearly and persistently constructed the written word as having primacy over being seen. Tonally, many of the writers sought to convey hurt when their written text was met with disbelief.
49 TNA MH 12/15801, 1607/1869.
50 Rothersthorpe Parish Chest.
51 This has also been observed for other socioeconomic groups; Lyons, *A History of Reading and Writing*, p. 95.
52 TNA, MH 12/12231, 29615/1888.
53 For context, see Lyons, *A History of Reading and Writing*, pp. 103–5.
54 TNA MH 12/5058, 20004/1851.
55 TNA MH 12/15488, 84438/1882.
56 TNA MH 12/14691, 44795/1882.
57 See Jones and King, *Pauper Voices*, Chapter 2.
58 TNA MH 12/15485, 83044/1878.

59 TNA MH 12/261, 16268/1866.
60 On encoding, see Marina Dossena, 'The study of correspondence: Theoretical and methodological issues', in Marina Dossena and Gabriella Del Lungo Camiciotti (eds), *Letter Writing in Late Modern Europe* (Amsterdam: John Benjamins, 2012), pp. 13–31, pp. 18–20.
61 For an important discussion of imposed identity, see Christophe Pons, 'The mystical and the modern: The uses of ordinary writings in identity construction by Icelandic spiritual mediums', in Lyons, *Ordinary Writings*, pp. 85–100.
62 Martyn Lyons, 'A new history from below? The writing culture of ordinary people in Europe', *History Australia*, 7:3 (2010), 59.1–59.9, p. 59.4. See also Lyons, *The Writing Culture of Ordinary People in Europe*, pp. 3, 35 and 67.
63 The latter phrase is that of Sheila Fitzpatrick, 'Supplicants and citizens: Public letter writing in Soviet Russia in the 1930s', *Slavic Review*, 55:1 (1996), 78–105, p. 86.

4

Common writers in German-speaking countries from the eighteenth century to the twentieth century as agents of a language history from below

Stephan Elspaß

Introduction

For a long time, the attention of historical as well as historical-linguistic research in the German-speaking countries was focussed on the social elites. Yet literacy was already widespread among various social classes from the early modern period onwards. It took a paradigm shift in historical research as well as in historical linguistics towards a view from below to recognise the intrinsic value of sources from the lower classes. In recent decades, sociohistorical as well as historical sociolinguistic researchers have brought to light and systematically investigated previously unnoticed handwritten sources by common (or ordinary) writers from various archives in Germany, Austria, Switzerland and also from destination countries in the great emigration waves, such as the United States and Brazil.

The sociohistorical and the linguistic dimensions of texts by common writers are closely intertwined. It is primarily the textual (i.e. linguistic) tradition that serves as a window to the 'extra-linguistic' past. At the same time, knowledge about social and communicative conditions in the past, which has been handed down primarily through language, is necessary to answer a central question in historical sociolinguistic research: Why did individuals from certain groups of the population write to certain addressees at a certain time, in certain situations and in the specific way that is documented in texts from the past? This connection between social history and historical sociolinguistics has two methodological consequences for research into the sociolinguistic history of writing, particularly with respect to the common writer. Firstly, linguists will strive for 'informational maximalism'; that is, 'the utilisation of all reasonable means to extend our knowledge of what might have been going on in the past, even though it is not directly observable'.[1] Secondly, it is inevitably necessary to consult original handwritten sources and to edit these sources diplomatically (in other words, produce exact transcriptions of the originals), because only in this way can variants of writing be revealed that allow a historical sociolinguistic analysis.

The aim of the present chapter is to show – to an interdisciplinary readership – what makes these texts so interesting for historical linguistics and what they contribute to a fresh view of the histories of our modern languages. In particular, I will try to demonstrate the central position of common writers in a 'language history from below', a research approach to language history which has moved away from the traditional narratives of language historiography. The history of German will serve as a case study.

The chapter is structured as follows. First, I will give a short overview of the range of surviving texts by common writers in the early modern and modern history of German. The following section will explain some basic ideas of a language history from below approach as well as the role that ego-documents by common writers play in it. The 'from below' approach will be demonstrated using the example of the language history of German in the long nineteenth century. The conclusion will briefly reflect on the position of a language history from below as part of a general history from below.

Common writers and their texts in the modern history of German

Up until the 1980s, researchers in German-speaking countries showed hardly any interest in the study of texts written by common writers, especially texts by writers from the lower social strata, as these texts were accorded neither literary nor cultural-historical dignity. Since the 1980s, social historians and historical sociolinguists have unearthed a wealth of hitherto ignored or even completely forgotten text sources from a wide range of text types. The following examples will illustrate the broad spectrum of writings 'from below' that already existed in the early modern period of German.

In 1590, Rebecca Lemp, a weaver's daughter from the southern German town of Nördlingen and one of the early victims of witch-hunts, wrote several secret letters from her prison cell to her husband in which she claimed her innocence. Her letters and the letters from her husband and children have survived because they were intercepted by court authorities.[2]

In 1591, Paulus Mairat, an impoverished weaver from Augsburg, commissioned a young weaver's apprentice (named 'Hännßle' in the court records) to write a blackmailing letter to a great nephew of the banker Jakob Fugger the Rich, in which he offered to protect Fugger from the allegedly imminent attack of fifteen witches if he agreed to send him a certain amount of money.[3]

In 1595, Hanns Mair, a bookbinder from Augsburg, wrote a short note in which he recorded the mayor's permission to visit a village outside the city walls for the purpose of drinking alcohol. More than sixteen hundred such notes from the municipal archive of Augsburg have been analysed.[4]

Anna Hainhofer, a widow of a citizen of Augsburg, confirmed in a short letter in 1604 that Margarete Ammann, a local healer, had successfully helped her with an ailment. She was one of dozens of women who wrote letters at the request of Ammann, who tried to defend herself against the accusation of quackery brought against her by the city's barbers' guild and the city's Collegium medicum.[5]

In his autobiography of 1657, Augustin Güntzer, a pewterer from the Alsace region, reflected on his years in the trade, which took him, like other journeymen of his time, through a large part of Central Europe.[6]

Caspar Preis, a farmer from Upper Hessia, kept a private journal from 1636 until 1667, the year of his death, in which he documented the events and devastation of the Thirty Years' War (1618–48) as well as experiences in his personal environment, such as illnesses, weather events and crop failures.[7]

Likewise, the hatter Michel Dominikus Kropp, from the town of Eschweiler in the Rhineland, wrote a journal between 1792 and 1807 in which he reported – among other things – events during the French occupation of the Rhineland.[8]

In Ludwig van Beethoven's conversation notebooks, which he used from 1818 onwards (after he had lost his hearing), there are several entries by unnamed housekeepers in which everyday errands are negotiated.[9]

Albert Böhme, a carpenter from the northern German city of Brunswick, and his wife Friederike exchanged 128 letters between August 1870 and June 1871, during the Franco-Prussian War, in which Albert participated as a common soldier at the age of twenty-four. His wife was twenty-three years old at the time.[10]

Pius G., a tailor from the Bavarian town of Dillingen, who was diagnosed with psychosis and in 1883, at the age of thirty-six, was transferred to the nearby psychiatric hospital in Irsee, wrote more than a hundred private letters as well as official letters (mostly letters of complaint and letters of appeal) to a wide range of addressees, including family members and doctors at the hospital.[11]

Some of these sources, which can be subsumed under the umbrella term 'ego-documents',[12] are individual finds, but others are examples from serial sources, particularly letters. For the period from the late eighteenth century to the twentieth century, which will be the focus of the main section of this chapter, letters by common writers have, for the first time in the history of German, survived on a scale that allows a representative insight into the writing practices of broad sections of the population and an alternative view of social history and linguistic history on the basis of textual testimony by common writers.

There are four types of letter, of which thousands of examples have survived: 'official' letters to authorities (e.g. letters of appeal by paupers); soldiers' letters; emigrants' letters; and patients' letters. But what makes these texts so important for linguistic history research? Apart from the fact that they are often little-known texts and offer interesting insights into everyday life in the past from the perspective of common writers, what added value do they have from the point of view of historical sociolinguistics? In the following section, I will try to demonstrate what their special potential is for an alternative historiography of language.

Recentring the angle of vision in language history

In historical sociolinguistics, a research strand has emerged since about the turn of the millennium in which researchers are striving for alternative perspectives and descriptions of language history, but especially of histories of major national languages based on texts by common writers. The trigger for this sociolinguistic turn in language historiography was unease with traditional accounts of the histories of present-day standard languages, which were perceived as too selective and teleological. Many older, but also some more recent, language histories appear selective because they concentrate on certain types of text and/or on certain layers of writer. Older textbooks and research literature on the history of the German language, for example, are based almost exclusively on literary texts; hence they are no more than histories of the German literary language. Moreover, much of the older, and even the more recent, literature on the history of the German language (like other language histories) also focusses on formal, mostly printed texts. And finally, the older scholarship almost exclusively considers texts written by professional or at least experienced scribes or – with regard to the history of German since about 1500 – printed texts.

Many of the older, as well as more recent, textbooks are highly teleological in their narratives of language histories as 'precursors' of today's standard languages and thus, in a certain sense, as their 'prehistories'. Watts called this the 'funnel view' of language history. Referring to the history of the English language, he wrote:

> The perspective on the history of the language is thus rather like a funnel, in which a number of varieties are poured in at the wide top of the funnel and standard English comes out of the narrow neck .... The fate of the original

varieties poured in at the top and others that may have arisen at a later stage are generally not taken into consideration.[13]

There is a consensus in historical sociolinguistics that such selective and teleological accounts of language history have been supported and promoted by some dominant linguistic ideologies. Most prominent in this context is the 'standard language ideology', which is 'a bias toward an abstract, idealised homogeneous language, which is imposed and maintained by dominant bloc institutions and which names as its model the written language'.[14] Historically, the standard language ideology has its roots in the ideology of the nation state, as Reichmann notes for the linguistic history of German:

> I would argue that the language historiography of German from its scientific beginning in the early nineteenth century until well into the second half of the twentieth century was not interested in an objective description of language reality. Rather, it aimed at convincing its readership of the existence of a specific, unique communication system called 'German', a system which is characterised by high structural, semantic and sociological (e.g. literary) standards and which is suitable for serving as a means of constructing or reinforcing identification and of solidarisation in a linguistic-national and cultural-national sense.[15]

I have termed this traditional linguistic perspective on language histories the 'language history from above' approach.[16] The above-mentioned unease with a historiography of language based on a view from above was mainly ignited by the neglect or even complete omission of such aspects as: the heterogeneity of textual traditions; the voices of the 'common people'; the role of oral language registers in the past and in language change more generally; the impact of social factors on language variation and change; the effects of contact between languages; dialects and their role in language change; the role of language ideologies in both individual text production and the normative and aesthetic evaluation of texts; the role of non-standard (often labelled 'deviant', 'not correct', 'bad', 'corrupted', etc.) varieties and variants in standardisation processes; individual linguistic repertoires (i.e. people's mastery of different languages and language varieties); and the social meaning of particular ways of writing (e.g. the attempt to elevate one's own style through the use of certain grammatical forms or formulae of literary language). In German, these include the use of the dative -e suffix or the genitive, or proverbs, biblical quotations and truisms, which are all, in some contexts, signs of an effort to produce an elevated style.

Adding to various other 'histories from below' (military, church, medical, etc.) and coinciding with the call for a 'new history from below',[17] I introduced a 'language history from below' as an alternative approach to language historiography.[18] It advocates a radical change of perspective from a 'bird's eye' to a 'worm's eye view',[19] in an attempt – as Lyons put it in his explanation of the 'Liddenbrock paradox' – 'to establish a new core which re-centres the historian's angle of vision.'[20]

This change of perspective in language history has a sociohistorical and a linguistic aspect.[21] From a sociohistorical point of view, it involves a shift in focus from the language use of experienced writers from the upper classes to the language use of common people, who have always constituted the vast majority of the population. From a linguistic point of view, the language history from below approach suggests an entirely different point of departure for the description and explanation of language in history than in traditional accounts from above. It proposes a shift to focus on oral registers in informal texts, which represent a 'language of immediacy' for common writers. In Koch and Oesterreicher's notion, 'language of immediacy' is characterised by a combination of universal communicative factors such as '(closeness to) spoken language', 'physical proximity of communication partners', 'temporal immediacy of the interaction', 'privacy', 'familiarity of the partners', 'intense involvement of communication partners', 'dialogic structure', 'free turn-taking' and 'spontaneous development of conversational topics'. Fundamentally, the shift to a language history from below entails the recognition of varieties and informal registers as linguistically unmarked (i.e. default) forms of human interaction. According to Koch and Oesterreicher's model, the opposite pole to the language of immediacy is conceived as the 'language of distance'. Accordingly, language of distance is represented by language in formal registers, which is derived from default forms and developed for the purpose of specialised communication, such as in formal and institutional contexts (e.g. religious rituals, newspaper articles or administrative texts).[22]

Prototypically, language in informal registers is represented by speech in oral face-to-face interaction[23] and, in the context of the history of present-day standard languages, by dialects. The chances of gaining access to such varieties and registers from the past are limited. There are no audio recordings of speech from before the invention of the phonograph in 1877. Researchers therefore resort to vernacular texts that are as close to historical speech as possible. Such texts can be 'speech-like (e.g. private correspondence), speech-based (e.g. trial proceedings) or speech purposed (e.g. plays)'.[24] Variational studies in historical sociolinguistics have concentrated on 'speech-like' texts, which primarily include historical private correspondence, but also ego-documents with a more monologic structure, such as diaries, autobiographies (e.g. Augustin Güntzer's text from 1657) and chronicles (e.g. Caspar Preis's text, written in 1636–67).[25] However, comparative studies have suggested that diaries are usually more formal or standard-like than private letters and hence have a lower degree of orality.[26] Consequently, letters are given preference for the investigation of language history from below. Among the different types of letter, private letters are preferred to official letters for two reasons. Firstly, official letters are less oral than private letters; they are based on asymmetrical communicative relationships – socially inferior people addressed socially superior people with a request, the fulfilment of which was usually in the hands of the latter.[27] Accordingly, in official letters to authorities, common writers are trying their hand at formal registers, in which they are less proficient than the more educated recipients. Secondly, and related to the aforementioned problem, there is the question of authenticity. Although the question of authorship – as with all historical documents – in principle affects all kinds of letter, it seems more likely that in the case of official letters, where a formal register was required and much could depend on its mastery, trained (and often paid) scribes were more likely to be consulted than in the case of private letters.

Furthermore, vernacular texts are particularly suitable for the study of language *change* from below, in linguistic as well as in social terms. In Labovian sociolinguistics changes from below are 'systematic changes that appear first in the vernacular, and represent the operation of internal, linguistic factors. At the outset, and through most of their development, they are completely below the level of social awareness.' Labov emphasises that language changes from below can emanate from any social class, 'although no cases have been recorded in which the highest-status social group acts as the innovating group'.[28] This, in turn, is of particular interest for the historical sociolinguist view of language history, because it suggests that texts by common writers are particularly suited to provide information about variation leading to language change.

A language history of German from below in the nineteenth century

For the German-speaking countries it is assumed that at the beginning of the nineteenth century about half of the population and at the end of the century almost the entire population was literate in the sense that they had at least basic reading and writing skills.[29] Reading skills, however, always exceeded writing skills. Large regional and gender differences applied. For example, illiteracy rates tended to be higher in Catholic areas of Prussia than in Protestant ones and were, initially, higher among women than among men. Many common writers who had once learned to write were seldom compelled to take up pen and paper in their daily lives. Nevertheless, it is fair to assume that in the nineteenth century a large part of the population was able to write simple letters; that is, they possessed what could be called a 'partly-schooled letteracy'.[30] Wars and migration movements provided an occasion, if not a compelling reason, for many to put their writing skills into practice. Accordingly, the largest body of surviving private letters from the nineteenth century predominantly written by common writers are letters from soldiers and emigrants and their relatives.[31]

The need to communicate in writing by letter rather than orally in order to maintain contact with friends and relatives in the distant homeland is illustrated in a letter by Catharina Mannott, a farmer's wife, from 1868. She finished her first and only surviving letter, written shortly after her arrival in the United States and addressed to her relatives, with the words: 'With this I must finish. This is my first letter that I am writing. Catharina must study hard.'[32] The Mannott family emigrated to the United States in 1868; Catharina, born in 1831, was thirty-seven years of age at the time. If her statement is to be trusted, this is the first letter that she had written since she left school, probably at around the age of fourteen as was customary for children of common people at the time. This interpretation is supported by her visibly unpractised handwriting and the spelling errors and cross-outs in her letter.[33]

Other letter writers also made it clear that writing letters was not an everyday routine for them but required special effort.[34] Time and again, writers complained that they could not find the time or leisure to write, or that they needed several attempts to finish a letter, among other things because various jobs got in the way. In a letter from 1850, a housemaid from Swabia complained about not receiving many letters from home, whereas she and her husband make an effort and 'sit down three to four times when we write to you'.[35] A farmer from the Lower Rhine area apologised for the delay in writing to his children by saying that he had to interrupt his letter to take measures to protect his vegetable crop during a sudden period of frost.[36]

Although private letters in general can be regarded as 'speech-like' types of text, a closer look at the language of nineteenth-century letters reveals that they often oscillate linguistically between several poles, among them: the pragmatic requirements of the concrete communicative situation – for example, to maintain contact with relatives or to ask them for money in financially difficult situations; written language traditions – for example, the formal conventions of correspondence such as salutations, closing formulae or health formulae, or the use of the conservative genitive case; the influences of spoken vernaculars – for instance, dialect words and the use of double negatives; as well as overarching tendencies in conceptual orality – for instance, widely used grammatical constructions like the progressive form with *am* + infinitive (*es ist am regnen* – 'it is raining') that are considered non-standard German. Illustrations and explanations of these factors will be given below.

Overall, the writers were guided by a communicative principle that applies to all intended linguistic action: 'Speak/write in such a way that you best achieve your communicative goal in the most economical way possible.' This overarching principle controlled the basic textual functions of the letters, which first and foremost included the maintenance of social contacts and information. In order to achieve these aims, the use of textual routines proved to be indispensable in the private correspondence of inexperienced nineteenth-century writers. Routine formulae, for example, formed the ritual framework of the text type 'letter' (salutation, closing formulae, etc.) and at the same time provided the writers with a kind of linguistic framework into which information could be incorporated and with which situational pragmatic purposes could be mastered. Such text-constituting formulae, which are not a feature confined to German letters alone, included phrases like 'I now take my pen in hand to let you know',[37] 'that we have received your letter in good health',[38] or 'herewith / with this I must close my letter'.[39] In addition to text-constituting formulae, common writers often used proverbs, biblical quotations, truisms and the like, primarily in the process of excusing or justifying themselves. In many cases, this was an attempt to use the argumentative power of general truths conveyed by such formulae. For instance, a thirty-year-old clothier from Hessia seemed to safeguard himself against the excessively high expectations of his father and his brothers by quoting the proverb *aller Anfang ist schwer* 'the first step is always the hardest'.[40] Many common writers used the biblical quote 'es fällt kein Haar aus Eurem Haupte, ohne des Herrn Wille' 'but not a hair of your head will perish without the Lord's will' (Luke 21:18) in different apologetic contexts. A twenty-two-year-old day labourer from the Moselle area employed this quote in connection with a whole series of formulae to justify his resistance to his family's wish that he return to his German homeland; the reason for this was that he had fled his country to avoid military conscription – which he would face again if he returned to Germany:

> If I, now accustomed to a free life in America, had to be a Prussian soldier and let myself be commandeered by everyone, it would certainly be the greatest misfortune for me. Everyone's fate is decided for him, and what will be will be. The Lord is our guide, and not a hair will fall from your head without the Lord's will.[41]

With regard to the analysis of grammatical features, it is noteworthy that such passages contain constructions that seem archaic and which are hardly used in non-formulaic parts of private letters. In the German emigrant letters, for example, dative singular forms of masculine or neuter nouns with the *-e* suffix and genitive attributes preceding a noun appear more frequently in formulae than in non-formulaic speech; for example, the *-e* suffix in 'Haupte' (formal dative form of *Haupt* – 'head') and the genitive form 'des Herrn' preceding 'Wille' (the Lord's will) in the biblical quotation just mentioned ('es fällt kein Haar aus Eurem Haupte, ohne des Herrn Wille').

The rather eclectic use of various forms of formulaic language in the letters points to different epistolary traditions used by common writers. It seems, as David Fitzpatrick[42] observed in Irish emigrant letters of the nineteenth century, that letter writers found such patterns in school textbooks of the time and in documents handed down from one generation of the family to the next, and that they mixed them with phrases from catechisms and sermons, from newspapers and popular writings; linguistically, the formulaic language was 'largely divorced from the substance of the letter' and can be interpreted 'as the cultural residue of seven centuries of rhetoric, instruction, imitation, and modification'.[43]

More interesting from a linguistic point of view – and for the view from below, in particular – are the grammatical and lexical forms of use in the non-formulaic parts of the letters, which seem to be much more influenced by oral rather than written linguistic traditions. Thus, we can observe a contrast between texts from above – the language of printed texts written by educated writers – and texts from below – private letters written by common writers in nineteenth-century German. Texts from above were oriented towards prescriptive grammar-book norms and, as a result, tended towards uniformity in grammar and spelling. Texts from below were linguistically characterised by lexical, morphological and spelling variation, syntactic flexibility and a polyfunctionality of grammatical forms such as prepositions and conjunctions. However, the grammatical variation of these texts was not arbitrary, but pointed in the direction of regular change that has been observed for the vernaculars of virtually all living languages. In essence, this change is leading in the direction of a reduction of grammatical complexity and an expansion of analytical forms.

The reduction of grammatical complexity is illustrated by two grammatical phenomena, namely the use of the dative *-e* suffix (already mentioned) and the prepositional case in German. Since the end of the eighteenth century and almost throughout the nineteenth century, grammars prescribed the use of the *-e* suffix for the dative singular of masculine or neuter nouns; for example, *auf dem Tische* (on the table), *auf dem Felde* (in the field). The codified forms in present-day grammars of standard German are forms lacking a suffix (*auf dem Tisch, auf dem Feld*), except for their rare use in idioms and other formulae, such as *im Grunde* (in essence), *im Stande sein* (to be able to). Whereas many nineteenth-century printed texts (literary texts, texts in newspapers and periodicals, legal texts, etc.) followed the prescriptive norm by using *-e*, the analysis of a sample of ninety emigrant letters written by common writers found that in almost two thirds of all relevant cases, the forms without suffix were used.⁴⁴ A similar discrepancy between prescription and usage existed in the area of prepositional case. As a prepositional case after *wegen* (because of), *während* (during), *anstatt/statt* (instead of), *trotz* (in spite of) and other prepositions, nineteenth-century grammars prescribed the genitive; the use of the dative – which requires less complex case marking – was stigmatised as incorrect. Quite predominantly, however – in more than 81 per cent of all relevant cases⁴⁵ – common writers used the dative or even the accusative (which was also considered incorrect); only educated writers used genitive forms in the majority of cases.⁴⁶

Such discrepancies between prescription and usage can also be observed in the area of syntax in the letters. The use of the double negation and analytical constructions with the auxiliary *tun* (to do) can serve as examples of grammatical constructions that were used for many centuries in vernacular speech, but stigmatised by prescriptive grammars since the eighteenth century. As in English and Dutch – but unlike, for example, in French or Russian – the use of a double negative has been considered incorrect in standard language for centuries due to a popular language myth that 'double negatives are illogical'.⁴⁷ Whereas they are virtually absent from nineteenth-century text in print and also from letters of educated writers, there are many examples of the use of double negatives in letters by common writers;⁴⁸ for example, 'kein geistiges getränk darf nicht verkauft werden' (no spirits may not be sold).⁴⁹ In non-standard varieties of German (especially in Upper German dialects), double negation is still commonly used today.

The construction with *tun* (to do) is another example of how the evaluation of certain syntactic constructions as 'standard' can vary widely in today's standard languages. For example, while certain constructions with do + infinitive are obligatory in standard English, equivalent constructions in German are considered non-standard; for example, in negative sentences such as 'den Herman Holle tuth […] nicht heieraten'⁵⁰ (Hermann Holle does not get married). Constructions with *tun* can serve an array of different functions in German, but in most cases the use of *tun* is deemed 'bad' German. Again, in spite of their stigmatisation in formal registers and in printed German, they are frequently used in letters, just as they are very common in everyday varieties of present-day German.⁵¹

We have seen so far that various grammatical phenomena were used in texts from below, which, despite their long history of stigmatisation in prescriptive grammar writing,⁵² were widely used by common writers and are still in use in standard and/or non-standard varieties of present-day German, not least because of their functional properties. Moreover, the analysis of nineteenth-century letters uncovered innovative constructions that originated in everyday language and have continued to be employed in present-day German, primarily in everyday spoken varieties. Two prominent examples are the progressive form with *am* + infinitive and the use of the conjunction *weil* (because of) with main clause word order. Typologically, German is considered a language lacking grammatical forms of aspect – 'aspect' understood here as a grammatical category of the verb, such as tense or mode, perhaps expressing a repetitive or progressive action. Researchers, however, are presently discussing whether a grammaticalisation of the *am* + infinitive construction to express progressive aspect is currently taking place. The conjunction *weil* was once used to introduce subordinate clauses only, but is now increasingly used with main clause word order. The usage of both constructions has become widespread in spoken everyday German and even spoken standard German, but is generally still considered non-standard in writing.[53] Both constructions, which are not mentioned by traditional grammars, represent 'natural' tendencies to expand the range of grammatical structures in German. It is noteworthy that both constructions have emerged from oral varieties of German, and in both cases the examples found in private letters of the nineteenth century are among the earliest evidence of their use.[54]

Finally, the case studies presented here shed an interesting light on the relationship between the typological description of German and its history of standardisation. Viewed from below, nineteenth-century German appears as a less inflectional language; that is, it used fewer morphological endings in words than Latin, for example. Rather, it appears as a language that exhibited more analytical structures than shown, for example, in printed texts of the time, and as a language that already developed aspectual structures. These observations confirm von Polenz's assumption that the standardisation of German and the rise of prescriptive grammar had a 'retarding' effect on its typological development and that

> German as a standard language today would have been less inflectional and more analytic – similar to Dutch and English – if its development during the period of German Absolutism and its cultivation by an educated middle class had not been so strongly governed by written language, by academia, by a focus on Latin, by a penchant for inflection, and by language ideology.[55]

Conclusion

Documents by common writers, which have been preserved and have become available for research in large numbers in the last three decades, have proved to be an important source for the social history of writing as well as for language history. I hope to have shown that the potential of researching such texts goes far beyond granting selective insights into what many scholars would still deem as 'marginal' areas of writing and literacy. From the selected findings presented in this chapter, it becomes clear that a language history from below, based on texts by common writers, is of eminent importance for describing and explaining present-day language variation and change. The uniformitarian principle – that is, the belief that a knowledge of linguistic processes that operated in the past can be inferred by observing ongoing processes in the present – is fundamental to historical linguistics. However, historical sociolinguists have suggested that it is at least as important to use the past 'to explain the present';[56] that is, to realise that it is necessary to have a view of the language of the past that is as comprehensive as possible and covers all layers of writing, in order to better understand the roots and developments of today's language. In this respect, the crucial potential of texts from below, written by common writers in the past, lies in their contribution to a language history of below as an alternative approach to the study of language in the past – which essentially constitutes part of a (new) history from below.

Notes

I dedicate this chapter to the memory of Wolfgang Helbich (1935–2021), the eminent German historian, who founded and supervised the *Bochumer Auswandererbriefsammlung*, now part of the *Deutsche Auswandererbriefsammlung*, the biggest collection of German emigrant letters (with over 10,000 individual letters). Without Helbich's pioneering work and the diplomatically edited letter collection, which he started in the 1980s, linguistic work such as the one reported on in the present chapter would not have been possible at the time. For more about this collection, now under the direction of Ursula Lehmkuhl, see www.auswandererbriefe.de.

1 Richard D. Janda and Brian D. Joseph, 'On language, change, and language change – or, of history, linguistics, and historical linguistics', in Brian D. Joseph and Richard D. Janda (eds), *The Handbook of Historical Linguistics* (Malden, MA, and Oxford: Blackwell, 2003), pp. 3–180, p. 37.
2 Elvira Topalović and Iris Hille, 'Perspektivierung von Wirklichkeit(en) im Hexenprozess: Geheimbriefe und Verhörprotokolle im Vergleich. Quellen, Transkriptionen, Übertragungen', www.historicum.net, 2007.
3 Helmut Graser, 'Quellen vom unteren Rand der Schriftlichkeit—die Stimme der einfachen Leute in der Stadt der Frühen Neuzeit?', in Stephan Elspaß und Michaela Negele (eds), *Sprachvariation und Sprachwandel in der Stadt der Frühen Neuzeit* (Heidelberg: Winter, 2011), pp. 15–48, see pp. 25–6 and 40–5.
4 *Ibid.*, p. 31.
5 *Ibid.*, pp. 27–8.
6 Augustin Güntzer, *Kleines Biechlein von meinem gantzen Leben. Die Autobiographie eines Elsässer Kanngießers aus dem 17. Jahrhundert*, ed. Fabian Brändle and Dominik Sieber (Cologne, Weimar and Vienna: Böhlau, 2002).
7 Wilhelm A. Eckardt and Helmut Klingelhöfer (eds), *Bauernleben im Zeitalter des Dreißigjährigen Krieges. Die Stausebacher Chronik des Caspar Preis 1636–1667* (Marburg an der Lahn: Trauvetter and Fischer, 1998).

8 Richard Pick, 'Ein Tagebuch aus der Zeit der Fremdherrschaft. Im Auszuge mitgetheilt von R. P.', *Annalen des Historischen Vereins für den Niederrhein*, 16 (1865), 127–58.
9 See, for example, Karl-Heinz Köhler, Grita Herre and Dagmar Beck (eds), *Ludwig van Beethovens Konversationshefte*, Vol. 9 (Leipzig: Deutscher Verlag für Musik, 1989), pp. 67 and 255.
10 Isa Schikorsky (ed.), *'Wenn doch dies Elend ein Ende hätte'. Ein Briefwechsel aus dem Deutsch-Französischen Krieg 1870/71* (Cologne, Weimar and Vienna: Böhlau, 1999).
11 Archiv des Bezirkskrankenhauses Kaufbeuren, File no. 936; cf. Markus Schiegg and Lena Sowada, 'Script switching in nineteenth-century lower-class German handwriting', *Paedagogica Historica*, 55:6 (2019), 772–91.
12 Gijsbert Rutten and Andreas Krogull, 'The observee's paradox: Theorising linguistic differences between historical ego-documents', *Neuphilologische Mitteilungen*, 122:1–2 (2021), 284–318.
13 Richard J. Watts, *Language Myths and the History of English* (Oxford: Oxford University Press, 2011), p. 291.
14 Rosina Lippi-Green, *English with an Accent. Language, Ideology, and Discrimination in the United States* (London and New York: Routledge, 2nd ed., 2012), p. 67.
15 'Ich behaupte aber, daß die Sprachgeschichtsschreibung des Deutschen, von ihrem wissenschaftlichen Beginn im frühen 19. Jahrhundert bis weit in die 2. Hälfte des 20. Jahrhunderts, mehr als durch das abbildtheoretisch motivierte Beschreiben objektsprachlicher Verhältnisse durch das Anliegen bestimmt ist, die angesprochene Leserschaft von der Existenz eines spezifischen, eigentümlichen, einmaligen Verständigungssystems ‚Deutsch' zu überzeugen, eines Systems, das mit hohen strukturellen, semantischen, soziologischen (z. B. literatursprachlichen) Gütequalitäten ausgezeichnet ist und das sich deshalb gut in den Dienst von Identitätsfindung oder -verstärkung, von Solidarisierung in einem sprach- und kulturnationalen Sinne stellen läßt.' (Oscar Reichmann, 'Nationale und europäische Sprachgeschichtsschreibung', *Mitteilungen des Deutschen Germanistenverbandes*, 48:4 (2001), 530–7, p. 533).
16 Stephan Elspaß, *Sprachgeschichte von unten. Untersuchungen zum geschriebenen Alltagsdeutsch im 19. Jahrhundert* (Tübingen: Niemeyer, 2005), p. 6; Stephan Elspaß, 'A twofold view "from below": New perspectives on language histories and language historiographies', in Stephan Elspaß, Nils Langer, Joachim Scharloth and Wim Vandenbussche (eds), *Germanic Language Histories 'from Below' (1700–2000)* (Berlin and New York: De Gruyter, 2007), pp. 3–9, pp. 3–4.
17 Tim Hitchcock, 'A new history from below', *History Workshop Journal*, 57:1 (2004), 294–8.
18 Elspaß, *Sprachgeschichte von unten*; Elspaß, 'A twofold view "from below"'.
19 Elspaß, 'A twofold view "from below"', p. 4.
20 Martyn Lyons, *The Writing Culture of Ordinary People in Europe, c.1860–1920* (Cambridge, UK: Cambridge University Press, 2013), p. 50.
21 Elspaß, *Sprachgeschichte von unten*, p. 20; Elspaß, 'A twofold view "from below"', pp. 4–5.

22 Cf. Peter Koch and Wulf Oesterreicher, 'Language of immediacy – language of distance: Orality and literacy from the perspective of language theory and linguistic history', in C. Lange, B. Weber and G. Wolf (eds), *Communicative Spaces: Variation, Contact, and Change. Papers in Honour of Ursula Schaefer* (Frankfurt: Peter Lang, 2012), pp. 445–7. [German original: Peter Koch and Wulf Oesterreicher, 'Sprache der Nähe – Sprache der Distanz. Mündlichkeit und Schriftlichkeit im Spannungsfeld von Sprachtheorie und Sprachgeschichte', *Romanistisches Jahrbuch*, 36 (1985), 15–43].
23 Peter L. Berger and Thomas Luckmann, *The Social Construction of Reality: A Treatise in the Sociology of Knowledge* (London: Penguin, 1966).
24 Terttu Nevalainen and Helena Raumolin-Brunberg, 'Historical sociolinguistics: Origins, motivations, and paradigms', in Juan M. Hernández-Campoy and J. Camilo Conde-Silvestre (eds), *The Handbook of Historical Sociolinguistics* (Chichester, UK: Wiley-Blackwell, 2012), pp. 22–40, p. 29.
25 Cf. Stephan Elspaß, 'The use of private letters and diaries in sociolinguistic investigation', in Hernández-Campoy and Conde-Silvestre, *Handbook of Historical Sociolinguistics*, pp. 156–69.
26 Rutten and Krogull, 'The observee's paradox'.
27 Marion Klenk, *Sprache im Kontext sozialer Lebenswelt. Eine Untersuchung zur Arbeiterschriftsprache im 19. Jahrhundert* (Tübingen: Niemeyer, 1997), p. 138.
28 William Labov, *Principles of Linguistic Change, Vol. 1: Internal Factors* (Oxford: Blackwell, 1994), p. 78.
29 Peter von Polenz, *Deutsche Sprachgeschichte vom Spätmittelalter bis zur Gegenwart. Vol. 3: 19. und 20. Jahrhundert* (Berlin and New York: De Gruyter, 1999), p. 51.
30 Tony Fairman, '"Lower-order" letters, schooling and the English language, 1795 to 1834', in Elspaß *et al.*, *Germanic Language Histories 'from Below'*, p. 34. Fairman defines 'letteracy' as the ability to write, in order to distinguish the basic writing skills of common writers – which can be ascertained on the basis of their texts – from 'literacy', their ability to read – which cannot be definitively determined; cf. *ibid.*, p. 32.
31 The Deutsche Auswandererbriefsammlung, archived in the Forschungsbibliothek Gotha, Handschriftenabteilung, is by far the largest collection of German emigrant letters, comprising over twelve thousand letters (cf. Auswandererbriefe Aus Nordamerika, www.auswandererbriefe.de, accessed 9 June 2023); another eight thousand letters are hosted by the German Heritage in Letters project at the German Historical Institute in Washington DC (cf. German Heritage in Letters, https://germanletters.org/, accessed 9 June 2023). The scope of soldiers' letters collections from the nineteenth century is considerably smaller. The collection of the Museumsstiftung Post und Telekommunikation comprises about a hundred letters from the nineteenth century (cf. Museumsstiftung Post und Telekommunikation, www.briefsammlung.de/feldpost-19tes-jh/, accessed 9 June 2023), compared to about twenty-two hundred letters from the two world wars (cf. Museumsstiftung Post und Telekommunikation, www.briefsammlung.de/feldpost-erster-weltkrieg/, www.briefsammlung.de/feldpost-zweiter-weltkrieg/, accessed 9 June 2023). Another extensive collection, consisting of about

twenty-seven hundred war letters and diaries, is maintained by the Bonn University Library (cf. Universitäts- und Landesbibliothek Bonn, 'Kreigsbriefe' (War letters), https://digitale-sammlungen.ulb.uni-bonn.de/ulbbnhans/topic/view/1468382, accessed 9 June 2023). For an exemplary edition of emigrant letters, see Wolfgang Helbich, Walter D. Kamphoefner and Ulrike Sommer (eds), *Briefe aus Amerika. Deutsche Auswanderer schreiben aus der Neuen Welt 1830–1930* (Munich: Beck, 1988). For an overview and linguistic analyses of war letters in German, see Marko Neumann, *Soldatenbriefe des 18. und 19. Jahrhunderts* (Heidelberg: Winter, 2019), pp. 59–67.

32 'Hir mit mus ich schließen dies iß mein eßß erß Brief zu schreiben. Catharina mus gut Studiren' (Deutsche Auswandererbriefsammlung, letter series Wohlers, letter by Margarethe Catharina Mannott from 1868.)

33 Cf. the excerpt from a copy of the original letter in Elspaß, *Sprachgeschichte von unten*, p. 55.

34 Cf. the title of the reader by Siegfried Grosse, Martin Grimberg, Thomas Hölscher and Jörg Karweick, '*Denn das Schreiben gehört nicht zu meiner täglichen Beschäftigung*' (Because writing is not part of my daily routine) (Bonn: Dietz, 1989). (The quote in the original letter contains several spelling mistakes: 'den das Schreiben gehört nicht zu meiner Tägliegen Bescheftigung', p. 13.)

35 'wir geben uns mehr mühe wir sitzen 3 bis 4 mal hin wann wir euch schreiben' (Deutsche Auswandererbriefsammlung, letter series Schwarz, letter by Maria Schano, née Klinger, from 1850).

36 'Lieve kinder ik heb dit briefje aan vangs Juni aan gevangen to schrijven maar doen moest ik weer met schrijven op hooren want dags voor Christi hemmelvaart doen bevroor ons bijna alles pullekes boonen en staak boenen.' (*Chronik der Familie Look*, Cleves, private printing, 1948, p. 27). The letter is written in Dutch, as this was the written language taught in school in the Lower Rhine area well into the mid-nineteenth century, although it had already belonged to the Kingdom of Prussia since the Congress of Vienna.

37 'ich ergreife die Feder, um euch wissen zu lassen' (cf. Dutch 'ik zal de pen opvatten [...] wij laeten uw weten', and Danish 'Jeg skriver dig til for at lade dig vide').

38 'dass wir Euren Brief in guter Gesundheit empfangen haben' (cf. Dutch 'dat wij die briever [...] hier in goede gesondhijd ontfangen').

39 'hiermit muss ich mein Schreiben schließen' (cf. Danish 'Nu maa jeg slutte min korte brev for denne gang').

40 'Lieber Vater u. Bruder wenn ich gesund bleibe dann verdiene ich hier ziemlich Geld denn es heißt aller Anfang ist schwer' (Deutsche Auswandererbriefsammlung, letter series Fritz, letter by Matthias Weitz from 16 July 1854).

41 'wenn Ich müsst des freien Lebens in Amerika gewohnt, preusischer Soldat sein, Mich von jedem komadieren lassen[,] Es würde gewiss das größte Unglück für Mich sein. de[nn] dabei bleiben würde Ich nicht. Es ist einem jeden sein Los beschieden, und was sein soll geschieht. Der Herr ist unser Führer, und es fällt kein Haar aus Eurem Haupte, ohne des Herrn Wille.' (Deutsche Auswandererbriefsammlung, letter series Bauer, letter by Franz Joseph Löwen from 7 October 1860).

42 David Fitzpatrick, *Oceans of Consolation: Personal Accounts of Irish Migration to Australia* (Ithaca, NY: Cornell University Press, 1994), pp. 501–2.

43 *Ibid.*, p. 496.

44 Elspaß, *Sprachgeschichte von unten*, p. 351.
45 Genitive and dative case marking can only be identified in prepositional phrases with masculine or neuter nouns; for example, *wegen des Mannes* (genitive)/ *wegen dem Mann(e)* (dative) (because of the man), *wegen der Männer* (genitive)/ *wegen den Männern* (dative) (because of the men). In feminine nouns, the genitive and dative forms are identical in the singular forms, for example, *wegen der Frau* (genitive/dative) (because of the woman), and can only be discriminated in the articles of plural forms; for example, *wegen der Frauen* (genitive)/ *wegen den Frauen* (dative) (because of the women).
46 Stephan Elspaß, 'Private letters as a source for an alternative history of Late Modern German', in Anita Auer, Daniel Schreier and Richard J. Watts (eds), *Letter Writing and Language Change* (Cambridge, UK: Cambridge University Press, 2015), pp. 47–8. The history of prescription and usage of such prepositional cases is described in great detail in the recent study by Megumi Sato, *Sprachvariation und Sprachwandel im 18. und 19. Jahrhundert. Untersuchungen zur Kasusrektion der Präpositionen* wegen, statt, während *und* trotz (Heidelberg: Winter, in press).
47 Jenny Cheshire, 'Double negatives are illogical', in Laurie Bauer and Peter Trudgill (eds), *Language Myths* (London: Penguin, 1998), pp. 113–22.
48 Elspaß, *Sprachgeschichte von unten*, pp. 277–80.
49 Private letter archive of G. Maresch, Bad Goisern (Upper Austria), letter by Katharina Hinterer, née Gamsjäger, from 31 July 1887.
50 Deutsche Auswandererbriefsammlung, letter series Kammeier, letter by Margarethe Winkelmeier from June 1867.
51 Elspaß, *Sprachgeschichte von unten*, pp. 254–67.
52 Cf. Winifred V. Davies and Nils Langer, *The Making of Bad Language. Lay Linguistic Stigmatisations in German: Past and Present* (Frankfurt am Main: Peter Lang, 2006).
53 Mathilde Hennig (ed.), *Duden, Sprachliche Zweifelsfälle. Das Wörterbuch für richtiges und gutes Deutsch* (Berlin: Duden, 9th edition, 2021), pp. 75 and 1036.
54 Elspaß, *Sprachgeschichte von unten*, pp. 268–75, 296–316.
55 'dass die deutsche Sprache als Standardsprache heute sicher ähnlich flexionsarm, also mehr nach dem analytischen Sprachbau wäre wie etwa das Niederländische oder Englische, wenn die deutsche Sprachentwicklung in der Zeit des bildungsbürgerlich kultivierten deutschen Absolutismus nicht so stark schreibsprachlich, akademisch, lateinorientert, flexionsfreundlich und sprachideologisch gesteuert verlaufen wäre'; (Peter von Polenz, *Deutsche Sprachgeschichte vom Spätmittelalter bis zur Gegenwart, vol. 2, 17. und 18. Jahrhundert* (Berlin and New York: De Gruyter, 2nd edition, 2013), p. 277). Cf. Stephan Elspaß, 'Language standardization in a view "from below"', in Wendy Ayres-Bennett and John Bellamy (eds), *The Cambridge Handbook of Language Standardization* (Cambridge, UK: Cambridge University Press, 2021), pp. 93–114.
56 Joan Beal, 'To explain the present: 18th and 19th-century antecedents of 21st-century levelling and diffusion', in Javier Pérez-Guerra, Dolores González-Álvarez, Jorge L. Bueno Alonso and Esperanza Roma-Martínez (eds), *'Of Varying Language and Opposing Creed': New Insights into Late Modern English* (Bern: Peter Lang, 2007), pp. 25–46.

5

Narrating injuries and injustices: life stories in the struggle for working-class rights in Britain, 1820–1945

T. G. Ashplant

Workers' life histories

During the nineteenth and early twentieth centuries, the occasions for – and invitations to – working people to utter their life stories to a wider public, in the hope that they might help to effect change, increased markedly. Pauper letters represented efforts by *individuals*, albeit with some community support and knowledge of the law, to make a claim on the state to alleviate their immediate personal circumstances by narrating the source of their material distress. They are examples of what Carolyn Steedman has termed 'enforced narratives'.[1] From the 1790s, the development of workers' organisations, with new models of campaigning and their own press, constituted a *collective* force which governments had to take account of. Under such pressures, Parliament initiated inquiries into working conditions, to which workers were invited to give testimony. A field of force was created, stretching between the state and those interest groups in civil society closer to it on the one hand, and working people and their organisations on the other, constituting a space within which plebeian life narratives could be variously elicited or proffered. These narratives differed widely: in who initiated them; in what role intermediaries played in their composition and publication; in what audience(s) they were aimed at, and with what intentions. I will use three examples – campaigns to limit factory hours; efforts to improve women's access to divorce and maternity care; and literary/political responses to mass unemployment – to explore changing patterns of such transactions between 1820 and 1945. Some key themes extend across the different forms of life narrative involved: the (often ambivalent or conflicted) roles of intermediaries in eliciting and deploying workers' stories; the threat of victimisation against those who spoke out; the complex relations between the spoken and the printed in the articulation of those stories; and the experiences of material deprivation, bodily trauma and injustice around which they often centred.

Child labour, working hours, factory discipline

As early nineteenth-century parliaments, faced with growing concern about the social problems resulting from rapid industrialisation and urbanisation, were increasingly pressured to intervene in economic and social life, they established official inquiries which actively solicited testimony from working people as representative of particular occupations. These developments involved a reciprocal interaction with groups of workers, who – though initially suspicious of this summons – increasingly saw such inquiries as opportunities to press the case for legislation to improve their working conditions, and developed new testimonial strategies to promote their own causes and to demand, influence or resist government initiatives.[2]

These inquiries featured contributions from, and battles over the authenticity of, workers' autobiographical testimony. The cases of Robert Blincoe, Charles Aberdeen and William Dodd exemplify the strategies workers used and many of the difficulties they faced. Robert Blincoe (born circa 1792) was sent as a parish orphan to a cotton mill where, while serving a fourteen-year apprenticeship, he both experienced and observed cruel ill treatment of the child workers.[3] The tortuous composition and publication history of Blincoe's memoir of this period is revealing. It was initiated by a campaigning radical journalist, John Brown, who in 1822 interviewed Blincoe, transcribed his oral narrative and planned to publish it.[4] When Brown's illness delayed this, hostile rumours were spread about his intentions; the written text was then outside Blincoe's control, squabbled over by conflicting political interests. This led to a brief rupture between Blincoe and Brown, but the interviews resumed in 1824. Two years later, Brown killed himself; but his papers survived and came into the hands of the radical publisher Richard Carlile. As part of a campaign against the ineffectuality of the most recent (1825) Act limiting child labour, Carlile serialised Blincoe's story in his paper *The Lion* in 1828, and then issued it as a separate book. Blincoe, who had not known of this plan, was at first angry but then accepted the explanation that Carlile had tried but had been unable to contact him before publishing. Four years later John Doherty, the leading trade unionist and editor of *The Poor Man's Advocate* (PMA), reissued the memoir. Only now was Blincoe able to approve the printed version, making minor additions and corrections.[5] The text can thus be seen as a collective product, created, published and circulated by the successive efforts of three radical journalists, two of them working men.

Blincoe's chief complaints concern the child workers' excessive hours, meagre food and filthy working conditions; the frequent, often sadistic, beatings with which they were disciplined; and the industrial injuries they suffered. His own resultant lameness he mentions only briefly.[6] Perhaps his greatest anger is directed at the deceit and injustice with which the authorities (parish officials, mill owners and overlookers, and local magistrates) treated him and his fellows.[7]

Brown's purpose in eliciting and writing up Blincoe's story was to help mobilise action against the mistreatment of child factory workers.[8] He insisted that the story he told was not exaggerated, mentioning the interviews he conducted with Blincoe and also his efforts to corroborate details of the narrative by questioning fellow workers.[9] As narrator, Brown's voice dominates the text, its language melodramatic (occasionally gothic) and moralising.[10] When Blincoe's words are presented as direct quotation, their register is very similar to Brown's own.[11] The narrative voice is that of an omniscient outsider of the scene it describes: it contrasts the repeated illusions of the child Blincoe (about possible improvements to, or escape from, his circumstances) with Brown's retrospective knowledge of how Blincoe is being (self-)deceived.[12] The effect is to demonstrate that naivety and lack of adult strength makes it impossible for even a determined and courageous child to defeat mill owners, who are supported by the collusion of parish officials and magistrates.[13]

The text was compiled in the early 1820s, and referred to events of the 1800s, when Blincoe had been an apprentice. Moreover, one specific evil of which it complained, the system whereby parishes supplied orphans as cheap labour for mill owners, had since been addressed by Parliament.[14] Nevertheless, Brown intended it to reverse the previous silencing of workers' voices in the campaigns over factory regulation; and Carlile in his preface stressed the need for working people themselves to tell their story.[15] Doherty's republication had the same intention, at a crucial moment in the campaign. He commissioned a woodcut portrait of Blincoe, showing his crippled limbs, which appeared on the cover of the reprint. At a major demonstration in support of the Ten Hours' Bill in August 1832, this image appeared on hundreds of banners.[16]

The campaigns for Factory Acts to limit the hours of work, from the late 1820s through the 1840s and beyond, saw an emergent clash between two modes of official inquiry. The parliamentary leader of the Ten Hours campaign, the Tory radical Michael Sadler, had secured the establishment of a Select Committee (SC) on Factory Children's Labour in March 1832.[17] The passage of the Reform Act shortly afterwards was followed at the turn of the year by the election of a new Parliament with greater representation of Members of Parliament (MPs) sympathetic to the manufacturers. By the time the SC's report began to appear in January 1833, the new Parliament, in response to claims that Sadler's choice of witnesses had been biassed in favour of the Ten Hours campaign, had established a Royal Commission (RC) to review the question.[18] Robert Gray has situated these two committees of 1832 and 1833 as representing 'competing models of social enquiry and legislative information'.[19] Sadler's SC certainly used leading standard questions, but this was normal SC procedure where a case was presented on behalf of some group interest. What was distinctive about Sadler's hearing was the presence of a large number of adult male workers, who could present the moral economy of their community which underlay its campaign.[20] These individual testimonies given at Westminster have to be placed in a wider context where, after public meetings in the textile districts in support of the Ten Hours campaign, 'the operatives told their tales of woe, fines, strapping, and oppressions'.[21]

The RC's proceedings, by contrast, were dominated by 'the visions of regulation and surveillance elaborated by some professional men and functionaries of the official state', which would come to shape the approach of many subsequent official inquiries.[22] The RC sought to re-examine several of the SC's witnesses.[23] Though he had not been a witness in 1832, Blincoe was summoned before one of the commissioners who visited Lancashire, to verify the claims in his now widely publicised text. He briefly recapitulated his own injury: 'I got deformed [at the cotton mills]; my knees began to bend in when I was 15; you can see how they are (*showing them*)'; but spent longer recalling injuries to others. He concluded with a precisely worded remark: '*I have a book written* about these things, describing my own life and sufferings. I will send it to you' (my emphasis).[24]

Charles Aberdeen, who had also been a parish apprentice in the same years as Blincoe, was likewise subjected to scrutiny. He had given testimony to the SC, including both his experiences as an apprentice and adult worker, and a detailed account of his victimisation for having supported the Ten Hours' Bill in defiance of pressure from his employer.[25] Called before the RC, he explained that since his sacking he had been living as a servant with Richard Carlile, making his living by selling pamphlets. Questioned on the accuracy of aspects of his previous testimony, he concluded: 'If I was in solitary confinement I could write a history of my life, and I could show up the factory system then.'[26]

Aberdeen's aspiration to 'write a history of my life' was realised a few years later by William Dodd. Dodd (b. 1804) was sent by his parents at the age of six to work as a piecer in a wool factory. The pressure of intense work on a child's body left him partially crippled, his legs bowed inwards at the knees. His repeated efforts to escape from the factory to other employment were continually thwarted by his bodily weakness; instead, he eventually secured less physically demanding work in the factory as a packer and bookkeeper. He embarked on a process of self-education, which led to his being elected secretary of his friendly society branch, and later a regional delegate to its national conference. A further attempt to escape from factory work by setting up as a tailor, initially successful, collapsed when a long-term work-related injury to his wrist required amputation of his forearm.[27]

Now impoverished, Dodd came to the attention of Lord Ashley, an MP and leading philanthropist who had taken up the cause of factory reform and was campaigning for a ten-hour day for adolescent and women workers. He supported Dodd in writing his memoir: *A Narrative of the Experience and Sufferings of William Dodd, a Factory Cripple. Written by Himself*, published in 1841 and dedicated to Ashley. On a personal level, the memoir combines an anguished account of Dodd's multiple injuries and the consequent thwarting of his attempts to find a new occupation and to marry, with a situating of himself as but one of many victims of the factory among his family, friends and workmates.[28] Politically, it combines acknowledgment of help and encouragement he has received from others, including even one of his employers, with an excoriation of the factory system, whose victims include even overlookers and masters.[29]

Ashley employed Dodd to collect further information about industrial conditions in the north; his reports were published as *The Factory System Illustrated in a Series of Letters to Lord Ashley* (1842). Ashley used these works as valuable evidence, while Dodd himself also played an active role in the campaign, his *Narrative* supporting the case for a reduction in working hours. However, as with Blincoe and Aberdeen, the direct testimony of workers continued to be contested. In a House of Commons debate in 1844, the reliability of Dodd's testimony was challenged by John Bright, an opponent of restraints on freedom of trade. He quoted some letters Dodd had written containing a confusing retraction of some of his work.[30] After Bright's attack, Ashley lost faith in Dodd.[31] It seems that intra- and inter-class tensions had ruptured a temporary alliance of convenience. Dodd, further handicapped by the recent loss of his arm, needed the employment Ashley offered, which also enabled him to publish his memoir. But the Evangelical Anglican Tory Ashley, while keen to use the evidence Dodd provided, was fighting not only for the Ten Hours' Bill, but also against the northern Dissenting cotton manufacturers. It seems to have been Dodd's refusal to attack certain cotton masters whom he respected which provoked his confusing retraction and, in turn, led to Ashley's abandoning him. In the latter's words, from 'My poor cripple ... is a jewel, his talent and skill are unequalled; he sends me invaluable evidence', Dodd became 'a mere matter of charity', who 'if he chose to come when the servants dined ... might have some dinner with them'.[32]

The focus of Blincoe's and Dodd's texts differs. Blincoe's primary target is the authority figures who tricked, abused or failed to protect him; his demand is for justice. Strikingly, when he addressed the medical factory commissioner, the bodily injury to which he drew attention was not the industrial injury (his bowed knees) which made him an iconic figure in the campaign, but instead the result of unjust punishment. 'I have seen the time when two hand-vices of a pound weight each, more or less, have been screwed to my ears ... Here are the scars still remaining behind my ears.'[33] For Dodd, whose injuries were more numerous and more severe, it is the machinery (in all senses) of the factory system which is targeted. His language foregrounds the literal and metaphorical intermeshing of bodies and machines. On Monday mornings, after the Sunday off: 'My joints were then like so many rusty hinges, that had laid by for years.' To describe the failing circulation of blood in distorted limbs such as his damaged arm, he used a similar mechanical analogy: 'our very life (for life depends upon the circulation of the blood), at best, is only like the half-extinguished flame of a gas-burner, when there is water in the pipes – it jumps and flickers for a little while, and then pops out'.[34]

Both Blincoe's and Dodd's memoirs, denouncing a system of which each was merely one sufferer, can be seen as examples of *testimonio*, as John Beverley has defined it. The narrator's situation is 'one that must be representative of a social class or group', and concerns 'a problematic collective social situation that the narrator lives with or alongside others'; the account is presented 'with an urgency to communicate, a problem of repression, poverty, subalternity, imprisonment, struggle for survival .... The position of the reader of *testimonio* is akin to that of a jury member in a courtroom.'[35]

It proved a struggle to defend the validity of their testimony when it was called into question. Blincoe, summoned before the RC, maintained the truth of his account, which was supported and publicly proclaimed by the Ten Hour mass movement. Dodd, his veracity and character challenged in Parliament, and abandoned by his aristocratic patron, then emigrated to America.[36] There, he published *The Laboring Classes of England* (1847), in which he recounted (under pseudonyms) both his own and Blincoe's testimony.[37]

Maternity assistance and access to divorce

In the late nineteenth century, significant changes were occurring in the public roles of women. Some middle-class women (often trained in professions or university educated) were seizing or creating new professional opportunities, in emergent forms of social work or as social researchers.[38] They developed – with varying degrees of success – a willingness to listen to and recount the experiences of working-class women.[39] A growing concern, in a period of increasing imperial rivalry, with the future health of the population made it possible for women researchers to emphasise motherhood – both social and biological – as important for the continuing strength of the nation, thereby justifying both their own role in the public sphere and the subject of their investigations.[40] The relationship between middle-class investigators and working women, and the narrating of the fruits of that relationship to an audience of policy makers and liberal readers, was complex. Contradictory identifications were created whereby women with new and sometimes insecure professional roles could use the situation of working women to explore indirectly some of the economic and gender conflicts they themselves faced.[41] The investigators, like women philanthropists of an earlier generation, presumed the right to ask questions.[42] As Eileen Yeo has suggested: 'their focus of concern or subject matter was often poorer women. Social science staged a fascinating theatre of encounter between women of different social classes'; yet 'the question of who was to think and act for whom was still very problematic and advocacy tended to outweigh any commitment to agency for poor women'.[43]

These developments intersected with some cross-class political alliances, as both middle-class and working-class women were drawn into the growing suffrage movement, or joined related campaigns to improve the workplace and domestic lives of working women. Yet such attempted alliances could produce very different approaches to valuing and presenting the testimonies they collected. Both the Fabian Women's Group (FWG) and the Women's Co-operative Guild (WCG) included socialist and feminist women who wanted the state to take some responsibility for the costs of motherhood; the WCG, in addition, wanted to challenge the concept of the family wage, so as to give working women some financial independence from their husbands. However, their different politics shaped how they collected and presented the testimony of the women they sought to help.

In 1913, the FWG published *Round about a Pound a Week*, the report of its investigation of the impact of poverty on new mothers in working-class Lambeth (a London district of the respectable working class, not the very poor).[44] The middle-class investigators worked from 1909–13 and interviewed forty-two families; their analyses were sympathetic to the women and emphasised that it was the poverty of life on an income of a pound a week, rather than any lack of knowledge or concern, that handicapped their mothering. However, their portrayal of the women's efforts at writing and compiling budgets was couched in patronisingly humorous terms, and the women's own voices are heard only in brief snippets.[45] The socialism of the Fabian Society looked to permeate the upper and middle classes with collectivist ideas and, thereby, shift public policy towards greater state intervention on behalf of the working class. This approach had little room for working women's own ideas and actions.[46]

The WCG was equally concerned to influence the formation of policy, but took a radically different approach. The Guild had been founded in 1883 to support the wives of working men who were co-operative members. It had in the region of ten thousand members by 1897 and thirty thousand by 1914.[47] In 1891 Margaret Llewelyn Davies – from an upper-middle-class Liberal radical background committed to public service, herself a socialist and feminist – became the movement's general secretary. Her class background might have suggested similar limitations to those of key figures in the FWG; but the character of her thirty years of work for the Guild, and the heartfelt testimonials paid to her by working women on her retirement, point to a much deeper and more democratic engagement with the conditions of working-class women's lives.[48]

In a history of the Guild's first twenty-one years, which she published in 1904, Davies described those from her own background who were involved in the Guild as women who 'must identify themselves with working-class interests, and come as interpreters of the needs and wishes of the workers'.[49] Under Davies's leadership, the WCG set itself the aim of educating working women to be able to play an active role, first within the co-operative movement itself, and then in the wider public sphere (especially local government). Recognising that many such women had internalised the view that they had no place in the public sphere, and lacked the experience or formal education to challenge this, the Guild established forms of training, especially in public speaking. It also developed what Gillian Scott terms a 'culture of affirmation' about working women's 'untapped capacity for public work'. One aspect of this was the provision, through its 'Women's Corner' column in the weekly paper *Co-operative News*, of a space in which working women could write about their own experiences.[50]

The effectiveness of this training can be traced in the memoir of Elizabeth Layton. On joining the Guild, she contrasted it with the philanthropic Mothers' Meetings she had previously attended. 'I was not used to working women managing their meetings …. I have boiled over many times at some of the things I have been obliged to listen to, without the chance of asking a question. In the Guild we always had the chance of discussing something.' She described her development from the first time she addressed the management committee of her local co-operative on behalf of her Guild branch (when she was so nervous that, standing behind her husband's chair, she nearly shook him off it) to the occasion, some three decades later, when she addressed a government minister on behalf of a WCG deputation.[51]

These various internal training initiatives, carried on over a twenty-year period, helped members to become active in the WCG itself, local co-operative societies, the Labour Party and the trade unions, and later to hold office in various public bodies, or become magistrates.[52] They also provided the basis for two major WCG incursions into the sphere of public policy making between 1910 and 1915, for the reform of the divorce laws and for maternity provision for working women – campaigns in which forms of life writing played a major role. Davies's democratic principles led her always to encourage the Guildswomen to articulate their own perspectives on, and remedies for, the conditions of their lives.

The RC on Divorce and Matrimonial Causes was established in 1909. The WCG collected evidence to support the case for reforms, having first consulted forty-one branches (on the two key questions of whether the grounds for divorce should be equal for men and women and whether divorce proceedings should be cheapened so that the law was within reach of the poor), and, in more detail, 124 Guild officials and former officials. As well as giving a statistical breakdown of the replies, the WCG's evidence, presented to the RC by Davies, included an appendix of personal testimonies, most about cases known to (or described merely as known to) the informant, but some recounting individuals' own experiences. One woman recalled: 'The tenth day after the baby was born [my husband] came home drunk and compelled me to submit to him. Of course I had no strength and was at his mercy.' Another described her husband 'holding a knife over me, but *never touching me*, because then, and only then, could I get a separation. He never lost himself enough to forget that .... I got a doctor to see him; he could not testify him insane. Saw the local magistrate. He, sorry as he was, could do nothing.'[53] Davies commented: 'I regret it is impossible to place before the Commission the manuscript letters – often many pages long, laboriously written after thought and consultation – which have been sent in, for the personality and attitude of mind of the writers are largely lost in printed extracts.'[54]

By eliciting and presenting working women's testimony *in writing*, the WCG had enabled them to present their case in (often painful) personal detail. The difficulty working women still faced in '*speaking* truth to power' became evident when the WCG's second witness, Eleanor Barton, was questioned by the commissioners. Barton was a working-class woman with years of experience within the Guild. 'Her effort to inform the commissioners about post-natal rape, involving as it did a struggle to find a vocabulary to discuss sexual abuse in a setting which lacked the necessary legal or cultural conceptual framework, is particularly striking.' Unable to break through the barriers of social status and the demands of propriety in addressing sexual questions, Barton instead referred the commissioners to doctors, who 'have this evidence and could give it more conclusively than one like myself'.[55]

When the Liberal government was preparing its major welfare reform, the WCG presented a detailed case for the inclusion of maternity benefit in the 1911 National Insurance Act. Initially defeated in its demand that this payment should be made directly to the mothers, it managed to secure this right in the 1913 amendment. The Guild then pressed for a scheme for the national care of maternity.[56] To support this campaign, following what Gill Scott has termed its practice of 'investigative agitation', questionnaires had been circulated to some 600 members who were or had been officers of the Guild; some 386 were returned.[57] Expanding what it had pioneered in collecting evidence on divorce, the Guild subsequently published a selection of these testimonies, as *Maternity: Letters from Working Women* (1915).

Davies contributed an introduction generalising the implications of the replies; but the power of the text lay especially in the women's letters, which, she commented, 'give for the first time in their own words the working woman's view of her life in relation to maternity'.[58] Clearly, the 160 letters published were chosen to make a case; and were no doubt edited (the originals do not survive). While many comprised short vignettes focussed specifically on pregnancy, childbirth, maternal health and childcare, others gave fuller accounts, or extended to brief life narratives giving a sense of how the questions of maternity with which the campaign was concerned fitted into the wider picture of the author's life.[59] They are painful to read even today. In Gloden Dallas' words, they tell of 'childbirth and death, exhaustion and self-sacrifice, of totally inadequate pre-natal care, of poverty, abortion, sometimes despair'.[60]

Taken together, these campaigns can be regarded as a two-pronged attack on the idea that the private world of home and family life occupied a separate sphere from the realm of politico-legal regulation. Their deployment of testimonial life narratives challenged the assumption that working women were unable to articulate their experiences in a manner which could bring about changes of policy. These writings can be contrasted with pauper letters. Women (as well as men) wrote such letters, as named individuals, to state or philanthropic authorities, with the aim of negotiating benefits on behalf of their own families. In the two WCG campaigns, the life narratives were respectively presented to the RC, and published, in both cases anonymously. Working women were invited to share, and thereby pool, individual accounts of experience which nevertheless collectively and powerfully demonstrated the impact of political, economic and legal inequality on their intimate lives.

Mass unemployment and unsafe working conditions

Following a brief post-war economic boom, Britain experienced mass unemployment for almost two decades from 1921. With the persistence of this problem, and growing political tensions in the face of the rise of fascism in Europe, individuals and groups on the political left (liberal, socialist and communist) launched initiatives to encourage workers to write creatively and vividly about their lives. The familiar difficulties of inter-class alliances between the gatekeepers of access to journalistic and publishing outlets and working men and women were cross-cut by fierce contemporary debates about the desirable politics and aesthetics of such writing.[61] A combination of the figure of the coal miner as the 'archetypal proletarian' and the fact that the coal industry was one of the worst hit of Britain's staple export industries, leading to sustained high levels of unemployment in some coalfields, opened a cultural space for the 1930s mining novels of Lewis Jones and Harold Heslop.

The writing and publishing career of the Welsh miner B. L. (Bert) Coombes (1893–1974) intersects with these projects.[62] From one perspective, Coombes' story suggests how little had changed for workers in the century since Blincoe and Dodd, as the themes of injustice and corporeal suffering are once again central. He and two fellow workers were asked to shore up the roof of a coal seam; though doubtful of the safety of this task, they went ahead under pressure of the need to earn their living. A sudden rockfall killed the other two miners. At the inquest, Coombes, fearing that if he mentioned their prior concerns the insurers would use this to evade paying death benefit, muted the evidence he gave. This incident impelled Coombes, then aged forty, to reveal the truth about the life of his community. Determined to make himself into a writer, he faced the familiar material constraints: finding time (as well as the long hours of his shifts, he had two children and was active in his union and St John's Ambulance), space (he wrote on the kitchen table) and even paper (many of his manuscripts were written on the backs of existing texts).[63]

However, through a combination of expanded adult education provision and a range of left-wing literary-political initiatives, new routes to authorship and publication had been created. Seeking to train himself as a writer, Coombes benefited from membership of a 'British Scribblers' writing circle (originally founded by two Oxford academics) and from the local classes of the National Council of Labour Colleges (a strongly left-wing adult education body).[64] His early writing comprised both political essays and fictional short stories – though these often had a strong autobiographical element.[65] His breakthrough came when John Lehmann, editor of *New Writing*, published his short story 'Flame' in 1937. Lehmann, keen to encourage working-class writers, mentored Coombes.[66] But his name was made with two successive publications in 1939. The first was the booklet *I Am a Miner*, published in the Fact series.[67] The second was his autobiography. The left-wing publisher Victor Gollancz, whose Left Book Club included several texts dealing with the crisis of unemployment, also sought direct working-class voices.[68] He was very enthusiastic about *These Poor Hands*, which was published as a Left Book Club 'Book of the month' in June 1939.[69]

A keen self-improver (after developing a love of music, he made his own violin), Coombes underplayed the more personal autobiographical elements within his narrative, choosing, like Blincoe, to narrate not individual success, but difficulties and injustices of the life he shared with others.[70] His primary aim was to dispel widespread ignorance of, and prejudice against, miners and their communities by documentary description of their lives.[71] Hence much of his writing comprised detailed accounts of miners' daily work, the physical risks they face and the inadequate protection they receive. Coombes highlighted three systemic factors: the pressure to keep up the pace of production at the expense of safety precautions; the miners' need to keep earning at all costs, with a consequent fear of victimisation if they challenged these demands; and the combination of injustice and ignorance which prevented adequate compensation for injury or industrial disease. Threaded through his narrative are asides – ironical or bitterly angry – pointing out the substantial profits made by the coal owners.

The deaths of two men just inches away became a haunting memory for Coombes; his accounts of his reactions suggest post-traumatic stress. He wrote about the incident several times.[72] Two versions appeared in 1939: in the autobiography *These Poor Hands* and, six months later, in the short story 'Twenty tons of coal'.[73] The similarities and differences between these accounts exemplify the bleeding into each other of fiction and documentary which Storm Jameson had explored in *Fact*.[74] Both versions simplify the original incident: the narrator escapes while just a single workmate, barely a pace away, is crushed. Moreover, concerned to avoid claims of libel, or Coombes' victimisation, Gollancz had asked him to rewrite the episode for *These Poor Hands*, as a reported incident.[75] In response, Coombes made it a story told to him by one fellow miner about another. This change, however, also achieves other effects. Coombes as autobiographer now distances himself from the event. He omits the post-traumatic nightmares with which the fuller account in 'Twenty tons' opens. In keeping with his strategy throughout *These Poor Hands*, this shifts the focus away from Coombes's individual reaction to the general point about the potential dangers and injustices which all miners face. If this incident echoes the work experiences of Blincoe and Dodd, a sentence in 'Twenty tons' inverts that of Blincoe and Aberdeen when questioned about their truthfulness before the RC. Reflecting on the forthcoming inquest, the narrator comments: 'If I appear stupid at the inquiry, as a workman is expected to be, then I will answer the set questions as I am supposed to answer them and "the usual verdict will be returned."'[76]

The book was generally well received (though some mainstream publications were troubled by its demand for change, while the communist left found it insufficiently radical).[77] In spite of such criticisms, it was very successful, selling more than eighty thousand copies in its first year, and being widely translated. This success gave Coombes a national profile. In 1941, the highly successful photojournalism magazine *Picture Post* opened its special number on post-war reconstruction, 'Plan for Britain', with Coombes' essay 'This is the problem'.[78] For the next fifteen years, Coombes had access to a range of publishing outlets, national and local, which he used to portray the character of his mining community more fully, for an audience ignorant of this world, while also pressing the political case for the nationalisation of the mines.

Testimony to injustice

The instances of working people's life writing discussed in this chapter come from three very different historical moments: the struggle to control emergent forms of industrialisation from the 1820s to the 1840s; a transformative moment in women's entry into public life from the 1890s to the 1910s; and the attempt to resist and think beyond the impact of mass unemployment on working conditions in the 1920s and 1930s. Nevertheless, some key similarities link these texts.

All required the help of middle-class intermediaries to bring their stories to the public.[79] Brown's *Memoir of Robert Blincoe* and Dodd's *Narrative* both depended on collaboration, though in radically different forms. The stories which the adult Blincoe had told to fellow workers were turned into a written text by the radical journalist Brown. After Brown's death, the worker-journalists Carlile (with Blincoe's eventual consent) and Doherty (with his active support) printed his narrative in the workers' own press as part of an organised worker campaign.[80] By contrast, the publication of Dodd's memoir, and the research for his second book, *The Factory System*, depended on a temporary and uneasy alliance with Ashley, a patron whose philanthropic support for the Ten Hours' Bill was entangled with his aristocratic Tory hostility to Whig manufacturers. When Dodd proved unwilling to further this second agenda, he was abandoned. Seventy years later, newly professional middle-class women (such as those in the FWG) could combine genuine sympathy with, and effective publicity for, the difficulties of working women with an inability to see them as articulate actors. The members of the WCG, by contrast, benefited from the exceptional commitment of an upper-middle-class woman whose socialist and feminist principles supported the building of skills necessary for full participation of working women in democracy. Though the Guild itself was politically neutral, some of its most active members, such as Eleanor Barton, were also involved in the socialist and suffrage movements.[81] Born a century after Blincoe, and sharing Dodd's love of books, Coombes had far greater opportunities than either, able to benefit from the expansion of adult education, and efforts by politically committed middle-class sympathisers to foster workers' writing. Such cross-class support was the more valuable, since all these narrators encountered or reported some form of the threats and intimidation which sought to silence working people who spoke out about their lives.[82]

Thematically, their narratives share a focus on the hardships, injustices and sometimes cruelty which marked their lives. This is figured in particular through the body, which is sometimes displayed, more often evoked, as testimony. Though made famous by the image of his knock-knees, when Blincoe gives evidence to the RC it is his ears that he points to, since they testify to the injustice and cruelty which is his central theme. Dodd, whose injuries were worse, explicitly proclaims himself a 'factory cripple'. Coombes's world, below and above ground, is peopled by men whose limbs and lungs are damaged by their work. The title *These Poor Hands* presents this in synecdoche. Blincoe's left forefinger was lopped off at the first joint. Dodd's hands bled for weeks from rubbing the wool cardings. When Coombes was playing the violin for inmates of a workhouse, its strings reopened stone cuts in his fingers, leaving them bleeding. He claimed: 'I have often to bandage men's hands before they can start to work. I have known a man work for weeks with splintered pieces of bone coming out of his finger.'[83] Coombes combines the themes of bodily injury and injustice in the opening pages of 'Twenty tons', where the narrator's trauma from seeing 'my mate smashed – right by my elbow' is intensified by his summons to the inquest where he will have to collude in an injustice.[84]

Whereas for the men injustice lay in the inadequacy of the law or the failure to enforce it, for the women it lay in the very law itself, which allowed husbands to demand sex from their wives whatever the effect on their health, while effectively denying women the possibility of divorce. Injustice lay also in the taboos which frequently prevented them from speaking of their suffering. One woman recalled a husband who 'all the way home threatened what he would do when we got there. I was not accustomed to talk to my neighbours. Shame held me silent. This he knew.'[85] Perhaps the chorus of such women's voices, orchestrated by the WCG and published anonymously, could be seen as a collective form of *testimonio*.

Notes

1 Carolyn Steedman, 'Enforced narratives: Stories of another self', in Tess Cosslett, Celia Lury and Penny Summerfield (eds), *Feminism and Autobiography: Texts, Theories, Methods* (London: Routledge, 2000), pp. 28–30.
2 '[Royal] Commissions created an environment for negotiations that had both literal and symbolic dimensions for political elites, and between them and the lower classes'; Oz Frankel, 'Scenes of commission: Royal commissions of inquiry and the culture of social investigation in early Victorian Britain', *European Legacy*, 4:6 (1999), 20–41, pp. 21.
3 Parish officials sent orphans for whose care they were responsible to factory owners as cheap labour, a practice euphemistically described as 'apprenticeship'. Janice Carlisle, 'Introduction', in James R. Simmons, Jr. (ed.), *Factory Lives: Four Nineteenth-Century Working-Class Autobiographies* (Peterborough, Canada: Broadview, 2007), pp. 43–4.
4 On Brown, see John Waller, *The Real Oliver Twist: Robert Blincoe: A Life that Illuminates a Violent Age* (Thriplow, UK: Icon, 2005), pp. 245–52, and 273–8.
5 John Brown's *A Memoir of Robert Blincoe, an Orphan Boy* (hereafter cited as Brown) is reprinted in Simmons, *Factory Lives*, pp. 91–179. For its complex composition and publication history, see *ibid.*, pp. 80–2, 88, 91–2 (Carlile's preface), pp. 93–4, 98 (Brown's account), pp. 326–7, 330.
6 On conditions: Brown, *Robert Blincoe*, pp. 111–15, 132–5, 140, 149–51, 154–5; on discipline: pp. 116, 141–6, 151, 156–7, 161; on injuries: pp. 122, 143, 166–8 (lameness). While his own experience is central, Blincoe gives examples of what happened to fellow workers (pp. 122–3, 146), insisting that others suffered worse (p. 163).
7 On injustice: Brown, *Robert Blincoe*: pp. 95, 104–5, 107, 124–5, 127, 130 (workhouse officials), pp. 131, 135–6, 148–9, 157–8, 161 (owners), pp. 136, 157–63 (magistrates).
8 Blincoe's experience showed that previous legislation was not being enforced: Brown, *Robert Blincoe*, p. 125.
9 On Brown's claim: Brown, *Robert Blincoe*, pp. 98, 137–8; interviews with Blincoe: pp. 95, 98; on corroboration: pp. 134, 136–8, 146–8. Carlile published letters of corroboration after he began serialising the memoir; one writer said he had heard many of Blincoe's stories before, when they were both apprentices: pp. 177–9.
10 On melodramatic elements, see Cassandra Falke, *Literature by the Working Class: English Autobiographies, 1820–1848* (Amherst, NY: Cambria, 2013), pp. 76–7.
11 Apparent quotations from Blincoe: Brown, *Robert Blincoe*, pp. 102, 105–6, 118–19, 120, 121.
12 On illusions: Brown, pp. 100–1, 103–5, 120–1, 164–5 (the adult Blincoe is a 'simpleton' in being taken in by a fortune-teller).
13 For a rare and temporary symbolic victory, see Brown, *Robert Blincoe*, pp. 151–4.

14 If inadequately: Carlisle, 'Introduction', pp. 44–5.
15 A parliamentary committee considering factory labour in 1816 had heard from no workers; that of 1819 from only a few (who were then victimised); Carlisle, 'Introduction', p. 45. Brown argued that Blincoe could have given evidence to the 1816 inquiry (pp. 98–9). Carlile, 'Publisher's preface', in Simmons, *Factory Lives*, p. 92: 'If a remedy be desired, it must be sought by that part of the working people themselves, who are alive to their progressing degradation.'
16 Waller, *Real Oliver Twist*, pp. 295–8, 310–1; image reproduced on p. 297.
17 A few days after Sadler's SC held its first hearing, Doherty published an extract from the memoir in *PMA* (21 April 1832), p. 112. On 9 June, *PMA* published (pp. 161–2) a brief biography of Blincoe (in a series of five such factory victims), with the woodcut portrait, and announced the forthcoming republication; Waller, *Real Oliver Twist*, pp. 294–5.
18 Frankel, 'Scenes of commission', p. 21.
19 Robert Gray, *The Factory Question and Industrial England, 1830–1860* (Cambridge, UK: Cambridge University Press, 1996), p. 60; Oz Frankel, *States of Inquiry: Social Investigations and Print Culture in Nineteenth-Century Britain and the United States* (Baltimore, MD: Johns Hopkins University Press, 2006), pp. 167–71. On the differences between SCs and RCs, *ibid.*, pp. 141–2, 162–3.
20 Gray, *Factory Question*, pp. 59–72, especially pp. 60, 66. 'Adult male working-class witnesses, recruited and briefed by the short-time committee network, were probably the recognised, and in some sense elected, representatives of their trades and communities'; *ibid.*, p. 66. Sixty of the seventy-eight witnesses were workers; Carlisle, 'Introduction', p. 23.
21 Gray, *Factory Question*, p. 63.
22 *Ibid.*, p. 61. On the early development of RCs, and the practices of their individual commissioners, see Frankel, 'Scenes of commission', pp. 20–9; and the same author's *States of Inquiry*, Chapter 4. On the different textual forms of SC and RC reports, see 'Scenes of commission', pp. 30–2.
23 On the tensions between Sadler's SC and the 1833 RC, see Frankel, *States of Inquiry*, pp. 147–8, 168–9.
24 *Second Report of the Royal Commission on Children's Employments in Factories*, Parliamentary Papers, House of Commons (henceforth HC) 1833 [519] xxi, D.3 (Lancashire District, medical report by Dr Hawkins), pp. 17–18 (original italics); reprinted in Simmons, *Factory Lives*, pp. 327–30.
25 *Report from the Select Committee on the Bill to Regulate the Labour of Children*, HC 1831–32 [706] xv, pp. 439–48; Simmons, *Factory Lives*, pp. 391–400; victimisation: Questions (Q) 9598–622.
26 *First Report of the Royal Commission on Children's Employments in Factories*, HC 1833 [450] xx, D.2 (Lancashire District, examinations by Mr Tufnell), p. 1; for the evidence of fellow workers who challenged his testimony, D.2, pp. 23–5; Gray, *Factory Question*, pp. 69–71. For the different conditions

under which workers and employers were questioned, see Frankel, 'Scenes of commission', p. 23.

27 William Dodd, *A Narrative of the Experience and Sufferings of William Dodd, a Factory Cripple. Written by Himself* (hereafter cited as Dodd), reprinted in Simmons, *Factory Lives*, pp. 181–222.

28 On his own injuries: Dodd, *A Narrative*, pp. 189–90, 208–9, 219–20; on finding a new job: pp. 193, 213–14, 219–20; on marriage: pp. 201–2, 211–13; on injuries to others: pp. 186–7, 195–6, 204–5, 209–10.

29 On help from others: Dodd, *A Narrative*, pp. 198–9; on the factory system: pp. 205, 209, 218; on its victims: pp. 210–11.

30 Hansard's account of this section of their debate, with Dodd's letters referenced therein, is reprinted in Simmons, *Factory Lives*, pp. 334–52.

31 Simmons, *Factory Lives*, pp. 48–53, 343–8.

32 Quotations from Ashley, 'Diary', 3 Dec 1841, cited in W. H. Chaloner, 'New introduction', in William Dodd, *The Factory System Illustrated* (London: Frank Cass, 1968), pp. v–vi, and the parliamentary debate, Simmons, *Factory Lives*, pp. 344–5; Kathleen M. Keating, *Beleaguered Memory: Nation and Narrative Forgetting in Nineteenth-Century British Literature*, Ph.D. thesis, University of California, Irvine, 1998, pp. 65–75, for the suggested cause of the rupture.

33 *RC Second Report*, p. 18, reprinted in Simmons, *Factory Lives*, p. 329.

34 Dodd, *A Narrative*, pp. 193, 209.

35 John Beverley, 'The margin at the centre: on *testimonio*', *Modern Fiction Studies*, 35:1 (1989), 11–28, pp. 14, 15.

36 The conflict over veracity has continued within modern scholarship: on Blincoe, see the criticisms of Stanley D. Chapman, *The Early Factory Masters: The Transition to the Factory System in the Midlands Textile Industry* (Newton Abbot, UK: David and Charles, 1967), pp. 199–209, and responses of A. E. Musson, *Trade Union and Social History* (London: Frank Cass, 1974), Chapter 9, and Waller, *Real Oliver Twist*, pp. 156–8, 382–4; on Dodd, see Chaloner, 'New introduction', pp. v–xiii, which simply endorses Bright's attack, and the response in Carlisle, 'Introduction', pp. 52–3.

37 Simmons, *Factory Lives*, pp. 348–52.

38 On this development, see Eileen J. Yeo, *The Contest for Social Science: Relations and Representations of Gender and Class* (London: Rivers Oram, 1996), Chapter 9; Deborah Epstein Nord, *Walking the Victorian Streets: Women, Representation, and the City* (Ithaca, NY: Cornell University Press, 1995), Chapter 7; Ellen Ross, *Love and Toil: Motherhood in Outcast London 1870–1918* (Oxford: Oxford University Press, 1993), Chapter 1; Sally Alexander, 'Introduction', in Maud Pember Reeves, *Round about a Pound a Week* (London: Virago, reprint, 1979, first published 1913 (hereafter Reeves), pp. ix–xxi.

39 Ross, *Love and Toil*, pp. 18–19, suggests that 'the characteristic mode of the women observers was aural'.

40 Nord, *Walking the Victorian Streets*, pp. 213–14; Yeo, *Contest for Social Science*, p. 246.

41 Ross, *Love and Toil*, pp. 20–1. Nord, *Walking the Victorian Streets*, pp. 208–9; she analyses the contradictions this produces within Reeves' text, pp. 224–7.
42 The Lambeth women were sometimes reluctant or forbearing: Reeves, *Round about a Pound*, p. 16. 'Their descriptions of the Lambeth women recall the notes of other "lady visitors"'; Nord, *Walking the Victorian Streets*, p. 223.
43 Yeo, *Contest for Social Science*, pp. 249, 258–9.
44 Reeves, *Round about a Pound*, pp. 2–3.
45 On number of interviews: Reeves, *Round about a Pound*, p. 176. On women reading and compiling budgets: pp. 12–14 (cf. Yeo, *Contest for Social Science*, p. 263); on limitations of language: pp. 16–17.
46 'The investigators constructed poor women as active if oppressed in the private sphere but in need of advocacy in the public sphere. In the final two chapters which analysed causes and remedies Pember Reeves gave the housewives little to say. She had fenced them out earlier by an assumption that their horizons were too limited to be of use'; Yeo, *Contest for Social Science*, pp. 263–4.
47 The members were predominantly the wives of respectable artisans: Parliamentary Papers 1912–13 XX, *Minutes of Evidence taken before the RC on Divorce and Matrimonial Causes* (Cd 6481) (hereafter *RC Divorce*), p. 149, Q 36, 976–8.
48 For Davies' background and values, see Gillian Scott, *Feminism and the Politics of Working Women: The Women's Co-Operative Guild, 1880s to the Second World War* (London: University College London, 1998), ch. 2; for retirement tributes, p. 42. 'Not only was she committed to helping women develop the skills for self-organisation and active citizenship in a democracy but she worked hard to open public space where poor women could speak for themselves. ... The politics of self-representation shaped Davies' investigative practice'; Yeo, *Contest for Social Science*, p. 266.
49 Margaret Llewelyn Davies, *The Women's Co-operative Guild, 1883–1904* (Kirkby Lonsdale, UK: Women's Co-operative Guild, 1904), p. 150.
50 Gillian Scott, '"As a war-horse to the beat of the drums": Representations of Working-Class Femininity in the Women's Co-operative Guild, 1880s to the Second World War', in Eileen Janes Yeo (ed.), *Radical Femininity: Women's Self-Representation in the Public Sphere* (Manchester: Manchester University Press, 1998), pp. 196–219, p. 198 (contrast with its early years), pp. 201–3; Scott, *Feminism*, pp. 55–7.
51 Elizabeth Layton, 'Memories of seventy years', in Margaret Llewelyn Davies (ed.), *Life As We Have Known It, by Co-operative Working Women* (London: Virago, reprint, 1982), first published 1931, pp. 1–55, pp. 40–1, 49.
52 Scott, *Feminism*, pp. 49–50, 103–4.
53 Individuals' experiences: *RC Divorce*, pp. 166–7, nos. 113–15, and p. 168, no. 117 (original emphasis). Davies accepted the offer to have the testimonies printed as an appendix to the minutes because 'the accumulated evidence is so effective': p. 162, Q 37,009. The WCG also reprinted its evidence as a separate book: *Working Women and Divorce: An Account of the Evidence Given on Behalf of the Women's Co-operative Guild before the Royal Commission on Divorce* (London: David Nutt, 1911).

54 *RC Divorce*, pp. 149–50, Q 36,980. The majority report of the RC accepted many of the arguments the WCG had made; but the religiously inspired minority report (which took particular exception to the Guild's proposals), blocked immediate action; Scott, *Feminism*, pp. 137–9. Not till 1923 were some, much more limited, reforms made.
55 Barton's evidence: *RC Divorce*, pp. 171–3, especially Q 37,147–161, quoted at 37,153. Scott, *Feminism*, p. 177.
56 Scott, *Feminism*, pp. 111–17.
57 Gillian Scott, 'Working out their own salvation: Women's autonomy and divorce law reform in the co-operative movement 1910–20', in Stephen Yeo (ed.), *New Views of Co-operation* (London: Routledge, 1988), pp. 128–53, p. 132. Margaret Llewelyn Davies (ed.), *Maternity: Letters from Working Women* (London: Virago, reprint, 1978) first published 1915, p. 191; the respondents were mostly wives of better-off manual workers: *ibid.*, pp. 2–3; Scott, *Feminism*, p. 128, n. 146.
58 Davies, *Maternity*, p. 3. For facsimiles of some letters: pp. 51, 63, 139. Their replies 'made many spirited proposals for remedial action and brought out themes not covered by [Davies' initial] guidance, some of which ended up at the centre of Davies' analysis'; Yeo, *Contest for Social Science*, p. 267.
59 For fuller accounts: Davies, *Maternity*, nos 95, 99; for brief life narratives: nos 5, 20, 44, 120, 134, 160.
60 Gloden Dallas, 'New introduction', in Davies, *Maternity*, p. i.
61 Christopher Hilliard, 'Producers by hand and by brain: Working-class writers and left-wing publishers in 1930s Britain', *Journal of Modern History*, 78:1 (2006), 37–64, highlights the difficulties of such collaboration and the frustrations it could create for would-be worker-writers.
62 For details on Coombes' life and literary career, see Bill Jones and Chris Williams, 'Introduction' to B. L. Coombes, *These Poor Hands: The Autobiography of a Miner Working in South Wales* (Cardiff, UK: University of Wales Press, 2002) first published 1939, pp. ix–xxxix; Jones and Williams, *B. L. Coombes* (Cardiff, UK: University of Wales Press, 1999).
63 Jones and Williams, 'Introduction', p. xi; Jones and Williams, *Coombes*, pp. 20–1.
64 Jones and Williams, 'Introduction', p. xi; Jones and Williams, *Coombes*, p. 23. The National Council of Labour Colleges had strong support from the South Wales Miners' Federation.
65 His first publication, in a Welsh Labour monthly in 1935, was a critique of the government's 'distressed areas' policy to tackle unemployment: Jones and Williams, 'Introduction', p. xii.
66 On Lehmann's role in encouraging working-class writing, see Hilliard, 'Producers', pp. 39, 51–6.
67 This periodical promoted a documentary style of writing: Storm Jameson, *Documents*, Fact 4 (July 1937), 9–18. The same issue reprinted verbatim an extract from an official report on the 1934 Gresford colliery disaster (pp. 45–9).

On B. L. Coombes, *I am a Miner*, Fact 23 (1939), see Jones and Williams, *Coombes*, pp. 40–6.

68 The Left Book Club published George Orwell's *The Road to Wigan Pier* (1937), Ellen Wilkinson's *The Town that was Murdered: The Life-Story of Jarrow* (1939), and Wal Hannington's *The Problem of the Distressed Areas* (1937).

69 On Lehmann's role in mentoring Coombes, and the respective roles of Lehmann and Gollancz (who had both been keen to publish the book) in helping to shape *These Poor Hands*, see Jones and Williams, 'Introduction', pp. xiv–xvii. Coombes dedicated the book to Lehmann.

70 Jones and Williams, 'Introduction', pp. xxvi–xxix. Some contemporary reviews criticised this failure to fit a personalised autobiographical norm: *ibid.*, p. xx.

71 Jones and Williams, 'Introduction', pp. xiii–xiv; *These Poor Hands* as *testimonio*: pp. xxix–xxx. Testimonio 'constitutes an affirmation of the individual self *in a collective mode*' (Beverley, 'Margin', p. 17, original emphasis). Coombes insisted that 'a writer should stay amongst his people and live the life he describes in his words'; Jones and Williams, *Coombes*, pp. 60–1. Falke, *Literature*, pp. 83–5, points out that by the time Doherty re-published his memoir, Blincoe (having survived loss through fire, bankruptcy and prison) had successfully established himself as a small businessman. Yet he chose to show solidarity with his community by not turning his narrative into a success story.

72 Jones and Williams, *Coombes*, pp. 17–19. B. L. Coombes, 'Twenty tons of coal', in New Writing, *NS III* (Christmas 1939), pp. 159–74, especially pp. 159–61, 173–4; B. L. Coombes, 'A miner's record-III', in *New Writing and Daylight* (summer 1943), pp. 129, 134–5.

73 B. L. Coombes, *These Poor Hands: The Autobiography of a Miner Working in South Wales* (London: Victor Gollancz, 1939), pp. 245–57.

74 The overall generic instability of these texts is clear. Coombes had first proposed a novel to Gollancz, who instead suggested an autobiography or 'direct description'; Coombes later described his text-in-progress as an autobiographical novel. 'Twenty tons' arose from a request by Lehmann for 'something from that last part' of the manuscript as it awaited publication; Jones and Williams, 'Introduction', pp. xiv–xv.

75 Jones and Williams, 'Introduction', pp. xvi.

76 Telling the truth would have put compensation for the dead man's family at risk; Coombes, 'Twenty tons', p. 174.

77 Jones and Williams, 'Introduction', pp. xvii–xx.

78 *Picture Post*, 10:1 (4 January 1941), 7–9. The issue included articles on 'Work for all' and 'Social security', foreshadowing what the Beveridge Report would recommend. On its impact, see Jones and Williams, *Coombes*, p. 69.

79 The conflicts and contradictions in the roles of intermediaries discussed above are likewise found in the compiling of *testimonio*: Beverley, 'Margin', pp. 18–21.

80 Blincoe in turn supported Doherty when the latter got into difficulties: Waller, *Real Oliver Twist*, pp. 305, 307–99, 323.

81 Scott, *Feminism*, pp. 176–82.
82 Brown, p. 98, recalled that when he fell ill during 1822–33, amid rumour and suspicion about his intentions, there were attempts to destroy his papers. When parish officials came to examine the treatment of their apprentices at the mill, fear of future punishment made Blincoe and his fellows remain silent. Aberdeen was victimised for supporting the Ten Hours' Bill. Dodd's letters to the Ashworths show his fear of loss of income if he spoke freely; Chaloner, 'New introduction', pp. ix–xi. In Coombes, *These Poor Hands*, pp. 256–7, the survivor of the rockfall had hesitated only once at the inquest, refusing to tell a direct lie in support of the cover story. Now he is looking to change pit, in fear of retaliation.
83 Brown, *Robert Blincoe*, p. 122; Dodd, *A Narrative*, pp. 189–90; Coombes, *These Poor Hands*, pp. 226–7; Coombes, *I am a Miner*, p. 70.
84 Coombes, 'Twenty tons of coal', p. 159.
85 *RC Divorce* p. 167, no. 114; cf. no. 115: 'Publicity has been my one dread, and I find I am not alone.'

6

Music and affective signalling in an immigrant letter from 1844

David A. Gerber

Introduction

The lines of music in Figure 6.1 were sent in a personal letter by Thomas Steel, a British physician of Scottish birth settled in the post-frontier Wisconsin countryside, to his sister Lilly, who resided in London. The letter is dated 5 November 1844. Thomas was then thirty-five, and Lilly was twelve years younger. I found this letter, which is unique for its transcription of music among the thousands of immigrant personal letters I have read, in Thomas Steel's voluminous correspondence – with both Lilly and his father James, with whom Lilly lived – at the Wisconsin State Historical Society.[1] I was then doing research for the book that appeared as *Authors of Their Lives: The Personal Correspondence of British Immigrants to North America in the Nineteenth Century* (2006).[2] The transcription appears at the very end of a letter dedicated to the usual content of immigrant letters. Though an educated, professional man who wrote well, Steel's concerns were those to be found in the letters of less experienced and literate immigrants: the multiple problems and material and social opportunities attendant on settling in a new society and learning the ways of its diverse peoples, the gradual forming of networks for mutual support and sociability of dependable friends, neighbours and co-workers, and the hope someday of family reunification. Steel was well practised in this genre. As we shall see, he had been an emigrant and an international traveller in the past, and he enjoyed an extensive correspondence with his sister and their father after his most recent emigration in 1843. Steel belonged to the professional middle class but, in his concern for writing personal letters about the common problems and opportunities of immigrants, he, too, was a 'common writer'.

The music, untitled and described only with the heading 'March', appeared towards the end of Steel's 5 November letter.[3] 'March' is obscured by its location at the very top of the page and, now, by fading ink. With the exception of the passage cited below and the usual formal salutation,

Figure 6.1 The transcription of music tentatively identified as *Caledonian March*, found in Thomas Steel's letter to his sister Lilly, 5 November 1844. All rights reserved and permission to use the figure must be obtained from the copyright holder, Wisconsin State Historical Society, WHI 38821.

the music constitutes the near-close of the letter. Steel was describing his eager anticipation of musical evenings in the future, when he was married to Catherine (Kate) Freeman, a local woman to whom he was engaged. He wrote:

> I picture myself how pleasantly we shall spend our winter evenings, Kate sitting on the side of the stove sewing and I reading aloud or playing the flute [and] a neighbor of ours sometimes comes over with his violin. As he approaches the house he commences with the tune which you will find on the opposite side.

Before closing, he commented briefly that 'our neighborhood' is now full of 'good company'. He did not lack, he told Lilly, for friends and companions, such as this fellow music-maker, perhaps British like himself, for he had begun to choose his closest friends from people of his own background. He painted a warmly domestic picture of how he might break the gloom of a dark evening on the northern prairie, where by early November winter threatened long before the formal change of seasons. Steel was often rushed for time in his letter writing, and it is apparent at times that he drew impatient toward the close of his letters and hurried to finish them. But that could hardly be the case here, for the time it took to transcribe this music was much greater than that it would have taken to close the letter with prose.

Steel left us with a complex task. Language is a symbol system, and so, too, is music. In this case, we have to interpret two symbol systems working in tandem. The music, in effect, takes over where the prose ends, but the prose remains the context for interpreting the music. I intend to explore the meanings of this transcription, which I think of as an instance of affective signalling. Without explicitly spelling out his purposes in prose, and perhaps not fully aware of some of them, he was nonetheless engaged in sending his intimate thoughts and emotions through music. Music is an ideal medium for accomplishing such purposes for at least three reasons that have been pointed out by the philosopher Jennifer Robinson in a deeply reasoned analysis of music and the emotions. First, like our emotions, music is a process that occurs in streams that meld often seamlessly and unpredictably into one another, and hence may be too complex, at times even contradictory, and too pressing to be patiently and effectively explained. (Think, for example, of the rendering of the crisis in the relationship of a couple in Alban Berg's *Transfigured Night*, in which competing threads fade and mesh in an unanticipated, stunning crescendo). Also, though music does not lend itself to infinite interpretation, what Robinson refers to as 'the expressive potential' of a piece of music permits a wider variety of responses than does prose. Finally, music lends itself to bodily changes: we feel music as we hear it, and hence, through the physiological state it creates, music may induce a mood that facilitates entering an emotional state.[4]

What was it that Steel sought to signal? What was it that might occur to his sister as the impact of the harmony, melody and rhythm receded, and their objective associations came to consciousness? Was he merely challenging Lilly to come up with the identity of the music? Did he believe she could identify it from that short transcription and that it was already familiar to her, perhaps on the basis of their having once played it together? (Lilly played the piano.) Why a transcription of music at that moment and not in any other letter during the course of over a decade-long correspondence? Was he, in fact, marshalling the emotions in the music to make a statement about his state of mind and being at that moment, and perhaps simultaneously to affect his sister's mood? Was he advancing ideas about their shared future?

In order to understand those purposes and meanings, this chapter proceeds to explore Steel's relation with his sister and his father as these were embedded in his biography and inscribed in his letters. I will then identify the music, which, given that this is a piece of informally and collectively composed communal music, has proved a challenge in itself. Next, with attention to how the emotions in music have an impact on the emotions of listeners, the essay seeks to answer the questions raised about Steel's purposes. Finally, the implications of the transcription for the larger project of analysing immigrant personal correspondence are suggested. Much is speculative, but the material is rich in opportunities for the exploration of the emotional life, under circumstances of long-distance separation, of this immigrant letter writer and the family he left behind in London.

Interpreting personal letters

My winding path to understanding Thomas's signalling is testimony, not only to the complexities of interpreting the emotional impacts of music, but also to the allusive, multiple meanings to be found in personal correspondence, and the necessity of frequent, repetitive readings and deep contextualisation to make sense of letters. Just as letters require theoretical and conceptual frames for analysis, they also require going back to the source again and again to understand the intentions behind the mobilisation of the language that letters contain. This is not only true of the individual letter itself, but also of the individual letter in the context of others written by the same correspondents and exchanged between the same parties. This axiom, returning to the source, certainly seems superficial wisdom, but it is much more elusive and demanding in practice than it may sound. In this case, I have been engaged for a number of years in making sense of the purposes of this brief transcription. It took multiple readings over years to place the music in the context of the Steel's 1844 letter and the corpus of his correspondence.

The Steel letters have much to recommend them as examples of intimate personal correspondence in the context of international migration.[5] The entire collection totals 480 letters. The majority were composed within an agreed-upon schedule of exchange (usually two letters a month), negotiated by the parties over the course of 1843–54. Furthermore, for 1845–46, the letters represent a rare three-way correspondence, exchanged between Steel, his sister and his father. Usually, collections of immigrant correspondence have only the letters of immigrants sent to family and friends in the homeland, not the letters sent in reply. If personal letters represent an intimate conversation on paper, the typical collection of immigrant letters leaves the researcher to imagine one end of that conversation, usually in the letters acknowledging and responding to the ones to which we do not possess access. In the Steel letters – some of which appear to have been brought together when Lilly and James eventually came to settle in Wisconsin and joined their saved letters to the letters that Thomas had saved – for at least a brief period many of these significant gaps in the conversation are explicitly filled in by the subsequent letters by both parties.[6]

This is certainly not to say that the work of interpretation is easily resolved in Thomas Steel's letters. Even with the more articulate immigrant letter writers, there remains a vast, indeterminate territory of interpretive confusion and guesswork resulting from combinations of poor, vague or hurried writing, conflicted and semi-conscious purposes and emotions, and barely articulated suggestions, half-truths and untruths of the sort that occasionally enter into correspondence. The popular opening sentence, 'We are well and doing well' or variations on it, often masked a world of difficulties – sickness, depression, death, debt, poor harvests, business reversals and unemployment – which correspondents were too proud, too emotionally unsettled, or too anxious about the effects of candour on their loved ones to commit to paper. If anything, in the two-party – in this case three-party – exchange, knowing what is hinted at or what is an untruth, for whatever benign or malign or simply confused reasons, complicates the problem of determining meaning. It adds multiple parties' writings to the work of decoding what each correspondent intended.[7] The rich potential of this collection complicates the task of interpretation of the musical transcription.

Thomas Steel: emigration, livelihood, family

An exploration of Thomas Steel's biography, and especially the narrative of his emigration and resettlement, is necessary to understand the personal dimensions of his letter writing.⁸ Born in 1809 in Scotland and educated in Scotland and in London, where the family relocated in order for his father to take up a job as a civil servant in the British government, Steel studied medicine at Glasgow University. He graduated in 1833. His was among the first cohorts at the university to take the modern four-year course of medical education.⁹ Against the advice both of one of his senior professors and of his father, in 1834 the young man set out for North America, where he tried unsuccessfully to establish himself as a doctor. Without contacts, a naive and inexperienced stranger, he met with discouragement in one town after another in both Canada and the United States, before running out of money in New Orleans and booking a ticket back to England. He left the United States deeply impressed by its dynamism and possibilities for the future, but penniless. Perhaps his father, who would combine an insistently directive but materially supportive relationship with his son throughout their adult relationship, suggested at that point that he develop a practical plan for the future. Soon after returning to England, Thomas signed on for two years as physician on a ship sailing between England and the East Indies. At the end of that contractual period, he practised medicine for six months among Europeans in China. While these years at sea and in Asia might seem a great adventure and foretell years of storytelling, Steel would never write about them in his letters, perhaps out of embarrassment at the circumstances that had driven him in the first place to sign on as a ship's doctor.

His course during the next seven years is unclear. He may have practised medicine in London, where his widowed father was living with Lilly, who was the last of the siblings at home. In 1843, Steel affiliated with a group of utopian socialists who wished to start a co-operative agrarian community in Waukesha County in the Wisconsin Territory, and he emigrated with them. In the manner of many such projects, soon after resettlement in Wisconsin, that intentional community failed for want of interpersonal harmony, experience in cultivating North American prairies and ideological coherence. Following a period of privation, in which he had to spend the winter in a one-room log cabin with a dozen or so other immigrants, Steel began the gradual process of resettling on his own, assisted by frequent infusions of cash provided by his father, enclosed in letters. He acquired land in order to farm, built a house in stages as he could afford to improve and expand it, and attempted to establish a profitable medical practice. Medicine never quite worked out. Though there were many settlers needing care and medicines – which Steel bought in nearby Milwaukee or that were sent him by his father from London – and he attempted to market his services, few could afford to pay him in cash and instead offered in-kind payments in eggs, chickens or vegetables. Many of them never paid anything. Routinely called to provide medical care to expectant mothers and injured farmers, often in the most adverse weather conditions and never with adequate compensation, Steel grew weary of being a doctor, even as he established a reputation for honesty and expertise, as one of Wisconsin's pioneer physicians. Though he regularly wrote his father to say he might quit medicine once and for all and concentrate on farming, he never left medicine, though he appears to have practised increasingly at home and to have made fewer house calls. Key to his resettlement project was establishing a household and family. He approached marriage practically, as needed for the success of his resettlement, but with a great deal of affection for his bride, Catherine, who was the daughter of an English settler who had been a cabinetmaker at Buckingham Palace.

For the first decade after returning to North America in 1843, while in the midst of his strenuous efforts at resettling, Steel was emotionally torn between building a life in Wisconsin and, as is evident in their frequent exchange of letters, his deeply felt obligations to his father and sister. The roots of his sense of responsibility were deeper than the usual family affections. Toward his father he felt some regrets for his confused emergence into adult life – a brief nineteenth-century version of 'failure to launch' – after his medical education. Then the collapse of the communal agrarian experiment necessitated that Steel endeavour to establish himself on his own, which would have been impossible without his father's constant subsidy for years. Like other immigrant letter writers who were new to farming and had little knowledge of the climate and soil of the American prairies, he continually underestimated his expenses. Steel regularly and explicitly acknowledged his father's generosity in his letters to James.

Toward his sister Lilly, he felt a different and perhaps even deeper regret. Within two years of the death of their mother in 1841, he had left her, a nine-year-old child, alone with their ageing father. James Steel seems to have been a somewhat grumpy man, set in his ways and opinions, though with a great deal of practical wisdom to offer. In relation to Thomas's siblings, in addition to the death of two older brothers, one in the year of Lilly's birth, there had also been at some unidentifiable moment the agonisingly drawn-out death from whooping cough of a three-year old sister, Eliza, which lingered in the background of the siblings' relationship. Thomas could only wonder what effects these deaths had had on a child such as Lilly, because they haunted his own mind to the extent that he would embrace Spiritualism, in full knowledge of the way it contradicted his scientific education. He sought to communicate with the departed spirit of his mother in a series of backwoods seances in the late 1840s and early 1850s, in the company of his wife and his neighbours. In those seances, he also enquired about the soul of little Eliza. His guilty feelings for the life he had led and was leading were also alleviated to the extent that at one seance he received a message from his mother that there was no place of eternal punishment beyond the grave.

Added to his concerns about Lilly was the fact that as she emerged into womanhood, her prospects seemed to narrow. Some of the young men in whom she was interested were themselves thinking of emigrating. She wrote at times, increasingly explicitly beginning in 1845, of experiencing low spirits and transient illnesses that might today be taken as signs of depression. Where was Thomas in the midst of his younger sister's difficulties? At sea (perhaps as much metaphorically and emotionally as physically), in India and in China, and now four thousand miles away in the Wisconsin Territory. The correspondence certainly shows Thomas's desire to rekindle a relationship with the sister he had left behind.

Thomas was a constant correspondent, deeply engaged with both his father and his sister. At times, he addressed James and Lilly in the same letter, but he also opened a separate stream of letters with his sister, in part for practical, strategic purposes. As is sometimes apparent in other family letter collections, sibling exchanges of personal letters might be organised as an informal conspiracy to influence, if not explicitly manipulate, parents, or to keep from them information that would cause anxiety and misapprehension.[10] In the midst of courting Catherine Freeman, with the intention to marry in the near future, Thomas anticipated his father's resistance to what would lead to additional household expenses. He recruited his sister's help, in a steady stream of letters to Lilly between July and November of 1844, in making the case for marriage, informing her about the emotional and material needs that would be satisfied by marriage and domesticity. In a long letter in July 1844, he wrote to Lilly of the need to influence their father to see that marriage was a practical step, not merely a romantic plunge into the unknown. In that letter Thomas outlined, as if engaging in a tutorial, a list of arguments in favour of this marriage.

The engagement and eventual marriage early in 1845 also solved one of Thomas's epistolary issues. He was often too preoccupied with his medical practice, additions to his house and farming to keep up correspondence with both Lilly and James, to whom it was necessary to account in detail for how he was spending his money and the purposes for which he needed ever more of it. Thomas had not only to explain the day-to-day decisions he made in using the money, but also to appear to solicit his father's advice, though this often seemed more an expression of filial piety than an effort at genuine consultation. He would sometimes append a paragraph on his plans to his letters for Lilly's consumption, and then soon admit in subsequent letters to feeling guilty for neglecting her and for 'selfish' letters that spoke only to his own needs. He soon put Lilly and Catherine in letter contact and, as the two women developed a sisterly relationship, felt less anxious about what neglect there may have been.

Yet Steel was not without a sense that his letters to Lilly were marked less by concern for her than by his own absorption in the projects of his resettlement. He was aware, too, that these very projects, as he acknowledged in a letter to his father in 1844, were taking money from his estate and leaving less for Lilly. Soon after resettling in Wisconsin, beginning in a letter in May 1844, Steel developed a view of the future that appears to have resolved his guilty feelings about both neglect for Lilly and his instrumental use of his father: he would encourage them to visit Wisconsin perhaps for a season or a year or two and see if they wished to settle permanently. His father could retire from government service and conveniently collect his pension through Canadian banks, while living as a gentleman farmer on lands that he and Thomas would purchase. Lilly could start a new life, away from the increasingly limiting circumstances she was experiencing in London. It is possible that Thomas and Catherine had begun to see one of Catherine's brothers as a suitable husband for Lilly, and that they took this possibility as an added benefit of a visit or permanent resettlement. After a decade of Thomas's cajoling, providing one argument after another and a variety of incentives to relocate (a comfortable house, the availability of consumer goods, cultural opportunities in the growing city of Milwaukee, a piano for Lilly to play and sociable neighbourhood companions), Lilly and James did come to Wisconsin permanently in 1854. James, who had been reluctant to relocate, especially fearing the consequences of the climate for his fragile health, died within a few years of immigrating. Lilly married Thomas's brother-in-law soon after coming to Wisconsin.

Thomas's letter of 5 November 1844 is testimony to his resettlement at that point in time and to the complexity of his relationships, as they gradually unfolded in his correspondence and the purposes that emerged out of them. In the manner of Steel's letters to his sister, he addressed a number of matters, rather randomly and in contrast to his sharply focussed letters to his father. To James Steel, Thomas mostly wrote of masculine commercial and professional matters: the frustrations of his medical practice, his need for money to build a house and buy farmland to cultivate, the fluctuating costs of materials and labour for homebuilding and farm-making, and his frustrating interactions with local government in buying property and in dealing with the public easements on his land that were sought for road construction. But in the letter of 5 November 1844 and other letters to Lilly, he spoke more frequently of matters that we may broadly construe as feminine. These concerned the quality of his life: his low or hopeful moods, his loneliness in the first years on the prairie, his emerging circle of friends, his need for a wife and then his engagement and marriage, and the availability of goods and commercial services as the frontier receded. He mentioned, too, that among the virtues of his wife-to-be's family was that one of Catherine's grandfathers was a Scot. And then, at the very end, there is that singular transcription of music.

Identifying the music

The music has been identified by academic music cataloguers and compilers of folkish music as in the British-American repertory, and they have assigned it several sharply contrasting titles in numerous musical variations: *Star of Bethlehem*, *The Caledonian March*, *Bonaparte Crossing the Rhine*, *Bonaparte's Retreat* and, less often, *Napoleon Crossing the Alps* and *The Dusinberry (Jutenberry) March* and, finally, the wildly improbable *Bonaparte Crossing the Rockies*. As Samuel P. Bayard, the editor of a classic compendium of instrumental folk tunes collected for decades in the backcountry of Pennsylvania, explains, that ambiguity was present in the genealogy of any particular piece of music he analysed, and so this particular piece was no different from many hundreds of other tunes that folk musicians played at fairs, picnics, church and fraternal lodge socials and impromptu get-togethers. It is the nature of this type of communal music that it was to be heard and then improvised upon, whether intentionally or not, as the spirit moved the musicians. Even when the piece of music was first encountered as sheet music or in tune books – which were expanding commercially and proliferating geographically across the United States at the time Steel was settling in Wisconsin – it would have been subject to improvisations and deviations in line with the momentary desires and the creativity, and limitations, of the players.[11] Steel himself might well have come by the music by ear and through sheet music (or handwritten copies of sheet music) simultaneously. It is not likely he would have been able to transcribe the tune on to paper from only a listening acquaintance with it. He knew how to play the flute for recreation, but there is no evidence of any knowledge on his part of musical composition.

Hence, though those who play piano tell me the tune *sounds* most like sheet music transcriptions from that time of *The Caledonian March*, the music may well have been, with improvisations, *Bonaparte's Retreat*, *Napoleon Crosses the Rhine*, *Star of Bethlehem* and other titles all in one, and a mixture of something else, too, added on occasion.[12] The earliest American printed versions I have found, which were done by the leading music publishers George Willig (sheet music, 1837) and Elias Howe (tune book, 1842), and known respectively as *Caledonian March* and *Caledonian March (1)*, might have been available to Steel, depending on local marketing and his own musical networks of fellow amateurs.[13] It is likely, as the description 'march' on the letter suggests, that Steel probably believed it to be *The Caledonian March*, and that through 'Caledonian' it meant something fond and familiar to him, given his Scottish roots.

This inference may well be assumed in light of Steel's ethnic evolution in Wisconsin. By a general sort of cultural evolution, he was becoming tricultural – some mix of Scottish, English and American. Yet by more or less conscious identification, Steel seems to have opted to be more Scottish as he integrated himself into American life – a familiar if at first seemingly paradoxical pattern of inventing ethnicity to facilitate situating oneself in an identity while accepting of necessity the demands of a different culture. Identities establish continuity and assure us through mobilising our memories and our personal stories that we continue to be the same person we always have been, even as our lives dramatically change.

Such an invention in the service of identity was based on two simultaneous psychological processes that worked on Steel during the early years of his residence in the United States. One involved understanding who he believed he was not and the other, who he believed he was. The first was a product of negotiating the ethnic diversity of the prairies, which were populated mostly by Americans, but also by smaller groups of recent European immigrants, among them Scottish and English people, and German, Welsh and Scandinavian people.[14] As he encountered them as his patients and his immediate neighbours, the Americans posed the greatest challenge for him, for they represented the mentalities and habits of the country in which he hoped to build a life for himself and his family. Culturally, they represented, for better or worse, the likely future of his children (there would eventually be eight). Steel was wary of his American neighbours, though not hostile to them. Many of them seemed to him morbidly distrustful of 'foreigners', always wary of being cheated, hostile to medical advice, unrelentingly money oriented, sectarian and religiously intolerant. He embraced American democracy in theory and briefly held public office, but in becoming an American citizen and engaging in limited public activism he was partly motivated by perceptions of the need to protect his newly acquired property. He joined the Universalist Church, the least evangelical and most theologically liberal branch of American Protestantism, in part to counteract the influence of American evangelicalism, which he regarded as narrow-minded and unprogressive.

In contrast, there was the familiarity of things recalled from life in Britain and the memories, from childhood and family, especially of Scottishness. The more he interacted with Others, the more Steel seems to have come to cleave to being Scottish. He had little sense of active engagement with a worldwide Scottish community, and his Scottishness was for the most part muted and episodic. It was the familiar sort of nostalgic, symbol-laden romantic nationalism rooted in a distant history that today's Scottish independence seekers see as a burden on their national aspirations.[15] They have long felt it necessary to unburden their national identity of both the shortbread tin (a familiar Scottish export) imagery of tartans and bagpipes, which doesn't speak to the complex genealogy of the Scottish people, and the legends of clans and heroic kings, like 'Bonnie' Prince Charlie, that they believe make Scotland's present politics harder to determine. But in the Scottish diaspora, such have been the associations that often kept Scottishness alive for emigrants.[16]

Steel's Scottishness was also a matter of connection to a community in the making on the Wisconsin prairies, and as such it was ultimately about ethnic belonging; that is, *groupness* among those resettling in a new country. In North America, to be sure, a Scot's ethnicity was more elusive than that of non-English-speaking European immigrant groups, for language and religion did not necessarily lead to perceptions of difference, whether on the part of the immigrants or those receiving them. (Even strongly accented English did not necessarily mark an individual as a recent arrival, as in a largely rural society, there would have been many long-standing relatively isolated pockets of varieties of accented English). But the desire for the familiar was one the Scottish, English and Irish Protestants could nevertheless experience, whatever their relative cultural similarities to Americans. Indeed, when similarities to Americans made these immigrants complacent, something jarring might occur in their relations with Americans, such as in Steel's case the politics involved in appropriating land adjacent to his own for a public highway, to remind them of their differences.[17] Steel early on showed that he favoured Scottish and, like his wife's family, English acquaintances. He celebrated Robert Burns' birthday, with music and readings of Walter Scott, Robert Burns and others, on frigid January evenings in the homes and cabins of other Scottish people, and was one year the organiser of the annual festival. It is possible that the unidentified neighbour coming up the pathway and playing his fiddle to announce his presence was himself Scottish, playing a tune that signalled their own ethnic connection.

The emotions in the music and the emotions signalled by the 'march'

Why put the music itself in this letter to his sister? How did the music work to signal his thoughts and feelings? Can we know the effects of this signalling on Lilly Steel? Jennifer Robinson assists us here by drawing a distinction between the emotions in music and the emotions we may take out of the music we hear.[18] This distinction is helpful in interrogating what Steel had in mind in transcribing the music for Lilly.

We have assumed that because Steel identified the music as a 'march', it is plausible that he had in mind *The Caledonian March*, a conclusion furthered by his identification with the homeland of his childhood. Yet he failed to title the music, leaving us to explore how the music was supposed to affect Lilly. We may begin with Steel's own response to the music, for that was probably the start of how he believed his sister would react. How does the music sound? What emotions and references seem buried in it?

Two considerations present themselves. First, a march is energising music. The generic title 'march', in itself is an imperative to action.[19] With its 4/4 cadence, *The Caledonian March* has a tempo that vitalises. While the music does not display the general characteristics that have been identified by the definitive *Grove Encyclopedia of Music* as characteristically Scottish, the lilt and the uplift (or bounce) of the telling opening embellishment that Steel himself, or whatever source from which he took the music, seems to have added to *The Caledonian March* sound distinctly like a Scottish dance tune.[20] The fiddle assisted mightily in furthering the feeling in the music: by the eighteenth century the fiddle (usually a violin) had come to replace the bagpipe as the principal instrument in the repertory of Scottish communal music.[21] As his imagined friend and neighbour walked up the path that evening, Steel may well have felt the surge of energy that came from a complex mix of nostalgia, belonging and friendship prompted by the music embedded in *The Caledonian March*. He could feel more secure in his life-in-the-making on the prairie, and take heart in the fact that his labours, for all of their difficulties, appeared at that moment to be fulfilling a variety of needs and goals.

Steel may have assumed that Lilly, through Scottishness and through his letters that mentioned his local friends, shared in a general way the groupness embedded in the music and in the immediate circumstances of its production that night. The music's inclusion might have had multiple purposes, though probably semi-conscious ones. It was a fond gesture that emphasised something they had in common – that is, music, and maybe the tune itself. Steel had promised Lilly that they would share music when she came to Wisconsin, and he would obtain a piano for her, or she could bring a small pianoforte with her. He signalled, too, that he did not want for familiar company and neither would she if she came to join him. If he did not want for familiar company, moreover, he was not lonely and bereft of community to pass hours that might relieve the burdens of his medical practice, farm-making and home construction. To that extent, his sister and father need not worry about him, however remote his location seemed to be and however trying its circumstances might seem, from his occasional complaints and constant need for cash to pay his bills and secure material foundations for the future. At that moment, he felt positive and hopeful about his life and energised in the face of its challenges.

As much as he might be inspired by the music, Steel could not know how his sister would react to it. One can imagine her sitting down at her piano in London and playing the tune. She might be moved to attempt to find a name for the tune she was playing, and through that identification to fill in some of the ethnic details surrounding her brother's purposes and plans and the quality of his life (printed variations of the tune were then available for sale, and perhaps were already popular, in Britain).[22] But it isn't clear that she would necessarily share in his positive emotions in doing so. In a collective setting, or contemplating the immediacy of a collective setting, the emotions in music may be contagious.[23] Its impact on a solitary performer or listener, lacking the stimulus of the collective setting, not to mention personal associations, is less obvious. Perhaps, catching her brother's upbeat mood as he contemplated a sociable music evening, she was indeed energised by the march and alive to acting on the possibilities of sharing the life they had in common and could continue to make as a reunited family in Wisconsin. Perhaps she might imagine the duo described in the letter as a trio if she came to Wisconsin. But it is also possible her occasional low spirits may not have been able to respond to the imperative of the 'march'. The Scottish pulse of the music might have produced a mournful mood that dwelt on family occasions lost in time and of intimate personal associations lost to sickness and death. Steel's fondly rendered nostalgia might well have been a source for his sister's pessimistic reverie. Nostalgia may assist people to move forward positively with their lives, but it does not necessarily have that effect on everyone recalling the past.[24] Unfortunately, we cannot know the impact of the transcription on Lilly Steel. The collection contains no correspondence acknowledging the music was received, let alone reacted to. What we do know is that the family reunion Thomas so desired took place. James and Lilly did eventually join Thomas in Wisconsin. There were probably thereafter many musical evenings.

The implications of the transcription for interpreting letters

The meanings for understanding immigrants and immigrant letter writing that may be derived from this casual musical reference are telling. The transcription certainly makes clear that, in Thomas Steel's example, even a brief rendering of music potentially has multiple ideational and psychological associations – or, in Robinson's suggestive formulation, 'cognitively complicated emotions'.[25] It reminds us, too, of the plasticity of letters in the hands of the deft but variously creative and technically skilful writers we encounter in immigrant correspondence. Certainly, not many immigrant letter writers at that time had Thomas Steel's bourgeois family background, extensive education and adept literacy, let alone his ability to transcribe music. But when mobilised by purposes deemed crucial to emotional well-being and practical comfort, many immigrant letter writers were capable of using what literacy they did possess to express explicitly, or signal more subtly, profound intentions, complex meanings and strong emotions.

Immigrant letters are often primarily mined for information in the service of constructing generalisations for understanding the masses of immigrants; for example, the work available, the wages artisans earned, new illnesses experienced in a foreign environment or the quality of the soil farmers worked and the prices of the crops they raised. That is all to the good, of course, from an analytical perspective. But these letters also furthered another project: sustaining vital, intimate connections rendered vulnerable by long-distance separation and kindling the hope of reunion. Long-distance separation in the context of experiencing profound changes in cultural and social circumstances threatened to sunder personal and social identities, furthering the isolation of emigrants and their alienation from their rooted memories. The first purpose of the letter was retaining contacts with family, kin and familiar associates. With its peculiar signalling, Thomas Steel's letter reminds us that our analytical agenda cannot be complete without attention to the intimate details of those private relations.

Notes

Reprint permission for the music has been granted by the Wisconsin State Historical Society. This essay is the result of a somewhat more complex research process than most historical work on epistolarity, because of its need to interpret the transcription of music. I do not read or play music, so I am especially indebted to those who assisted me in identifying the musical transcription in Thomas Steel's letter. In April, May and June 2022, both Marcella Branagan and Carolyn Korsmeyer played on the piano various printed, nineteenth-century music renditions from around the time of Steel's letter and compared them to the transcription in the letter. In 2006, when I first began inquiries into this music, John Bewley of the University at Buffalo Music Library solicited the assistance of the Music Library Association email list and drew the responses of his colleagues Paul Wells, the director of the Center for Popular Music in Murfreesboro, Tennessee, and Drew Beisswenger, Music Librarian at Missouri State University in Springfield, Missouri. Both Wells and Beisswenger suggested a range of titles without settling on one from among them (John Bewley to David A. Gerber, 27 February 2006, email in the possession of David A. Gerber).

1 Wisconsin State Archives, Madison, WI, Wis Mss 51PB, Thomas Steel (1809–96) Papers 1660, 1834–1909.
2 David A. Gerber, *Authors of Their Lives: The Personal Correspondence of British Immigrants to North America in the Nineteenth Century* (New York: New York University Press, 2006).
3 At this time Thomas Steel did not have access to envelopes, which were just then beginning to come into use. Like other letter writers, therefore, he folded his text into an envelope-like enclosure and sealed it with either glue or paste or, as in the case of this letter, sealing wax, which had the virtue of an additional layer of security. If the seal was broken, it would be apparent that the privacy of the letter had been breached. Traces of sealing wax are found in the illustration in Figure 6.1. The music transcription was inside the sealed letter.
4 Jennifer Robinson, *Deeper than Reason: Emotion and Its Role in Literature, Music, and Art* (Oxford: Clarendon, 2005), pp. 311, 325, 337, 403, 405, 411.
5 I devoted a chapter, 'Dr. Thomas Steel: The difficulties of achieving the reunited family', to Steel and his family correspondence in *Authors of Their Lives*, pp. 309–35.
6 On gaps in immigrant letters and related methodological problems, Wolfgang Helbich and Walter D. Kamphoefner, 'How representative are emigrant letters? An exploration of the German case', in Bruce S. Elliott, David A. Gerber and Suzanne M. Sinke (eds), *Letters across Borders: The Epistolary Practices of International Migrants* (New York: Palgrave Macmillan, 2006), pp. 29–55.
7 David A. Gerber, 'Acts of deceiving and withholding in immigrant letters: Personal identity and self-presentation in personal correspondence', *Journal of Social History*, 39:2 (2005), 315–30.
8 Western Historical Company, 'Thomas Steel', in *History of Waukesha County, Wisconsin, Containing an Account of Its Settlement, Growth, and Resources* (Chicago: Western Historical Company, 1880), pp. 930–1; Women's Auxiliary of Waukesha County Medical Society, 'Steel, Thomas, M.D.' (Waukesha, WI, no date), pp. 119–21, in Thomas Steel Papers, Wisconsin Historical Society, Wis Miss 51PB.
9 School of Medicine, Dentistry and Nursing, Glasgow University, 'A significant medical history', www.gla.ac.uk/schools/medicine/mus/ourfacilities/history/19thcentury/, accessed 30 May 2022.
10 Gerber, *Authors of Their Lives*, pp. 191–2.
11 Samuel P. Bayard (ed.), *Dance to the Fiddle, March to the Fife, Instrumental Folk Tunes of Pennsylvania* (University Park: Pennsylvania State University Press, 1982), pp. 1–12; Richard Crawford, *America's Musical Life: A History* (New York: W. W. Norton, 2001), pp. 139–55; Richard J. Wolfe, *Early American Music Engraving and Printing: A History of Music Publishing in America from 1787 to 1825, with Commentary on Earlier and Later Practices* (Urbana: University of Illinois Press, 1980), pp. 38–67, 68–87. The eminent folklorist Allan Jabbour went further in identification based on his fieldwork on the dozens of individualised titles given by vernacular musicians to *Bonaparte's*

Retreat; Alan Jabbour (ed.), *American Fiddle Music: From the Archive of Folk Song* (Washington, DC: Library of Congress, 1972), pp. 16–17.

12 Bayard, *Dance to the Fiddle, March to the Fife*, pp. 94, 256, cross-references *The Caledonian March*, *The Star of Bethlehem* and *The Dusinberry (Jutenberry) March* as the same tune, but going by these different names.

13 Paul Wells, Center for Popular Music, to John Bewley, University at Buffalo Music Library, 27 February 2006, email in the possession of David A. Gerber; George Willig, *Caledonian March*, Philadelphia (attributed to 'A Professor'), 1837; and Elias Howe, *Caledonian March (1)*, Boston, 1842 (attributed to 'A.P. Knight and H. Seipp of the Boston Brigade Band'), 1842, https://tunearch.org/wild.Caledonian_March%281%29, accessed 3 March 2022.

14 In 1850, 64 per cent of the population of Wisconsin was composed of people born in the United States. There are no data on the ethnic composition of the population of either the state or individual counties, by individual foreign nation or individual ethnic group. 'Wisconsin', *Seventh Census of the United States*, p. 924, www2.census.gov/library/publications/decennial/1850/1850a/1850a-45pdf, accessed 17 June 2022. My understanding of the composition of Steel's immediate area is anecdotal, based on remarks in his letters.

15 For another example, more self-consciously understood, of this romantic attachment in the diaspora to Scottish cultural nationalism, see 'Mary Ann Woodrow Archbald: Longing for her "little isle" from a farm in Central New York', in Gerber, *Authors of Their Lives*, pp. 281–308.

16 Gerry Hassan and Rosie Ilett (eds), *Radical Scotland: Arguments for Self-Determination* (Edinburgh: Lauth, 2011); Neil Davidson, *The Origins of Scottish Nationalism* (London: Pluto, 2000); Murray G. H. Pittock, *Scottish Nationality* (London: Red Globe, 2001) and *The Invention of Scotland: The Stuart Myth and the Scottish Identity, 1638 to the Present* (London: Routledge, 2014); T. M. Devine, *The Scottish Nation, 1700–2000* (London: Allen Lane, 1999).

17 Observations made persuasively by two pioneers in the study of British immigration to North America; see Charlotte Erickson, *Invisible Immigrants: The Adaptation of English and Scottish Immigrants in Nineteenth Century America* (Ithaca, NY: Cornell University Press, 1972), pp. 2–3; Wilbur Shepperson, *Emigration and Disenchantment: Portraits of Englishmen Repatriated from the United States* (Norman: University of Oklahoma Press, 1965). For more recent discussion, see Gerber, *Authors of Their Lives*, pp. 19–28, and William Van Vugt, *Britain to America: Mid-Nineteenth Century Immigrants to the United States* (Urbana: University of Illinois Press, 1999).

18 Robinson, *Deeper than Reason*, p. 358.

19 William H. McNeil, *Keeping Together in Time: Dance and Drill in Human History* (Cambridge, MA: Harvard University Press, 1995).

20 Kenneth Elliott and Frances Collinson, 'Scotland. Instrumental Music', in Stanley Sadie (ed.), *The New Grove Dictionary of Music and Musicians*, Vol. 17 (London: Macmillan, 1980), pp. 70, 71.

21 *Ibid.*, pp. 70, 77.

22 Printed versions of a tune called *The New Caledonian March* and dating respectively from 'between 1840–1855' and as early as the eighteenth century are located in the National Library of Scotland. The eighteenth-century version closely resembles what was known in the United States as Elias Howe's 1842 transcription of *Caledonian March 1*. *New Caledonian March*, in *Davie's Caledonian Repository of Favorite Scottish Slow Airs, Marches, Strathspeys, Reels, Jigs, Curious Ancient Airs, Variations, and Etc., Etc., Expressly Adapted for Violin* (Aberdeen: George Cornwall, between 1840 and 1855); and the transcription of *The New Caledonian March* in the John Glen Collection of Scottish songs and music (eighteenth and nineteenth centuries); https://digital.nls/uk/special_collections_of_printed_music/archive/104998973, accessed 26 February 2022.
23 Robinson, *Deeper than Reason*, p. 390.
24 David A. Gerber, 'Moving forward and moving on: Nostalgia, significant others, and social reintegration in nineteenth century British immigrant personal correspondence', *History of the Family*, 21:3 (2016), 291–314.
25 Robinson, *Deeper than Reason*, p. 345.

7

Pen, paper and peasants: the rise of vernacular literacy practices in nineteenth-century Iceland

Sigurður Gylfi Magnússon and Davíð Ólafsson

Introduction: a vernacular writing revolution

In the introductory chapter of her book *The Rise of Writing*, Deborah Brandt juxtaposes the two central aspects of literacy practices and how they were regarded differently from the founding of the American Republic onwards.[1] In the minds of the founding fathers, reading was considered an imperative prerequisite for liberty and citizenship. The same urgency was, however, not bestowed upon mass writing.

If, as the founders reasoned, people's literacy developed through their reading and people's democracy developed through the same skill, then people's writing and the civic protections around it mattered less from a political or educational perspective. Reading was the dominant literacy skill, the skill of consequence, and democratic values tacitly relied on its standing as such. From the founding of the Republic onwards, these assumptions about reading as dominant and writing as recessive conditioned the ways in which mass literacy was supported, experienced, regulated and valued.[2] In her book, Brandt explores contemporary literacy practices in the context of digital communications and an economy based on the manufacturing of knowledge, ideas and data, rather than things: 'In this economy texts serve as a chief means of production and a chief output of production, and writing becomes a dominant form of manufacturing.'[3] Brandt has described the rise of the productive side of literacy, the writing side, as 'a second stage of mass literacy'.[4]

Albeit on a totally different scale and in the context of disparate cultural, political and technological conditions, Iceland experienced a rise of writing as a second stage of mass literacy in the nineteenth century. The hierarchy that placed reading as the primary literate skill and writing as secondary had been a feature of educational policies throughout the early modern era, and writing ability did not become part of Iceland's formal educational requirements until 1880. Prior to that time, however, scribal practices had been on the rise.

This chapter argues for a vernacular writing revolution in the long nineteenth century in Iceland, set between two institutional literacy campaigns.[5] We propose to emphasise the *agency* of the manuscript culture itself: its scribes, collectors, texts and the manuscripts as objects. We will take account of various written documents from the second half of the nineteenth century, penned by people of modest social status and little formal education. We will study them both as examples of, and sources on, literacy practice which have their origins in everyday experience but were not regulated by the formal rules and procedures of dominant social institutions.[6] Everyday experience and the desire for education are the soil in which vernacular literacy practices are rooted; these practices draw on and contribute to vernacular knowledge. We will highlight the role of scribal activity within the popular literary culture of the long nineteenth century in Iceland and propose that these practices can best be understood in the context of everyday life.[7] Additionally, we will explore how elements of agency are embedded in scribal practices as 'participatory culture', in the sense that media scholar Henry Jenkins has presented the term.[8] By giving agency to its ordinary participants and attention to hitherto overlooked source material, we will examine how manuscript exchange – the scribal community – as a sociocultural network questions the traditional view of the development of literacy, education and communication in Iceland. Our focus will mostly be on two 'barefoot historians'; tenant farmer and popular scribe/scholar Sighvatur Grímsson Borgfirðingur (1840–1939) and farmer Halldór Jónsson (1873–1912). In addition, we will discuss their connections with a number of other 'brothers in arms' who took part in an endless quest for material to collect, copy and produce for their local community and society at large.

The term 'barefoot historians' was formerly used by a group of German social historians who were exponents of *Alltagsgeschichte* – the history of everyday life.[9] When we refer to barefoot historians, we mean poor peasants and farmhands who sat and copied manuscripts day in and day out even though most of them had a hard time keeping themselves and their families alive. One thing they all had in common was that they lived with long-term poverty; some also suffered from severe ill health. But their culture was rooted in fertile soil, and on that they founded their visions of a better future.

Peasant writers and their output and impact

In the nineteenth century a new world opened up to the common people of Iceland – the world of the written word.[10] As in much of northern and western Europe, literacy – both reading and writing – gradually became widespread skills.¹¹ That is not to say that all at once everybody had the opportunity to gain literacy skills and start to write; nor, by any means, that prior to that time society had been entirely bookless. It will, however, be argued here that in nineteenth-century rural society a cultural state came into being which may be termed 'scribal culture', where handwritten materials played an essential role in the creation, collection and dissemination of knowledge, entertaining material and ideas, as well as in communication between individuals and in personal expression. While cultural infrastructure hardly existed, the potential for developing literary practices was present in the nineteenth century, and growing numbers of people seized that potential eagerly and shaped scribal culture through their own contributions, large and small. Even those who could neither read nor write had a share in scribal culture – for every person who listened to stories or verse read aloud from a handwritten manuscript may be said to have been a participant, no less than the reader, copyist or writer of the text.

This transmission of texts was rhizomatic, following Deleuze and Guattari's metaphor, based on a botanical term for complex systems of roots that are both non-hierarchical and multinodal. The idea of the rhizome can be usefully applied to describe the state of ordinary writing in nineteenth-century Iceland. Each act of manuscript transmission had links to an infinite number of others in a continuous web of textual circulation; some are obvious, others traceable, but most of them are and will remain invisible. This network of communication was performed by different agents.¹² By that, we mean any individual or group that influences, in one way or another, the ways in which literature is produced, consumed, regarded or discussed by other members of society. In nineteenth-century Iceland, it seems, many of these roles were filled by lay scholars, dedicated amateurs who took it on themselves to cater for the needs and guide the tastes of other people from the same background as themselves.¹³ Some of the peasant poets, scribes and collectors of the time can be viewed as 'literary institutions' in their own right, on an equal footing with the publishers and printing houses, schools and writers of the 'official' literary world.

These people's thirst for knowledge, and the importance of their activities for the community at large, cannot be overestimated. Although these peasant writers were usually working people, taking an active part in the daily routines of their family farms, every spare moment of their lives seems to have gone into intellectual activity – reading, writing, calculating and speculating about their surroundings. These lay scholars were very often keen collectors of books and manuscripts, possessing or handling far more than one would ever expect of poor rural farmers and labourers. They took time off work if necessary to write up material they had not seen before, to ensure that it would not be lost to the community. It was often an expensive, arduous and time-consuming occupation, and the gains were neither obvious nor certain. One has to wonder why they took all this trouble.[14]

These barefoot historians did not operate alone and in isolation. Together they constituted an informal grouping, exchanging material, organising meetings and providing each other with mutual support. The collaboration among members of the group was so extensive and their productivity so great that we know they exercised considerable influence on the general population around them, functioning as a sort of quasi-institute of cultural affairs.

To give an idea of the methods and activities of these lay scholars, it is worth quoting from the diary of Magnús Hj. Magnússon (b. 1873), one of the best known of the West Fjords group.[15] Magnús gained national recognition after his death as the model for one of the characters in Halldór Laxness's epic novel *Heimsljós* (The Light of the World), published 1937–40. Magnús's diary provided Laxness with one of his main sources. The passage in question is for 28 February 1899, and Magnús is recording his activities for the day:

> Fair weather, clear skies and no wind. This month I copied out the *Rímur of Jesus Christ's Childhood*, or *Rímur of Mary*, written in 1654 by the Rev. Guðmundur Erlendsson, pastor at the farm of Fell in Sléttuhlíð in the district of Hegranes. This poem is hard to get hold of. In this county [Ísafjörður] I know of only two copies, one of them in the possession of Sighvatur at the farm of Höfði, the other being the one I have copied.[16]

Magnús mentions here some of the members of the 'school' he belonged to, in particular the 'super scholar' Sighvatur Grímsson of Höfði, originally from the Borgarfjörður region. Sighvatur's vast output was of central importance to the 'West Fjords Academy'. He was an extremely prolific copier of manuscripts and left a diary spanning over sixty years and a large amount of other material. His writings shed considerable light on the worldview of the nineteenth-century peasant class.[17] The text shows that one of Magnús's conscious aims was to save rare material from destruction, in this case a religious poem from 1654. Elsewhere Magnús compiled a list of all the lay scholars and copyists he was aware of, and came to the conclusion that at the time of writing there were something like 210 of them scattered around the country. These people formed the core of the informal network of the barefoot historians.

The records reveal that the picture found in the West Fjords region was repeated in Skagafjörður in the north-west. Here, again, we find a vigorous and unbroken succession of lay scholars and barefoot historians, extending from the late seventeenth century up until modern times. The activities and outlook of the Skagafjörður group have been the subject of detailed investigation by literary historian Viðar Hreinsson and bear many of the same characteristics as the West Fjords group, and we can safely assume that some kind of connection was maintained between the two throughout the nineteenth century.[18]

In the first half of the nineteenth century, a remarkable group of popular scholars coalesced in Skagafjörður around the figure of Sheriff Jón Espólín (b. 1769). Its members were mostly ministers of the church, public officials and farmers, all united by a shared interest in history and the compilation of annals. Another barefoot historian, Gísli Konráðsson, who lived most of his life on the island of Flatey off the west coast, acted as a sort of link between the 'Skagafjörður Academy' and the 'West Fjords Academy', being both a central member of the circle around Espólín and a mentor and friend to Sighvatur Grímsson. This impressive coterie of scholars seems to have fuelled a powerful interest in writing among the young people of Skagafjörður. One significant result, according to Kristmundur Bjarnason, the most important modern historian to research the subject, was that Skagafjörður was almost universally literate well before the implementation of the Education Act of 1880. 'The youth of the region was held up as a proud example', he wrote, noting that 'manuscripts were handed on from one person to another, from farm to farm, for the purpose of copying, and young people showed great eagerness in being able to express themselves in this way.'[19]

The cultural importance of these 'informal institutes', such as the groups around Jón Espólín, Gísli Konráðsson and Sighvatur Grímsson, raises a number of questions. Precisely how much influence did they have on popular attitudes in the first half of the nineteenth century? The output and sheer energy of these men is undeniably remarkable and deserves our admiration. But, when all is said and done, how important were they?

Icelandic popular culture at the time was too complex and multi-stranded to allow for precise and unequivocal answers to these questions. But one thing is certain: the barefoot historians played a major role in the dissemination of written material in every district of the country and, in many instances, won the respect, gratitude and friendship of their communities for their efforts. This was often all they won. Many of these men sat and copied manuscripts day in and day out – mostly on their own initiative and occasionally working on commission – material that was later handed on from person to person, home to home. And for many, both rich and poor, this material became the principal source of knowledge, information and entertainment in a country where print publishing was small-scale and limited in scope.[20]

In rural Iceland, formal institutions of the kinds on which modern historians tend to concentrate were only one of the channels through which the popular desire for knowledge and education was served – and in most cases not even the main one. For the majority of people, especially children, there were compelling psychological factors that came into play. Reading and education provided a way of coping with the emotional stress that formed part of daily life, and became an important tool in many people's tactics for mental and spiritual survival. Without the network of barefoot historians and the sort of 'People's press' they established to provide the materials, there would have been no way of satisfying this popular hunger. The activities of these poor farmers, farmhands and lay scholars are probably largely responsible for the fact that the Icelandic peasantry in general took great pride in their own reading and writing abilities, many of them capable of producing texts that can stand the most exacting examination, including diaries, autobiographies and letters – both personal and public. It was all part of the peasant mechanism for survival.

Rather than being circumscribed by formal or informal geographical limits, networks of this kind were built up around personal contacts and the shared interests of individuals. At the heart of such groups lay the exchange of manuscripts, whether literary texts, historical or other informational material, or even personal writings. Letters, which themselves form a significant part of the scribal culture of the nineteenth century, were the primary medium for these communications, alongside deliveries of manuscripts and personal meetings among those who belonged to the network.

All the men we have mentioned so far – Magnús, Halldór (together with his brother Níels) and Sighvatur – kept diaries over the course of many years. For example, Magnús Hj. Magnússon began his in 1893 when he was nineteen years old and kept it up until his death in 1916, for a total of twenty-four years. The diary fills 4,351 pages of quarto, in excellent handwriting and containing exhaustive details of his daily toils over these years, plus his reflections and poetry. The diary is interesting not only because Magnús maintained it so scrupulously and used it to record his opinions, attitudes and feelings for people and animals, but because it reflects a life course that was constantly strewn with thorns. Magnús stood, in a sense, on the cusp between the old world and the new.[21]

The reason it is possible to follow the life courses of Halldór and Níels Jónsson in detail is that both left behind them enormous amounts of written material in the form of diaries, letters and other sources.[22] The brothers provide one example, among many, of how the barefoot historians went about their business. Halldór, for example, started his diary in 1888 as a seventeen-year-old farmer's son from a poor community in the remote north of Iceland. For two years prior to this, he had already been recording various bits of information relevant to the management of the farm. He kept his diary up to the day of his death in 1912. Alongside this, he wrote various pieces describing his ideas and speculations, as well as practical material about himself and the running of the farm. Five large volumes of this kind have been preserved. Also from his hand we have fifteen collections of poetry containing copies of poems taken from both printed and manuscript sources (see later discussions). In total, these sources amount to a massive corpus, particularly in view of the fact that the writing was done under difficult conditions in traditional turf farmhouses, often in extreme cold and with no light, by a man who had to labour with his hands every day of the year. It should also be said that all of Halldór's literary activities are characterised by great precision and accuracy, as well as being in an elegant and aesthetically pleasing hand.

In a recent book, Davíð Ólafsson has demonstrated that diary writing in the nineteenth century testifies to the growth and expansion of manuscript culture among the Icelandic peasantry, as reading and writing skills gradually became widespread, although public educational and cultural institutions did not keep up with that development. Nineteenth-century diarists included many well-known names from Icelandic history – clerics, officials, poets and scholars – as well as many people of the lower classes – farmers, fishermen, labourers, farmhands and casual workers – some of whom we have dealt with in this chapter.[23]

From devotional reading to popular writing

The quest for popular literacy in eighteenth-century Iceland was profoundly linked to the premise of knowing and understanding 'God's Word'.[24] Lutheran doctrine asserted that every adult individual should be able to approach the word of God directly, rather than through a priest or other mediator. The ability to read was therefore a prerequisite for pious devotion, along with the availability of religious texts in the vernacular, and in this way literacy grew as a by-product of religious instruction. The heading of the 1746 *Tilskipun um húsagann* (Edict on household discipline), which decreed that every child should learn to read before his or her confirmation, suggests a strong relationship between obedience and reading. Primary reading instruction was mostly carried out at home by parents and supervised by the local pastor. Lessons usually started when children were five or six years old, and the process was concluded with the rite of confirmation around the age of thirteen. This project resulted in near-universal literacy, in terms of the ability to read, in Iceland by the end of the eighteenth century.

The rudiments of this configuration of primary education were effective into the last quarter of the nineteenth century. The literacy campaigns of the mid-eighteenth century had aimed only at spreading the capacity to read, while the ability to write was not considered essential for people's salvation.

It was not until 1880 that writing ability became part of Iceland's formal educational requirements with a new, and more secular, decree.[25] Its first article reads: 'In addition to the educational responsibility incumbent upon the clergy, they shall ensure that all children fit to do so in the judgement of the pastor and verger learn to write and to do arithmetic.'[26] This law prefigures a second institutional literacy campaign implemented with new educational laws in 1907, which decreed four years of mandatory education for every child. The trajectory towards a modern schooling system was, however, slow, and youngsters in rural areas were at best educated by peripatetic teachers or during short stays at the local pastor's house, while household instruction was the dominant form of primary education.[27]

There were, however, a substantial number of ordinary Icelanders who acquired the skill of writing and employed it for various purposes throughout the eighteenth and, in particular, the nineteenth centuries, as we have already shown. This happened without much institutional input and had a significant impact on everyday Icelandic culture. Between and alongside the two institutional campaigns, we highlight the *agency* of the manuscript culture itself – demonstrated by the scribes and collectors – and the manuscripts as objects.[28]

The vernacular tradition of autodidacticism was to a great extent propelled by scribal production and the circulation of handwritten reading material. First-hand accounts, or ego-documents, of self-taught writers often deal with the problems with which the autodidact was faced, such as the lack of primary schools and competent teachers. Parents and guardians could provide only the minimum level of instruction; they often lacked interest in literary matters, and in some cases were even openly hostile towards such endeavours. Then there was the lack of printed secular reading material. The cases of many self-taught writers emphasise the importance of informal education and the availability of handwritten reading material. They reveal the shortcomings of the educational system, the conflicting attitudes towards learning in society and the strength of individuals' pursuit of knowledge and entertainment. The texts reveal that the world of vernacular literacy was much broader and more variegated than the narrow output of printed material would suggest. It was through manuscripts that knowledge was chiefly produced, gathered, and mediated within the context of everyday cultural practices and without formal authoritative command. One important aspect of this 'vernacular writing revolution' was the advent of ego-documents, which include diaries, autobiographies, memoirs and related genres, written by ordinary people, particularly in the second half of the nineteenth century.

For our argument for a vernacular writing revolution in nineteenth-century Iceland, we employ the model of 'vernacular literacy practices', coined by linguist David Barton and social psychologist Mary Hamilton in their 1998 book *Local Literacies: Reading and Writing in One Community*.²⁹ 'Vernacular literacy practices,' Barton and Hamilton claimed, 'are essentially ones which are not regulated by the formal rules and procedures of dominant social institutions and which have their origins in everyday life.'³⁰ In other words, we highlight the role of scribal activity within the popular literary culture during the modern period in Iceland and suggest that these practices can best be understood in the context of everyday life.³¹

In this way, vernacular literacy practices differ from dominant literacy practices, which are associated with schools or other institutions of learning. Vernacular literacy is rooted in the home; it is integrated into other everyday activities and can rarely be separated from its use – scribes, collectors, texts, and the manuscripts as objects and can best be understood as part of everyday life.

Manuscript culture – the production, dissemination and consumption of handwritten material – played a substantial and often leading role in the literary and cultural practices of rural communities in nineteenth-century Iceland.³² Manuscript culture involved, in one way or another, a large number of participants – not only the scribes who created individual manuscripts and their commissioners and owners, but also the copyists who transcribed them, the readers who borrowed them and last but not least those who heard stories read aloud and ballads chanted from handwritten books.

Popular scribes and collectors as agents: 'in-between spaces'

One essential aspect of the common literacy practices of ordinary people in nineteenth-century Iceland was the relentless composition, collection and circulation of popular poetry. Literary historian Viðar Hreinsson has, in a paper on Icelandic-Canadian poet Stephan G. Stephansson, described the traditions of popular poetry in nineteenth-century Iceland:

> The composition of occasional verse was widely practised. It served the function of popular entertainment and was used to commemorate an event or a person, as well as to capture aspects of everyday reality, be it weather, nature, livestock (mainly horses), news, fashion, knowledge, courtship and sexuality, alcoholic drinks and songs. The most popular verse was the *lausavísa* – a single verse, usually in quatrains – often composed spontaneously in jest, to get the upper hand in a debate, devastate the opponent in an invective, or simply to seize and capture the moment .... The different compositions of the *alþýðuskáld* [popular poet] were mostly preserved, copied, and passed around in manuscript as well as orally; many of them are highly intricate in form. Popular poetry, versifying, was thus traditionally a vital part of daily life and exchange between people who believed that the best way to record reality was to bind it in metre and rhyme.³³

This practice is manifested, for instance, in the importance attached by many to collecting all the verse they could get hold of – especially poetry which had not been printed. A case in point is the fifteen-volume anthology of the works of nearly two hundred poets accumulated by Halldór Jónsson, who specially prioritised collecting unpublished verse by nineteenth-century folk poets. Each volume usually contains a miscellany of verses by a range of poets, some extending up to four hundred pages.[34] Some of these poets are represented in numerous volumes.

One of those poets was a certain Tómas Guðmundsson (1828–95), nicknamed *víðförli* (the far-travelled) or *Geirdælingur* (of Geiradalur). Poems by him are to be found in ten volumes out of fifteen. One of them, number five, contains only verse by Tómas, written out on 173 pages. Thus Halldór, as a prolific scribe and collector, performs both the role of a community scribe (mediator) and the collector of material that would otherwise largely be lost. Tómas, who belonged to the class of vagrants or wanderers, died of exposure when travelling from one farm to another. He would carry his belongings on his shoulders, stuffed into an old pair of trousers that he used for a bag according to one of his contemporaries, Einar Jochumsson. Einar reports that Tómas had

> gorged himself in reading various scholarly writings that I have never looked at. Greek and Roman literature, chivalric tales and romances, had children out of wedlock, drunk immeasurable quantities of rum, brandy and other liquor he got hold of. And wandered back and forth through the four regions of the country, with his patched breeches, full of his spiritual and physical nourishment … and at his breast he carried the material in his big volume of poetry, which he had named *Amlóði* [Weakling]. And it is very sad that such a magnificent publication!! should not have been made public. All must surely understand this, as such a versatile man as Tómas has worked on it for most of his life, and practised his inherent poetic talents by reading the great literature of the world.[35]

Halldór Jónsson had become acquainted with Tómas in his youth, when the latter was drifting through the district where Halldór grew up. They were probably drawn to each other due to their shared literary interests, and Halldór reports in his diary that he wrote up almanacs for Tómas, and did other tasks for him, in exchange for poetry that he added to his mounting collection.[36] Shortly after Tómas's sudden death in 1895, Halldór set out to collect poetry by him, which was disseminated in manuscript form in the region. In a letter to his brother Níels in February 1898, Halldór writes that he generally sits writing, as he has received many poems he has not copied before – including a large quantity, weighing three and a half pounds, that he has bought from the son of the late Tómas.[37]

A little more than a year later, Halldór again makes reference to these transcripts in a letter to his brother:

> I have now got what exists of poetry by Tómas Guðmundsson – it was a total of about nine pounds of papers and such, that I received from his son Guðmundur. But it is difficult to deal with – mostly loose sheets and small notebooks, in among the diaries and so on, the poems are scattered here and there, written in pencil and faded, much of it obviously written here and there, out in the open air. I have written up about twenty sheets of them, and that is just a drop in the ocean. It will be enough to make two or three volumes of poetry, if I live to copy it all.[38]

Halldór also writes about his collection of Tómas's verse in his diary at that time. On 20 June 1898, for instance, Halldór is on a farm where Tómas has often been, and notes: 'I got quite a lot of poems by the late Tómas Guðmundsson, which have been kept here since he died.'[39] On two occasions Halldór records that he has been sent a large parcel by his brother Ísleifur: on 4 February 1899 'a huge amount of poems of Tómas Guðmundsson, three pounds, thirty poems. Postage one *króna*, which Leifi [Ísleifur] paid', and on 27 February 'probably about five pounds of poems by Tómas Guðmundsson'. Other diary entries in February 1899 recount how Halldór set about classifying and organising the poems, and prepared himself to copy them in chronological order.

In addition to devoting an entire volume of his vast anthology to Tómas Guðmundsson's verse, Halldór also included more of his poems in other volumes, and in this way he succeeded in saving a large amount of Tómas's verse for posterity.[40] These examples illuminate the diligence of scribes as individuals in collecting and preserving folk verse in the latter half of the nineteenth century; and also the importance of the extensive network they built up among themselves and outside the group. As stated above, Tómas was a vagabond and drunkard who made little effort to preserve his verse; but his poems survived here and there, on farms where he stayed, because they were used and recited routinely by members of the household on winter evenings. Halldór, on the other hand, succeeded through his diligence and resourcefulness in collecting that verse together and producing a handwritten book of poetry, which circulated from farm to farm. That was the modus operandi of the barefoot historians: they tracked down material that interested them, organised it and made it into books that preserved it, handwritten by them.

Sighvatur Grímsson Borgfirðingur was also proactive in his collection of the writings of lesser-known contemporary poets. Among them was poet and pauper Jón Jónatansson, much of whose surviving poetry came into collections due to Sighvatur's efforts in collecting and copying it. Extant letters from Sighvatur to Jón provide a vivid insight into their interaction and Sighvatur's attitude to society. The cultural role played by him and other poets and lay scholars, the barefoot historians, is implicit in every word. Sighvatur starts a letter to his friend on 26 December 1902 by saying he has no time to write to him, 'but I want to make a gesture, at least'. He recalls a previous conversation about a certain poem of Jón's which he is keen to acquire, adding that he would be interested in getting his hands on any of his poems and verses,

> for I keep together all that I acquire of your writings, but there are so few items I have acquired, lamentably. You should sit down and write up everything possible of your poetry, whether good or bad, to make books, and place it in a safe place, so it is not lost – for it is all well done, and it would be a great shame if it were lost.[41]

Sighvatur's aim is both to preserve and to promote Jón's writings, so that they will be available in perpetuity, in manuscript copies or in print. 'In this way,' writes Sighvatur in his later letter of 1906, 'I have raised memorials to more than myself alone: your name will live as long as mine, my good old friend.'[42] In that work, time is of the essence, and the letter concludes as it began, on the day after Christmas 1902:

> I would be happy to keep on chatting, but I must stop now. I have such a huge amount to do, for all my letters – sixteen of them – must be ready this evening, as if possible a man is leaving for Ísafjörður in the morning, and it is nearly ten at night, and seven letters yet unwritten. I have written two like this in an hour, but I am now fully sixty-two years old.[43]

A substantial part of Sighvatur's extensive archive consists of a collection of hefty anthologies containing works of various poets, of different times and genres. This includes a 664-page compilation of assorted poetry named *Hít* (literally 'Bottomless pit'), brought together by Sighvatur in the early 1890s.[44] A considerable section (pp. 62–251) of this weighty compilation of nearly 150 poems is made up of poetry drawn from his childhood and adolescent days at Skipaskagi (Akranes) in the 1840s and 1850s, and thus reflects the literary milieu of the hamlet and its vicinity. Here Sighvatur revisits the cultural scene of his childhood and adolescent years: his own early compositions and transcripts, his father's poetry and some of the local poetry that formed the backdrop of daily life during his upbringing.[45] Several examples of direct encounters between young Sighvatur and various local poets found in *Hít* bear witness to transmission between oral and scribal media. In addition to local poets, Sighvatur's miscellany also contains examples of poetry by others, copied from manuscripts available at Akranes.[46]

Another of Sighvatur's later assemblages, also from the 1890s, gives further insight into the literary dynamism at Skipaskagi during his adolescence, and notably the tradition of *ljóðabréf* (verse letters).[47] These anthologies from the early 1890s contain strong indicators of the vibrant cultural environment at Skipaskagi four decades earlier and of the status of popular poetry in everyday life at the time. These and other examples of local literary activity at Skipaskagi and its vicinity portray dynamic textual exchange between the poets and other literary enthusiasts.

These instances of copying and collecting popular poetry and occasional verse demonstrate the role of these prolific scribes and scholars as mediators in between the spheres of popular culture and formal cultural institutions like archives and outlets of print publication. Their aspiration was not only to accumulate or distribute reading material but to facilitate new paths for peasant writing. The change in their position consisted primarily in their seeing the possibility of their works being safely preserved in archives and collections which were developing and growing at that time. In the end, much of their writings has found its way into such collections.

Postscript: manuscript culture as a sociocultural umbrella

One of the principal features of the literary work of the barefoot historians was the combination of historical knowledge, general knowledge, prose and poetry. The preservation and dissemination of historical, and to some degree collective, memory, without intervention by authorities or cultural/educational bodies, through text is thus a central aspect of the work. In addition oral dissemination and scribal practices coalesce in many cases in a peasant narrative culture. The material that belongs to the local tale tradition or vernacular lore is diverse in nature; in many cases it has been stored in the memory for decades, or was even passed down from generation to generation for centuries before finally finding its way into a manuscript or book. The basis of the tradition of vernacular lore (quite apart from its entertainment value) is the notion that specific events not only have meaning for the person involved, but also have something to say to others who live in similar conditions. Every story is thus widely applicable, although they are almost always identified with a named individual. But a personal viewpoint can be discerned in this material, because it is generally drawn from the memory of those who tell the story, which adds an individual flavour. The vernacular lore tradition can thus prove an interesting field for studies of the status and formation of the self as well as many other subjects relating to the scribal community.

The 'local tales' are sometimes seen as a uniquely Icelandic genre, which brings together different types of text and spans various vital phenomena of human life such as annals, topography, genealogy, biography, accounts of events and histories of regions and districts, and even of specific farms. *Sagnarit* (books of local tales) are grounded in the gathering of resources, both in written and oral form. In that way, the methods and attitudes of lay scholars were passed on in their writing from group to group and from generation to generation, and in due course enjoyed a flowering in the nineteenth century, when ordinary people gained access to writing materials: paper, pens and ink.

This literary tradition rose to a higher level in the twentieth century, with the ever-growing publication of material of this nature on the general market – as it enjoyed great popularity. We have gained some insight into this process in accounts of the lives of the men discussed here, when they began to publish their work for a wider public. As the twentieth century progressed, this genre remained popular among the reading public in Iceland – with adjustments to take account of the market and its dictates.

History professor emeritus Ingi Sigurðsson has addressed this same tradition, writing on the principles of his own discipline:

> In the nineteenth century a unique peasant tradition of writing tales evolved. Account must certainly be taken of the fact that the distinction between peasant history-writing and other history-writing was never very clear. As the century progressed, the development of history as an academic discipline influenced the historical writing of most university-educated Icelanders, while peasant history remained closer to the old Icelandic tradition in writing of tales, which has features modelled on Old Icelandic literature. The subjects of peasant histories are rarely large-scale; they tend to deal with individual people, events in the history of specific communities, and memorable occurrences. They are invariably rooted in oral traditions, but written sources are used increasingly during this period. The *sagnaþættir* are a remarkable manifestation of peasant tale-writing. Gísli Konráðsson played the major role in their development.[48]

Ingi views the local tale tradition and other lay historiography as individual endeavour rather than cultural practice. He did not observe the important quasi-institutional element which characterises the work of the barefoot historians. In this chapter, our thesis is precisely that a kind of 'counter-institution' was in existence – but an institution for all that. Study of such a phenomenon demands consideration of the question of how the 'institution' defined and viewed itself, so to speak – what someone had to do in order to be recognised as a 'real popular scribe', what feats they had to perform into order to be admitted to the network of the barefoot historians and, finally, what hierarchy – if any – existed within the group. These are all matters we have sought to address and answer, directly or indirectly, in this chapter.

It must be borne in mind that those who worked within the local tale tradition – vernacular lore – often attained a position of influence within their own districts, though their 'fame' was on a small scale. Such material, collected and written by barefoot historians, was hugely popular in the eighteenth, nineteenth and twentieth centuries, and it rose to respectable status thanks to the systematic efforts of scribes such as Sighvatur Grímsson Borgfirðingur, Magnús Hj. Magnússon and the brothers Halldór and Níels Jónsson. But, first and foremost, we are dealing with a 'participatory culture', in the sense that media scholar Henry Jenkins and his collaborators have presented the term – a culture in which the audience is not only a passive consumer, but also makes its own contribution.[49] Jenkins has described it in his recent writings, taking account of his studies of contemporary digital culture: 'A participatory culture is a culture with relatively low barriers to artistic expression and civic engagement, strong support for creating and sharing creations, and some type of informal mentorship whereby experienced participants pass along knowledge to novices.'[50]

The barefoot historians were important participants in such cultural practice – they were agents who were connected to others via acts of manuscript transmission. Every such act has links to an infinite number of others through connections between nodes that constitute a network, with endless possibilities for onward connections to other networks. The objective of this chapter has been to explore the circumstances and conditions in which the scribes worked, and the qualities of the material they produced: its nature, and how it was handled by these peasant scribes. We have also focussed on tracing how knowledge passed from person to person and generation to generation, and was conducive to spectacular literary achievement by these lay scholars – the dissemination of knowledge derived from the local tale tradition, vernacular lore, which played a vital role in daily life and culture in Iceland.

Notes

We are grateful for the support we have enjoyed from the Icelandic Centre for Research (Rannís, no. 184976-051 – Grant of Excellence) during our research.

1. Deborah Brandt, *The Rise of Writing: Redefining Mass Literacy* (Cambridge, UK: Cambridge University Press, 2015).
2. *Ibid.*, p. 2.
3. *Ibid.*, p. 3.
4. *Ibid.*, p. 11.
5. Sigurður Gylfi Magnússon and Davíð Ólafsson, *Minor Knowledge and Microhistory: Manuscript Culture in the Nineteenth Century* (London: Routledge, 2017), pp. 89–104.

6 Davíð Ólafsson, *Wordmongers: Post-Medieval Scribal Culture and the Case of Sighvatur Grímsson*, Ph.D. thesis, University of St Andrews, 2008; Sigurður Gylfi Magnússon and Davíð Ólafsson, 'Barefoot historians: Education in Iceland in the modern period', in Klaus-Joachim Lorenzen-Schmidt and Bjørn Poulsen (eds), *Writing Peasants: Studies on Peasant Literacy in Early Modern Northern Europe* (Odense: Landbohistorisk Selskab, 2002), pp. 175–209; Sigurður Gylfi Magnússon and Davíð Ólafsson, 'Minor knowledge: Microhistory, scribal communities, and the importance of institutional structures', *Quaderni storici*, 47:140(2) (2012), 495–524.

7 Sigurður Gylfi Magnússon, *Wasteland with Words. A Social History of Iceland* (London: Reaktion Books, 2010).

8 Henry Jenkins with Katie Clinton, Ravi Purushotma, Alice J. Robison and Margaret Weigel, *Confronting the Challenges of Participatory Culture: Media Education for the Twenty-First Century* (Cambridge, MA: MIT Press, 2006).

9 'Everyday life history' started out, however, as a grassroots movement. Geoff Eley described it as follows: 'Much of the activity is conducted by amateurs and semi-professionals – "barefoot historians", in the commonly used expression, which captures the distinctive mixture of zeal, anti-academism and popular politics so important to the elan of much of the broader movement' (Eley, 'Labor history, social history, *Alltagsgeschichte*: experience, culture and the politics of the everyday—a new direction for German social history', *Journal of Modern History*, 61: 2 (June 1989), 297–343, p. 298). Alf Lüdtke also wrote about going 'barefoot', referring to the methods of staying 'closer to the soil and hard rock of reality – an insight often forgotten among "institutionalized" scholars and scientists' (Lüdtke, 'Introduction: What is the history of everyday life and who are its practitioners?', in A. Lüdtke (ed.), *The History of Everyday Life: Reconstructing Historical Experiences and Ways of Life*, trans. William Templer (Princeton, NJ: Princeton University Press, 1995), pp. 3–40, p. 29.

10 Magnússon and Ólafsson, *Minor Knowledge and Microhistory*; Ólafsson, *Wordmongers*; Matthew J. Driscoll and Margrét Eggertsdóttir (eds), *Mirrors of Virtue: Manuscript and Print in Late Pre-Modern Iceland*, Bibliotheca Arnamagnæana XLIX: Opuscula XV (Copenhagen: Museum Tusculanums, 2017).

11 On the spread of literacy and the development of peasant book culture in Europe and elsewhere, see David Vincent, *The Rise of Mass Literacy: Reading and Writing in Modern Europe* (Cambridge, UK: Polity, 2000); Harvey J. Graff, *Literacy Myths, Legacies, and Lessons: New Studies on Literacy* (London and New York: Routledge, 2011); Robert A. Houston, *Literacy in Early Modern Europe: Culture and Education 1500–1800* (London and New York: Routledge, 2nd edition, 2014). On new research on manuscript culture and literacy practices in recent centuries, see Davíð Ólafsson, 'Post-medieval manuscript culture and the historiography of texts', in Driscoll and Eggertsdóttir (eds), *Mirrors of Virtue*, pp. 1–30. See also a detailed review of this publication, placing it in the context of the history of research in the field in recent decades: Sigurður Gylfi Magnússon, 'What takes place, when nothing happens? The importance of late modern manuscript culture', *Scripta Islandica*, 69 (2018), 149–75.

12 Gilles Deleuze and Félix Guattari, *A Thousand Plateaus: Capitalism and Schizophrenia*, trans. Brian Massumi (Minneapolis, University of Minnesota Press, 1987); Ólafsson, *Wordmongers*, pp. 191–5.
13 Davíð Ólafsson, 'Scribal communities in Iceland: The case of Sighvatur Grímsson', in Anna Kuismin and Matthew J. Driscoll (eds), *White Field, Black Seeds: Nordic Literacy Practices in the Long Nineteenth Century* (Helsinki: Finnish Literature Society, 2013), pp. 40–9.
14 Sigurður Gylfi Magnússon, 'Tales of the unexpected: The "textual environment", ego-documents and a nineteenth-century Icelandic love story – an approach in microhistory', *Cultural and Social History*, 12:1 (2015), 77–94.
15 Sigurður Gylfi Magnússon, *Emotional Experience and Microhistory: A Life Story of a Destitute Pauper Poet in the Nineteenth Century* (London: Routledge, 2020).
16 National and University Library of Iceland, Manuscript Department (henceforth NULI) Lbs 1673 4to – Dagbók Magnúsar Hj. Magnússonar (Diary of Magnús Hj. Magnússon), 28 February 1899.
17 Ólafsson, *Wordmongers*; see also Matthew Driscoll, *The Unwashed Children of Eve: The Production, Dissemination and Reception of Popular Literature in Post-Reformation Iceland* (Enfield Lock, UK: Hisarlik Press, 1997).
18 See, for example, Viðar Hreinsson, 'Íslenska akademían: Kotungar í andófi', *Skírnir*, 173 (1999), 255–88.
19 Kristmundur Bjarnason, 'Alþýðufræðsla í Skagafirði fram undir síðustu aldamót: Nokkrar athuganir', in *Gefið og þegið: Afmælisrit til heiðurs Brodda Jóhannessyni sjötugum* (Reykjavík: Iðunn, 1986), pp. 221–46, p. 227.
20 Sigurður Gylfi Magnússon and Davíð Ólafsson, 'In the name of barefoot historians: In-between spaces within the Icelandic educational system', in Cristiano Casalini, Edward Choi and Ayenachew Woldegiyorgis (eds), *Education Beyond Europe: Models and Traditions before Modernities* (Leiden: Brill, 2021), pp. 324–44.
21 Magnússon, *Emotional Experience and Microhistory*, pp. 3–13.
22 Part of the argument presented by Sigurður Gylfi Magnússon in his work – for instance, in his Icelandic book whose title translates as *Education, Love and Grief* – is that an important element of the informal education that occurred during the winter evenings was the creation of an emotional outlet in the lives of Icelandic children. That is the reason the two brothers were drawn to reading and writing. See Sigurður Gylfi Magnússon, *Menntun, ást og sorg. Einsögurannsókn á íslensku sveitasamfélagi 19. og 20. aldar*, Sagnfræðirannsóknir 13 (Reykjavík: Háskólaútgáfan, 1997), pp. 55–68.
23 Davíð Ólafsson, *Frá degi til dags. Dagbækur, almanök og veðurdagbækur 1720–1920*, Sýnisbók íslenskrar alþýðumenningar 27 (Reykjavík: Háskólaútgáfan, 2021).
24 Loftur Guttormsson, 'The development of popular religious literacy in the seventeenth and eighteenth centuries', *Scandinavian Journal of History*, 15:1 (1990), 7–35.
25 Loftur Guttormsson, 'Læsi', in Frosti F. Jóhannesson (ed.), *Íslensk þjóðmenning, 6 Munnmenntir og bókmenning* (Reykjavík: Þjóðsaga, 1989), pp. 118–44, see pp. 136–7.

26 *Stjórnartíðindi 1880* A, 6–9. 'Auk þeirrar uppfræðsluskyldu, sem prestar hafa, skulu þeir sjá um, að öll börn, sem til þess eru hæf að áliti prests og meðhjálpara, læri að skrifa og reikna'.
27 On the development of popular education since 1880, see Loftur Guttormsson (ed.), *Almenningsfræðsla á Íslandi 1880–2007*, vols 1 and 2 (Reykjavík: Háskólaútgáfan, 2008).
28 Davíð Ólafsson, 'Vernacular literacy practices in nineteenth-century Icelandic scribal culture', in Ann-Catrine Edlund (ed.), *Att läsa och att skriva: Två vågor av vardagligt skriftbruk i Norden 1800–2000*, Nordliga studier 3, Vardagligt skriftbrug 1 (Umeå: Umeå Universitet and Kungl. Skytteanska Samfundet, 2012), pp. 65–85.
29 David Barton and Mary Hamilton, *Local Literacies: Reading and Writing in One Community* (London: Routledge, 1998).
30 *Ibid.*, p. 247.
31 Ólafsson, 'Vernacular literacy practices in nineteenth-century Icelandic scribal culture', pp. 65–85.
32 Ólafsson, *Wordmongers*; Magnússon and Ólafsson, *Minor Knowledge and Microhistory*.
33 Viðar Hreinsson, 'Unheard thunder: Stephan G. Stephansson', in Guðrún Björk Guðsteins (ed.), *Rediscovering Canadian Difference*, Nordic Association for Canadian Studies Text Series 17 (Reykjavík: Nordic Association for Canadian Studies, 2001), pp. 74–5.
34 NULI Lbs 1870–1884 8vo – Kvæðasafn Halldórs Jónssonar; Sigurður Gylfi Magnússon, *Menntun ást og sorg*, pp. 128–33.
35 Einar Jochumsson, *Hrópandi rödd til Tómasar Guðmundssonar þess víðförla* (Ísafjörður: published by the author, 1894), cited in Lárus Jóhannsson, *Andvaka. Lífshlaup og ljóð Tómasar skálds Guðmundssonar Geirdælings hins víðförla* (Dýrafjörður: Vestfirska forlagið, 2012), pp. 50–3.
36 Magnússon, *Menntun, ást og sorg*, pp. 128–9.
37 *Ibid.*, p. 128.
38 *Ibid.*, p. 129.
39 NULI Lbs 1864 8vo – The diary of Halldór Jónsson: 5 February 1898.
40 Lárus Jóhannsson, *Andvaka*, p. 6.
41 NULI Lbs 2255 4to – Letter from Sighvatur Grímsson to Jón Jónatansson, 26 December 1902.
42 NULI Lbs 2255 4to – Letter from Sighvatur Grímsson to Jón Jónatansson, 19 November 1906.
43 NULI Lbs 2255 4to – Letter from Sighvatur Grímsson to Jón Jónatansson, 26 December 1902.
44 NULI Lbs 2289 4to – Sighvatur Grímsson, *Hít*, 1891–1892.
45 *Ibid.*
46 NULI Lbs 2289 4to – Hjálmar Jónsson, 'Eptirmæli eptir Sigurð skáld Breiðfjörð orkt af Hjálmari Jónssyni í Bólu, eptir handrit Lýðs skálds Jónssonar'.
47 NULI Lbs 2291 4to – Sighvatur Grímsson, Collection of *hrakningarímur* (ballads of hazardous sea journeys) and *ljóðabréf* (verse letters), collected and

copied by Sighvatur Grímsson in spring 1890 from various older manuscripts, including several items in his hand dating from the mid-century.
48 Ingi Sigurðsson, 'Þróun íslenzkrar sagnfræði frá miðöldum til nútímans', *Saga*, 38 (2000), 9–32, p. 18. See also Ingi Sigurðsson, *Íslensk sagnfræði frá miðri 19. öld til miðrar 20. aldar*, Ritsafn Sagnfræðistofnunar 15 (Reykjavík: Sagnfræðistofnun, 1986).
49 Jenkins, *Confronting the Challenges of Participatory Culture*.
50 *Ibid.*, p. xi.

8

Questioning 'the common writer': ordinary writings from the Emagusheni trading station in Pondoland, 1880–84

Liz Stanley

Introduction

The idea of the common writer has considerable analytical utility in focussing on the production and circulation of everyday forms of writing by the mass of people with very varied literacy skills, rather than those of an educated elite.[1] In doing so, it raises interesting questions about the multiple ways in which everyday, ordinary writings are formulated and used and the analytical implications of this.[2] A key question concerns the association of the common (or 'ordinary') writer with social position and/or education, as people of humble status rather than the middling or upper sort.[3] This may hold true in many European contexts, but in parts of the world which over the nineteenth and early twentieth centuries experienced the arrivals of large numbers of migrant settlers, it requires detailed investigation to establish whether it remains so in these different circumstances.

In colonial contexts in Africa, North America and Australasia, settlers originally from across the entirety of the European class structure, though often with few literacy skills in formal terms, could find themselves in circumstances in which the written word was an everyday necessity because it enabled communication across great distances between people and places.[4] Functional forms of literacy abounded as a consequence. And as the settler colonial population increased, so its activities began to have an impact on Indigenous populations too. This occurred in many regions of southern Africa, and the question arises as to whether this new and different context gave rise to variations in what were ordinary writings and who were ordinary writers. This question is explored here around the example of ordinary writings produced in Pondoland in the 1880s.

The polity of Pondoland was on the south-east coastal area of what is now South Africa, between the Cape to the west and Natal to the east.[5] It was fully independent until the death of its powerful and effective King

Faku in the 1860s, was then de facto divided between his two senior sons, and was eventually annexed by the Cape in 1894. Discussion here concerns a busy trading station (a general store combined with distance sales and servicing people in a large area) located on a main travel route close to the eastern border between Pondoland and Natal, with a high level of written exchanges facilitating the range of commercial and related activities in which it engaged. Trading stations were often liminal places, where ideas about power and authority could come under question and relationships between insiders and outsiders, the Indigenous and the colonial, could be both complex and volatile.[6] These features can be discerned regarding this Pondoland station, and as discussion will show, they gave rise to changing patterns of interrelationship among the people associated with it, as demonstrated by the many documents that survive.

The trading station operated from 1880 through to the 1950s. Its records, now archived, span this entire period and include letters, orders, bills, receipts, accounts, ledgers and other items.[7] It was established in 1880 by brothers Josiah Pleydell Bouverie and William Bouverie, and then taken over at the start of 1883 by Michael Hurley O'Donnell. Initially referred to as Fort William and Untamvana, it was subsequently renamed Emagusheni, with this early phase of activity culminating at the end of 1884 with a court case against O'Donnell, an Irish republican and anti-imperialist, for gun-running.

Emagusheni's extensive documents for the earlier decades of its activities evidence the presence of white hunters, traders, storekeepers, colonial officials, missionaries and many black people from the MPondo elite – hundreds of people overall. The white group included those who were dependent on or directly employed by the Great King Mqikela and his ruling elite, acting as diplomatic agents, secretaries and general factotums. The backgrounds of the other white people represented, many of whom held anti-colonial and pro-MPondo views, were diverse, as were their writing skills overall, with no clear-cut relationship between social status of origin and writing competence.

The land that the trading station was located on was the Great King Mqikela's, with locally resident counsellors and wider family acting as observer-caretakers on his behalf. The Wesleyan mission in the area ran schools, including for girls, resulting in basic literacy skills for a large number of MPondo women and men. Also some of the MPondo elite had attended Lovedale College, which provided higher-level education.[8] Consequently the backgrounds of the many black writers represented in the collection were less diverse but generally of considerably higher status in local terms than the whites.

Emagusheni's voluminous records show a wide variety of writing practices by both black and white contributors. The everyday, ordinary writings produced by these people are related in complex ways to notions of social status, including racial categorisations as understood through the lens of the later history of South Africa and the apartheid system. As a result, thinking about the 'common writer' as a person of low status, and 'ordinary writings' as those produced by such persons, needs to be suspended and a detailed investigation carried out on the writing practices involved and what they add up to. Doing this shows the importance of time, place and circumstances, suggests a different understanding of 'ordinary' writings, and puts an interesting question mark over the idea of the common writer – points returned to in the concluding section.

The Emagusheni documents

The Gallagher collection holding the Emagusheni trading station papers is a very large one of eighty-three archive boxes, organised by type of document and in year sequence, adding up to many thousands of often lengthy items. The early period is as well covered as the later, with nine boxes for the first period of its existence to the end of 1884. These documents show that writing and exchanging letters and related forms of communication facilitated a wide range of activities on the part of people from diverse European *and* Indigenous African backgrounds. None of them possessed any marked literacy skills, but they were able nonetheless to use the written word well enough to proficiently conduct and record many business and related activities. These include orders of imported wholesale merchandise, records of goods purchased, receipts for taxes on goods crossing the border, order books, inventories of goods, account books and a voluminous correspondence. The latter involved many contributors who wrote letters to each other in order to transact activities of different kinds, predominantly business ones about purchases, but often mixed with political and interpersonal concerns too; and, while focussed on the task in hand, there is frequently an 'oiling the wheels' aspect in maintaining relationships.

The largest component of the Emagusheni collection consists of inventories, orders, receipts, accounts and similar records, all concerning goods bought and sold and related matters. The next-largest component consists of the letters. But rather than representing conventional letter writing of a personal kind, these letters are transactional in character and often criss-cross the borders with other genres of writing, like orders, accounts and receipts. Also, while usually focussed on their performative aspects, they evidence the varied ways in which these different forms of writing, overwhelmingly by people unskilled in writing, were used to carry out complex transactions in addition to the purchasing of goods.

The letters for discussion in this chapter have been selected from records of the years 1883 and 1884. As already noted, Michael O'Donnell took over control of Emagusheni at the start of 1883, and by the end of 1884 the Natal court case against him for gun-running had been conducted. These years form the start and end point of discussion here, with a one in ten sample of letters considered out of just under a hundred filed for this period. These are examined in depth and show that the writers and addressees were connected through multiple activities and not just through purchases from the trading station alone.

In what follows, these letters are discussed in the chronological order in which they were written. All of the letters are provided in full and exact variorum transcriptions, thus including underlinings, mistakes, omissions and any crossings out. Questionable readings of words are indicated with '?' in front of the word in question. Archive referencing information is provided in the accompanying endnotes.

Border exchanges

The idea of border exchanges is used in two different but connected senses here. The letters discussed often sit on the borders between one subgenre of writing and another, and show the competence of the writers in managing these complexities, through what and how they wrote. They were also written by people who were living and working close to the geographical border between Pondoland and Natal, with the different interests and competing authorities that existed there regarding matters of authority and sovereignty – something they needed to take into account.

In short, the trading station was a 'contact zone' in the analytical sense, wherein relationships could be made and remade, with the role of writing and reading playing a significant part in fashioning those relationships.[9] As their content makes clear, these letters are exchanges, moments in a dynamic in which transactions were started and concluded and wider information conveyed, and they were generally conducted with the expectation that there would not be a written response, but instead some practical activity as part of the transaction.

Letter 1[10]

?Edilohloryanemi
January 4th 1883

dear
Mr O'Donnell & Bou
will you please obliged me lend me 1 lbs coffee & 2 lbs Sugar and bottle of ?Brown?beer

I Remain
Yours very truly
Umhlangwaso i Seakora

This letter was written in January 1883 by Umhlangwaso, a very senior figure in the Pondoland ruling hierarchy and in effect its ruler, given that the Great King was often seen to be drunk and incapacitated. Umhlangwaso is also referred to in a letter discussed below, written by Hamilton McNicholas (Letter 7); and his senior wife also wrote letters, and one of these will be discussed later too (Letter 4). Other letters from him also exist, and the content of this one seems typical. In general, letters in the collection by a writer who is different from the person authorising them have this indicated in their phrasing (e.g. 'the King has asked me'), so this letter was almost certainly written by Umhlangwaso himself. As these comments suggest, it was those who received an elite education in mission schools and at Lovedale College, including women from this group as well as men, who wrote the letters now in the collection.

The handwriting as well as content of this letter suggests a measure of skill and competence but also some uncertainty. The content is seemingly addressed to two people, O'Donnell and Bouverie ('Bou' is how Umhlangwaso wrote it), but this most likely indicates that it was being directed to the trading station as such, rather than addressing these two men personally, with a number of people in addition to them involved in expediting transactions in the store. And tacitly, the store supported face-to-face transactions and also responded to orders such as this one arriving on paper, with goods then dispatched in the care of a messenger.

Umhlangwaso's letter has various of the attributes of formal letter writing, including its dating and content, and its sign-off – after 'I Remain Yours very truly', he provides his full name in an honorific sense. These formal attributes are frequently applied in diverse ways, as with the stray 'dear' at the start. However, it proficiently does the job of work needed, to expedite the request ordering the coffee, sugar and beer. It is of note that Chief Umhlangwaso was writing his own letter here, so perhaps he was in a different place from where his diplomatic agent (a European who acted as secretary, administrator and general factotum in dealings with the white community) was when it was written.

Letter 2[11]

Emfinsdiswani
March 9 1883

Dear Mr O'Donnell

Please please send
^none^   1   pr Women's Boots 5s good
^Sent at 9/6^   1 pr Boots 12s   "
^None^   1 Lamp Glass for hanging ^lamp^
^3/-, 4/-^   1 Glass Butter Dish
send wholesale & retail?prices [torn, word unreadable] of these articles

Yours faithfully[12]

This March 1883 document is addressed to O'Donnell and has the structure of a letter, with an address and date at the start, a personal address and a formal sign-off at its end. It belongs to a mixed genre, having some attributes of an order and a receipt. The body of the letter consists of orders for goods in a kind of inventory, together with the request that wholesale and retail prices for them should be supplied as well as the goods. It has also been used as a return receipt or account, with the action taken recorded in a different handwriting as indicated by the insertion symbols, as with '^Sent at 9/6^'. In its mixture of purposes this document is, if not prototypical, still one of the major forms that letter writing takes in the collection.

The signature at the end has been frayed away and so the name of the writer is not known. However, are there ways in which some characteristics of the writer can still be discerned? In particular, is there any way of telling whether the writer was one of the educated black elite, or one of the various whites who purchased goods from the trading station?

The 'Please please' at the start suggests that the writer is being careful to be polite and observe the conventions in this respect, but is unsure as to how polite to be. This is rather similar to a 'please' at the start of the letter from Mrs Umhlangwaso discussed later (Letter 4), and also the 'dear' at the start of Chief Umhlangwaso's letter, discussed earlier (Letter 1). So there is a clear possibility that such politeness might indicate black people writing, because a personal address would have been expressed in such terms orally in MPondo society. Nothing can be added to this surmise through considering the handwriting, as this is rather unformed and similar to much else in the collection, and could be by anyone not very used to writing. Consequently the jury must remain out regarding the likely identity of the writer.

Letter 3[13]

Plough Hotel PMBburg
Sep 10th 1883
J.P.B

No doubt you have seen the Papers see how Mcdonald has comited him self I have taken an action against him Dukes is my man, the same who defended the Kaffer & made a fool of Dr Gordon in a crowded court shepstone could not take the matter up as he is town solicitor, not news shepstone don't think much of my case hope things are going on well I bought a donkey for 40/- I will send him out as soon as Possible

Yours truly
M.H. O'Donnell

The writer of this September 1883 letter, Michael O'Donnell, was, as noted earlier, an Irish republican. In addition to his more mundane activities around the trading station, he was involved in gun theft and gun-running for the Pondoland chiefs in their attempts to counter colonial incursions from Britain and its local colonies. The letter was sent from Pietermaritzburg in Natal, judging by the initials provided at the letter's head, and the addressee was Josiah Playdell Bouverie, the elder of the Bouverie brothers associated with the trading station. They were members of a merchant family that shipped goods into Natal and then sold them across southern Africa. The brothers were the initial owners of the trading station; then for a time they acted with O'Donnell when he took over, in the period which is the focus of the present discussion. Shepstone was one of the powers that be in Natal and elsewhere, and with his son he also acted as agent, sometimes for the colonial powers and sometimes for Indigenous rulers in the Pondoland/Natal area.

The content is a mixture of the news that O'Donnell had taken out a legal action against McDonald (a hunter operating in the area), of 'not news' in the shape of Shepstone thinking that his legal case would not succeed, and of information about the donkey he would send to the trading station. The court case brought by the Natal authorities against O'Donnell for gun-running took place in 1884, leading to his acquittal, but what the legal action against McDonald refers to in this letter is not known.[14]

Overall, O'Donnell's letter is short and observes the conventions of the day, although there are some non-standard aspects like the imperfect capitalisation of names, misspelling of a difficult word ('comited'), 'him self' as two separate words, and a lack of commas in the later part of the letter. These things may indicate either lack of practice or lack of time to observe the conventions more closely. The letter also shows something of the relationship between O'Donnell and Bouverie – an easy familiarity is suggested here, although other letters indicate some tension about the other white men who used the trading station as their base and occupied O'Donnell's rooms when he was away.

Letter 4[15]

Please Sir

to give that Boy 1 lb of Sugar I will pay you Sir on Monday you must wait for me till I have change Because I send it one?pun[d] to this Morning at ?Magushen to Mr Oakes to get change for him.

I am your obt. Servant
Mrs Umhlangwaso
Esilongwani
17 Novbr 1883

This November 1883 document by Mrs Umhlangwaso is an order for goods and a promise to pay, and also a letter. It is addressed in general terms and in the politest of ways: 'Please Sir'. It has an equally polite sign-off and signature, and concludes with the address it was sent from and the date. The signature is itself formal in an interesting way, with 'Sir' matched here by 'Mrs'. Mrs Umhlangwaso has a number of letters in the collection. As this example indicates, she did not run her own messages; someone did this for her, signalling a person in a lower social position than she, probably the same boy who is fetching the sugar. In fact Mrs Umhlangwaso was a relative of the Great King and kept an eye on his property in the area, which included the land that the Emagusheni trading station was on, so the messenger referred to might well have been directly working for her but indirectly working for the King. Her husband, as noted earlier, was also one of the King's most senior counsellors and a notable power in the land, and a number of letters from him also survive in the records.

Mrs Umhlangwaso has to be addressed by title as well as her marital name. In gender terms this is notable because it is an indication of equivalence with the Sir who is addressed, and it is highly performative in this. It demonstrates that it is not possible to address her in a familiar way; it *does* the equivalence; it is the material accomplishment of it. Any response on paper would have required the storeman to have addressed her either as Dear Madam or Dear Mrs Umhlangwaso. And Mrs Umhlangwaso signs her name thus in her other communications too, so there is never a possibility of being familiar with her.

148 *The common writer in modern history*

Letter 5[16]

I cannot tell you what I like to say therefore I will as soon as possible I will come a se you and hope that we will arrange matters in I friendly feeling

Hoping that you will spent Merry Xmas

With regards
I Remain
WH Boshoff

This short 1883 letter from W. H. Boshoff has no punctuation and in a formal sense contains mistakes as well. It bears comparison with that by Mrs Umhlangwaso. The sense is nonetheless quite clear: the writer is unable to convey what he wants in a letter and therefore will come to see the addressee in person. The addressee is not named and nor is there a date, although it is in the 1883 sequence of documents and the addressee is perhaps Josiah Bouverie.

It is also likely that Boshoff was writing in his second language, as a Dutch or more likely an Afrikaans speaker, and early Afrikaans (*taal*) had no written form until later, so he would not have been proficient in writing it anyway. In this he would have been in the same position as most black people, including Mrs Umhlangwaso, in the sense that when they wrote the letters now in the collection, they did so in their second or third languages, some of which at the time did not have written forms.

Letter 6[17]

Great Place
26 December 1883
Mr Bouverie

Dear Sir
The Chief Umquikela Sends bearer to you for 2 blankets (two) and 2 bottles of Brandy
& by so doing will oblige him
yours truly
for Chief Umquikela
W Johnson

PS. The Chief Umquikela wishes you to meet me at Thomas's place on Saturday in reference of Major Giles's letter

over

The Chief wishes you to pay unto bearers your license for the insuing year ending 31 Decr 1883

By order
of Chief Umquikela
W. Johnson
Trading License £5.0.0
Liquor License under consideration whither to be granted or not
Hoping you had a Merry Xmas

^Went & saw Chief & settled all about Licenses to my intire satisfaction
4 Janry 1884^18

This complex document was written at the end of December 1883 by W. Johnson, then acting as the diplomatic agent on behalf of the Great King, whose name is rendered here phonetically: Umquikela. Its addressee is most likely Josiah Bouverie, as he was more involved in the day-to-day running of the trading station than his brother William. It has a formal structure which follows epistolary conventions, although it has an 'out of place' feature, given the otherwise impersonal gravity of content, in ending with 'Hoping you had a Merry Xmas'. It is in fact a compendium document with a number of aspects to it. It combines an order for goods in the shape of blankets and brandy, a request or demand for a meeting to discuss 'Major Giles's letter', a requirement that payment be made for the renewal of a trading licence and a statement that a liquor licence might or might not be granted. It is notable that the writer is not the originator of the letter, who is the 'Chief' referred to, and so it uses removed phraseology, as in 'The Chief wishes you to pay unto bearers', because Johnson is writing as a proxy for the chief. Although not differentiated from other chiefs referred to in letters, clearly the addressee would know full well that as the originator of this letter lived in the 'Great Place', which signified kingship, they were in formal terms the key political figure in Pondoland.

The content includes stock phrases, like 'by so doing will oblige him' and 'By order'. There are also indications of an imperfect knowledge of grammar, and spellings like 'insuing' and 'intire' are either leftovers from an earlier period or, more simply, spelt phonetically as pronounced. At the same time, there are also signs of grammatical proficiency, as in the use of apostrophes, the most notable being 'Giles's'.

Overall, the document is a mixture of the formal, conventional and grammatically correct, combined with the informal and indications of lack of formal proficiency. It is particularly interesting in its mixture of genres. It is a letter that does not require a written reply but a practical response in the shape of blankets, brandy, payments and a meeting; it is an order for goods; and it is a formal notification about two licences in the gift of the Chief – that is, the Great King. At the end of the document, in another hand, there is an insertion dated 4 January 1884, where the recipient has recorded the meeting and its outcome – that the liquor licence had been granted.

The letter writer, Johnson, was the diplomatic agent of the Great King – that is, he was a kind of administrative secretary – and so the indications of his imperfect knowledge of such things as spelling and grammar and punctuation are interesting. Such agents were in practice not usually very educated men, but drawn from the ranks of the flotsam and jetsam of those white people who could read and write at a basic level or better, and were in such places at a time when an intermediary between Indigenous rulers and the colonial presence was needed. They ranged from the almost illiterate and incompetent through to the highly professional, of whom the best-known example now is Theophilus Shepstone, who worked mainly in Natal and is referred to in a number of letters.[19]

Letter 7[20]

to me.

I do not think Umhlangwaso will be able to go up to the Umquidini, But I think ask me to go. I will wire and let you know when O'Donnell can come

The Chief wishes you to tell your Brother that he must come and get his Blankets also the payment as the man has now paid who took them – he also wants you to send him some Gin on the strength of it. And please send me a flask of <u>good gin</u> and give the Bearer to understand it is not for the Chief or otherwise he will give it to him –

Yrs sincerely
EB Hamilton McNicholas

The beginning page or pages of this letter are missing and the edges are frayed and torn, and it commences *in media res* as a consequence. The addressee is not specified in what remains; this is not O'Donnell, but is perhaps the younger Bouverie brother, William. The writer, Hamilton McNicholas, was the agent then working for the Great King, and his letters frequently mention senior chief Umhlangwaso, also referred to in this example. He had succeeded Johnson, writer of Letter 6, who had died suddenly at the start of 1884, and McNicholas acted as agent not only for the Great King but also for men in the next tier of the political hierarchy as well.

The letter has a marked informal tone apart from in its sign-off. Grammatically and in other ways its form is correct with regard to spelling, punctuation and mode of expression. Its content is concerned with a transaction involving blankets, payments being made, and gin that can be bought on the strength of this. It contains the strong implication that the Chief referred to, who is the King rather than Umhlangwaso, would commandeer gin that was actually for McNicholas unless it was kept from him. It also shows that there were different qualities of gin available via the trading station, both good gin and presumably the not so good, so this is likely to have been a popular item for purchase.

Letter 8[21]

Jan 4th 1884
Mr J. Bouverie

Dear Sir
The chief Umkila ask me to write to you for 15/ worth of Gin cash sent & also he says you can make him a little present his it all the money he got.

Yours very Truly
Chief Marsupla

This document is a letter by proxy, originating from the Great King but expedited by having been physically written by a relatively minor chief, Marsupla, on King Umkila's behalf. This suggests that those lower down the hierarchy of chiefs were in a sense Indigenous diplomatic agents working on behalf of the Great King in their area of Pondoland, and could play a role similar to that carried out by Johnson and McNicholas, commented on earlier. Its content and mode of expression are proficient in making the point and conveying what was needful, which is making a purchase of gin as well as the extraction of a 'little present'.

There is an interesting trickster aspect here in the 'little present' expected or rather required from the storekeeper, who would have been very aware that granting licences was dependent on the King's approval, thus making such overtures very difficult to resist. Many of the communications ordering goods from both black and white people concern alcohol and in particular gin, either as part of an order or as the sole item requested. This suggests that the annual liquor licence, referred to earlier, was important to the business, so losing the King's approval would have been a matter of consequence.

Letter 9[22]

Umtamvuna Drift
7 Nov 1884

Received from J. P. Bouverie Esq the sum of Five Shillings stg – for 1 Pack (containing 3 saddles) crossing this drift.

£-.5.0

Lavington Evans
On behalf of
Paramount Chief, Pondoland

This November 1884 document starts with an address and date, and ends with a formal sign-off. No response is envisaged and its content is confined to recording and acting as a record of a transaction. It looks like a letter, but its content is that of another kind of ordinary writing – a receipt. It records the payment of the required tax on a pack item, three saddles, which crossed the river drift that formed the border between Pondoland and Natal. Lavington Evans was the border tax collector acting on behalf of the King for goods entering, while there was a Natal official acting in respect of goods moving in the opposite direction, and many other communications from Evans are on file.

This document, then, has the conventional structure of a letter, but apart from its beginning and ending it is otherwise the spare receipt recording payment. It sits at the boundary of what is and what is not a letter and shows the dexterity with which the writers could make use of the letter format to expedite different activities in these ordinary writings.

Letter 10[23]

Harding
December 1884

Dear Sir

Owing to the rain & other causes I was unable to send you other wagon away before today. I am sorry I have no lime pine to send you. Hoping goods will arrive safely & wishing you a Merry Xmas I am

Yours truly
Horace Downey
Acct will render you at end of April

The last letter for discussion is dated December 1884 and was written by a man who worked as a blacksmith in the local area and also provided a range of other services. It has the formal attributes of a letter, beginning with an address and date, and ending with a formal signature, followed by something which is a postscript although not marked as such. Its addressee is not known but is probably O'Donnell. It is brief and grammatically correct, there are no obvious mistakes and it proficiently conveys everything needful. Its content explains a delay, states that a request for limed pine cannot be fulfilled and ends with a polite wish that things will arrive safely and that a happy Christmas will be had. Although details vary greatly, it is prototypical in showing the proficiency of the brief communications often found in the collection.

The letters in the Emagusheni collection discussed here display a number of important features worth drawing together. They are all demonstrably letters, in having a number of the formal characteristics which indicate 'the letter' rather than another form of writing. But at the same time, many have other components which means that they hover on the borders with other forms of writing. The complexities of what the writers want to convey complicate what on the surface might seem very simple communications, but which have multidimensional aspects that become apparent when considered closely.

The wide range of contributors who wrote the letters in the collection is also notable and includes many of African backgrounds as well as white; and even more notably, those who are Indigenous Africans are of a much higher status in local terms than the whites. This requires reading on two levels, in particular keeping in mind that the white presence was on a grace and favour basis and, for instance, licences could be removed or not renewed if requests were not fulfilled and 'presents' were not provided. Close scrutiny also shows the strong network aspects, which are tacitly present but are not spelled out by the writers because such things could be taken for granted by them and their addressees. This is indeed a network with close associations between the people involved; discussion has shown that all the people who wrote or were addressees of the letters discussed, and also the people mentioned in contents, were connected with each other.

The common writer and ordinary writings

What do these letters and their interconnections convey about the common writer and ordinary writings? For those whose familiarity with letters comes from those written by members of cultural and political elites (such as writers and prominent politicians) from the imperial metropoles, the Emagusheni letters may seem simplistic and lacking finesse. However, as discussion has shown, even those which are very spare in content often appear to perform complex tasks when we attend to the details of composition and content. Letters showing greater finesse would not have been able to accomplish so readily what these examples do, which is to expedite practical transactions in the context of 1880s southern Africa and in particular the circumstances prevailing in Pondoland.

This raises another point, that it is important to consider the idea of 'ordinary' writings in a context. There is no general category of 'the ordinary'; it all depends on the situation. What constituted ordinary among the intelligentsia of the imperial metropoles, for example, would not have been ordinary among the hoi polloi producing the Emagusheni letters in

Pondoland. In this context, the letters discussed here are the quintessence of ordinary writings, for they were routinely produced in great volume and were necessary to conduct the ordinary business of everyday life for the people involved and the trading station itself. Moreover, in their focussed and performative aspects they closely resemble other South African letters, which typically have very similar characteristics.[24] Time, place and context had an important impact on the structure and shape as well as on the content of the letters; not only did these factors influence the formal conventions of letter writing, and the transaction of business around this particular trading station, but also, and more generally, they influenced the response to great distances between sender and recipient and the practicalities of everyday life in the prevailing circumstances of the settler colonial presence.[25]

Earlier I commented that the Emagusheni letters call for an interrogation of the idea of the common writer itself. There are three important aspects to consider here. Firstly, the black writers represented in what is overall many hundreds of letters across the Emagusheni collection are not 'common' folk in a European sense in the 1880s period, but members of an elite group. They are educated and literate and competent users of the letter writing form, albeit with deviations or departures from conventional rules and requirements. Such departures often seem the product of specific purpose, rather than lack of knowledge or competence, and they reflect prevailing practices and conventions among the MPondo, with a key example being what might at first sight seem exaggerated expressions of politeness.

Secondly, although nominally simple, many complexities are found when looking closely at these letters. An important aspect here concerns the markers of status they contain in such things as formal names and titles, and using proxy writers acting on behalf of the person originating a letter. What comes across is that the writers or originators had an awareness of their social and political standing, and while observing polite forms they were also concerned to impress this on their addressees. They may not have been insisting on ceremony, but they do imply an awareness of status divisions and that their position in the social hierarchy was by no means inferior. This was indeed a contact zone in the analytical sense, where understandings of status and authority could be volatile, negotiable and change over time.

Thirdly, since the ground-breaking work of Thomas and Znaniecki on migrant letters, there has been an awareness that letter writing registers in a very quick way wider changes occurring in the context of writing.[26] This provides interesting insight into the trading station letters, for this period was one of great changes in the making in Pondoland and southern Africa more generally.[27] What evidence do the Emagusheni letters provide about this? It is clear that if a parallel exercise was carried out on its letters from, say, the 1920s, 1930s and 1940s, then a very different picture would emerge.²⁸ The letters would then be written predominantly by white people with higher levels of writing skills; and a smaller number by black people would be marked by imperfect literacy, rather than the proficient functional literacy that characterises the letters of the 1880s, while expressions of social confidence and politeness would be replaced by subservience markers. The mission school and Lovedale College produced educated people, whose letters are represented in the earlier period of 1883 and 1884 and focussed on here. These letter writers were harbingers of an emergent black bourgeoisie, a group that would thereafter be demolished by a series of legal and practical measures, leading first to the institutionalisation of segregation and then to the apartheid system.²⁹

This 1883–84 period in the life of the Emagusheni trading station, then, marks a particular point when the racial structure of South Africa could have developed in a very different way from how it later actually did so. The letters discussed, along with the greater number referred to in more general terms, show the complexities of the ordinary writing practices that the writers engaged in and illuminate aspects of the changes occurring, and they provide a backcloth to the changes that happened subsequently. They are uncommon letters indeed.

Notes

1 For important contributions which have influenced discussion here, see David Barton and Nigel Hall (eds), *Letter Writing as a Social Practice* (Amsterdam: John Benjamins, 2000); David Barton, Mary Hamilton and Roz Ivanic (eds), *Situated Literacies* (London: Routledge, 2000); Mary Hamilton, David Barton and Roz Ivanic (eds), *Worlds of Literacy* (London: Multilingual Matters, 1994); Martyn Lyons (ed.), *Ordinary Writings, Personal Narratives: Writing Practices in Nineteenth and Early Twentieth-Century Europe* (Bern: Peter Lang, 2007); Martyn Lyons, 'A new history from below? The writing culture of ordinary people in Europe', *History Australia*, 7:3 (2010), 60.1–60.9; Martyn Lyons, *The Writing Culture of Ordinary People in Europe, c. 1860–1920* (Cambridge, UK: Cambridge University Press, 2013); Martyn Lyons, 'Writing upwards: How the weak wrote to the powerful', *Journal of Social History*, 49:2 (2015), 317–30.

2 For insightful discussions of the development of diverse ordinary writing practices in formerly non-literate societies which have been drawn on here, see Jack Goody (ed.), *Literacy in Traditional Societies* (Cambridge, UK: Cambridge University Press, 1975); Jack Goody, *The Domestication of the Savage Mind* (Cambridge, UK: Cambridge University Press, 1977); Jack Goody, *The Logic of Writing and the Organization of Society* (Cambridge, UK: Cambridge University Press, 1986); Jack Goody, *The Interface between the Written and the Oral* (Cambridge, UK: Cambridge University Press, 1987).

3 On the 'middling sort' and other class groupings, see the key work by Margaret Hunt, *The Middling Sort: Commerce, Gender, and the Family in England, 1680–1780* (Oakland: University of California Press, 1996). Also helpful in providing a review of everyday usages is Jonathan Barry and Christopher Brooks (eds), *The Middling Sort of People: Culture, Society and Politics in England 1550–1800* (London: Macmillan, 1994).

4 For important contributions and overviews, see Karen Agutter, 'Exploring the migrant experience through an examination of letters to *The New Australian*', in Catherine Dewhirst and Paul Scully (eds), *The Transnational Voices of Australia's Migrant and Minority Press* (London: Palgrave Macmillan, 2020), pp. 151–67; Ewa Barczyk, 'Polish migrant memoirs and letters: Documenting the World War II diaspora', *Polish American Studies*, 77:2 (2020), 84–5; Marcelo Borges and Sonia Cancian (eds), *Migrant Letters: Emotional Language, Mobile Identities, and Writing Practices in Historical Perspective* (London: Routledge, 2019); Bruce Elliott, David A. Gerber and Suzanne M. Sinke (eds), *The Epistolary Practices of International Migrants* (New York: Palgrave Macmillan, 2006).

5 Important work on the Pondo economy and polity for the period under discussion which has been drawn on here includes: William Beinart, 'European traders and the Mpondo paramountcy, 1878–1886', *Journal of African History*, 20:4 (1979), 471–86; William Beinart, *The Political Economy of Pondoland 1860–1930* (Cambridge, UK: Cambridge University Press, 1982); Walter Bramwell, *Loyalties and the Politics of Incorporation in South Africa: The Case of Pondoland, c. 1870–1910*, Ph.D. thesis, University of Warwick, 2015; Norman Etherington, 'Review of the political economy of Pondoland 1860–1930', *African Affairs*, 83:330 (1984), 128–9; Timothy Stapleton, *Faku: Rulership and Colonialism in the Mapondo Kingdom, 1780–1867* (Waterloo, Canada: Wilfrid Laurier University Press, 2001). See the map in Figure 1 in Beinart, *Political Economy of Pondoland*, p. 472.

6 A useful compendium and overview of trading stations in the broad area is provided by Mike Thompson, *Traders of the Transkei* (Natal: Brevitas, 2012).

7 For the archive collection, see Gallagher Family KCM 95/11, Killie Campbell Library, Durban, South Africa. There is a helpful inventory. All references to letters in the collection come from KCM 95/11 in the Killie Campbell Library, Durban. Gallagher inherited the trading station from Michael O'Donnell, who was his maternal uncle.

8 For a helpful discussion of Lovedale College and its race politics, see Paul Rich, 'The appeals of Tuskegee: James Henderson, Lovedale, and the fortunes of South African liberalism, 1906–1930', *International Journal of African Historical Studies*, 20:2 (1987), 271–92. For a different view, focussing on protests, see Liz Stanley, 'Protest and the Lovedale Riot of 1946: "Largely a rebellion against authority"?', *Journal of Southern African Studies*, 44:6 (2018), 1039–55.

9 For the founding discussion of this concept, see Mary Louise Pratt, 'Arts of the contact zone', *Profession* (1991), pp. 33–40; Mary Louise Pratt, *Imperial Eyes: Travel Writing and Transculturation* (London: Routledge, 2007). See also Joseph Harris, 'Negotiating the contact zone', *Journal of Basic Writing*, 1:1

(1995), 27–42; Jon Stratton and Devadas Vijay, 'Identities in the contact zone', *Borderlands*, 9:1 (2010), 1–15.
10 KCM 95/11, Gallagher 7, 9278, Umhlangwaso to M. O'Donnell and J. Bouverie, 4 January 1883.
11 KCM 95/11, Gallagher 39, 9198, Unknown to M. O'Donnell, 9 March 1883.
12 Torn, and name missing; ^inserted^ words are in a different handwriting.
13 KCM 95/11, Gallagher 7, 9300, M. O'Donnell to J. Bouverie, 10 September 1883.
14 There are few letters mentioning the gun-running case, and information comes from comments in passing.
15 KCM 95/11, Gallagher 7, 9308, Mrs Umhlangwaso to Sir, 17 November 1883.
16 KCM 95/11, Gallagher 2, 9188, W. Boshoff to J. Bouverie, no date but November or December 1883.
17 KCM 95/11, Gallagher 2, 9191-2, W. Johnson to M. O'Donnell, 26 December 1883.
18 ^Inserted^ words are in a different handwriting.
19 For Shepstone's activities in Natal and Transvaal, see the detailed discussion in Thomas McClendon, *White Chief, Black Lords: Shepstone and the Colonial State in Natal, South Africa, 1845–1878* (Rochester, NY: University of Rochester Press, 2010).
20 KCM 95/11 Gallagher 3, 9216, EB Hamilton McNicholas to unknown, page/s missing, no date, but following the death of Johnson, therefore after December 1883.
21 KCM 95/11 Gallagher 8, 9343, Marsupla to J. Bouverie, 4 January 1884.
22 KCM 95/11 Gallagher 9, 6405, L. Evans to J. Bouverie, 7 November 1884.
23 KCM 95/11 Gallagher 7, 9319, H. Downey to Dear Sir, December 1884.
24 See the Whites Writing Whiteness project research at www.whiteswritingwhiteness.ed.ac.uk, accessed 9 June 2023. See also Liz Stanley, 'The scriptural economy, the Forbes figuration and the racial order: Everyday life in South Africa 1850–1930', *Sociology*, 49:5 (2015), 837–52. This discusses the key characteristics as performativity, the absence of affect and the expectation of practical responses rather than letter replies.
25 On South African settler colonial letters, see Stanley, 'The scriptural economy', pp. 837–52; Liz Stanley, 'Settler colonialism and migrant letters: The Forbes family and letter-writing in South Africa 1850-1922', *The History of the Family*, 21:3 (2016), 398–428. See also the Whites Writing Whiteness research at www.whiteswritingwhiteness.ed.ac.uk, accessed 9 June 2023.
26 The 1996 compendium edition provides a useful overview of this highly influential research, carried out in the first decade of the twentieth century. See William Isaac Thomas and Florian Znaniecki, *The Polish Peasant in Europe and America: A Classic Work in Immigration History*, ed. E. Zaretsky (Urbana: University of Illinois Press, 1996), first published 1918. For their methodological approach in particular, see Liz Stanley, 'To the letter: Thomas and Znaniecki's *The Polish Peasant* and writing a life, sociologically', *Life Writing*, 7:2 (2010), 139–51.
27 On changes in South Africa with particular regard to thinking and practice on race matters, see Paul Maylam, *South Africa's Racial Past: The History and*

Historiography of Racism, Segregation and Apartheid (London: Routledge, 2017). Also helpful is Saul Dubow, *Racial Segregation and the Origins of Apartheid in South Africa, 1919–36* (New York: Springer, 1989).

28 As shown by preliminary research on the boxes in the collection for these decades. See KCM 95/11, boxes 70 to 83.

29 For a cogent discussion of this repressive political process, see Beinart, *Political Economy of Pondoland*.

9

Madlands: Vincenzo Rabito as a writer

David Moss

Introduction

What exactly is the *Terra matta* (Madlands) which, first as a book, then a play and most recently a film, has entered into Italy's cultural life over the last fifteen years? How should we treat the book's writer, a semi-educated roadmender from Chiaramonte Gulfi in eastern Sicily who spent the years of his retirement on his autobiography and died in 1981? Although he is often taken to be a unique case, how much does what he wrote differ from the many other texts by 'primitive writers' which have appeared in recent years and have been collected in archives set up for them? How should we incorporate the editors, protagonists and directors who have brought Rabito's work further into the public domain and have given their distinctive slants to the writer's personality and life? Thanks to those people who directed and produced their own versions of what he had written, there seems to be more than a single author – and more than a single text – in public view.

I want to focus on three questions. First, how is the author portrayed, by himself and by his editors? Second, how are the resources available for publication, play and film – resources which were not available to the writer himself – used to present the work and distinguish the particular message each wants to convey? Third, given the difference between the time when Rabito was writing and the times when the play and film appear today, how is the relation between past and present portrayed in the various versions? Other questions arise but these three are the ones I shall deal with in this chapter.

Terra matta and its questions

The public history of *Terra matta* is clear. In 2007 Einaudi published under that title an abbreviated version of an untitled 1,027-page autobiography, typed in the late 1960s by Vincenzo Rabito. Rabito's original text, written between 1967 and 1970, is held at the Archivio Diaristico Nazionale (ADN) in Pieve Santo Stefano in eastern Tuscany, where it was awarded the archive's annual prize, the Premio Pieve, in 2000.[1] This prize is awarded by a combination of amateur readers and professional scholars to the best non-professional autobiographical text received in the previous year. In 2007 the version published by Einaudi, edited by the archivist Luca Ricci and the novelist Evelina Santangelo, rapidly became a bestseller, was mentioned as a possible candidate for the Premio Strega (a prestigious literary award) and has been in print in all formats ever since. In 2009 a stage version was produced by Vincenzo Pirrotta, followed in 2012 by a film (entitled *Terramatta*) directed by Costanza Quatriglio. The film was shown at the Venice Film Festival, where it won the first of several national and international prizes.

Terra matta's unsparing description of life on the brutal north-eastern front in 1917 – where Rabito had served as a member of the last group called up to fight, *i ragazzi del novantanove* (the ninety-nine boys) – earned it a special place in the centenary exhibitions in 2015 to mark Italy's entry into the First World War. Locally, the name 'Terra matta' was used to rechristen the street in Chiaramonte Gulfi where Rabito had lived and a square in Marina di Ragusa, and to provide a name for some local wines and for chocolate from nearby Modica. Thirty years after Rabito's death, one of his sons encapsulated his life and the unexpected success of his autobiography by having the term 'writer' engraved on his tombstone.

Given the current interest in life writing, this summary raises the kind of questions which are common in literary and critical studies. Are we dealing with an autobiography or perhaps a chronicle or a memoir? Why should someone usually described as semi-literate, sometimes as illiterate, have chosen to devote his retirement to producing a vast text of almost half a million words? Who was it written for and for what reasons? What sort of text did he actually write – just a confusing array of words, spellings and styles that any uneducated person would produce in a language he used to speak, or perhaps something with a more complex organisation? Why did the abbreviated text enjoy its extraordinary popular success in a post-war Italy, so vastly different from the one which Rabito described? What differences from the original text did the stage and screen versions introduce which would guarantee an equally successful impact as a play and a film? Are there specific aspects of the play and film versions – staging, music, visual features – which play their own distinctive part in showing us what the author and his life looked like? Any volume selected for Einaudi's prestigious Supercoralli series – it had published translations of works by Paul Auster, José Saramago and Philip Roth in 2007 – should surely expect to attract widespread professional interest.

Few of these questions have been addressed at any length. Reviewers have naturally praised the author's achievement in managing to write his life down at all, especially at such extraordinary length, and have recognised the documentary value of the 'history from below' in his account of wartime and colonial experiences. But 'popular literature', the category of non-professional writing into which Rabito's work falls, had rarely attracted much interest from literary scholars beyond appreciation of the writers' achievements in writing down their lives. Its texts do not belong in any literary traditions: they circulated at most only within the writer's family; and none of its writers had read any texts by their fellow members of the genre.

Those difficulties, clear enough after the book's publication, become still more complicated after 2008. Apart from the theatre and film use of the abbreviated text and their addition of the visual and aural resources of stage and screen to frame the story and its characters, the role of the interpreter is complicated by the revelation at a conference on *Terra matta* that once his son had taken away his original text, Rabito had then written a second autobiography, in a similar style but even longer, amounting to around 1,600 pages beginning from his birth and breaking off just a few days before his death.[2] The reasons for redoing his life story are not clear: Rabito never expressed them and it may be that the pleasure of typing was one he was reluctant to abandon. This second chronicle is held by the family, his sons, and is effectively out of reach for most outsiders, even for the basic task of comparison.[3] To what extent does the second version correspond to the first version? That is a tricky question. Even at the very outset the first page of the two versions gives different places for Rabito's birth, and some of the details in that second life are simply invented.[4] Indeed the famous phrase often regarded as summarising Rabito's view of his own life – 'La sua vita fu molto maletratata e molto travagliata e molto desprezata'[5] (It was a life of great ill-use, affliction and scorn) – did not appear in the second version; it is better taken as his specific comment on his mother-in-law's view of him, not a verdict on his own life. No doubt these and similar issues make for a good story, but they also lead us to wonder whether the same might be the case for many of the striking episodes recounted in the earlier version.

What is the actual documentary value of what Rabito tells about his early life, war and colonialism?

How to analyse *Terra matta*

This combination of different resources in presenting Rabito's life suggests a different object for analysis. So far the appreciation of *Terra matta* has concentrated on the single figure of Vincenzo Rabito and his remarkable achievement – his life as he describes it in his first text. But what we really have in *Terra matta* – the story that most people know – is a life story spread across three portrayals in different media. The first portrayal is Rabito's text. The original text stored at the ADN, is consultable but not removable; that makes detailed consultation and analysis extremely hard. The later autobiography, held by the family in Ragusa, is not publicly available although some extracts have been given to students for their university theses. The text that most people know is the edited version of Rabito's text, published by Einaudi. The second portrayal is the play version conceived and performed by Vincenzo Pirrotta, which has been staged in many places in Italy and overseas.[6] The third portrayal is the version used in the film, now also available on DVD and broadcast at various times on national television channels.[7] The original typescript occasionally appears in the film but only as decoration, not as an object of analysis. The two original texts are immobile and with very limited access. The third part – the media version which has probably attracted most attention – is mobile, available in Italy and overseas to anyone interested in Rabito himself but not especially keen to see what he had written. But if we are going to analyse *Terra matta*, how can this composite array of texts, each one different from the others, portrayed in a separate medium with its specific resources and worked on by different sets of participants, best be presented and the questions mentioned above addressed?

One way to understand those materials, aiming to connect the separate (and perhaps contradictory) ways in which Rabito's life has survived for us, is to treat the three texts as parts of a triptych. In effect we see what more than half a century ago the film critic André Bazin described as the future of adaptation:

> all things considered, it's possible to imagine that ... the notion of the unity of the work of art, if not the very notion of the author himself, will be destroyed. ... [T]he (literary?) critic of the year 2050 would find not a novel out of which a play and a film had been 'made', but rather a single work reflected through three different art forms, an artistic pyramid with three sides, all equal in the eyes of the critic.[8]

So instead of the standard focus on Rabito himself, we should look at *Terra matta* from a contrasting perspective – as a triptych in the form anticipated by Bazin of an overarching and hard-to-access textual original with its three descendants presented in different media.

Triptychs, mostly artistic, come in different forms. Some are sequences, the later parts commenting on the earlier ones. Others present different groups who belong to a single institution or who mark historical moments between the three parts (a standard format for religious triptychs). Some remain largely inscrutable, their intention unspecified by the artist and obscure to his later analysts. Most triptychs are the work of a single creator or at least produced by his or her studio under that creator's direction. But *Terra matta* offers something different. The edited story, the play and the film were produced in their different media by separate creators, none of whom knew either each other or Rabito himself and none of whom was from his home territory. All had read the published book and the film editors had also seen the stage version, but none of them was in contact with the others. What we therefore have are three sequences, played out differently: the man in a text (a partial version since only the first autobiography is considered); the man and music; and the text and music with visual resources.

The open text

Most reviewers treat *Terra matta* as a recent creation, begun once Vincenzo Rabito had retired and moved to Ragusa. Rabito himself is usually portrayed as self-educated and barely able to read or write. But in fact the story begins very much earlier. If we treat what he wrote as truthful – something he insists on at various points in his two texts[9] – then he was a born raconteur, keen to illustrate his life and its episodes for whatever local audiences he could find. His repertoire of experiences was large. His life between 1912 and 1945 went as follows: he began life as a boy working in the country (*caruso*) and then was called up as a soldier on the eastern front near the river Piave; after the war he worked in a tomato factory and then became a skilled worker digging stone, worked for several years on laying the rail tracks on the line ending in Chiaramonte Gulfi and spent two years or so in Africa working in the countryside; then he spent part of the Second World War years in Germany as a helper in a mining area, then went back to Chiaramonte for countryside work, and finally achieved (as a married man) the position of roadmender there, which he held until retirement. Materials for entertaining stories are therefore likely to have been in abundance for someone who took himself and his colleagues both seriously and ironically.

In fact both versions of *Terra matta* have plenty of references to his reading and writing as well as visits to theatres. He appreciated the visits he made to Florence immediately after the war's end, as with the electric light one could read the newspaper.[10] Likewise, in his second autobiography he recalled how a hospital visit to Trapani and help from its Red Cross nurses enabled him to read and write, building on his initial introduction when he tried to copy what his elder sister was writing for school. Likewise his later relations with his sons away on service leave or at university were pursued by weekly letters on his part. His letters may of course have been brief and basic, but their very existence suggests someone for whom writing was not unfamiliar. Similarly, his regular attendance at one of the three cultural clubs in Chiaramonte's main square, where newspapers were a staple diet, again suggests that even the reading of the day's events was quite common. There is of course most of the first version devoted to his work and travel, but surprisingly little about sex and women. These issues, always tied to particular people, appear more regularly in his second autobiography, something which his son Giovanni identifies as part of a broadening stance towards life as well as the assumption of his role as a writer addressing anonymous readers.[11] Moreover, during the last twenty years of his life he kept a small diary, noting down briefly the events of each day – but they and the letters he had received were all destroyed by his widow after his death. So the two versions of his life story are all we have of Rabito's life history.

There remains the question of why he should have given *Terra matta* a form so different from the standard norms and styles of writing. The original text occupied 1,027 mostly A4 pages, each with up to fifty lines of text, with no breaks at all between paragraphs or sentences, no capitals or apostrophes, no spaces above, below or beside the text, no proper use of the punctuation – semicolons, commas, question marks or exclamation marks – with which Rabito separated almost every word (see Figure 9.1).[12] Each group of fifty pages, written on both sides, was then put into a folder which he bound, and he occasionally gave it a title (e.g. 'la guerra'). The same format was used for the second autobiography, mostly A5 pages, occupying eighteen folders, of which one, *Cantastorie*, told stories of love, betrayal and vendetta that he had heard from a travelling storyteller in Florence, and another contained a third version of what would become *Terra matta*. Rabito had read the tales of chivalry and *Il conte di Monte Cristo* as well as having regular contact with the newspapers. We can therefore assume that his writing – the use of Italian, Sicilian and personal coinings for his terms, plus the punctuation (using the four marks from the bottom left keys of the Olivetti typewriter) – was not entirely eccentric, despite the varied ways in which, even on the same page, he wrote down terms like 'Sicily'.

So is this really something recognisable as an autobiography? Rabito mostly uses the term *portamemoria* (memory marker) to describe what he is doing – compiling a record of events that are, in his words, truthful. He acknowledges that his wife will certainly be upset by the harsh comments he makes about her own kin.[13] In fact, of autobiographic material relating to the author there is not very much, very little that will help us decide what sort of person he was. He acknowledges his own readiness to get angry and to fight on behalf of what he sees as dishonest to himself, but his readiness to confront the dangers to Italian society is limited. He mentions some of the major events but, as in the case of the murder of Moro, confines himself to a brief deprecation.[14] In politics, he gave his vote to

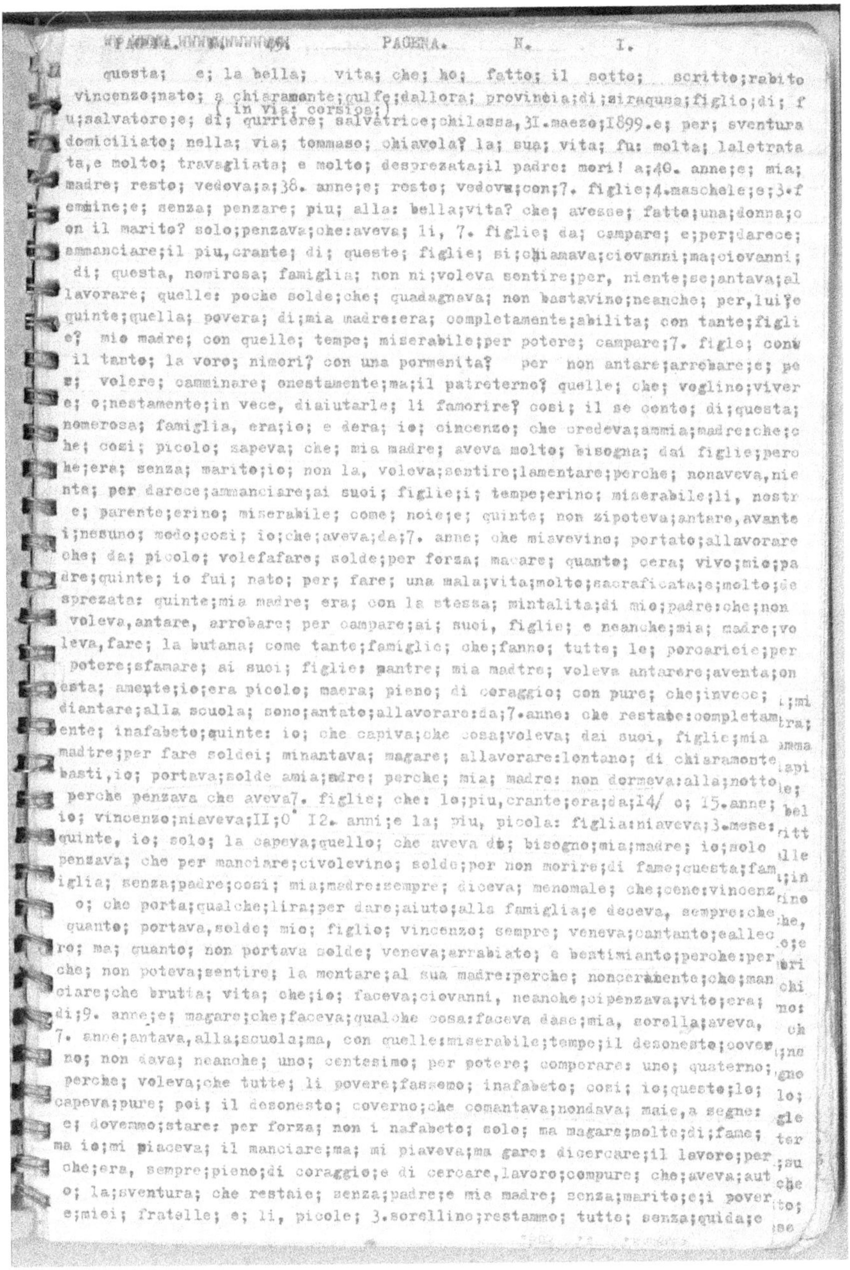

Figure 9.1 Vincenzo Rabito's autobiography, p. 1. All rights reserved and permission to use the figure must be obtained from the copyright holder, Giovanni Rabito.

several different parties – two of his older sons stood locally for Democrazia Cristiana (Christian Democrats) and for Movimento Sociale Italiano (the neo-Fascist Italian Social Movement) – but his book contains no detail on any local political figure or event; he himself never stood for office nor took any active role in his town's public life. He had no individual perspective that he wanted his autobiography to promote, nor did he want his descriptions of life in rural Sicily to be transmitted to successor generations – these are the two classic routes to animate why people decide to write down (parts of) their lives.

On the page

How could this massive text be turned into something that a publisher would seriously consider, given that his son had already tried to do so without success? Once the Pieve Prize had been awarded, the animator of the move towards eventual publication of the text was Luca Ricci, the senior archivist at the ADN. He had no theoretical skills in editing but had the valuable experience of turning several texts into publishable pieces. He secured investment from outside funders (in particular from the Neapolitan shipowner, Lucio Zagari, who had already had contact with the ADN), who agreed to provide ten million lire to support his work on the transcription of Rabito's text. Identifying two possibilities – publication by a large commercial company or by a specialist enterprise interested in linguistics – Ricci opted to produce an edition which could have been used by either possible destinee. He identified 532 specific episodes that Rabito described – on work, war and the colonial enterprise – and decided to cut out around half of them, reducing the work by about half. Much of what he excluded were sections with an incomplete or confusing narrative, alongside many pages vilifying his mother-in-law and his wife for their treatment of him. Sending his copy out had no greater success than Giovanni Rabito had had, with publishing houses either acknowledging the value of the text but maintaining it could not be published or failing to reply altogether. The only positive response came from Einaudi, whose fiction editor, Paola Gallo, agreed to publish it provided that further work was done by the Einaudi novelist and editorial consultant Evelina Santangelo, herself from Palermo.[15]

Santangelo's first response to the text in 2004 was bafflement, confronted by Rabito's eccentric prose and style. However, her further work in turning the text into literature identified three specific dimensions: Rabito's expressive language ('il rabitese'); the identification of key moments ('le radure'); and the vision, ascribed to Rabito, that he considered his text as a 'casa', a home where he could finally and uniquely describe himself and what he had lived through in his own terms. Each of these raised problems. First, the focus on Rabito's writing pushed her into acknowledging the author's skill in bringing out the narrative power in the moments, well described elsewhere, that shaped his view of the world. Keeping his irony and intelligence as central features was essential, preventing his text from becoming simply a display of the editor's skills. Second, the focus on the 'radure' (clearings) was a way of ignoring many of Rabito's preliminary and confusing attempts to get it right and bringing out the narrative power of his descriptions. Third was the sense that the text (and of course its first oral version to local audiences) was Rabito's way of presenting his life and his ambitions as what he really felt. Santangelo identified the many attempts by Rabito to create a home – in Africa, in Chiaramonte Gulfi – and noted that he had regularly encountered difficulties and threats that he could resist but not finally overcome. His text, written in his own house in Ragusa, represented his 'last home', a place in which he has, however inconsistently his writing achieves this, the final say over what goes in. He insists at many points on the truth of what he is writing and on the difficulties that it will cause his wife and her family.[16] But for his editor, there lies the key narrative power that his text had to convey. 'Listen to the voice which animates the text' – that was what the founding father of the ADN, Saverio Tutino, advised the readers and that was the idea that Ricci and Santangelo agreed to follow.

This edition of Rabito's text, under the title *Terra matta*, appeared in midsummer of 2007. It was immediately received with unexpected plaudits, becoming a best-seller (15,000 hardback copies were sold in three months) and remaining in Einaudi's catalogue as hardback, paperback and e-edition ever since. In fact, this published text – which Rabito never saw or approved of – differed in its spelling, punctuation, organisation and balance of events from what he had actually written. Nonetheless, it made Rabito's text readable, indeed accessible to many Italians who would not have been able, or interested in trying, to follow the largely inaccessible original. The only detours followed by the editors have been legal: names and places have been replaced in order to prevent the descendants of some of those named from considering legal action against Rabito's heirs.[17]

What Ricci and Santangelo have done is to provide a script for versions on both stage and screen, effectively a text in Italian, with terms from Sicilian interspersed here and there but followable by anyone knowing Italian. But because of the text's openness, the messages of each version of Rabito's work are rather different. Consider the titles which have been given to it since Rabito himself left it untitled. In the ADN library, Rabito's original text is called *Fontanazza*, a title proposed by his son Giovanni, who used the name of the hamlet where Rabito's parents had worked and who thought that the contents echoed Silone's classic account of peasant life, *Fontamara*.[18] The version sent to Einaudi by Ricci and Santangelo from the

ADN in 2005 was called *Terra matta in Sicilia*, but the publisher, not wanting to give it too regional a connotation, reduced that to *Terra matta*, using a term found a few times in the text. The film is different again. Its title, *Terramatta: Il Novecento italiano di Vincenzo Rabito analfabeta siciliano* (Italy's twentieth century as seen by the illiterate Sicilian Vincenzo Rabito), gives a national perspective in 2012 on what had previously been signalled as a local and then a regional matter. In this last case, the value of the newsreel and other material gives Rabito's own description a solid basis.

On the stage

Terra matta first appeared on stage in March 2009 at the Teatro Stabile in Catania (Sicily). Its creator and protagonist in the role of Rabito was Vincenzo Pirrotta, an *autore-attore* (author-actor) from Partinico in western Sicily, and an innovator in theatrical production, interested in particular in how major European texts can be translated into Sicilian drama. This is partly because of his double theatrical apprenticeship, first as a graduate of the Istituto Nazionale del Dramma Antico and then as a disciple of Mimmo Cutticchio, who has worked with Sicilian puppets and puppet theatre. The combination of classical training and folk culture gives Pirrotta's work a special attraction. His achievements have been acknowledged by Chiaramonte Gulfi, which made him an honorary citizen in June 2016 and permitted him to stage a performance of *Terra matta* locally. It was performed again in the same year in Catania and has travelled to other Italian cities and abroad.

Watching Pirrotta dance onto the stage in the opening sequence, bursting with life, reveals a key to how the central character is going to be played. The enthusiasm with which he begins to recount his life from the earliest age, his work, his local bosses and so on, brings an animation to his performance which is very different from the slightly more relaxed style of the autobiography. This is a Rabito full of verve, a 'ragazzo piccolo ma pieno di coraggio' (just a little boy but one full of courage) as he describes himself, ready to handle the awkward moments which confront him and to ensure the outcome is the least damaging possible. The things that inspired Rabito Pirrotta takes as grotesque, performing accordingly with exaggerated movement of the body and demonstrating this through the absurd costumes of other characters and the theatrical staging of their interactions.[19] Humour, usually in the form of irony, is present throughout. This form of theatre occupies the full ninety minutes of the show – the cavortings, the occasional charm when Rabito meets his beloved mother, the lethal murders of the two world wars. In effect the action covers only the first part of his life, up to the end of the war – thereafter his life at home as a roadmender is ignored, as is the intensity of his relation with his mother-in-law, who had died in 1951 but is proclaimed by Rabito himself as the reason for trying to set the record straight so many years later.

Representing the world through which Rabito travelled, the stage provides the circuit for the events. The central area, occupied by Rabito, is surrounded by a partly raised platform on which the external actors appear. In particular the barber and the carabiniere, characters not part of Rabito's text but invented by Pirrotta, take up roles which bring the external world and its powers onto the stage. The stage is a symbol of Rabito and his world. It also provides space for one of the topics in the young Rabito's life: music – his involvement in informal groups that played music in private houses and barber shops after hours.[20] Mentions of this appear regularly in the text but it becomes a critical dimension in the very different stage and screen versions. Music – eighteen separate pieces played by up to five musicians, directed by Luca Mauceri and composing principally violin, cello, piano, drums and an accordion – follows Rabito's life essentially up to 1945, ignoring his later life when he became employed as a roadmender at Chiaramonte Gulfi. The titles of the pieces make this clear: *In viaggio* (On my way), *Un vero catanese* (A real Catanese), *nostalgia di Chiaramonte* (nostalgia for Chiaromonte) and so on. In the first piece, the tensions create a waltz with elements of both melancholy and irony, and this junction of tragic and comic elements is maintained throughout the pieces.

On the screen

The film, entitled, as mentioned earlier, *Terramatta: Il Novecento italiano di Vincenzo Rabito analfabeta siciliano*, was first presented at the Venice Film Festival of 2012 in the Young Films section, where it was awarded the first of several prizes. The prospect of turning Rabito's autobiography into a film had originally been proposed by Chiara Ottaviano, co-founder of a small public history organisation, Cliomedia Officina, in Turin. She had suggested the idea of a film to the Taviani brothers (acclaimed filmmakers) but had not been able to persuade them.[21] In her subsequent meeting with the director Costanza Quatriglio, she had found a willing enthusiast. Quatriglio had already produced several films – including *Écosaimale?* in 2000 and *L'isola* (The island) in 2003 – which made the life of a central character the key element. Many of those characters were awkward marginals, unable to place themselves well in their local societies, almost invisible in many respects, sometimes children, sometimes fishermen. In this respect the figure of Vincenzo Rabito was extremely appropriate – someone exposed to every kind of difficulty but determined to come out on top and able, in his autobiography, to see the various, usually conflicting, aspects in those situations. As he himself said, 'Se all'uomo in questa vita con ci incontro avventure non ave nienta darracontare' (If a man has no adventures in this life, he has got no stories to tell). The story that he wrote contains many different *avventure* in which he finds himself in serious trouble but which he can surmount, often full of acknowledgements of his own disasters, with at least some semblance of his worth intact.

What sort of film could be made of this long autobiography? Ottaviano's first idea was to use *Heimat* – the fictional story of families brought into a war in which they were on the margins – as a model. However, the costs of such a film were going to be prohibitive and rejection by the Taviani brothers meant this idea had to be revised. Discussions with Quatriglio, who had experience in making documentary films, pushed the idea of a documentary to the forefront, using Rabito's memories as the basis of the film and engaging personal participation by inhabitants of Chiaramonte and Ragusa. The film's concern therefore is with the representation that Rabito made of his life, not the life that he actually lived. Indeed Quatriglio has indicated that it is the 'materiality' of the text that attracted her and that the wonder she experienced in seeing it was something that she wanted to convey to the film's spectators. As Quatriglio says, 'The true key to making the film ... was the materiality of the writing'.[22] The key to the film is therefore the autobiography itself, pages of which are shown immediately and in close-up to get the viewers to appreciate the heavy-handedness of the writing (this was the first time Rabito had used a typewriter for anything beyond a letter). Sometimes the images are solid and point us to the term that is used to define each of the sixteen chapters from which the film is composed. At other times the text is diaphanous, drifting across other images so that reality and its representation by Rabito are interlinked – a particular case is the river Isonzo, full of corpses when Rabito was a soldier there, but placed in a kind of rural calm when he returns fifty years later to see the place again.

What is particularly important is the deliberate intention to give the text a timeless quality, remote from the world and essentially invisible. Nothing is said about its origins, nor about the involvement of Rabito in the writing nor about the ways in which what Rabito wrote has been transformed into an Einaudi bestseller. The originals are essentially out of reach for most spectators: Rabito's original, *Fontanazza*, in the library at Pieve Santo Stefano; his second version, *Terra matta* no. 2, in the possession of his sons. The film reveals nothing of the relations between Rabito and his mother-in-law – she died in 1951 but her bitter quarrels with Rabito are not mentioned at all except for an elliptical comment that his marriage to her daughter was the worst moment of his life. The text is certainly a *portamemoria* for Rabito but at several points he returns to the idea of correcting his mother-in-law's apparently appalling vilifications.[23] It is a tricky issue since his mother-in-law came from a complicated family. In effect, following her elder sisters' examples, she had been the third lover of a local notary with whom she had produced three children, adding to those she had had with her husband.

This situation had presented her with a number of difficulties, and she then vented her frustration on her son-in-law, whom she regarded as inferior to the social class of her other children. He had been ignorant of all this when he married her daughter, but soon discovered the ways in which he had been tricked.

In dramatic contrast to the stage version, Rabito himself only appears in a brief episode at a party in his house. His voice is taken by Roberto Nobile, an actor with a considerable reputation spanning many different kinds of production. Although born in Verona, he had been brought up in Ragusa, where he became a close friend of Rabito's son Giovanni. He had also been able to see pages of what Rabito had written and the versions then attempted by his son. His voice, hoarse but brilliantly evocative, recounts the events in Rabito's words, taking very much the stance of someone looking back on what had happened with a strong sense of irony, even at his own expense. In particular, Rabito impresses the viewer with his determination to ensure that his sons are educated properly, since he knows that education is the way ahead in this 'belle ebiche' (these fine times) that had transformed Italy in the post-war years. Rabito here is audible but not visible, someone who is looking backwards rather than forwards, as indeed the opening sequence of the film – the hammering of typewriter keys on the heavily pitted pages – suggests. In this respect, what becomes visible is the text itself, which Quatriglio hopes will induce in the viewer the kind of wonder that she herself felt in front of it. We glance at the pages as they are presented on the screen and marvel at the energy that it must have taken Rabito to produce them.

The music throughout the film reproduces an international focus, taking us away from Chiaramonte Gulfi and projecting us into the world far beyond. As the composer of the music, Paolo Buonvino, says, the musical styles adopted were deliberately very different:[24] church bells, pop songs and electronic music all appear, their conjunction ready to immerse the viewer in two ways. First, there is almost nothing which gives away the regional origins of Rabito's life. There is a complete contrast with the music on the stage, essentially Sicilian and full of both instrumental music and content from that repertoire. Second, the mixture of ancient and modern music, juxtaposed without further comment, leads us to the impression of a strange illustration of past and present.

Some other examples of the contrast between past and present: the view of Gorizia in 1920, destroyed by war, is immediately followed by a view of the contemporary city, full of people and traffic; a brief portrait of Sicilian agriculture in the 1950s is followed by contemporary scenes of a very distant world; and the slow observation of a Fascist building from a contemporary highway is accompanied by the triumphal sound of Mussolini's voice. This intertwining of past and present in the same images is one of the ways in which Rabito and his text are brought to life today, regardless of the times of his youth, now long ago, that he is recounting.

About 40 per cent of the film is devoted to archival clips and photos from the years 1915–68, mainly shots from wartime and colonial Africa. This realistic base, taken mainly from resources at the Istituto Luce and the Archivio Audiovisivo del Movimento Operaio e Democratico as well as from several local photographers (Giuseppe Leone in particular), provides Rabito's story with the weight of a history inscribed in the national archives. But alongside the historical element comes a wealth of images of people directly connected with Rabito – notably his sons – and while not asked to comment on his writing, they provide a sense of the local realism which is vital for the text. In this way, national and local realisms can coincide, supporting whatever interpretation Rabito himself makes. In fact, his text more or less declines any particular political perspective. He voted for different parties in different elections but little of the text gives any serious impression of deep understanding of political life.

The uniqueness of *Terra matta*

How exceptional is Rabito's text? Reviewers, mostly in the cultural pages of newspapers, have generally reckoned it to be unique; others have taken a different view. For example, Antonio Gibelli, founder of the Ligurian Archive of Popular Writing in Genoa, has declared *Terra matta* 'tutt'altro che un fenomeno isolato e inspiegabile, semmai il prodotto di una pratica diffusa' (anything but an isolated and inexplicable phenomenon, rather the product of a widely diffused practice).[25] Given that such writings are non-professional (the Genoa archive contains mainly letters home from ordinary soldiers and emigrants), preserved by the goodwill of descendants, it is impossible to say just how diffused the practice of keeping a written record of one's life was and how often individuals made such records. If we take the case of the ADN, we find that it received 6,472 texts in the thirty odd years between 1984 (the year of its foundation) and mid-2012. They are texts written by people of many different kinds: aristocrats, professionals, workers, military officers, criminals, drug addicts, peasants, artisans and the victims of domestic, terrorist or wartime violence. If we confine our sample to the forty-four people from Rabito's region with a similar lack of educational experience, we find that they provided 15 per cent of 375 texts from Sicily received by the ADN. How diffuse this experience was is hard to say, although we can deduce that recording in writing some feature of one's life was by no means exceptional. Rabito's text is perhaps rather longer than most, although half of the others received ran to at least 100 pages, seven to more than 300 pages, and one to 12,100 pages.[26] But it is at least on standard paper, different in that way from Clelia Marchi's description of her life on a double bedsheet or from Carmelo Campanella's writing down parts of his life on pieces of old sacking.[27]

Terra matta is not the first text of its kind to be treated with national acclaim. Einaudi published an earlier non-professional account, Tommaso Bordonaro's La spartenza (The departure) (1991) dealing with his life between Sicily and the USA, and Il Mulino provided Sbirziola's Fovero, onesto e gentiluomo. Un emigrante in Australia 1954–1961 (2012).[28] The works of Pietro Ghizzardi (1906–86), a self-taught worker from Viadana in Reggio Emilia, offer us his view on the world; his autobiography, Mi richordo anchora (I still remember) (2016), has been published and his paintings have been exhibited.[29] The ADN has long had an arrangement with a publishing house, currently Milan's Terre di Mezzo Editore, to publish the winners of its annual prize, although in most cases these are only very rarely semi-literate authors like Rabito. Where Terra matta is unusual is, first, in how widely it has been treated in different media and, second, how many awards that both the text and the film have gained. The award of the Premio Pieve for Rabito's text, plus the several awards (national and international) that the film has achieved, give Terra matta a special place in the world of non-professional writing.

One reason for this is external. Einaudi published the text in 2007, the play was launched in 2009, and the film appeared in 2012. This period coincided with the preparations to commemorate Italy's entry into the First World War in 1915; here Rabito's early life history has a special place. A considerable proportion of the text dealt with grassroots life at the front on the Piave, where Rabito had been a private assigned to the collection of Italian corpses. His stories of his 'avventure' there gave the film a special place, which is why it was selected for the museum display commemorating 1915 in Rome. No other account of the war at the grassroots level could match Rabito's often terrifying picture, although there are many small-scale portrayals, especially in letters, about the war.[30] Indeed, the play and film were reduced – to ninety minutes and seventy-six minutes, respectively – so that the proportion devoted to the war in each becomes larger, especially in the film, where the insertion of external scenes adds to the portrayal. At such length, the views of someone from the world of south-east Sicily, far from the front and its local cultures, offers a particular portrait of what the war was like. Rabito's description of what he had to do, often resulting in considerable disrespect to others and to himself, is a unique picture of life on the trenches, day in, day out.

As the title of this paper notes, Rabito is commonly described as a writer, and that is how most of the people who know his name think of him. But as we have seen, the words that people have read or listened to are not those that Rabito wrote. Those words are preserved in texts in two places – at the ADN and by the Rabito family – which makes detailed analysis and discussion of them very difficult. Those original texts are essentially reliquaries from whose presence the three public versions of the text – page, stage and screen – are derived.[31] Moreover, even when we take the three derivatives themselves, we can see that the interpretations by the editors and directors offer very different views of Rabito himself. He left us two texts, written with himself as the reader; and while he surely would not have disapproved of what has been made of them, he would have been pleased that his voice, if not the words he had typed, had reached a wider audience than he could ever have imagined.

Notes

I would like to express my gratitude to many people who have helped me to better understand Vincenzo Rabito and his text. In particular my thanks go to Chiara Ottaviano, Costanza Quatriglio, Luca Ricci, Vincenzo Pirrotta, Natalia Cangi, Evelina Santangelo and Paola Gallo, and to Rabito's sons, Turi, Tano and Giovanni, for their unstinting help.

1. For a brief account in English of this archive and the annual prize, see Martyn Lyons, *The Writing Culture of Ordinary People in Europe, c.1860–1920* (Cambridge, UK: Cambridge University Press, 2013), pp. 28–32; see also the ADN's website: http://archiviodiari.org/, accessed 9 June 2023.
2. A detailed account of the language used by Rabito in this second text is provided by Laura Brignon, *Traduire la litterature brute: le second tapuscrit de Vincenzo Rabito*, Ph.D. thesis, Universite Toulouse-le-Mirail – Toulouse II, 2017).
3. I am very grateful to Giovanni Rabito and Laura Brignon for access to photocopies of the full second version.
4. David Moss, 'Vincenzo Rabito's *Autobiography No. 2*: An interview with Giovanni Rabito', *Journal of Modern Italian Studies*, 19:3 (2014), 309–10.
5. Vincenzo Rabito, *Terra matta* (Turin: Einaudi, 2007), p. 3.
6. A later play, the first in a three-part series, was invented and performed by Stefano Panzeri. It has been presented in several places, but I will not be considering it here.
7. At the time of writing (February 2022), there is a provisional agreement to produce a new film of *Terra matta* with an Italo-American company and Gabriele Salvatores as the possible director.
8. André Bazin, *Bazin at Work: Major Essays and Reviews from the Forties and Fifties* (London: Routledge, 1997), pp. 49–50.
9. David Moss, 'Introduction', *Journal of Modern Italian Studies*, 19:3 (2014), 223–40, p. 226.
10. Rabito, *Terra matta*, p. 136.
11. Moss, 'Vincenzo Rabito's *Autobiography No. 2*', p. 311.
12. Moss, 'Introduction', p. 225.
13. Vincenzo Rabito, *Autobiography No. 2* (Unpublished typescript), p. 1449.
14. Aldo Moro, a leading Christian Democrat politician and former prime minister, was kidnapped, held for ransom and eventually murdered by the Red Brigades in 1978.

15 Ricci's detailed account of his work is outlined in Luca Ricci and Evelina Santangelo, 'From *Fontanazza* to *Terra matta*', *Journal of Modern Italian Studies*, 19:3 (2014), 252–67. The following details from Santangelo's work are also taken from there.
16 Moss, 'Vincenzo Rabito's *Autobiography No. 2*'.
17 Ricci and Santangelo, 'From *Fontanazza* to *Terra matta*', p. 260.
18 Ignazio Silone, *Fontamara* (Harmondsworth, UK: Penguin, 1934), first published 1933.
19 Stefania Rinini, *Le maschere non si scelgono a caso* (Corazzano: Titivillus, 2015), p. 97.
20 Gaetano Pennino and Maurizio Piscopo (eds), *Musica dai saloni. Suoni e memorie dei barbieri di Sicilia* (Palermo: Nuova Ipsa Editore, 2009).
21 Chiara Ottaviano, 'From *Terra matta* to *Terramatta*; and beyond', *Journal of Modern Italian Studies*, 19:3 (2014), 268–83.
22 Bernadette Luciano and Susanna Scarparo, 'Directing *Terramatta*. An interview with Costanza Quatriglio', *Journal of Modern Italian Studies*, 19:3 (2014), 284–92, p. 287; see also Alessandro Puglisi, 'L'epica del quotidiano. Intervista a Costanza Quatriglio', *Sul Romanzo*, 3:4 (2013), 74–8.
23 Rabito, *Terra matta*, p. 225.
24 Maria Lombardo, 'Paolo Buonvino. Partitura per macchina da scrivere', *La Sicilia* (9 August 2012), 24.
25 Antonio Gibelli, 'Antonio Sbirziola: fatica del vivere e forza della scrittura', introduction to Antonio Sbirziola, *Fovero, onesto e gentiluomo. Un emigrante in Australia, 1954–1961* (Bologna: Il Mulino, 2012), p. 19, note 12.
26 This monster text claimed to retail how many times the author, Antonio Sileci from Grammichele, had betrayed his wife over the past eight years and the strategies he used to hide his betrayals. The most valuable source on the ADN's library is Luca Ricci (ed.) *Archivio diaristico nazionale: Inventario*, vols 1 and 2 (Rome: Ministero per i beni e la attivita culturali: Direzione generale per gli archivi, 2003), which provides a brief summary of the content of every item.
27 Clelia Marchi, *Il tuo nome sulla neve. Gnanca na busia* (Milan: Il Saggiatore, 2014); Campanella, a former cow herder who died aged ninety in 2022, used pieces of sacking (which he called 'i papiri di carta') to set down his thoughts on life, stories and poetry. A brief account can be found in Marta Occhipinti, 'Storia del contadino che scriveva memorie sui sacchi di carta', *La Repubblica*, 22 February 2022, p. 12. Fuller accounts, by Chiara Ottaviano and Gianni Guastella, can be found at the Archivo degli Iblei's website: www.archiviodegliiblei.it, accessed 9 June 2023.
28 Tommaso Bordonaro, *La spartenza* (Turin: Einaudi, 1991); Sbirziola, *Fovero, onesto e gentiluomo*.
29 Pietro Ghizzardi, *Mi richordo ancora* (Macerata: Quodlibet, 2016).
30 Excellent accounts of many different kinds which reflect the war's impact are held in the Archivio della Scrittura Popolare in Trento.
31 David Moss, '*Terra matta* on the screen: Film in the form of reliquary', *Flinders University Languages Group Online Review*, 5:1 (2016), 9–17.

10

Copying, citing and creative rewriting: the transmission of texts and ideas in Finnish handwritten newspapers

Kirsti Salmi-Niklander and Risto Turunen

Introduction

The historical study of texts circulating between newspapers, journals and books has gained momentum during the last decade, mainly because of the wider 'digital turn' in humanities.[1] The combination of cheap computing power, mass digitisation of original sources and novel tools of computational analysis has enabled scholars to form a better understanding of printed texts moving across time and space. Recent findings show, for example, that 'scissor-and-paste journalism' – taking texts from other sources and reprinting or re-editing them with or without citing the original source – was not a temporary phenomenon at the beginning of print capitalism, but rather a practice characterising modernity at large.[2] In fact, the volume of text reuse in the press seems to have increased between the late eighteenth and the early twentieth centuries.[3]

Digital approaches to the history of text reuse have thus far focussed on printed materials, but in this chapter, we scrutinise the relation between printed and handwritten newspapers. Our analysis shows how texts taken from the printed word were reproduced in Finnish handwritten newspapers in the early twentieth century. There are a few occasional observations on the nature of text reuse in handwritten newspapers,[4] but the evidence is still patchy because tracing text reuse effectively would require that all relevant sources were in machine-readable form. By combining systematic distant reading of large digital corpora consisting of printed texts and careful close reading of handwritten newspapers, this chapter serves as a step towards the big picture of text transmission between printed and manuscript media.

Handwritten newspapers bloomed in many rising civil societies and communities of Europe and North America in the course of the long nineteenth century, when increased mass literacy, the diversification of organisational life and expansion of democratic ideals invited common people to express their ideas in public.[5] The handwritten newspaper was probably the most easily accessible public medium for the common people who did not write for a living, and whose own writing differed too much from the standard literary language to be published in print.[6] Thus, studying handwritten newspapers can reveal the role of ordinary men and women in the making of modern 'viral' culture, where texts, ideas and objects began to spread at an accelerating pace.[7]

In Finland, handwritten newspapers were edited in upper- and middle-class families, in schools and in student societies during the nineteenth century. They were adopted in popular movements (the temperance movement, the agrarian youth movement and the labour movement) at the end of the nineteenth century. The heyday of handwritten newspapers can be dated to the early twentieth century, when they were edited in hundreds of local communities in Finland.[8] This was a relatively late period for the widespread use of the manuscript medium compared with many other countries. The long-lived popularity of handwritten newspapers was due to both political events (the censorship and restrictions on political activity during the so-called Russification periods, and the rise of the labour movement) and strengthening literacy.

We will focus on two handwritten newspapers edited during this period: *Valistaja* (Enlightener), published in the industrial town of Högfors (since 1929 Karkkila) in southern Finland in 1914–25; and *Kuritus* (Discipline), published in the agricultural village of Niinivedenpää in eastern Finland in 1909–11 (see figures 10.1 and 10.2). Both papers were part of the vibrant literary culture of the Finnish labour movement – *Valistaja* was the organ of the local social democratic youth organisation, founded in 1906, and *Kuritus* operated formally under the debating society of the local workers' association, founded in 1909.

Writing and editing handwritten newspapers was a collective process, since several people participated in the creation of individual texts. Each issue was supposed to have at least an editor-in-chief and, if possible, one or two assistant editors. The number of contributors (people sending submissions) varied, and pseudonyms were commonly used.[9] According to archival sources, ninety-nine young people, fifty-eight men and forty-one women were involved in the production of *Valistaja* between 1914 and 1925.[10] In *Kuritus*, most texts could not be linked to a specific person because of pseudonyms and anonymous writing, but, in general, men seemed to write about twice as often as women.[11]

The texts of *Kuritus* and *Valistaja* were produced as one single manuscript copy and published by being read out aloud at meetings and social evenings. This was a common practice for Finnish handwritten newspapers. The contributions were expected to be original, but many texts were in fact copied or modified from printed periodicals or books, as our analysis shows

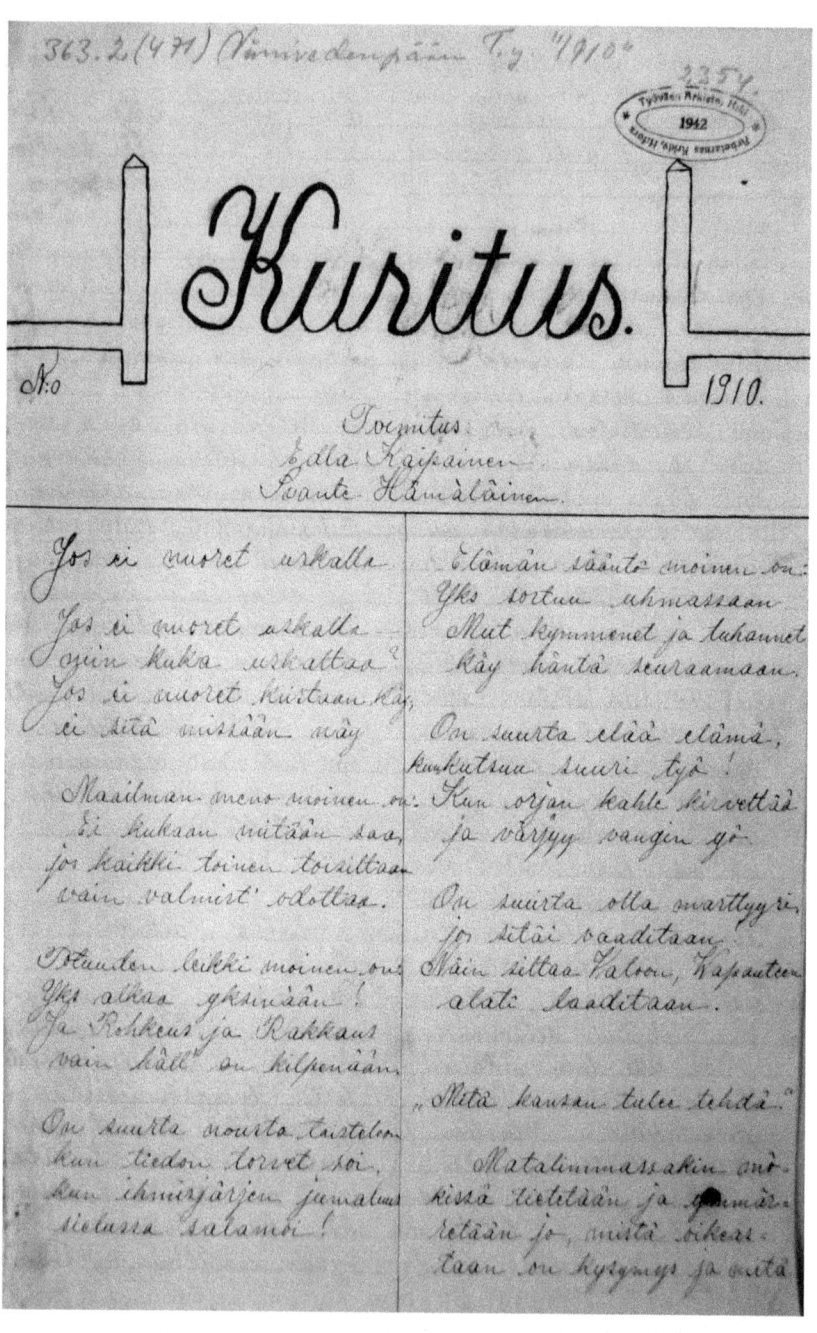

Figure 10.1 *Kuritus*, 21 August 1910 (Työväen Arkisto – Finnish Labour Archives – photo Risto Turunen). All rights reserved and permission to use the figure must be obtained from the copyright holder.

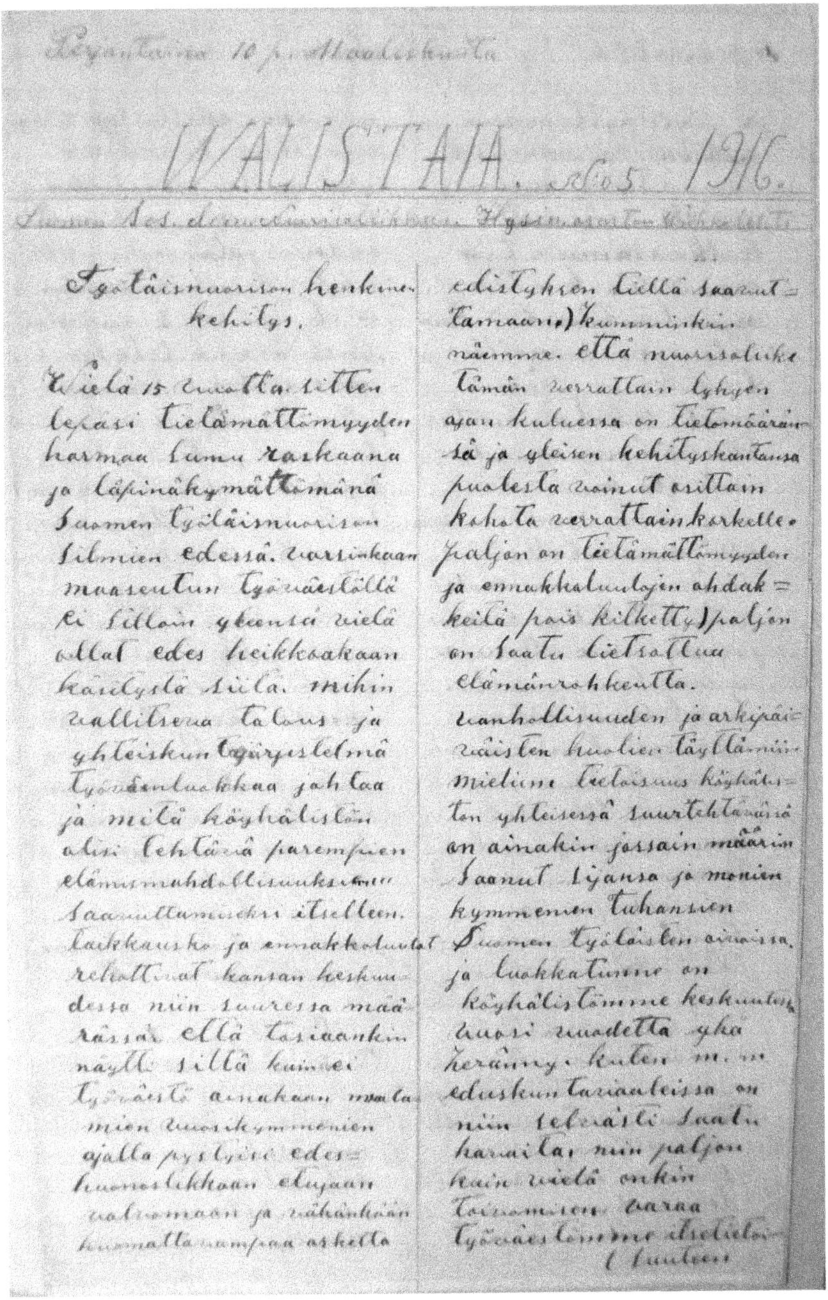

Figure 10.2 *Valistaja*, 10 March 1916 (Työväen Arkisto – Finnish Labour Archives – photo Risto Turunen). All rights reserved and permission to use the figure must be obtained from the copyright holder.

in the following pages. A large part of the texts in *Kuritus* and *Valistaja* are 'original' in the sense that they depict and discuss local events, or present individual reflections of political events or tensions in the community. Intertextual links to literature and the printed press can be observed in these essays, commentaries and 'local event narratives'.[12]

To understand the scale and quality of text reproduction among common writers, we have analysed all handwritten texts published in *Valistaja* in 1914–15 (153 texts in twenty-one issues and two fragments) and in *Kuritus* in 1909–11 (270 texts in thirty-three issues). Our quantitative analysis provides basic information on the extent of text reuse, the main sources of textual loans and the average time intervals between publication of the original texts and their reproductions. We have included in the analysis both those texts which were copied directly or almost directly and more creative re-editions and reproductions. In our qualitative analysis, we study more closely some individual texts to shed more light on the quantitative findings. We are especially interested in those smaller and bigger variations that took place when texts moved from print to the handwritten media.[13]

The big picture of text reproduction

In order to find text reproductions effectively, we read every text published in our handwritten newspapers and then used key word searches in the digital collections of the National Library of Finland. In most cases, the original text could not be found with the title given in the handwritten version, so we had to search for individual key words or combinations of key words. Table 10.1 summarises the main results of our quantitative analysis. In our dataset of two handwritten newspapers, the share of texts that are reused, measured by the number of reused texts (regardless of their length) divided by the number of all texts published, was 18.9 per cent for *Valistaja* and 15.6 per cent for *Kuritus*. The number of reused texts is greater than we initially expected (29 for *Valistaja* and 42 for *Kuritus*), and the true amount is even higher, for not all the possible original sources are included in the materials digitised by the National Library of Finland. For example, both handwritten newspapers contain references to the printed organ of the social democratic youth movement (*Työläisnuoriso*), which has not yet been digitised but can be studied on microfilm.[14]

In addition, there are several handwritten texts with subtitles such as 'copied' or 'adaptation', which suggests they have been taken from print versions, but we were not able to find the original sources. The original sources might be some of the periodicals or books which have not been digitised or digitised only to a limited extent.[15] We also soon realised that our

Table 10.1 Text circulation in two Finnish handwritten newspapers

	Kuritus	*Valistaja*
Years analysed	1909–11	1914–15
Texts published in total	270	153
Reused texts as a share of all texts	15.6% (42/270)	18.9% (29/153)
Reused texts as a share of texts found in the Digital Collections of the National Library of Finland	81% (34/42)	75.9% (22/29)
Original sources of reused text	Newspapers: 61.9% (26/42) Periodicals: 19.0% (8/42) Others: 19.0% (8/42)	Newspapers: 37.9% (11/29) Periodicals: 37.9% (11/29) Others: 24.1% (7/29)
Time between the original and its reproduction	Average: 858 days Median: 278 days Maximum: 5,196 days Minimum: 3 days	Average: 483 days Median: 167 days Maximum: 5,005 days Minimum: 31 days

categorisation of texts into 'original' and 'reused' was not without problems, because there are several texts that contain both reused quotations and originally created text, a technique we analyse more carefully later in the chapter. Although our quantitative estimation of the amount of text reuse is approximate at best, it makes one thing clear: handwritten texts should not be read in isolation, but in the context of the wider literary culture of the time. In other words, focussing only on the immediate textual context of handwritten newspapers could easily lead to mistaken interpretations that overemphasise their imagined 'authenticity'.[16] On the other hand, rewriting texts adopted from printed sources and adapting them to the local community can be seen as a creative process. The copying and adapting process gives an indication of the reception of these texts.

The distribution of original sources is not identical in the two handwritten newspapers: in *Kuritus*, the vast majority of reused texts originate from printed daily newspapers, whereas in *Valistaja*, periodicals are an equally important source. There is a difference related to the fact that *Valistaja* contains more fiction than *Kuritus*, and literary journals (such as *Nuori Voima* and *Nyyrikki*) offered good opportunities for circulating fiction. Another interesting difference in the sources can be found by looking more closely at newspaper circulations: while *Kuritus* adopted most of its newspaper texts from the socialist labour press and they were often political in nature, *Valistaja* more frequently copied light-hearted short stories from non-socialist newspapers. All in all, the reused texts cover a wide spectrum of literary genres: poems, political speeches, short stories, essays, anecdotes and aphorisms.

Finally, Table 10.1 reveals novel information on the temporality of handwritten reproductions. The average interval between the publication of the original text and its reproduction was 858 days for *Kuritus* and 483 days for *Valistaja*. However, here the median is a much better measure to describe typical circulation, because it is not affected by outliers: based on this measure, in most cases, the time gap was considerably less than one year. Although circulations completed in the short term dominated handwritten newspapers, the range of temporal intervals is quite impressive: the fastest circulation we identified took only three days, whereas the slowest took fourteen years to get from print to manuscript media.

The fastest case was tied to the topical political events in 1910: the Duma, at which the Finns had no political representation, enacted a new law on imperial legislation which limited Finnish autonomy.[17] This law generated a hostile reaction among the Finns in general, and we can see that working people contributing to handwritten newspapers were agitated, judging by their writing.[18] Someone copied an opinion piece with the title 'Missä Suomen kansan pelastus?' (Where is the salvation of the Finnish people?) from the leading socialist newspaper *Työmies*. According to the main argument, the Russians were trying to destroy Finnish autonomy and the only salvation was an 'economic reform', but the domestic bourgeoisie was foolishly preventing progress in Finland. The original had been published on 14 April 1910, followed by its handwritten reproduction on 17 April 1910.[19]

The slowest case we found in our sample of handwritten newspapers was taken from a Christian journal that offered pedagogical advice for teachers and parents. The original article, 'Nykyajan sivistysrientojen vaarallisuus' (The dangers of contemporary education activities), appeared in 1896; it warns against the lust for entertainment, mentioning plays, dances and raffles, which had become common in social evenings, arranged by different educational organisations at the end of the nineteenth century. Worst of all, people no longer kept the Sabbath holy – newspapers had even begun to appear on Sundays.[20] The handwritten reproduction of this originally disapproving text appeared in 1910. One important and ironic sentence was added at the very end, which changed the whole meaning of the text:

> These are bad, sad and scary omens for the educational activities of our people, and if there will be no improvement in these matters, then the growing youth of our nation and the future of our people will be in ruin, *into which it has gone at a dizzying pace during these last decades.*[21]

The original intention of the text in the 1890s had been to condemn young people having reckless fun in the name of educational activities, but the added sentence in the new version, and especially its publication on *Sunday* 24 July 1910, indicate that agrarian socialist youth did not take the criticism in the original text seriously, but instead re-published the text because its outdated message sounded amusing in a twentieth-century context.

It is interesting to compare the temporal patterns of text reuse in handwritten newspapers and text reuse in print papers, which also plagiarised each other's texts. In *Kuritus* and *Valistaja*, text reproduction took less than a year in 65 per cent of cases. According to one large-scale study on the Finnish press, the time gap between the first and last appearance of the reused text was less than one year in 85 per cent of the cases. However, there were also texts that spread with a much slower rhythm in the print media – even texts that were able to travel from the late eighteenth century all the way to the early twentieth century.[22] Our analysis shows that text reuse after a long time gap was not limited to print, but was a common practice also in the manuscript media.

Based on our quantitative analysis of a limited corpus of two handwritten newspapers, it seems that: (1) the extent of text reuse is surprisingly large; (2) the original sources used are diverse, although printed newspapers stand out in number; and (3) the typical reproduction took less than a year. While we consider this elementary information useful in order to better understand the relation between manuscript media and print, numbers do not tell us much about the actual proletarian literary agency that ultimately produced the patterns identified in our quantitative analysis. Next, we delve deeper into the literary techniques of text reproduction with a close reading of individual texts which working-class writers either directly copied or re-edited from printed sources.

Techniques of reproduction

The techniques of handwritten text reproduction can be divided roughly into three categories: texts copied word for word, texts cited partially and edited, and texts rewritten and recontextualised. In the issues of *Valistaja* in 1914–15 and *Kuritus* in 1909–11 which are analysed in this chapter, many of the texts copied word for word from printed newspapers are short anecdotes and aphorisms. An example of a longer text copied almost word for word is the essay 'Mitä on työ?' (What is work?), which was published in seven different newspapers and periodicals between September 1913 and April 1914. None of these were socialist newspapers. In *Valistaja*, it was included in the issue of 2 October 1914, signed with the pseudonym 'Petar' and annotated as a 'partial quote'. The essay follows the printed versions quite exactly, discussing work as an activity useful for society. Women who fill their life with fantasy and reading novels and men in white-collar jobs who are 'helpless as children' in any physical work are depicted as examples of 'useless work'.[23] However, the last paragraph of the newspaper article is left out in *Valistaja*: it refers to the 'Finnish week', a promotional event for Finnish industry, organised annually by Suomalaisen Työn Liitto (Association for Finnish Work) from 1913. The Finnish week and the association were related to the struggle for Finnish independence.[24]

Another essay in the same issue of *Valistaja* (2 October 1914), 'Tee se nyt!' (Do it now!) was also cited directly from printed newspapers.[25] This is a short 'self-help'-style essay, which underlines the phrase 'Do it now!' as a key to success. Both essays were copied from non-socialist periodicals, and their content is not directly linked to the ideals of the labour movement. *Kuritus*, on the other hand, relied more on socialist newspapers when reproducing texts from print sources. For example, someone directly copied an emotional speech given by socialist Member of Parliament Oskari Tokoi in the parliamentary debate on imperial legislation in 1910. Tokoi argued that the Russian authorities 'encouraged the Finnish Parliament to commit state suicide' with its new laws. This speech had been reused widely in the labour press[26] and, based on its handwritten reproduction, was also considered important at the grassroots level of the labour movement. However, the speech was shortened considerably in the hands of agrarian working people: only the first long paragraph, condensing fifteen paragraphs from the original, was reproduced for the handwritten version.[27]

Many fictional texts in *Valistaja* were directly copied from printed sources. One example is the short story 'Tehtaan kukka' (Factory flower), which was published in *Valistaja* on 25 February 1921 with no reference to the original source. The text was cited word for word from the original text written by Kyösti Korvenjärvi (a pseudonym),[28] published in *Kevätmyrsky*, the annual literary journal of socialist youth organisations.[29] As Kirsti Salmi-Niklander has commented, the text is not actually the same in *Kevätmyrsky* and *Valistaja*: the story is placed in a fictional industrial community, but readers and listeners have reinterpreted it in the context of the Högfors ironworks. *Kevätmyrsky* has not been digitised, nor has the literary journal *Nyyrikki* (published since 1905), which was widely read by working-class people. By randomly searching microfilms in *Nyyrikki*, Kirsti Salmi-Niklander found several which had been partially copied or re-edited in *Valistaja*.[30]

The transmission of texts from print to manuscript media was not confined to Finnish territory, for some texts were able to cross the Atlantic Ocean. *Kuritus* published one text which claims that 'the eyes of the working people in the whole world are focussed on the Finnish proletariat'. Once again, this text deals with the upcoming elections, and once again it originates from a previously published print version. However, the specific source is rather unique: a letter sent by a Finnish working man from the United States. In his public letter to the labour newspaper *Savon Työmies* (Working man from Savo), the man describes the dreadful conditions endured by those labouring Finns who had migrated to America in search of a better life. This part of the letter is completely ignored in the handwritten reproduction, but the part concerning Finland is copied with minor modifications. For example, the pronoun is changed from singular 'I' to collective 'we' and, at the very end of the text, 'the devil' is replaced with 'chains':

Printed version:

I count on Finnish workers, that they stand firm, for they have prevailed before, why not now. [...] This group I trust, I know that when the peoples awake from their misery, even the devil is afraid of them.[31]

Handwritten version:

We count on Finnish workers, that they stand firm, for they have prevailed before, why not now. [...] This group we trust, we know that when the peoples awake from their misery, even the iron chains must be broken in front of them.[32]

The meaning of a reused text could also be changed simply because of the time delay between the original and its reproduction. An illuminating example can be found in a text in *Kuritus* from November 1909. The handwritten text entitled 'Koston päivä on tullut' (The day of vengeance has arrived) encourages working people to vote in the forthcoming parliamentary election in February 1910. However, this piece of socialist election propaganda had been published originally in a printed labour newspaper just before the general vote of May 1909. Some minor changes were made for the new handwritten version, such as replacing the term 'köyhälistöluokka' (proletarian class) with 'köyhälistö' (the proletariat), and 'kapitalistiluokka' (capitalist class) with 'porvarit' (the bourgeoisie). What is more interesting here is how almost identical textual content was later reactivated in a different political context; that is, the vote in 1910 instead of in 1909.

In fact, one typical technique in handwritten text reproduction involved the modification of key terms. Here are two excerpts from an article on winter unemployment, originally published in the organ of the Christian labour movement and later reproduced in *Kuritus*:

Printed version:

By joining the Christian labour movement, anyone who wants true improvement can work towards the removal of the root causes of cold and hunger, or at least their mitigation.[33]

Handwritten version:

By joining the Social Democratic Party, anyone who wants true improvement can work towards the removal of the root causes of cold and hunger.[34]

This reproduction clearly shows how proletarian socialists adopted texts from their direct political opponents (e.g. the Christian labour movement) and, with only small lexical variations, changed the intention of the original text. Similarly, one writer in *Kuritus* had read a Christian poem celebrating the power of God and decided to transform it into the service of socialist class struggle: 'Christ's little flock' in the original was replaced by 'the great flock of socialism'; 'the white horse' was transformed into 'the red banner'; and 'darkness' had to make way in the new handwritten version for the more concrete evil of 'slavery'.[35]

Some texts went through a more profound process than simply switching the name of the preferred political movement or changing key phrases. Kirsti Salmi-Niklander has described this process as 'localisation', a term which has been used in folkloristic research referring to the adaptation of oral narratives to a new community. 'Fictionalisation' is a parallel textual process, referring to the use of images, quotations and means of narration adopted from the printed press and fiction.[36] Even more accurately, this process could be identified by the terms decontextualisation and recontextualisation, which have been applied to both folklore performances[37] and media texts.[38] In the process of decontextualisation, the original contextual details referring to place, social class, ideology or cultural artefacts are removed so that the text can be recontextualised in a new cultural, social and ideological environment.

Even though the folkloristic terms localisation, decontextualisation and recontextualisation can be applied to the process of copying and editing in handwritten newspapers, the process of reading and writing is in many ways different from oral performance. The editors of handwritten newspapers were often aware of the norms against plagiarism. Copying a printed or manuscript text by hand is a concrete act which involves social and material practices.[39] However, even those texts which were directly copied from printed sources were recontextualised in the process of the oral performance of handwritten newspapers.

A concrete example is a short story named 'Pajasta' (From the forge), published in *Valistaja* on 2 October 1914. The story takes place in a blacksmith's forge, where the narrator enters to have a discussion with the blacksmith. Most of the story consists of the blacksmith's monologue on his passionate relationship with his work. The original version of this story was discovered with the help of the digital newspaper archive, in a literary review published in the provincial newspaper *Satakunta* on 28 April 1904.

The review presents two recent books by the writer Iivo Härkönen, and quotes the short story 'Pajata' (In the forge), published in the collection *Tulia ja muita kuvauksia* (Fire and other stories) the same year.[40]

Iivo Härkönen's story has been re-edited quite a lot in *Valistaja*. In the following quotations, those phrases which are only included in Iivo Härkönen's original story – that is, not in *Valistaja* – are indicated with italics:

> Oh how difficult this work is, it is the most difficult work in the world *under the sky*. Iron is the hardest material in the world. *It has been created from the breast milk of the Nature-Maidens* (Luonnottaret), *the ore of the earth and the mist of the sky, that is why it is so hard*. You need to forge and tap it, hit, treat and harden it before it becomes a useful object. [...]
>
> You might think that this forge is a miserable place to be. *Here nothing changes, neither is there light – I mean the light of God*. By no means, yet this is sooty work, and we have another time order here. There is neither night nor day here, but anyway it is good to be there. Here fire is the whole world. *Fire is the spirit of the forge, huge and powerful*, the trolls of darkness which otherwise like to dwell amidst the soot and slag do not dare to live here.

The references to Kalevala, Finnish mythology and Christian religion are deleted in the *Valistaja* version. In Finnish mythology, three Nature-Maidens ('Luonnottaret') create iron out of their breast milk. 'The origin of iron' is included in the traditional incantations and in the ninth song of *Kalevala*, the epic poem compiled by Elias Lönnrot.[41]

In Iivo Härkönen's collection, 'In the forge' and all other stories are situated in Raja-Karjala (Border Karelia, the easternmost part of Karelia). One indication is the name of the blacksmith, 'rautio', which refers to the Karelian dialects. This is a very interesting example of recontextualisation in handwritten newspapers. It is also an example of ideological reinterpretation. Kirsti Salmi-Niklander has discussed the *Valistaja* version of this story as an expression of the basic elements of industrial work, especially in the ironworks: soot and sweat, fire and time.[42] These basic elements appear in other texts of *Valistaja* and in the local oral tradition of Karkkila. 'In the forge' represents the physical work as a source of joy, pride and passion, even when it is dirty, heavy and frustrating. This is to some extent contradictory to the socialist discourse of industrial work as 'slavery', monotonous toil and suffering. This contradiction was also experienced between generations of workers. The Högfors ironworks (founded in 1820) had a very patriarchal and hierarchical community, where sons followed their fathers into employment there. The work required skill and it was a source of pride, even of passion, for many experienced workers. Many workers of the older generation did not understand the idea of an eight-hour workday, which the labour movement and the younger workers promoted. For them, the work was a way of life.[43]

A later example of editing and recontextualisation is the short story 'Hyvä ja paha ihminen' (A good and a bad human being), which was included in an undated fragment of *Valistaja*, probably dated 1925. The original version was written by Aino Malmberg and published first in her short story collection *Totta ja leikkiä* (True and play) (1903) under the title 'Hyvä tyttö ja paha tyttö' (A good girl and a bad girl).[44] The minor change of the title was one form of recontextualisation. The short story was re-published in *Työläisnuoriso* on 19 June 1914.[45] In *Valistaja*, only the first half of the story has been preserved. It was re-edited so that it could take place in a working-class community, by leaving out some details, such as the fact that one of the characters is a male student.

In a later study of digital newspapers, Kirsti Salmi-Niklander discovered a few more 'missing links' between the different versions of this story. It was published in two other socialist periodicals: *Vapaa Sana* on 18 February 1914 and *Työläisnainen* on 30 July 1914. The story is also included in the programme of the recitation tours of actresses Elli Tompuri (Hamina, 1916, Kouvola and Tampere, 1919, and Helsinki, 1923) and Heidi Blåfield (Helsinki and Viipuri, 1916).[46] There are also a few references in newspapers to the performances of this story at social evenings.[47] Public and semi-public oral performances were one important way of mediating and circulating texts.

In both *Kuritus* and *Valistaja*, we have also found examples of texts which are apparently original pieces of writing, but which utilise quotations, ideas, plots or characters adopted from printed texts. One example is a tragic love story entitled 'Onneton rakkaus' (Unhappy love), published in *Valistaja* on 12 February 1915. It is signed with the letter 'a'. Quite probably the author was the editor of the issue, Agda Nieminen. The main character is Irja, a working-class girl living with her mother and happily courting Rikhard. However, Rikhard disappears, and after some time Irja receives a letter from him, in which he curtly and coldly says that he cannot marry Irja because she is a poor girl, and that instead he is going to marry the daughter of a wealthy businessman. Irja is desperate, and secretly attends Rikhard's wedding. Afterwards she sneaks into the house where the wedding reception is starting and starts a fire with an oil lamp. The results are tragic: the bride and her father die in the fire, many guests are severely burned and Rikhard is fatally injured. Dying, Rikhard begs Irja to forgive him. Irja drowns herself in the sea, asking forgiveness from her mother.

'Unhappy love' is a melodramatic and in many ways stereotypical story: a young man who deceives a poor girl and marries a rich girl is a common plot in many broadsides, in short stories published in socialist and literary periodicals, and also in Finnish literary fiction of the late nineteenth and early twentieth centuries. In most cases, these stories and songs end with the poor girl's suicide, and quite rarely in her active revenge. The arrival of a betrayed partner at an ex-fiancée's wedding is a common plot in nineteenth-century broadsides, but the betrayed partner is in almost all cases male.[48]

'Unhappy love' has some resemblance to a story entitled 'Inkerin kosto' (Inkeri's revenge), which was published in *Nuoriso* on 26 March 1915. In this story, Yrjö is the deceitful partner, a medical student who leaves his poor fiancée Inkeri to marry a rich girl. Twenty years later a young girl enters Yrjö's office, tells him that she is Inkeri and Yrjö's daughter, and shoots him. A tragic love story with Irja and Rikhard as the main characters was published in *Käkisalmen Sanomat* on 19 and 26 September 1912, but the plot is completely different from 'Unhappy love' in *Valistaja*; the latter was compiled from stereotypical textual elements, but the author created a fresh interpretation with an unconventional solution.

We have found cases in *Kuritus* too that demonstrate how an idea taken from a print version could be extended and creatively combined with other ideas. There is, for example, a piece about working women's liberation, drafted by the female pseudonym 'Liena'.[49] She reasons that the main thing preventing working women from joining the struggle for freedom is lack of information: 'But now: *It is great to rise into the struggle, when the trumpets of knowledge are playing. When the divinity of human reason is lightning inside the soul.* Having knowledge is the greatest weapon in the freedom struggle of the working woman.'[50]

Our italics in this quotation highlight that this proletarian woman was not afraid to use poetic language to strengthen her political arguments. A search in the Finnish newspaper corpus reveals that her expressive words did not rise authentically from the local community; rather, a small extract had been borrowed from the non-socialist author Ilmari Kianto, who had composed a long poem for a song and sports festival organised by a nationalist youth organisation in 1908. Two weeks before the quoted text above appeared in *Kuritus* in 1910, the last verse of Kianto's poem had already been published in *Kuritus* as an independent text.[51]

In literary history, Kianto is not famous for this poem but rather for his best-selling novel *Punainen viiva* (Red line), which describes the breakthrough of socialism in the Finnish countryside. Kianto portrays the voters of the Social Democratic Party as simple-minded and naive people who could be easily manipulated by travelling agitators.[52] Perhaps Kianto would have painted a richer image of agrarian socialism had he known how agrarian working women used his ideas from print to serve their own political agendas. After quoting a snippet of Kianto's poem, 'Liena' advises her comrades to read literature that 'makes a working woman think about her own inferior condition' and 'encourages her in the struggle for the happiness of the whole proletariat'.

Conclusion

In this chapter we have systematically analysed the scale and quality of textual transmission between print and manuscript media. The results show that the scale of text reproduction was surprisingly large in our sample of two handwritten newspapers, at 15.6 and 18.9 per cent. Geographically, instances of reuse originated mainly from Finnish printed publications, but we also found handwritten texts which originated from the United States. Considering the time delay, we found that most reproductions were less than one year old, but the slowest case we found took fourteen years to travel from print to a handwritten newspaper. However, it is possible that we have not traced all the relevant versions, because of gaps in the digitised materials.

In fact, the main limitations of our quantitative study are twofold. First, it is evident that our analysis, based mainly on key word searches in the digital archives of the National Library of Finland, could not find all the texts circulating between print and handwritten newspapers, since not all the printed materials are yet available in machine-readable form. Although more than 99 per cent of newspapers and journals have been digitised, the majority of Finnish books are still accessible only as physical copies. Thus, the connections between handwritten newspapers, schoolbooks and fiction and non-fiction literature need to be pinpointed more carefully in further research.

Second, based on the corpus of only two handwritten newspapers produced over a few years, it is impossible to evaluate the overall popularity of individual texts copied from print versions. If we had a large-scale corpus of handwritten newspapers, we could quantify which texts are the most 'viral'; that is, the ones that are reproduced in several handwritten newspapers. Previous research indicates that there were indeed some texts that were able to spread to many working-class communities.[53]

Our qualitative close reading of handwritten texts revealed rich diversity in the techniques of text reproduction. In addition to direct copying, some texts were shortened and either gently or heavily edited. In the most interesting cases, the text was fully rewritten in order to match the local conditions. The proletarian writers could intentionally change the meaning of the copied texts by changing key words or phrases, by deleting an important sentence, or by adding their own ironic comment at the end. We have also shown how performing a text copied from print in a new environment – that is, not silently in the privacy of one's home, but by reading aloud in the presence of fellow working people – could alter the interpretation of the same textual content. We argue that all texts in handwritten newspapers, even those which are copied directly from printed sources, are recontextualised in the process of copying by hand and oral recitation.

Above all, these findings blur the strict border between passive copying and authentic creative writing. Ellen Gruber Garvey has argued that scrapbooks are a form of active reading, shifting the line between reading and writing: 'Readers become agents who make and remake the significance of their saved items.'[54] Parallel processes can be observed in handwritten newspapers. Far from being mere consumers of print media, industrial and agrarian working-class people took part in the creation of modern society by making their own choices. Copying, editing, rewriting and commenting on texts, images and ideas from printed sources are a vital aspect in the development of literacy practices and becoming a modern citizen.

Notes

1 For text reuse, see Ryan Cordell, 'Reprinting, circulation, and the network author in antebellum newspapers', *American Literary History*, 27:3 (2015), 417–45; Hannu Salmi, Jukka Sarjala and Heli Rantala, 'Embryonic modernity: Infectious dynamics in early nineteenth-century Finnish culture', *International Journal for History, Culture and Modernity*, 8:2 (2020), 105–27. For the digital turn in historical research, see Adam Crymble, *Technology and the Historian: Transformations in the Digital Age* (Champaign: University of Illinois Press, 2021).

2 Stephan Pigeon, 'Steal it, change it, print it: Transatlantic scissors-and-paste journalism in *Ladies' Treasury*, 1857–1895', *Journal of Victorian Culture*, 22:1 (2017), 24–39.

3 See Figure 5 in Salmi *et al.*, 'Embryonic modernity'.

4 Kirsti Salmi-Niklander, *Itsekasvatusta ja kapinaa. Tutkimus Karkkilan työläisnuorten kirjoittavasta keskusteluyhteisöstä 1910- ja 1920-luvuilla* (Helsinki: Suomalaisen Kirjallisuuden Seura, 2004), pp. 175–9, 417–20; Risto Turunen, *Shades of Red: Evolution of the Political Language of Finnish Socialism from the Nineteenth Century until the Civil War of 1918* (Helsinki: Finnish Society for Labour History, 2021), pp. 337, 352–4, 399, 409–10.

5 Heiko Droste and Kirsti Salmi-Niklander, 'Handwritten newspapers: Interdisciplinary perspectives on a social practice', in Heiko Droste and Kirsti Salmi-Niklander (eds), *Handwritten Newspapers: An Alternative Medium During the Early Modern and the Modern Period*, Studia Fennica Historica 26 (Helsinki: Finnish Literature Society, 2019), pp. 19–21. In North America, handwritten newspapers coincided with some other alternative educational practices, such as scrapbooks (Ellen Gruber Garvey, *Writing with Scissors: American Scrapbooks from the Civil War to the Harlem Renaissance* (New York: Oxford University Press, 2013)) and so-called 'amateur journalism' (Jessica Isaac, 'Graphing the archives of nineteenth-century amateur newspapers', *Book History*, 19 (2016), 317–48).

6 Kirsti Salmi-Niklander, 'Käsinkirjoitetut lehdet. Yhteisöllisen kirjoittamisen ensiaskeleita', in Lea Laitinen and Kati Mikkola (eds), *Kynällä kyntäjät. Kansan kirjallistuminen 1800-luvun Suomessa* (Helsinki: Suomalaisen Kirjallisuuden Seura, 2013), pp. 384–412; Christian Berrenberg and Kirsti Salmi-Niklander, 'Handwritten newspapers and community identity in Finnish and Norwegian student societies and popular movements', in Droste and Salmi-Niklander (eds), *Handwritten Newspapers*, pp. 131–46; Hrafnkell Lárusson, 'Handwritten journals in nineteenth- and early twentieth-century Iceland', in Droste and Salmi-Niklander (eds), *Handwritten Newspapers*, pp. 147–69.

7 On viral modernity, see, for example, Salmi *et al.*, 'Embryonic modernity'.

8 Salmi-Niklander, 'Käsinkirjoitetut lehdet'; Kirsti Salmi-Niklander, 'Small stories, trivial events – and strong emotions: Local event narratives in handwritten newspapers as negotiation of individual and collective experiences', in Monika Tasa, Ergo-Hart Västrik and Anu Kannike (eds), *Body, Personhood and Privacy: Perspectives on Cultural Other and Human Experience*, Approaches to Culture Theory 7 (Tartu: University of Tartu Press, 2017), pp. 163–78; Risto Turunen, 'From the object to the subject of history: Writing factory workers in Finland in the early twentieth century', in Droste and Salmi-Niklander (eds), *Handwritten Newspapers*, pp. 170–92.

9 Salmi-Niklander, 'Käsinkirjoitetut lehdet', pp. 384–412.

10 Salmi-Niklander, Itsekasvatusta ja kapinaa, p. 70.

11 Turunen, *Shades of Red*, p. 76.

12 Salmi-Niklander, *Itsekasvatusta ja kapinaa*, pp. 175–9; Salmi-Niklander 'Small stories, trivial events'.

13 Kirsti Salmi-Niklander wrote her doctoral dissertation (*Itsekasvatusta ja kapinaa*) during the time when digitalisation of Finnish newspapers was at a very preliminary stage. For her doctoral thesis, she went through some of the newspapers and periodicals that working-class young people commonly read at that time and which were available on microfilm or as original prints. This was a very time-consuming process, but nevertheless she found some texts which were directly copied or re-edited from printed sources (Salmi-Niklander, *Itsekasvatusta ja kapinaa*, pp. 175–9). For this chapter, she has gone through some of the previously analysed materials, and made new searches with the digital materials provided by the National Library. Similarly, Risto Turunen used five different handwritten newspapers in his monograph on Finnish socialism (*Shades of Red*), but he did not systematically analyse textual reproductions in his sources. Now he has focussed on one newspaper in order to search for textual reproductions as comprehensively as possible.

14 *Työläisnuoriso* had been published since 1911. It was suppressed in December 1914, but was replaced by a temporary periodical, *Nuoriso*, in 1914–16.

15 Based on a search in the digital collection of Finnish newspapers, there are currently (December 2021) only around 1,300 books in Finnish from the years 1890–1915 in machine-readable form. For the same period, there are 275,120 newspaper issues and 47,732 journal issues in Finnish in machine-readable form. Available at the National Library of Finland; see https://digi.kansalliskirjasto.fi/search?set_language=en, accessed 9 June 2023.

16 Cf. Jari Ehrnrooth, *Sanan vallassa, vihan voimalla. Sosialistiset vallankumousopit ja niiden vaikutus Suomen työväenliikkeessä 1905–1914* (Helsinki: Finnish Historical Society, 1992), www.doria.fi/handle/10024/167619, accessed 23 February 2023.
17 Pertti Luntinen, *F. A. Seyn: A Political Biography of a Tsarist Imperialist as Administrator of Finland* (Helsinki: Finnish Historical Society, 1985, pp. 179–82).
18 Turunen, *Shades of Red*, p. 423.
19 *Työmies*, 14 April 1910; *Kuritus*, 17 April 1910.
20 *Rauman Lehti*, 2 May 1896.
21 *Kuritus*, 24 July 1910.
22 Hannu Salmi, Petri Paju, Heli Rantala, Asko Nivala, Aleksi Vesanto and Filip Ginter, 'The reuse of texts in Finnish newspapers and journals, 1771–1920: A digital humanities perspective', *Historical Methods: A Journal of Quantitative and Interdisciplinary History*, 54:1 (2021), 14–28.
23 Salmi-Niklander, *Itsekasvatusta ja kapinaa*, p. 288.
24 See Mikko-Olavi Seppälä, *Vuosisadan kampanja: Suomalaisen Työn Liitto 1912–2012* (Helsinki: Suomalaisen Työn Liitto, 2012).
25 *Kotimaa*, 22 January 1913; *Kajaanin lehti*, 30 May 1913.
26 *Työmies*, 9 May 1910; *Sosialisti*, 9 May 1910; *Kansan Tahto*, 10 May 1910; *Savon Työmies*, 10 May 1910.
27 *Kuritus*, 3 July 1910.
28 'Kyösti Korvenjärvi' was one of the pseudonyms of the contributors of the handwritten newspaper *Itseopiskelijat* (Helsinki Social Democratic Youth Society). See *Helsingin Sos.-Dem. Nuorisoseuran vuosikirja* (Porvoo, Finland: Työläisen Kirjapaino, 1915), p. 34.
29 *Kevätmyrsky* VIII (1919), p. 28.
30 Salmi-Niklander, *Itsekasvatusta ja kapinaa*, p. 177; *Nyyrikki*, 8 September 1919; *Valistaja*, 26 November 1919. *Nyyrikki* has only been digitised since 2016, but the earlier issues are available on microfilm.
31 *Savon Työmies*, 6 May 1909.
32 *Kuritus*, 19 December 1909.
33 *Tähti*, 10 December 1909.
34 *Kuritus*, 26 December 1909.
35 *Kotimaa*, 8 December 1909; *Kuritus*, 1 January 1910.
36 Salmi-Niklander, *Itsekasvatusta ja kapinaa*, pp. 176–7; Kirsti Salmi-Niklander, 'Manuscripts and broadsheets: Narrative genres and the communication circuit among working-class youth in early twentieth-century Finland', *Folklore*, 33 (2006), 112–13; Lauri Honko, 'Four forms of adaptation of tradition', in Lauri Honko and Vilmos Voigt (eds), *Adaptation, Change and Decline in Oral Literature*, Studia Fennica 26 (Helsinki: Finnish Literature Society, 1981), pp. 19–21.
37 Richard Bauman and Charles L. Briggs, 'Poetics and performances as critical perspectives on language and social life', *Annual Review of Anthropology*, 19:1 (1990), 59–88.
38 Andrew Peck, 'A problem of amplification: Folklore and fake news in the age of social media', *Journal of American Folklore*, 133:529 (2020), 329–51; see also Garvey, *Writing with Scissors*, p. 47.

39 Salmi-Niklander, *Itsekasvatusta ja kapinaa*, pp. 175–6; Salmi-Niklander, 'Manuscripts and broadsheets', p. 113.
40 Another review of Iivo Härkönen's book was published in the Karelian newspaper *Laatokka* on 31 August 1904.
41 On 'Origin of iron', see Avoin Kalevala, http://kalevala.finlit.fi/items/show/27, accessed 23 February 2023; Matti Sarmela, *Finnish Folklore Atlas: Ethnic Culture of Finland 2*, trans. Annira Silver (Helsinki: Matti Sarmela, 4th partially revised edition, 2009), pp. 342–4.
42 Kirsti Salmi-Niklander, 'Soot and sweat: The factory in the local tradition of Karkkila', in Sakari Hänninen, Kirsti Salmi-Niklander and Tiina Valpola (eds), *Meeting Local Challenges – Mapping Industrial Identities* (Helsinki: Finnish Society for Labour History, 1999), pp. 131–43; Salmi-Niklander, *Itsekasvatusta ja kapinaa*, pp. 288–9.
43 Salmi-Niklander, 'Soot and sweat', pp. 133–7; Salmi-Niklander, *Itsekasvatusta ja kapinaa*, pp. 288–96.
44 The short story was first published in the Christmas album *Nuori Suomi* (Young Finland) XII, 1902.
45 Kirsti Salmi-Niklander, 'Pahan tytön viimeiset sanat. Työläisnuorisoliikkeen sukupuolikeskustelua 1900-luvun alkupuolella', in Sanna Aaltonen and Päivi Honkatukia (eds), *Tulkintoja tytöistä* (Helsinki: Suomalaisen Kirjallisuuden Seura, 2002), pp. 185–206; Salmi-Niklander, *Itsekasvatusta ja kapinaa*, pp. 417–18.
46 *Helsingin Sanomat*, 11 February 1916; *Haminan Lehti*, 17 October 1916; *Karjala*, 9 December 1916; *Wiipuri*, 10 December 1916; *Tammerfors Aftonblad*, 17 February 1919; *Aamulehti*, 18 February 1919; *Kouvolan Sanomat*, 28 March 1919; *Uusi Suomi*, 10 June 1923.
47 *Wiipuri*, 11 January 1903; *Wiipurin Sanomat*, 17 January 1903.
48 Kirsti Salmi-Niklander, 'Lennart ja Fanny Lemmenlaaksossa', in Marjatta Rahikainen (ed.), *Matkoja moderniin* (Helsinki: Suomen Historiallinen Seura, 1996), pp. 117–38; Salmi-Niklander, *Itsekasvatusta ja kapinaa*, pp. 398–9; Salmi-Niklander, 'Manuscripts and broadsheets', pp. 119–21. The comparative analysis is based on the anthology of Finnish ballads and broadsides by Anneli Asplund and Dave Steadman (eds), *Balladeja ja arkkiveisuja: suomalaisia kertomalauluja = Ballads and broadsides: Finnish narrative popular songs* (Helsinki: Suomalaisen Kirjallisuuden Seura, 1994) and the archival collection of folksongs and broadsides copied from young girls' manuscript songbooks from the early nineteenth-century in Karkkila at the Folklore archives of the Finnish Literature Society (SKS. Ul. Pyhäjärvi. Ida Lusenius. KT 355. 1965).
49 This text has also been covered in Turunen, *Shades of Red*, pp. 352–4.
50 *Kuritus*, 4 September 1910, italics added.
51 Turunen, *Shades of Red*, p. 354.
52 Ilmari Kianto, *Punainen viiva* (Helsinki: Otava, 1909).
53 Turunen, *Shades of Red*, pp. 337–8.
54 Garvey, *Writing with Scissors*, p. 47.

11

Choreographing correspondences: how the state shaped soldiers' mail in the US Army and the Red Army during the Second World War

Brandon M. Schechter

The Second World War was one of the most disorienting events in human history. Millions of people were displaced, drafted and killed, while the geopolitical balance shifted to a bipolar world led by two formerly regional powers – the United States and the Soviet Union. Total war made demands on all of society and ripped newly minted citizen-soldiers from their communities, disrupting all manner of personal relationships. For most of their service, the only bridge that servicemen and their families had was the mail, and all belligerents put particular emphasis on providing their citizens with a reliable mail service. Mail was seen as absolutely vital to morale. Soldiers' mail in both the US and USSR was free, but the state interjected itself in a variety of ways into the intimate relationships of its citizens.

This chapter will provide an overview of how the state choreographed correspondences in the two largest allied armies in the Second World War, with a special emphasis on how chaplains in the US Army and political workers in the Red Army were (often literally) on the frontlines of this process.[1] The ways in which they operated reveal much about the technological, social, and political differences between these two regimes but also reveal surprising similarities. I have discussed Red Army soldiers' letters as a genre elsewhere, but here the primary concern is to show how constraints and conscious state interventions shaped what was often the only form of communication available to soldiers and to compare how two very different regimes mounted these interventions.[2] While many of the contrasts are predictable, there were a number of remarkable similarities as two states executed what may have been the single largest censorship campaign in world history. We will see how the very physicality of letters, regimes of censorship, and ways that specialists embedded in military units interacted with soldiers' mail ran the gamut from inert to consciously interventionist choreography by the state.

This chapter stems from a larger project comparing the work of chaplains in the US Army and political workers in the Red Army. The US and the USSR embedded specialists among their troops to make sense of the war and provide spiritual solace. In the US Army, the rising status of the chaplaincy reflected a desire to serve soldiers' spiritual needs, keep them moral and connect them with their home communities during a war in which religion and citizenship were increasingly intertwined.[3] In the Red Army, political workers, initially called military commissars, were instituted in 1918, described as 'not only the direct and immediate representative of Soviet power, but also, most importantly, the bearer of the spirit of our party, its discipline, fortitude and bravery in the struggle to implement its stated goals'.[4] Political workers monitored potentially traitorous elements, spread the party's word, inspired soldiers and instilled discipline.[5] The commissar was supposed to be 'the father and soul of a unit', as declared by Stalin, who had himself served as a commissar during the Civil War. Commissars were 'the moral leader of their unit, the first defender of its material and spiritual interests'.[6] Both chaplains and political workers engaged in what can best be described as pastoral work in service to both soldiers and the state, and soldiers' mail could be as important as the Bible or *The Communist Manifesto* to their work.

A fundamental task of both chaplains and political workers was the establishment and maintenance of bonds between soldiers and society, most importantly their home communities. The Red Army had no regular system of home leave. Once deployed overseas, US servicemen were unlikely to see their loved ones again until discharge. As a result, mail, as the only means for soldiers to communicate with loved ones, became central to morale and to the pastoral work of both chaplains and political workers. By interjecting themselves into personal correspondences, chaplains and political workers influenced how soldiers and families saw the war and made it their job to help soldiers maintain relationships with those for whom they were risking their lives. Mail was an issue of public interest, and in neither army was it considered to be private. The act of correspondence was patriotic, just as the content of letters was supposed to be.

The centrality of mail to soldiers' morale was announced at the front and on the home front. William R. Arnold, the Chief of Chaplains of the US Army, announced to families in 1942:

> A great deal of the chaplain's attention is occupied with mail. Where he can assist his men with difficult letters, he does so. Where he can be of service to parents inquiring about the welfare of their sons, he is more than glad to. When a soldier is sick, it is the chaplain who writes his letters home. And right here, let me urge the fathers and mothers of sons in service to join in the bond between the soldier and his chaplain. Write to your son's chaplain and tell him

about your boy. Simply address the letter to 'The Chaplain' and post it to the same address you use for your son's mail.[7]

Around the same time, the Political Department of the Red Army was emphasising the keen importance of mail. High-level discussions told of the importance of mail in political work, and the military press ran articles on how best to use correspondence.[8] Andrei Orlov, the commissar of the 11th Guards Rifle Division, told interviewers in June 1942:

> Now our goal was to show that it is a poor political worker who isn't approached by Red Army soldiers with their letters. Why doesn't the politruk [political officer] know that Red Army man Petrov has received a letter and not answered it? Why doesn't he know that Private Petrov's family isn't writing? What is he doing to fix this? Is he in touch with his family, with local organisations? Here people are experienced, battered, but when they get a letter from home some valve starts to work better in their body. If a soldier can't write, the politruk should come and help him write, connect him with his family. If the family isn't well accommodated, then the regimental, divisional or corps commissar needs to help out in any way possible.[9]

We see in both cases that connections between family and the front were considered vital to morale and something of keen interest to pastoral work.[10] But before letters could serve this purpose, they had to be written and pass through censorship.

Writing and sending letters

The particular difficulties faced by the US and USSR in providing mail service led to two physical forms of letter that became iconic and specific to the war. The need to provide relatively quick mail delivery to a US army deployed overseas from the South Pacific to Iceland, along with a truly impressive technological infrastructure, gave birth to 'V-mail', short for 'Victory Mail' – a microfilmed letter reprinted in the country of arrival – being the state-approved form of mail connecting US service personnel with their friends and families (see Figure 11.1). A dramatic shortage of everything, and paper in particular, led to envelope-less pieces of paper folded into triangles being the predominant form of mail connecting Red Army soldiers with their kith and kin. This section discusses the physicality of these forms and the impact that they had on soldiers' ability to express themselves, as well as a few details of how this affected connections between front and home.

Both armies provided free mail for their soldiers. In the US Army, V-mail was free to send from the military and cost civilians three cents for standard

198   *The common writer in modern history*

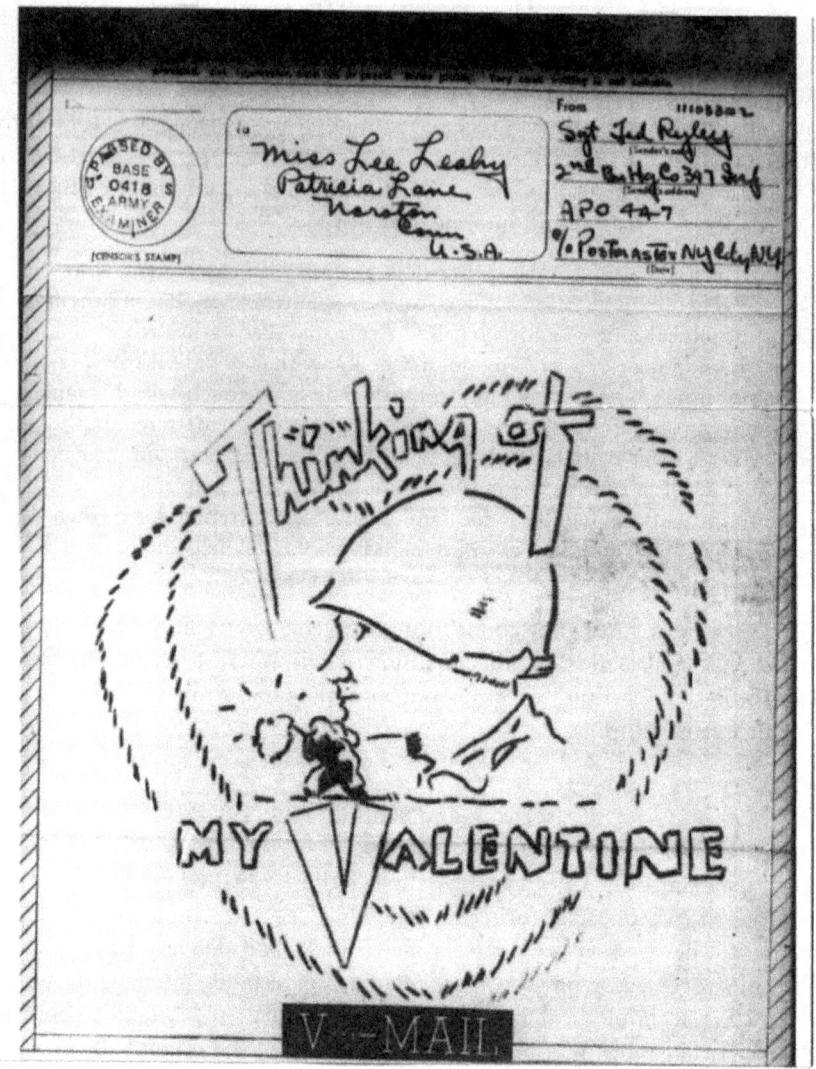

Figure 11.1 V-mail Valentine drawing from Sgt Jed Ryley, of 397th Infantry regiment in France, to Miss Lee Leahy in Noroton, CT, with army censor's stamp in top left corner, circa 1945 (US Postal Museum, Floyd S. Leach collection 0.260305.50.17.2, via Creative Commons).

mail or six cents for air mail within the US.[11] US Army personnel were forbidden to use civilian post, as that would circumvent the censor, while in the Soviet Union all mail was subject to censorship during the war. (In the US all international mail was subject to censorship, but domestic civilian mail was left largely untouched.)[12] Letters to the army were free in the Soviet Union if a soldier used the triangle method, though mail in envelopes was subject to postage.[13] So what were these two distinct forms and what do they tell us?

Early in the war, the US government understood that mail could take up a crippling volume of its shipping in a conflict in which its army would be an expeditionary force requiring vast amounts of equipment. As the US was by far the most mechanised of any combatant during the war (it alone had replaced all horses with machines by 1942 and many officers wrote their letters on typewriters rather than by hand), it was decided that instead of sending paper letters, it would encourage soldiers and their families to use technology borrowed from the British Airgraph service. A standard form was filled out and then photographed on microfilm, dramatically reducing the size of letters to be shipped. An article in *The New York Times* announcing the first delivery of V-mail stated that 150,000 regular letters took up thirty-seven sacks, while the same quantity of V-mail took only one sack. The president himself received the first V-mail letter, in a publicity stunt aimed at attracting people to its use. V-mail was also the fastest and most secure form of correspondence, travelling overseas by air while the original letter was held until a copy was delivered at its final destination.[14] V-mail was fast, reliable and utilised cutting-edge technology, but it was not without its limitations.

V-mail required the writer to compose within the limited space of one page, and readers had to squint to make out the miniature letter (5¼ by 4 inches) they later received.[15] (If the letter could not be processed, it could also be mailed as it was, being folded into an envelope.) This inherently reduced the amount that could be written, but also encouraged short, frequent correspondence in line with wartime propaganda that called on those on the home front to (as a wartime poster put it): 'KEEP HIM POSTED. Make it short. Make it cheerful.'[16] As Martyn Lyons has shown in his work on the correspondence of soldiers during the Great War, a major function of mail in these situations was simply to provide proof of life and many soldiers were probably uncomfortable expressing themselves in writing.[17] Several form letters with holiday or birthday greetings appeared in V-mail format, becoming essentially customisable postcards.[18] The fact that V-mail was a blank page meant that drawings (sometimes racy, sometimes humorous) were a common part of V-mail. However, some complained that the format led to shallow, postcard-like messages.[19] For longer, more meaningful communication, one had to use standard post, which would take much longer to reach its recipient. V-mail remained the most reliable and expeditious form of mail, with over one billion V-mails sent in the course of the war, although regular mail was still much more popular.[20] In short, V-mail in particular and letters generally were akin to soldiers' rations, whose purpose was to satiate needs as economically as possible, or as one modern observer put it, they were 'the instant messaging service of World War II'.[21] The limitations of this form of connection were reflected in a wartime song that lamented: 'I wish that I could hide inside this letter [...] I'd V-mail this female to you'.[22] Women attempting to do the next best thing – send kisses via V-mail – created 'the Scarlet Scourage [sic]' as lipstick gummed up machines.[23] Automation took much of the human element out of communication.

In contrast to the US, a state with cutting-edge infrastructure waging war far beyond its borders, the Soviet Union, which fought most of the war on its own vast territory, faced a very different set of obstacles in realising its wartime postal service. Many soldiers had nowhere to send a letter to – either their families were under German occupation or they had been evacuated to an unknown address. A paper shortage meant that soldiers often had to scrounge to find something to write on. An August 1942 report to the Political Directorate lamented that 'due to the lack of paper, [soldiers] write letters on newspapers and all sorts of scraps'.[24] Even at the end of the war, a propaganda article noted that soldiers were still using fragments of newspapers, 'trophy' paper (in theory German, but in practice anything foreign-produced), propaganda broadsides, the paper used to wrap ammunition or rations, or whatever was at hand to write to their loved ones. Pages torn from notebooks for schoolchildren seem to have also been particularly common.[25] There was discussion of including paper as part of a soldier's regular rations, but this never became official policy.[26] Soldiers for the most part simply folded whatever paper they could find into a triangle with the address written on one side (see Figure 11.2). The lack of standardisation meant that Red Army letters could be several pages long and appear on a wide array of paper formats. They knew that their mail would be read by others, and the triangle format made it easier for the censor (and often political worker) to open it and read the contents. As we will see later, and as was true in other situations, there was no assumption of privacy in this correspondence.

Red Army soldiers' letters often repeated propagandistic terms – perhaps to show loyalty and perhaps because of the discomfort of many with the written word (something many of the American Allies also felt).[27] Observers noted that Americans seldom expressed 'flag-waving' sentiments.[28] The Red Army's mail infrastructure reflected the improvised, spartan methods that defined Stalinism, while the US solved its issues through the massive deployment of technology, reflecting its relative wealth and distance from the war. Soldiers' letters looked very different as a result. Of even greater import than the physical constraints on correspondence for soldiers in both armies were the censorship regimes imposed on these correspondences.

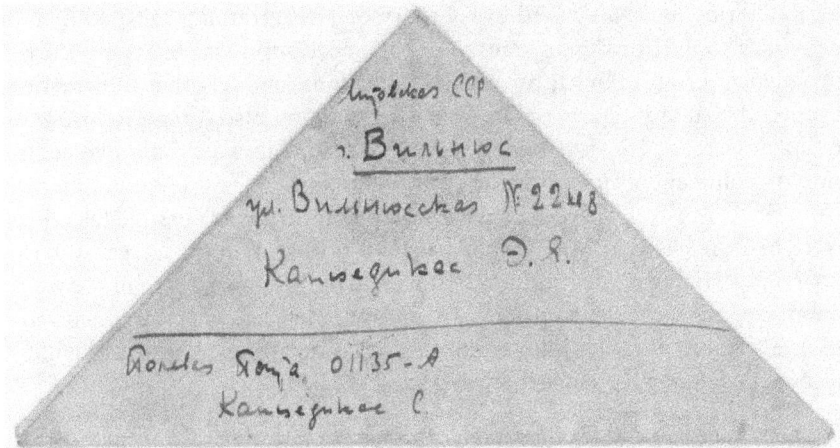

Figure 11.2 Triangle letter from Solomon Kantsedikas, probably in Latvia, to his wife Elisheva in Vilnius, 11 June 1945 (Blavatnik Archive, New York MISC 095.584). All rights reserved and permission to use the figure must be obtained from the copyright holder, Blavatnik Archive, New York.

Censorship

Censorship played a tremendous role in shaping the correspondence of all belligerents during the war. There were significant overlaps in the goals and methods of US Army censorship and Red Army censorship, but also some interesting contrasts.

One fundamental difference was how comfortable each regime was with censorship as a concept. In his 1945 report to the president, Byron Price, who ran the US Office of Censorship (which primarily censored civilian mail), declared:

> Everything the censor does is contrary to the fundamentals of liberty. He invades privacy ruthlessly, delays and mutilates the mails and cables, and lays restrictions on public expression in the press. All of this he can continue to do only so long as an always-skeptical public is convinced that such extraordinary measures are essential to national survival.[29]

Censorship was an uncomfortable necessity of war, at odds with a free society.

In the Soviet case, on the other hand, censorship of the media had been a hallmark of Stalinism since before the war. Lavrenti Beria, head of the People's Commissariat of Internal Affairs (Narodnyi Komissariat Vnutrennikh Del – NKVD), issued an order calling for the censorship of all Red Army and Navy mail in February of 1940, framing censorship as a necessary tool '[f]or the prevention of the penetration via Red Army correspondences of anti-Soviet, provocative, libellous, and or other information against the state interests of the Soviet Union, and also – the disclosure of military secrets'.[30] A stated goal of Soviet censorship was 'the implementation of political control' over the mail.[31] The logic here was quite different from the US case, where criticism of the government was possible (elections were held in 1944) and where the safeguarding of military secrets was the goal of and only justification for censorship. In the Soviet case, on the other hand, censorship was just as concerned with what political sentiments soldiers expressed as it was with controlling military secrets, and it was willing to punish soldiers for what they wrote.

What was universal was the fear that soldiers would try to keep their families informed of their whereabouts and that this could lead to tragedy, as expressed in the wartime mottos 'Loose lips sink ships' and 'Ne boltai' (Don't blab). US soldiers were instructed by a pamphlet to 'THINK! Where does the enemy get his information – information that can put you, and has put your comrades, adrift on an open sea; information that has lost battles and can lose more, unless you personally, vigilantly, perform your duty in SAFEGUARDING MILITARY INFORMATION?'[32] Both regimes feared that soldiers would boast to their loved ones about the information they were privy to in a period in which it was in short supply, leading to disastrous consequences as someone was always listening and mail passed through many hands.

Soldiers were instructed as to what information they were forbidden to write about – including anything about their unit, location, commanders and the effects of enemy operations. In the US case there was particular concern about discussion of ports and ship movements, as their troops had to cross oceans patrolled by submarines to distant theatres of battle. The US Army forbade soldiers to write home to the families of fallen comrades until they had received official notification from the state, while in the Red Army soldiers were encouraged to correspond with their deceased comrades' families. Both forbade discussing losses in terms of numbers or percentages. Both regimes could censor postcards – in the US case for fear of disclosing location, in the Soviet case for fear of exposing Soviet citizens to foreign influences, as any Nazi imagery and foreign text were subject to censorship (although they provided state-approved patriotic postcards and let through information about participation in major operations and geographical locations which could have a positive impact on the morale of those at home, a similar process happening in the US after D-Day).[33] Both regimes forbade soldiers to write in code, and it was the censor's task to ferret out and destroy coded messages.[34]

The way that soldiers received information about what was subject to censorship varied. Red Army personnel, serving in an army which suffered from acute shortages and in a state that was enduring a decades-long paper shortage, seemed to have received information about censorship orally, usually from their commanders and political workers. They were often ignorant about what was allowed and what was not. Aleksandr Lesin recorded in his diary in 1942 that he overheard with embarrassment a commander listing forbidden subjects, all of which he had just written home about.[35] Red Army soldiers were constantly reminded that the guarding of state and military secrets was key among their duties, but many clearly did not understand the state's capacious understanding of what constituted a secret.[36] A report from Stalingrad in 1942 reminded command staff of the need to continue work among soldiers, repeating what not to write, and a 1944 article repeated much of this information.[37]

The US Army had more resources to drive its messages home. Soldiers received pamphlets, but also watched films such as the cartoon *Private Snafu: Censored*, in which a boastful soldier repeatedly tries to send information about his front to his girlfriend, repenting after a 'technical fairy fourth class' reveals in a dream sequence the disastrous results of this endeavour.[38] In the US case, censorship was about self-discipline and the soldier was encouraged 'to impose his own additional rules'.[39]

In the US Army, it was common for chaplains in particular and officers more generally to censor soldiers' letters, with additional base censors stationed at military facilities and in the rear. Anything judged a military secret would be excised, and letters with many violations could be destroyed. Because much of the censorship was done by people that soldiers interacted with, offenders could be set right in personal interventions. Soldiers who wanted to write about personal matters that could be embarrassing placed their letters in a 'blue envelope' where it would be reviewed by base censors who had no connection to the soldier. Officers' mail was always censored outside their own unit.[40] In the US Army we see both a faith in officers to properly censor mail and room for privacy that was absent in the Red Army.

American soldiers seemed to have accepted the necessity of censorship. A 1944 article presenting the results of a survey conducted in the Pacific found that 64 per cent felt that censorship was 'about right' and only 33 per cent found it 'too strict'. Some complained that they could not send home pictures or information about their location, and that rules regarding censorship varied according to unit. Others noted that 'blue envelopes' were largely unavailable (only one in fifty of those surveyed had used one in the previous month). Perhaps most surprisingly, some of those surveyed complained that officers '[made] public, laugh[ed], joke[ed] and criticise[d] what [was] written', punished soldiers if text had to be excised, censored letters on a 'purely moral basis', due to 'hard language', or even took 'it upon themselves to return the letter because of family or girlfriend arguments. They then give you a lecture on how you should speak in your letters'.[41] While American soldiers were not subject to prosecution for what they wrote, the lack of privacy in correspondence could lead to humiliation and punishment at the hands of those who censored them.

Red Army censorship was conducted anonymously and could have much more serious consequences for soldiers. Military censors were tasked with sorting letters into two categories – Authorised and Confiscated. The former could be forwarded to their address with any information subject to censorship blacked out. The presence of sensitive material was considered to be the result of honest mistakes by soldiers unaware of censorship rules, as we have seen above. Confiscated letters were much more consequential, as they included information considered to be defeatist, libellous and/or anti-Soviet, including criticism of the Soviet leadership or statements of German superiority. These were to be forwarded to the NKVD and could lead to interventions ranging in severity from a soldier being taken aside for a political chat to fix their mood, to prosecution as a traitor or defeatist.[42]

Soviet censorship was often ineffective. Military censors in the Red Army were overworked, quickly reading around five hundred letters a day, only having time to skim each letter. They often lacked the technical means to properly black out text. Most disturbingly for Soviet officials, censors were frequently under-educated, as the more qualified cadres had been mobilised for political work. A 1943 survey found censors who didn't know who the head of the Soviet state was and were unsure about who the Soviet Union was at war with.[43] Reports throughout the war saw failures to properly censor letters, including censoring official letters to heads of state, censoring letters in ways that made the offending material obvious or, even worse, the forwarding of letters subject to confiscation.[44]

Whether due to shoddy censorship or soldiers' learning to write appropriate letters, available censorship reports show a very small percentage of Red Army letters requiring intervention. Reports from the 57th Army in April of 1942 showed that of 130,084 letters that underwent censorship, only 246 were confiscated, and of those only 62 were sent to the NKVD. Many of the confiscated letters (124) were simply written on German trophy paper, others included unofficial death notices, and some simply had no return addresses. The confiscated letters were burned.[45] A report on perlustrated letters from the 30th Army during the battle of Kursk found that only 21 out of 55,315 letters expressed 'negative statements', declaring the rest to be 'of a patriotic character'.[46]

Finally, censorship occurred in a variety of languages in both armies. Some US soldiers were the sons of immigrants whose families could not read English. Their letters, whether in Yiddish, Italian, Spanish or another tongue, had to be censored. Chaplain Morris Kertzer recalled how a base censor warned a Yiddish-speaking soldier not to write home about his *momzer* (Yiddish for 'bastard') of a commander. One enterprising soldier taught Yiddish to soldiers in New Guinea, as many spoke this language, but had never learned to read and write it, which cut them off from their families.[47]

In the Soviet case, years of encouraging education in native languages and making Russian a mandatory school subject only in 1938 led to soldiers writing home in a vast array of languages, all of which required censorship, and this could slow down the processing of soldiers' mail. Some soldiers switched to Russian so that their letters would pass more quickly, and all soldiers had to know enough Russian to write addresses.[48]

This leads to a final difference in the amount of information soldiers' letters in both armies contained, relating to the addresses themselves. No letter could be mailed without a return address in either case, leading to accountability for one's words (letters without return addresses were automatically censored). US addresses contained much more information than Red Army addresses. A US Army address gave the soldier's rank, full name, serial number, company, regiment and an Army Post Office number, followed by 'US Army'.[49] Early in the war, the Soviet mail system contained much of the same information, but never the soldier's rank. In autumn 1942 the Red Army switched to a system of Field Post in which a soldier's address consisted only of their name and a field post number, to make it more difficult for enemy agents to divine any information from captured mail.[50]

While censorship served to safeguard military secrets in both armies, its importance and functions within the Soviet regime were much greater than in the US case. Censorship was part of a larger complex of monitoring soldiers' moods and controlling the information that passed between correspondents. Both political workers in the Red Army and chaplains in the US Army had an uninvited window into soldiers' correspondences, as chaplains often served as censors themselves, while political workers could both be privy to information censored from letters and take it upon themselves to read soldiers' mail.

Guiding hands

In early 1944, Chaplain Israel Yost recalled how he: 'spent some time censoring letters for enlisted men, a task I often assumed during the lulls between battles; the ways the Hawaiians expressed themselves were often humorous, making this an enjoyable chore'.[51] Censoring letters allowed him to know much more about the soldiers whose needs he was to serve, combining the state's need to censor mail with the soldiers' need for a figure who knew their problems and could offer solace. While Red Army political workers were not trusted to censor soldiers' mail, they did monitor their moods and often inserted themselves into correspondences without soldiers' permission. For instance, numerous complaints about material hardships by soldiers' families – something that early in the war political workers were supposed to help soldiers address – eventually led to censorship of this information in letters. After these topics became subject to censorship, a system of attending to these needs via the political apparatus was created. For example, if a soldier's family had not received firewood or housing that they were entitled to, this was to be blacked out of the letter, but the political worker of the unit would fill out forms to rectify the issue, ideally without the soldier ever knowing.[52] Chaplains likewise tried to solve a variety of bureaucratic problems for soldiers and monitored their mail.

The 1941 chaplain's manual encouraged the establishment of 'a threefold bond; the chaplain knows the soldier and those interested in him, and a regular correspondence chain may be started by which the chaplain is brought into clear touch with the soldier and his former life environment and consequently is better able to be of assistance to him'. Chaplains were encouraged not only to keep the kin of soldiers informed as to their progress in service but also to write to local newspapers to 'stimulate … a genuine interest in the soldier away from the home town' and 'forge a bond of sympathy and interest for the Army'.[53] In the US case, maintaining morale on the home front was especially important, as Chaplain Gittelsohn wrote in the war's immediate aftermath:

> Every chaplain spends no small proportion of his time making contacts and writing letters that are aimed primarily at the home front … because he necessarily understands the very direct and immediate relationship between the morale of Private First Class Johnny Jones in Company C, and the morale of Jones's mother or wife back in Indiana.[54]

Mail was undeniably central to the morale of troops in both armies, and the ways in which chaplains and political workers influenced and utilised correspondence demonstrated significant overlap but also contrasts.

In the US case, there was a strong emphasis on teaching folks at home to write the correct type of letters. These were letters that didn't demoralise soldiers, but rather elevated their mood. Many a young wife found herself living with her husband's family in his absence, in very tense situations. Rumours of infidelity spread by kin who never approved of their son's or brother's choice could send soldiers into a spiral of anxiety and depression. Some parents continued to treat their mobilised sons as small children.[55]

Opinion polls among troops showed that 'letters from home, especially those telling about other soldiers who had come back from overseas or about soldiers who had not gone overseas allegedly having a "soft" time in the States' could have a demoralising effect on those deployed overseas.[56] Chaplains helped mediate this confusion by explaining to family members at home what the proper kind of letter looked like – bereft of bad news, without rumours and speculation that might distract a soldier, and light on details about family conflicts. Chaplain Gittelsohn recommended 'writing at once to the offending parent or wife, explaining politely but firmly, diplomatically but unmistakeably, what they are doing to their son or husband', and encouraging them to address their concerns first to the chaplain and only *then* to their loved ones.[57] If Red Army censors excised demoralising information about the material conditions of soldiers' families, chaplains encouraged civilians simply not to write about their emotional issues, while censoring the letters that soldiers sent home.

Chaplains and political workers functioned as intermediaries between families and soldiers. Their priorities were shaped by the nature of the societies they represented. The US military drew men from a society with free speech and (for white men) robust civil rights. As a result, many civilians wrote to the military to complain about perceived mistreatment of their relatives in the service, a situation that chaplains often stepped in to resolve. As one noted: 'the chaplain, who in most cases as a civilian in uniform is suspended somewhere between the dual worlds of the military and the civilian, can help interpret each to the other, thereby strengthening morale at home on which morale at the front so largely depends'.[58]

Both sets of specialists counselled soldiers who received bad news. Chaplains frequently broke the news of the death of loved ones at home or on other parts of the front. The army encouraged civilians to contact the chaplain with tragic news so that the soldier could immediately find solace in the chaplain's counsel rather than face tragedy alone.[59] Chaplains also acted as mediators in the case of 'Dear John' letters, in which wives or girlfriends ended relationships over the mail, often having already found someone new. Some recount counselling soldiers whose wives had been unfaithful or left them, sometimes writing angry letters to the women in question. Chaplain Clyde Kimball recorded in his diary: 'Had to write another letter to another wife who has been playing around and fallen in love with a man at home. I wrote her that I felt the same way about her as a striker; both are stabbing soldiers in the back.'[60]

These letters played into fears of disconnection from the home front that seemed detached from the war and unable to comprehend the sacrifices of soldiers. The fact that the US was undergoing a period of economic growth was a source of tension for soldiers, many of whom felt they would be better off as war workers.⁶¹ This type of resentment was difficult to express in the Red Army, with its rhetoric of a unified camp fighting off fascism, and due to the fact that soldiers received more resources than civilians, who were suffering serious material deprivation.⁶² Chaplains often advised their charges to try and repair their marriages.⁶³ In the Red Army unfaithful spouses could lose substantial benefits in the case of divorce, but Soviet official culture made scant mention of this possibility, emphasising instead the wife whose love was so strong it had a talismanic power.⁶⁴

In the Red Army, managing civilian expectations was less of a concern than ensuring the morale of soldiers and providing material assistance.⁶⁵ First, the Red Army was drawn from a society that had undergone a series of mobilisations (most notably in the Civil War and the Socialist Offensive) that had asked significant sacrifices of citizens. Requests for discharges or questioning of army policy that chaplains fielded would simply be inconceivable for Soviet citizens to write. Second, as the war progressed, much of the negative information was supposed to be censored out of the letters via a complicated and constantly shifting set of guidelines.⁶⁶ Red Army soldiers had to navigate their relationships with kinfolk during the war, but the more desperate material situation of Soviet civilians meant that many often had more pressing priorities than difficult family situations.

Both sets of specialists chastised soldiers who failed to write home, and aimed to connect soldiers with loved ones, or in their absence, establish pen pals.⁶⁷ Both could write to the local press in a soldier's hometown. Political workers helped soldiers find the addresses of family members among the millions of Soviet citizens who had been evacuated.⁶⁸ Both chaplains and political workers assisted in securing benefits and sending home soldiers' pay, in the US case sometimes to keep them from gambling it away.⁶⁹ It was not uncommon for chaplains to receive mail from concerned relatives seeking information about a loved one who hadn't written for an extended period of time and encouraging them to write.⁷⁰ Political workers often co-ordinated group letters, known as *Nakazy*, to a factory that had manufactured their weapons or a locality they were drafted from or defending, vowing to end the war more swiftly and securing public bonds between the front and rear in ways that would have rung hollow to American soldiers.⁷¹ The closest to this practice among US troops was when chaplains arranged the mass-mailing of generic holiday cards, a practice especially common around Mothers' Day.⁷²

While the chaplain was more explicitly concerned with the home front, both chaplains and political workers were deeply interested in the contents of correspondence. Throughout the war, political workers were encouraged to draw on exemplary 'patriotic letters'. These often included harrowing descriptions of life under occupation, stories of murdered wives, siblings and parents, children saved from slavery or execution by the advance of the Red Army, or family members' descriptions of their exemplary labour for the front.[73] The military press printed many of these letters in division-level newspapers and encouraged political workers to centre them in their work. Efim Shchedryi, a low-level political worker, described how he worked with letters:

> If a soldier gets a letter, it has already become a rule that he tells me about it, shares with me his most intimate dreams. If the letter is something of general interest, then we read it out loud. The joyful news that one receives becomes common joy. On the other hand, any unpleasant communication inspires sympathy from each soldier. That's the routine at the front, where people are connected with an indestructible friendship.[74]

Stories of horrors visited on relatives of people you lived with or of the herculean labour of a comrade's wife rang true and served to inspire soldiers who knew that the regime was often less than honest with them. These letters could become central to meetings held before major operations and could be used to pressure soldiers.[75]

While the ritualisation of soldiers' mail was more characteristic of Soviet pastoral work, the culture of shared mail was similar in the US Army, if more voluntary. As one soldier told opinion pollsters: 'If one man gets a letter from home over there, the whole company reads it. Whatever belongs to me belongs to the whole outfit.'[76] A significant portion of chaplains' pastoral work was helping soldiers process information they received in letters from home, as we have already seen.[77] In both armies, the practice of shared news from home helped to bind together diverse soldiers into a community with shared emotional investments, while also maintaining connections with the communities they had been torn from. In the Red Army, where soldiers were often moved from unit to unit without a stable social world, this was all the more important.[78]

The interest that chaplains and political workers took in soldiers' letters could be used to pressure them. In the US Army this was generally positive reinforcement – corresponding with family members to ensure them that their son was doing well, and often speaking of their exemplary religious faith or spiritual growth, especially if they had converted or were baptised.[79] In the Red Army, letters were used as both carrots and sticks. It was an established practice for political workers to write home to the families of undisciplined soldiers, who would often receive scolding letters from their loved ones. Sometimes such a letter left unsent was held over the soldier as a form of blackmail. Political workers would also send home letters of praise for soldiers who had earned decorations, often with a portrait of the soldier, which was imagined to have tremendous resonance on the home front.⁸⁰ These letters could end with phrases such as 'We thank you for raising such a bold and fearless warrior', including the family in the soldier's feat.⁸¹ A culture of echoing official propaganda appeals to destroy the enemy in personal correspondences was also used by political workers. Efim Shchedryi wrote in 1944: 'One of our soldiers gets a letter, his son writes: "Papa, beat the fascists harder and come home victorious." In my individual conversations I often ask this soldier: "How are you fulfilling the instructions your son sent you in the last letter?"'⁸²

How could one refuse their son's instructions to kill Germans? The culture of correspondence in the Red Army was not centred on helping civilians understand the military as much as using civilian connections to pressure soldiers, informing family members of the heroism of their relatives, providing evidence of the necessity of the war and supporting the rhetoric of a united community with anecdotes drawn from soldiers' hometowns.

Finally, it was a common occurrence for soldiers to appeal to chaplains and political workers to help find the right words in their letters home. Compare these statements, the first by a chaplain and the second from an article for political workers:

> One Catholic chaplain whom I know was even asked once to write a love letter. The boy knew how he felt toward the girl all right, but 'shucks' he 'wasn't ever much good at fancy words anyway.' So, would the padre mind if the boy just told him how he felt and let the chaplain choose the right words?⁸³

> communist Gushchin ... was able to befriend many Red Army soldiers. They share with him their joys and sorrows, their most intimate thoughts. Soldier Dzhalbogaev, for example, lets the agitator read his personal letters from his wife. At Dzhalbogaev's request Gushchin has more than once helped him write responses.
>
> – You are an agitator and have mastered the gift of speech – Dzhalbogaev appeals to Gushchin – Help me compose a letter to my wife, so I can express my feelings with all of my heart. ⁸⁴

Both sets of specialists were assumed to have access to special knowledge that taught one how to live and both were supposed to be eloquent and more educated. As a result, inarticulate soldiers, many of whom were uncomfortable with the written word, would often appeal to them for help.⁸⁵

Conclusion: cheerful letters

On 9 May 1944, Chaplain David Eichhorn wrote to his family: 'I hope that, as part of your share in the war effort, you will keep writing as often as you can, so that you will help keep your daddy in good spirits, no matter where he may be.' A few lines later he warned: 'I wish I could write more that would be of interest to all of you but many things which I should like to write about are in the realm of the forbidden and so I must content myself and you with vague generalities.'[86]

Those responsible for censorship chafed at how it limited their ability to communicate with loved ones, even as they encouraged them to write often even under these limitations. One of Eichhorn's counterparts in the Red Army expressed similar sentiments. Solomon Kantsedikas, a political officer, had to admit in a letter to his wife Elisheva in 1943:

> You often ask me to tell about myself, my life. This is a fairly difficult task, because we are forbidden to write about the most interesting things. My personal life boils down to the battle life of the unit and the worries connected mostly with the family situation.[87]

In the course of the war he wrote home dozens of letters assuring Elisheva that he was confident he would live to see her again. On 19 May 1945 he could finally tell the truth:

> Now I can confess to you directly that during the war I didn't hope to return, to remain among the living, you see all my comrades perished, and I didn't spare myself in battle. And we should be grateful to you for my survival, 'you simply knew how to wait'. Therefore I bow deeply before you and give thanks from myself and our numerous offspring.[88]

As a political officer, he was part of the apparatus that choreographed correspondence between loved ones on behalf of the state, and while he was a dedicated communist, he knew himself how much had to be left unwritten in the hope that his deepest thoughts and sentiments subject to censorship could finally be shared. Both Eichhorn and Kantsedikas survived the war and reconnected with their families. Both seem to have avoided using the most expeditious forms of mail – V-mail and triangles, respectively – in order to enjoy longer communications with their loved ones. They were both, after all, in part charged with choreographing these correspondences and were perhaps more keenly aware than others of their limits.

Notes

I would like to thank Martyn Lyons, Charles Shaw, Yuri Slezkine and Milyausha Zakirova for feedback on this chapter. All translations are by the author.

1 For a comparison of mail in the Wehrmacht and the Red Army, see Jochen Hellbeck, '"The diaries of Fritzes and the letters of Gretchens": Personal writings from the German–Soviet War and their readers', *Kritika: Explorations in Russian and Eurasian History*, 10:3 (2009), 571–606.

2 Brandon M. Schechter, *The Stuff of Soldiers: A History of the Red Army in World War II through Objects* (Ithaca, NY: Cornell University Press, 2019), pp. 195–210.

3 On chaplains, see Ronit Y. Stahl, *Enlisting Faith: How the Military Chaplaincy Shaped Religion and State in Modern America* (Cambridge, MA: Harvard University Press, 2017); Michael Snape, *God and Uncle Sam: Religion and America's Armed Forces in World War II* (Woodbridge, UK, and Rochester, NY: Boydell, 2015).

4 L. D. Trotskii, *Kak vooruzhalas' revoliutsiia T.1: 1918* (Moscow: Vyschii voennyi redakstionii sovet, 1923), pp. 190–1.

5 Ibid., pp. 102–8, 119–20, 184–5 and 190–4.

6 'Voennye komissary Krasnoi Armii', *Propagandist Krasnoi Armii*, 14 (1941), 4–7, p. 7.

7 William R. Arnold, 'We are strong in spirit', in Ellwood C. Nance (ed.), *Faith of Our Fighters* (St Louis, MO: Bethany, 1944), pp. 100–1; *The Chaplain*, Technical Manual (TM) 16-205 (War Department, 1941), pp. 50, 64–5.

8 Rossiiskii gosudarstvennyi arkhiv sotsial'no-politicheskoi istorii (RGASPI) f. 88, op. 1, d. 960, l. 20; Tsentral'nyi arkhiv obshchestvennykh dvizhenii Moskvy (TsAODM – Central Archive of Social Movements, City of Moscow) f. 3, op. 52, d. 124, ll. 50–62, in A. N. Ponomarev (ed.), *Aleksandr Shcherbakov: Stranitsy biografii* (Moscow: Glavarkhiv Moskvy, 2004), p. 319.

9 Nauchnyi arkhiv Instituta rossiiskoi istorii Akademii nauk Rossiiskoi Federatsii (NA IRI RAN) f. 2, r. I, op. 30, l. 235.

10 For more details on the Soviet case, see Schechter, *Stuff of Soldiers*, pp. 195–210.

11 *Army Postal Service, Field Manual* (FM) 12-105 (War Department, 1943), pp. 4–5, 53. See also 'To pay or not to pay', Victory Mail exhibit, National Postal Museum: https://postalmuseum.si.edu/exhibition/victory-mail-using-v-mail/to-pay-or-not-to-pay, accessed 23 February 2023.

12 Byron Price, *A Report on the Office of Censorship* (Washington, DC: United States Government Printing Office, 1945), pp. 6–7, 13; *Secrecy in Wartime*, US War Department Pamphlet No. 21-1, 29 July 1943, p. 3: https://penelope.uchicago.edu/Thayer/E/Gazetteer/Places/America/United_States/_Topics/history/_Texts/US_Government/War_Department/Pamphlets/21_dash_1/pamphlet*.html, accessed 23 February 2023.

13 Schechter, *Stuff of Soldiers*, p. 196.

14 'Roosevelt gets two messages opening Overseas Service V-mail', *The New York Times* (13 June 1942), p. 17; *FM 12-105*, p. 54.

15 For an excellent online exhibit on V-mail, tracing letters from writing to delivery, see Smithsonian National Postal Museum, 'V-mail: Service in Action booklet': https://postalmuseum.si.edu/exhibition/victory-mail-operating-v-mail/v-mail-service-in-action-booklet, accessed 23 February 2023.

16 Available at National Archives Catalog: https://catalog.archives.gov/id/514797, accessed 23 February 2023.

17 https://catalog.archives.gov/id/514797, consulted 23 February 2023.

18 Martyn Lyons, *The Writing Culture of Ordinary People in Europe, 1860–1920* (Cambridge, UK: Cambridge University Press, 2013), pp. 71, 84–6. Ironically, sending 'safe arrival' telegraphs was expressly forbidden; *Secrecy in Wartime*, p. 3.
19 Judy Barrett Litoff and David C. Smith, *Since You Went Away: World War II Letters from American Women on the Home Front* (New York: Oxford University Press, 1991), p. 123.
20 Smithsonian National Postal Museum, 'V-mail': https://postalmuseum.si.edu/exhibition/the-art-of-cards-and-letters-military-mail-call/v-mail, accessed 23 February 2023.
21 SOFREP, 'V-mail, the instant messaging service of WWII', 22 April, 2022: https://sofrep.com/news/v-mail-the-instant-messaging-service-of-wwii/, accessed 23 February 2023.
22 Charlie Tobias and Nat Simon, *I Wish That I Could Hide Inside This Letter* [song] (New York: Shapiro, Bernstein, 1943).
23 Smithsonian National Postal Museum, 'V-mail's limitations': https://postalmuseum.si.edu/exhibition/victory-mail-using-v-mail/v-mails-limitations, accessed 23 February 2023.
24 TsAMO (Tsentral'nyi arkhiv Ministerstva oborny – Central Archive of the Ministry of Defence), f. 32, op. 920265, d. 5, t. 2, l. 574 in N. I. Borodin and N. V. Usenko (eds), *Glavnye politicheskie organy vooruzhennykh sil SSSR v Velikoi Otechestvennoi voine 1941–1945 gg.: Dokumenty i materialy*, Vol. 17-6 (1–2) of Russkii arkhiv: Velikaia Otechestvennaia (Moscow: TERRA, 1996), p. 158.
25 Schechter, *Stuff of Soldiers*, p. 200.
26 RGASPI, f. 17, op. 125, d. 200, l. 172.
27 Schechter, *Stuff of Soldiers*, pp. 208–9.
28 Samuel A. Stouffer, Edward A. Suchman, Leland C. Devinney, Shirley A. Star and Robin M. Williams Jr, *The American Soldier. Volume I: Adjustment during Army Life* (Princeton, NJ: Princeton University Press, 1949), pp. 430–50; *Volume II: Combat and Its Aftermath*, pp. 150–70, quotes 1: p. 431, 2: p. 150.
29 Price, *Report on the Office of Censorship*, p. 1.
30 GDA SB Ukraïni (Galuzevii derzhavnii arkhiv Sluzhbi bezpeki Ukraïni – Sectoral State Archive of the Ukrainian Security Service), f. 9, spr. 208-sp, ark. 12–16, in V. Litvinenko and V. Ogorodnik, 'Viddili viis'kovoï tsenzuri ta politichnogo kontroliu NKVD–NKGB SRSR u Chervonii armiï ta Viis'kovo-mors'komu floti (kin. 1930-kh – berezen' 1946 rr.)', *Z arkhiviv VChK-GPU-NKVD-KGB*, 1:42 (2014), 150–3, p. 150.
31 GDA SB Ukraïni, f. 9, spr. 208-sp, ark. 17–20 in Litvinenko and Orgorodnik, 'Viddili viis'kovoï tsenzuri', p. 153.
32 *Secrecy in Wartime*, p. 1.
33 Schechter, *Stuff of Soldiers*, p. 198; Price, *Report on the Office of Censorship*, p. 15.
34 *Secrecy in Wartime*, p. 1; Schechter, *Stuff of Soldiers*, p. 197.
35 Aleksandr Lesin, *Byla voina: Kniga-Dnevnik* (Simferopol: Tavriia, 1990), p. 49.

36 *Rukhovodstvo dlia boitsa pekhoty* (Moscow: Voenizdat, 1940), pp. 18–21, 27–32.
37 TsA FSB RF (Tsentral'nyi arkhiv Federal'noi Sluzhby bezopasnosti Rossiiskii federatsii – Central Archive of the Russian Federation Federal Security Service), f. 14, op. 5, d. 96, l. 83–91, in *Stalingradskaia epopeia* (Moscow: Zvonitsa-MG, 2000), pp. 141–7; 'Pishite pravil'no adres', *Gvardiia*, 30 May 1944, p. 2.
38 War Department, *Private Snafu in 'Censored'* [video] (US National Archives, 1944): www.youtube.com/watch?v=xltO0Xcdm1s, accessed 23 February 2023.
39 *Secrecy in Wartime*, p. 1.
40 Ibid., p. 3; *FM 12-105*, p. 5.
41 'What soldiers think about censorship', *What the Soldier Thinks*, 6 (May 1944), 1–2.
42 Schechter, *Stuff of Soldiers*, p. 197. Information about the arrest or punishment of family members was also subject to censorship.
43 GDA SB Ukraïni, f. 9, spr. 216-sp, ark. 11–12 zv. In Litvinenko and Ogorodnik, 'Viddili viis'kovoï tsenzuri', pp. 206–8; GDA SB Ukraïni, f. 9, spr. 220-sp, ark. 21–2 zv. in Litvinenko and Orgorodnik, 'Viddili viis'kovoï tsenzuri', pp. 255–8; GDA SB Ukraïni, f. 9, spr. 220-sp, ark. 7–8, in Litvinenko and Orgorodnik, 'Viddili viis'kovoï tsenzuri', pp. 252–4.
44 Schechter, *Stuff of Soldiers*, pp. 198–9.
45 TsA FSB RF, f. 14, op. 5, d. 96, l. 83–91, in *Stalingradskaia epopeia*, pp. 141–2.
46 TsA FSB RF, f. 40, on. 28, d. 29, l. 70–2, in A. T. Zhadobin, V. V. Markovchin and B. C. Khristoforov (eds), *'Ognennaia duga': Kurskaia bitva glazami Lubianki* (Moscow: Moskovskie uchebniki i Kartolitografiia, 2003), pp. 31–2.
47 Morris N. Kertzer, *With an H on My Dog Tag* (New York: Behrman House, 1947), p. 129.
48 Schechter, *Stuff of Soldiers*, p. 199.
49 *FM 12-105*, p. 8.
50 *Pamiatka krasnoarmeitsu i krasnoflottsu ob adresovanii pochtovoi korrespondentsii* (Moscow: Voenizdat, 1941); 'Pishite pravil'no adres', *Gvardiia*, 30 May 1944.
51 Israel A. S. Yost, *Combat Chaplain: The Personal Story of the World War II Chaplain of the Japanese American 100th Battalion* (Honolulu: University of Hawai'i Press, 2006), p. 111.
52 Schechter, *Stuff of Soldiers*, p. 198.
53 *TM 16-205*, pp. 64–5.
54 Roland B. Gittelsohn, *Pacifist to Padre: The World War II Memoir of Chaplain Roland B. Gittelsohn, December 1941–January 1946*, ed. Donald M. Bishop (Quantico, VA: Marine Corps University Press, 2021), p. 122.
55 Ibid., pp. 122–7.
56 Stouffer, *American Soldier, Volume I*, p. 186.
57 Gittelsohn, *Pacifist to Padre*, p. 125.
58 Ibid., p. 127.
59 *TM 16-205*, p. 32; Clyde E. Kimball, *Diary of My Work Overseas* (Nashua, NH: E. E. Kimball, 1947), p. 185; Russell Cartwright Stroup, *Letters from the Pacific: A Combat Chaplain in World War II* (Columbia: University of

Missouri Press, 2000), p. 71; Yost, *Combat Chaplain*, p. 52; Gittelsohn, *Pacifist to Padre*, pp. 125, 135; Kertzer, *With an H on My Dog Tag*, pp. 46–7.
60 Kimball, *Diary of My Work Overseas*, p. 82. See also Alton E. Carpenter and A. Anne Eiland, *Chappie: World War II Diary of a Combat Chaplain* (Mesa, AZ: A. Anne Eiland, 2007), pp. 10–11; Yost, *Combat Chaplain*, p. 218; Stroup, *Letters from the Pacific*, p. 158; Kertzer, *With an H on My Dog Tag*, p. 33.
61 Stouffer, *American Soldier, Volume I*, pp. 89, 149, 167, 450, 460, 565; Gittelsohn, *Pacifist to Padre*, p. 78.
62 Schechter, *Stuff of Soldiers*, pp. 86–9. For the state of the field on the Soviet home front, Wendy Z. Goldman and Donald A. Filtzer, *Fortress Dark and Stern: The Soviet Home Front during World War II* (New York: Oxford University Press, 2021).
63 Gittelsohn, *Pacifist to Padre*, p. 128; Yost, *Combat Chaplain*, p. 218.
64 Most famously, Konstantin Simonov's song 'Wait for me!' (*Zhdi menia!*).
65 See, for example, Ivan Vaganov, Igor' Vaganov, *Stalingrad – ot porazheniia do pobedy (iz dnevnika partorga)* (no place: Ridero, 2017), pp. 135–8.
66 For a very thorough document collection on censorship guidelines, see Litvinenko and Ogorodnik, 'Viddili viis'kovoï tsenzuri', kin. 1930-kh – berezen' 1946 rr.
67 A. Shipov, 'Patrioticheskie pis'ma', *Agitator i propagandist Krasnoi Armii*, 13–14 (1943), 38–41.
68 Schechter, *Stuff of Soldiers*, p. 202.
69 Stroup, *Letters from the Pacific*, p. 21.
70 Kimball, *Diary of My Work Overseas*, p. 55.
71 Schechter, *Stuff of Soldiers*, pp. 202–3.
72 Stroup, *Letters from the Pacific*, p. 17.
73 TsAODM, f. 3, op. 52, d. 124, ll. 50–62, in Ponomarev, *Aleksandr Shcherbakov*, p. 319; Shipov, 'Patrioticheskie pis'ma'.
74 Efim Shchedryi, 'Zametki agitatora', *Agitator na fronte* (Moscow: Voenizdat, 1944), p. 35.
75 *Ibid.*, pp. 35–7; V. Olizerenko, 'Mitingi mesti', *Agitator i Propagandist Krasnoi Armii*, 9–10 (1943), 29 28–32; RGASPI, f. 17, op. 125, d. 171, ll, pp. 32–43.
76 Stouffer, *American Soldier, Volume I*, p. 99.
77 Kertzer, *With an H on My Dog Tag*, p. 32.
78 Schechter, *Stuff of Soldiers*, pp. 41–4.
79 Stroup, *Letters from the Pacific*, p. 31.
80 Jochen Hellbeck, *Stalingrad: The City that Defeated the Third Reich* (New York: Public Affairs, 2015), p. 47. See also NA IRI RAN, f. 2, r. III, op. 5, d. 2-a, l. 49; Sarsen Amanzholov, *Opyt politikovospitatel'noi raboty v deistvuiushchei armii* (Ust'-Kamenogorsk: Reklamnyi daidzhest, 2010), pp. 48–9; A. Losev, 'Individual'nyi podkhod v politicheskom vospitanii', *Propagandist Krasnoi Armii*, 9–10 (1941), 65–7.
81 Shchedryi, 'Zametki agitatora', p. 35.
82 *Ibid.*, p. 35.
83 Gittelsohn, *Pacifist to Padre*, p. 47.

84 N. Kharitonenko, 'Individual'naia beseda agitatora', *Propagandist Krasnoi Armii*, 4 (1942), 25–6.
85 S. Khirkov, *Iz opyta raboty rotnoi partorganizatsii* (Moscow: Voenizdat, 1943), pp. 19–20. This recalls the practice of soldier scribes used by illiterate soldiers in the Great War; Lyons, *The Writing Culture of Ordinary People in Europe*, p. 50.
86 David Max Eichhorn, *The GI's Rabbi: World War II Letters of David Max Eichhorn*, ed. Gregg Palmer and Mark S. Zaid, with introduction by Doris L. Bergen (Lawrence: University of Kansas Press, 2004), pp. 57, 59. The US Army Corps of Chaplains recruited clergy from recognised Protestant, Catholic and Jewish denominations to serve soldiers' spiritual needs.
87 Blavatnik Archive, Kantsedikas Family Letters, MISC095.114: www.blavatnikarchive.org/item/6905, accessed 23 February 2023.
88 Blavatnik Archive, Kantsedikas Family Letters, MISC095.562: www.blavatnikarchive.org/item/10075, accessed 23 February 2023. Kantsedikas was engaging in a strategy long used by soldiers to avoid troubling their loved ones. See Lyons, *The Writing Culture of Ordinary People in Europe*, pp. 84–5.

12

'Dear Prime Minister': the rhetoric of apology and affiliation in letters to Robert Menzies, Australian Prime Minister, 1949–66

Martyn Lyons

Writing upwards

On Boxing Day 1949, Reg Longden of Ballarat (Victoria) was driving home through South Australia when his car broke down and he found himself stranded for several days near Riverton. He was about seven hundred kilometres from home, with very little money. He telephoned his friends and family in Ballarat, but they were away from home and could not help him. Who could he turn to? Who *does* one turn to in a tight spot with little money and no immediate assistance in sight? Reg turned to his prime minister. He sent him a letter appealing for emergency assistance, hoping for a good response since he had driven a car for his local Liberal Party branch at the recent general election. He wrote:

> No doubt you will be surprised to hear from me in this way, but the fact is I am in one hell of a mess.
>
> I have had car trouble at the above [he gave an address in Riverton], and have to hang on here until Wed or Thurs with exactly 4 pounds.
>
> Would you be good enough to wire me at Riverton Post Office 8 pounds until my affects are clear [*sic*].[1]

Reg Longden did not receive the eight pounds he wanted, but he did get a reply in which the Prime Minister hoped he had successfully returned home. Today, when public trust in politicians throughout the western world has sunk below sea level, it is to say the least unusual to find an individual appealing directly to his prime minister in a personal emergency during the Christmas holiday period. The prime minister in question was Robert Menzies, and Reg Longden's letter was one among thousands which Menzies received, answered, carefully filed and eventually left to the National Library of Australia in Canberra.

Robert Menzies received over 22,000 letters during his record-breaking second term of office as Australia's Prime Minister (1949–66). The corpus is an example of 'writing upwards', a distinctive epistolary genre in which the weak wrote to the powerful, to praise them, berate them, abuse them or perhaps wish them a happy birthday. From this perspective, the Menzies correspondence takes its place alongside the correspondence of other twentieth-century leaders which has already attracted scholarly or popular interest (the Belgian monarchy, Hitler, Mussolini, Mitterrand, Obama).[2] Of these, Mitterrand and Obama provide the closest parallels with the Menzies correspondence, although there was a vast difference of scale between the huge volume of mail they received and the number of letters sent to Menzies. Mitterrand received about a thousand letters daily, and Obama as many as ten thousand per day.[3]

In some ways, writing to a political leader in a constitutional democracy was slightly different from petitioning a dictator or an absolute ruler like the Tsar of Russia. For one thing, the leader had been elected, and the individual correspondent knew that his or her vote counted for something. This gave them an ounce of power, which perhaps led some of them to adopt a very familiar or even hectoring tone. Nevertheless, there was some continuity between letters received by elected leaders like Mitterrand, Menzies and Obama and those received under other, less democratic regimes. Correspondents all thought writing was an important medium; they all assumed that their leader was accessible and could remedy their personal wants and grievances.[4]

The Menzies letters share some features of the correspondence received by all the twentieth- and twenty-first-century leaders I have mentioned. Menzies, like his counterparts, had a special secretariat to deal with his incoming correspondence and, like François Mitterrand, he tried to reply to them all. His replies were inevitably standardised, even if he often departed from conventional protocol and made his own personal interventions. Although many of the leaders studied, including Menzies, made good use of public radio broadcasts, they all, again like Menzies, relied heavily on the written word as a means of cultivating their support base. The letters they received belong to a particular genre – the genre of writing upwards, embracing any kind of correspondence or petitions addressed to employers, church authorities or politicians.[5]

Writing upwards describes the multiple ways in which poor, desperate or indignant people addressed their superiors. The description implies nothing about the tone of the letters, which could be grovelling, supplicatory or menacing; it refers simply to an inequality of status, between a prime minister and an ordinary citizen. 'Deference, demands, supplication' – this was how Camillo Zadra and Gianluigi Fait summarised their collection of studies on writing to the powerful.[6] Letters to authorities usually adopted a deferential tone which recognised their own inferior status, they often sought some personal advantage and sometimes they did so in begging language. But this was not always the case. Writings to the powerful might be abusive or obsequious, or they could denounce neighbours, conspirators and corrupt officials. Occasionally they demanded nothing, but seem simply to have been a cry for attention or a plea for reassurance. Sometimes the writer assumed a network of reciprocal obligations and reminded a superior authority of its duty to fulfil earlier promises. The underlying condition of all writing upwards was social or political inequality between the correspondents. For poor people addressing powerful forces, it was wise to be deferential and cautious. As James C. Scott has argued, however, expressions of loyalty and obedience should not be taken at their face value, because deferential language could disguise a deeper insubordination.[7]

Correspondents writing upwards did not always seek a personal favour; sometimes they had other, less self-interested objectives. They wrote to denounce a corrupt official or to congratulate a superior on achieving something of which they approved. They put their faith in letter writing to cut through bureaucratic obstacles and directly reach out to a higher source of power. Sometimes their language was obsequious and self-effacing – a common tactic of the weak seeking the favour of the mighty. They borrowed and reproduced the language of their superiors, possibly unconsciously, in order to ingratiate themselves. Letters to Menzies belong to and also enrich the history of this enduring scribal phenomenon.

In this chapter I concentrate on two of the rhetorical strategies writers used to engage the sympathetic attention of the Prime Minister. In the first, which I call the rhetoric of apology, writers practised a form of self-abasement which exaggerated the status gap between themselves and Menzies. At the same time, it reflected a genuine difficulty in working out the correct protocols for addressing politicians in power. The second strategy, the rhetoric of affiliation, was mobilised to establish the writer's personal credentials based on their previous connections with Menzies. First, however, I briefly present the corpus of correspondence.

The corpus

The main corpus of the Menzies correspondence analysed here consists of 19,363 letters. I have set aside dozens of boxes of invitations to functions and speaking invitations which Menzies usually declined. If I had included them, they would have brought the total number of letters in his mailbag to at least 22,000 items. The correspondence includes letters of all sizes, telegrams, air letters, 'with compliments' slips and cards for different occasions – birthdays, Christmas, Easter, bon voyage cards, welcome home cards and small visiting cards bearing a scribbled message. Ordinary writers did not always obey the standard rules of epistolary etiquette, and they exploited any material which came to hand. Some correspondents simply tore a page from a ruled exercise book. Bill Newling, a former bus conductor, wrote to Menzies on a piece of brown wrapping paper.[8] The archive is a great leveller: missives like Bill Newling's piece of brown paper sit side by side with the occasional telegram from Her Majesty Queen Elizabeth II.

My qualitative commentary on the correspondence is based on my reading of all 19,363 letters; there has been no triage or selection. Some questions, however, demand statistical answers and for this quantitative part of my analysis some sampling has been necessary. To this end, I have conducted a simple statistical survey of three sample years, one at the beginning of the period (1949–50, 863 letters), one in the middle (1958, 1,623 letters) and one near the end (1964, 1,195 letters). Altogether, these three years provide a total of 3,681 letters, which is a solid sample of 19 per cent of the main series of correspondence. The figures cited below are based on an analysis of these years, punctuating the sixteen years of Menzies' long, unbroken term.[9]

A few essential elements of the profile of Menzies' correspondents can be briefly summarised here. Thirty per cent of letters were from collective bodies – ministries, embassies, churches, businesses and other non-government organisations. Although my study does not neglect these sources of letters, I am more interested in the letters from private individuals, which made up the remaining 70 per cent of the corpus.

Men wrote most of the letters, perpetuating an imbalance which has probably existed since the very beginnings of all written communication. It reflects the historical male domination of politics, public administration and capitalist enterprise. Even if we only consider letters from private individuals, 71.7 per cent were written by men, compared to 28.8 per cent by women, with a small residue of cases where the author's gender cannot be determined.[10] This disproportion remained fairly consistent across the years. The first characteristic of the ordinary writer's profile thus emerges: the writer was more than twice as likely to be a man than a woman.

There was a strong overseas presence in the Menzies correspondence. The number of overseas correspondents fluctuated, but overall they were responsible for one in five of all letters (21.3 per cent). 'Londoners love Mr Menzies', reported Norma Norris when she returned home to Warburton (Victoria) after her holiday in England in 1964, and British correspondents regularly addressed Menzies on a range of topics, including the possibility of an assisted passage to Australia.[11] British correspondents, some from Conservative Party circles and others would-be emigrants, dominated the cohort of overseas writers, accounting for 45.4 per cent of all letters of foreign origin and rising to over 50 per cent of them in two out of the three sampled years. The USA produced just 22 per cent, and British Commonwealth countries like New Zealand and Canada dominated the rest. In fact almost two thirds (64 per cent) of overseas letters originated from Britain or the Commonwealth, which is a good indication of Menzies' personal network as well as of his general world-view.

Letters with an Australian postmark outnumbered overseas letters by about three to one, accounting for 76.9 per cent of the sample. They originated overwhelmingly from Victoria (35.2 per cent of Australian letters) or New South Wales (30.5 per cent); in fact Menzies was far more likely to receive a letter from England than one from either Queensland, South Australia, Western Australia, Tasmania or the Northern Territory. The vast majority of ordinary writers (82 per cent) sent only a single letter each, most often a single page. There was a remarkably high rate of reply from Menzies' small secretariat. If we exclude from the statistical sample all messages that clearly did not seek a reply, such as thanks-for-your-condolences and other goodwill cards, the very high share of 74.1 per cent of letters received a response.

The rhetoric of apology

Menzies' time was precious, and the writer could not presume to encroach on it without apologising for doing so. 'Of course', wrote one woman from Chatswood (New South Wales), 'I know that my thoughts are not of the least importance in your busy life.'[12] The unfortunately named Mrs Pain began with these words: 'Firstly I wish to say: "I apologise for this personal letter", as I just know how every minute of your valuable life is being taxed; but my request is so urgent and very <u>sad</u>.'[13] Such apologies were essential preludes to a plea for assistance or a demand for serious attention. A Mrs Brown similarly offered the standard apology: 'I am reluctant,' she wrote, 'to trespass on the limited time of Australia's busiest man.' She soon overcame her reluctance, however, and a two-page letter followed about the problems she encountered in installing a telephone line.[14] Writers apologised for pestering the Prime Minister or for their apparent impudence in writing to him. One writer took up his pencil and tried to bypass the usual approach channel by addressing his letter to Heather Menzies, the Prime Minister's daughter, in these terms:

> Please forgive me for writing this letter, you probably get a lot of begging and in fact, unpleasant letters, so I won't blame you if you don't encourage me, I ask you to believe me, that I won't annoy you or pester you in any way, your word is law to me, so, if you choose to ignore this I'll simply know I'm not worthy of your help.[15]

This correspondent was so engrossed in his self-effacing apology that he failed to arrive at the real point of his letter. He received a reply inquiring what exactly it was that he wanted.[16]

Many writers struggled to find the appropriate form of address. Sixty-five different forms of greeting were used in 1958, and sixty-four in 1964 – testimony to a general uncertainty. Occasionally a writer felt authorised to adopt a familiar tone and, in 1958, 100 letters opened with 'Dear Bob'. Sometimes the conventional apology was offered as if to a close acquaintance. Mrs Williams of Warrnambool (Victoria) wrote of her prayers for Menzies, the problem of loafers in the trade unions and the difficulty of living on a pension, and she signed off with: 'Well good night Dear Friend and thank you again I hope I have not given you a headache.'[17] Familiarity, however, could be a provocation, and this seemed to be the case with the angry correspondent who began 'Bro Menzie'.[18] If familiarity was not appropriate, the writer had to decide whether to address Menzies by his name (as in 'Dear Mr Menzies') or his title ('Dear Prime Minister') or a combination of both, as in 'Dear Mr Minister'. Deferential modes of address (including 'Dear Sir' and variations thereof) were popular. Gladys Spickett, writing from England, experienced a common dilemma, writing: 'I am not sure if I am addressing you in the right manner but I can assure you that I am very sincere.'[19] She addressed him as 'Dear Mr Menzies' so she need not have worried. Mr Punjabi, on the other hand, had no problem when he wrote from Gujarat to ask for Menzies' autograph: 'My Dear Chacha, This little letter of mine may come to you as surprise [sic], but my dear Chacha how can I tell you that my hand, Can not be prevented to write something to you to achieve my long cherished desires.'[20] 'Chacha' in Hindi means paternal uncle. It was used to address independent India's first Prime Minister Jawaharlal Nehru, for example, as 'Chacha Nehru'. Here it suggested affectionate respect and deference to a wise elder. Mr Punjabi had found the perfect solution to a common problem.

In apologising for writing to Menzies, authors expressed an exaggerated sense of their own insignificance. As one cricket fan put it, Menzies was 'higher up the batting order than I am'.[21] A young Indian correspondent defined himself in these self-deprecating terms: 'I am a teen-aged Indian boy [...]. My hobby is to correspond with internationally important men, whom I consider would not disappoint or ignore me, irrespective of their exhaulted [sic] and busy jobs, since I know that I am nothing but a tiny drop in the human-ocean.'[22]

José Barredo similarly introduced himself as a Filipino father of seven children, and asked Menzies for a second-hand transistor radio for Christmas, with the exaggerated modesty characteristic of supplicatory letters: 'At first,' he wrote, 'I was too shy indeed writing this believing that you, being the greatest man of that great country in earth, wouldn't mind answering this futile missive from a humble and poor peasant.'[23] Elsewhere in the letter, he refers to living in a deprived 'barrio', suggesting an urban residence, so the 'peasant' reference might be a flourish, but the humility it expressed was part of the standard rhetoric of writing upwards.

Housewives were especially prone to insist on their own irrelevance, like Mary Stewart in London, who began 'Although a mere, insignificant English housewife', before recommending that a royal residence be set up for Queen Elizabeth in Australia.[24] Recent immigrants expressed a kind of false reluctance to address Menzies, as if they were butting in on a national conversation that was not yet entirely their own. Ed Vieglais, who was possibly of Latvian origin, wrote: 'At first I want to beg excuses for myself that I dare to annoy you with my letter about a matter what of course [sic], is not my task, especially, for I am just a migrant here.'[25] He wanted to complain about the number of crime stories reported in the Australian daily press.

Father Murphy SJ of Newman College (University of Melbourne) wrote at Easter asking Menzies to 'Forgive a person of no consequence breaking in on the Pascal Peace of a person of much consequence (destined, I hope, to be even more)'.[26] He was certainly of enough consequence for Menzies to arrange a lunch meeting with him to discuss university affairs, and Murphy later wrote a letter of thanks, assuring Menzies that he had a number of unsuspected well-wishers – unsuspected, perhaps, because they were to be found in rarefied Catholic circles. Menzies' own Presbyterianism was well advertised, but he always maintained many friendly contacts within the Catholic Church.

The unequal status of correspondents when writing upwards could be turned into an asset. It offered an opportunity to challenge the recipient. Edward Hampel addressed Menzies thus, as if he were spoiling for a fight: 'Are you big enough to listen to an ordinary working man? If not, you should throw this in the waste-paper basket now.'[27] Menzies was sometimes told that it was his duty to take an interest in what ordinary people were saying and thinking. It was to his advantage to hear from humble and insignificant writers, because he needed to keep in touch with the mood of voters. 'Probably,' wrote A. E. Hyland, a retired Trade Commissioner, on the topic of revaluing the currency, 'you and those with whom you have been discussing the matter on which I am writing have covered all I am about to say, and yet as one of the ordinary people I feel there might be interest to you in a little, perhaps, of it.'[28] Not in spite of their anonymity, but rather *because* of it, some writers felt Menzies *needed* to be interested in what they had to say, because they were representative of those whose voices were rarely heard. Mr Kempe wrote about industrial unrest in 1955:

> I am writing this in the hope that you may find time to read a letter from an ordinary citizen, as I feel that in your position you may not come into contact with the man in the street as often as might be desirable, and therefore you may miss out to a certain degree on Public Opinion.[29]

In these cases the standard rhetoric of apology was turned inside out; the letters argued not that they intruded into the Prime Minister's valuable time but rather that, in his exalted but remote position, Menzies needed to make time to read them in order to keep in touch with ordinary Australians.

Writers offered many excuses for their poor handwriting and lack of epistolary expertise. Lack of education prevented Mrs Hurrell from writing as well as she might have wished. She was grateful for her pension and told Menzies so on one sheet of lined paper, writing in biro with no margins or punctuation. She concluded her letter: 'I had to learn myself Sir I never went to school hope you can understand this dreadful scribble.'[30] Mr Houghton of Canterbury (New South Wales) apologised because he felt weak after his accident, and E. Campbell of Kootingal (New South Wales) simply wrote in telegramese: 'Excuse scrawl badly crippled by disease.'[31] Writers were sick, or their sight was poor and this made their hand unsteady. 'I know the writing is a bit wobbly, but that's from the medicine I'm taking', was sixty-four-year-old Margie Cantor's excuse, but she promised dutifully to vote Liberal at the next election if she was alive to see it, 'because I like to be governed by gentlemen not rogues'.[32] They pleaded they were in a hurry, like Edna Smith, who apologised as she was rushing off to 'church'.[33] She underlined the word 'church' as if to signal that this was a cast-iron excuse. They were rushing, perhaps to catch the mail, like Gordon McKillop, who wrote: 'Sorry, no typewriter or time to re-write in correct phrase.'[34] For Beryl Danahay, the mere thought of writing to the Prime Minister was enough in itself to bring on a nervous state which produced 'wobbly' writing.[35] The quality of the paper was also a potential cause of embarrassment, and writers begged forgiveness for running out of good-quality notepaper; there was none to hand or it was too late at night to go out and buy some more.[36] Leonard Jones wrote to Menzies on the back of his own eviction notice and hoped he would understand his predicament because 'God is urging me to write to you'.[37]

The range of excuses offered for poor paper or wobbly writing indicated that, for many, letter writing was an unfamiliar task, accomplished only through a considerable physical and mental effort. Once having determined to try, they came up against another handicap: writing to an eminent prime minister made the task doubly intimidating. There were many reasons for 'writer's block', but this fear informed all of them. Mrs McNaughton had sponsored an English family in the 'Bring out a Briton' campaign and wondered why they had not appeared. She wrote to Menzies in trepidation: 'Trembling, I approach the head of our government, yet confident that you will give me your earnest attention for one moment.'[38] Writing to Menzies could bring on a fever and could be a health hazard. 'My heart is exceeding the speed limit (according to medical orders)', wrote another woman, adding 'my auld hand is rather shakey with nervousness!'[39] Margie Cantor, already mentioned, confessed that she had written three letters and destroyed them all before she finally overcame her inhibitions and communicated her suspicion that the Ministry of Health was being defrauded.[40] Writing to the Prime Minister could be an ordeal which led correspondents into very unfamiliar territory.

At least they were grateful for Menzies' accessibility, and they praised him for it. Joan Lewis, a would-be emigrant from Britain, was amazed to receive a reply from Menzies, and she wrote to his secretary Hazel Craig:

> Your letter from the Prime Minister Mr Menzies came as a complete surprise to me to-day. I never knew it was possible that such a person so high in the country, and with so much work and worry as well, that Mr Menzies has, could possibly take notice of a housewife. I don't really know how to start to thank you.[41]

British correspondents assumed that this unusual degree of friendliness was a national characteristic. E. Porter, seeking to emigrate from England, sent a query about the Assisted Passage Migration Scheme, writing: 'It may seem a colossal nerve for anyone to write to the Prime Minister of Australia ... but – nothing venture, nothing gain. Anyway, having visited Australia I know that even the highest ranking people are approachable.'[42] In fact, Menzies had a personal reputation for being available. Reminding him of this was a rhetorical strategy designed to make Menzies pay attention and, if necessary, take action.

The rhetoric of affiliation

Writers adopted subtle tactics to justify their personal approach to Menzies. Their letters developed narratives in which they had some previous contact with him. Perhaps they had met him or a member of his family in the past, although the writer realised that Menzies was unlikely to remember the encounter. Or perhaps their paths had crossed at some point because they had lived in the same area, or belonged to the same professional organisation or church congregation. The Scottish connection, as we shall see, was a favourite method of claiming a common interest which authorised them to write to Menzies with a small request. This was a powerful network which provided one of the anchoring rhetorics of the correspondence: it was based in a mutual experience, ancestry or connection which demonstrated the writer's affinity with Menzies and claimed they were both united in the same cause.

Stewart McInnes of Geelong College had several claims to Menzies' attention, and he condensed them all in a few sentences. Firstly, as he told Menzies, he had once spotted the Prime Minister at a cricket test chatting to (former Australian batsman) Don Bradman, and then there was more, as he wrote: 'You knew my uncle years ago when you were practising law. I live in Camberwell Vic and You visited my parents one night when we used to live at Colac. I heard you speak at a Speech night at Strathmere Girls' School in Melbourne where my sister was boarder.'[43] McInnes evoked a shared enthusiasm for cricket, acquaintance with a relative, the legal profession, previous geographical proximity in the Melbourne suburbs and a school event to establish his right to be heard; all these mapped out a common territory where he and Menzies shared an interest or where they had 'met' each other without Menzies' realising it.

One British businessman wrote and even addressed Menzies as 'Dear Bob', on the strength of private conversations they had enjoyed on board the 'Queen Elizabeth', presumably on the long voyage to Southampton.[44] Mrs R.J. McGarvie wrote: 'After all, we both went to the same church "Trinity" in Camberwell – years ago.'[45] It may have been years ago, but the reminder enabled Mrs McGarvie to establish an essential link which would give her privileged access to Menzies.

A letter from Mrs Muriel Webster of Hughesdale (Victoria) provides a final illustration of this kind of claim to personal affinity. She wrote to ask Menzies to help her pay a security bond for her two teenage sons who were in jail, and her letter began:

> It is some years since I knew you in Ballarat, but I attended St Andrew's Kirk and was a friend of your sister Belle and also my family by the name of McKillops were friends of your family and also your relations the Harry Adams. Perhaps you would remember my sister the pianist of Ballarat.[46]

She and Menzies were, she claimed, old acquaintances, former members of the same Presbyterian congregation, and furthermore she used to know Menzies' sister and, in case Menzies was still mystified, their two families had been good friends. She had established her personal credentials, which was an important way of justifying her request, even if it was an impossible one for Menzies to satisfy. On some occasions, secretary Hazel Craig would first ask Menzies if he actually knew the correspondent, before drafting a reply to their letter. She needed to verify their claims to affinity, which would influence the tone of the response they received.

Correspondents cited the Scottish connection whenever possible to establish a link with Menzies, and they did so all the more readily because Menzies frequently advertised his Scottish ancestry. He visited Scotland on trips to Britain and he would often turn up to Robert Burns commemorations in Melbourne. He was a member of the Melbourne Scots Club and the Royal Caledonian Society, and fellow members of these clubs used this as a springboard from which to launch a greeting or a request. Every time that Menzies visited the United Kingdom for a Commonwealth Prime Ministers' conference, Scottish nationalist organisations tried to recruit him for the cause of Scottish independence.[47] He consistently ignored them.

Women knitted him clan tartan scarves.[48] Another sent him a gift of heather.[49] An Inverness art dealer sent him an original 1820 print of the Menzies clan, to congratulate him on his 1949 election victory.[50] One correspondent asked Menzies to get him some books on Scottish country dancing – and, if possible, autograph them – because he could not afford to buy any himself.[51] Correspondents knew that the ancestral home of his clan, Castle Menzies, still stood in Perthshire, and a few had been there. Helen Pepys was one – she fondly remembered picking snowdrops as a child in nearby Aberfeldy.[52] The vicar of St David's at nearby Weem, where Menzies' grandfather was born, asked for help with the restoration of his church, and Menzies responded with a donation of £10.[53]

The Scottish network was also a Presbyterian connection, and Menzies' fellow religionists often played the Presbyterian card. As his followers well knew, Menzies had married Patti Leckie in Melbourne in Kew Presbyterian Church, and this affiliation was often recalled. Edith and Margaret Drummond asked Menzies to pay a visit to their namesake, a Presbyterian minister in Edinburgh. 'I am not writing to you as our Prime Minister,' they wrote, 'but rather as a friend – a fellow Presbyterian – a fellow Scot and a loyal supporter of the cause of Liberalism.'[54] In their view, that made three good reasons why Menzies should oblige them. Presbyterian Church elders regularly offered congratulations and prayers for Menzies' success.[55]

Besides all the correspondents who claimed Scottish ancestry, voters in Menzies' own Melbourne constituency of Kooyong also had a strong basis for making a claim on the Prime Minister's time. Constituents appealed for his intervention either to install or improve a telephone line to their home or business, to cut through bureaucratic tangles and eliminate delays. Menzies always referred these cases to the Postmaster-General for a report, and his sponsorship of their inquiry produced results, or at the very least an explanation of why the petitioner should be patient a little longer. Camberwell Business Men's Club, for instance, wanted his intervention to secure better local post office facilities.[56] Father McNamara of East Kew asked for Menzies' assistance to persuade a local bank to give him a loan to build a new church. In support of his request, he reminded Menzies of the Catholic Church's role as a bulwark against communism.[57] Menzies received several dozen letters annually which can be clearly identified as either coming from his Kooyong constituency or else related to local constituency matters. In 1958, the number of Kooyong or Kooyong-related letters rose to 185, or 13.5 per cent of all Australian letters. The number fell away later as the demand for new telephone lines was satisfied. As a good constituency member, Menzies would respond to requests from individuals, local businesses and church organisations. At Christmas 1953, he obtained permission for Kew shopkeepers to erect an illuminated Christmas tree outside the Kew Post Office, to raise funds for the Children's Hospital and the Kew Mental Hospital. The electricity bill for the Christmas lights was covered by the Postmaster-General.[58]

Other ways of performing the rhetoric of affinity can be briefly summarised. Menzies had made many contacts in the legal profession before he had entered politics, and a few correspondents traded on this connection. Since Menzies was an honorary master of Gray's Inn in London, the law opened up another international network for him. Menzies was a member of several gentlemen's clubs, including the Savage Club of Melbourne, of which he became president. He received messages and requests from other 'Savages', as they called themselves, claiming affinity on this score. The Liberal Party network across Australia, including Liberal parliamentarians, frequently claimed his attention.

Lastly, there was a network of ex-servicemen and their organisations which petitioned Menzies. Strictly speaking, this cannot be called a case of affinity, since Menzies had never served in the armed forces – something often held against him. Army veterans and their relatives, however, wrote of their hardships and of sacrifices for the nation in wartime to which they presumed Menzies would be sympathetic. Victoria Brown, asking for a better deal for pensioners, wrote of 'We who gave our sons and brothers and husbands to fight for this "Wonderful" Country and who helped to make the country what it is today'.[59] A writer would frequently introduce himself as a veteran of one or both world wars, before further identifying himself as a Scot or as a voter in Kooyong. He or she might then go on to give their age, as if this too earned them an audience, and a mother or a war widow would stress how many children she had brought up. On this register Mrs Hardy pleaded for a pension for her ninety-two-year-old mother, asking accusingly: 'My mother had three sons at the war, I wonder what they fought for?'[60]

When Alexander MacClure wrote to Menzies about his war disability pension, he used several rhetorical ploys, but he began by identifying himself as a war veteran, prefacing his appeal with 'As an ex-member of the

1st and 2nd A.I.F.' – in other words he had fought in both world wars. He now suffered from pulmonary tuberculosis as well as duodenal ulcers and stressed his history of patriotic sacrifice for the country. 'We did not fight for the Country,' he added, 'as a prelude to selling out to the Communists', and he informed Menzies that he had always supported the Liberal Party ever since he first cast his vote as a front-line soldier in France.[61] Just to make sure he left no stone unturned in his appeal for help, he told Menzies that he also belonged to the clan McLeod.

Without sacrificing an ounce of sincerity, Menzies' correspondents were nevertheless artful writers. They adopted a variety of rhetorical ploys to establish their credentials. In order to justify their approach to the Prime Minister, they inserted themselves into the networks which they felt were most significant to him – the Scottish connection, the Presbyterian church, the Kooyong constituency, the legal profession or the Savage Club. If possible, they played on several of these registers in the same letter, adding where appropriate the plea of the army veteran or the war widow to explain why they were especially worthy of consideration. These were some of what Steven King calls the 'anchoring rhetorics' on the basis of which requests were formulated.[62] Having presented their curriculum vitae, what exactly did correspondents ask for in their letters of supplication? Their requests will be reviewed in the next section.

Asking for a favour

In 1903, a seventeen-year-old American wrote to ask the King of Belgium to help him buy a new elephant to replace one that had died, thus depriving the young man of the small income he made from giving elephant rides.[63] Requests to Menzies half a century later tended to be less exotic but perhaps they were sometimes more practical. As we have already seen, requests from Kooyong constituents to have a telephone line installed produced results, even if, as one supplicant admitted, asking the Prime Minister to get a telephone installed seemed like taking a sledgehammer to crack a nut.[64] Schoolchildren overseas who asked Menzies to send some Australian stamps also received a favourable response. Menzies received many pleas for help from those who considered themselves eligible for a War Service Pension, a Widows' Pension or an Ex-Serviceman's Home Loan. These were diverted to the appropriate civil service department.

There were constant demands for Menzies to grant an audience, receive a delegation or arrange a personal interview. Writers always hoped for direct access to the highest political level, which was why they wrote in the first place, but they were rarely accommodated. Menzies' time was too valuable, unless a very influential person or business interest was involved. To protect his time, he made it a rule never to give personal interviews while Parliament was in session.

Correspondents asked Menzies to write them a letter of introduction, especially if they were travelling to Britain and hoping to facilitate a few key meetings. He often obliged, although sometimes this was impossible. Walter King, for example, a former mayor of Concord (New South Wales), asked for a letter of introduction to Winston Churchill. Hazel Craig replied, apologising for the fact that 'the Prime Minister of Great Britain is not as accessible as our Prime Minister is and Mr Menzies is unable to do as you ask'.[65]

Visits to England spawned a multitude of requests for access to the Queen or a royal event. There were requests to organise an invitation to a Royal Garden Party for the writer, an invitation to the royal enclosure at Ascot racecourse, or to the Trooping the Colour ceremony. All such requests were channelled through Australia House in London. One Londoner asked Menzies to procure an autographed photograph of the Queen herself.[66] The chance of seeing the Queen during her visit to Australia in 1954 was another reason to write to Menzies for privileged access. One thing Menzies could sometimes achieve for supplicants was to get them tickets to a London cricket test, which he did for a couple who wanted to see Australia play at The Oval in 1953.[67]

On many occasions, however, Menzies could not satisfy a correspondent's request because the law could not be subverted on their behalf. When one Englishwoman asked for help in getting her Pekinese puppy out of quarantine, there was little that could be done.[68] Similarly, another Englishwoman wanted to take three pet cockatoos to Tasmania, but again Menzies would not circumvent quarantine regulations.[69] Several correspondents expected Menzies to help them in conflicts with the tax office or another government department. When problems like this arose, Menzies referred the letter to the relevant department.[70]

Letters sought an entry into Menzies' family and domestic life. Wendy Solling wanted permission to paint his daughter Heather's portrait, which was also declined, although the artist had by then had several successful exhibitions of her work.[71] Madge Lyons, former cook at the King's Head pub in Sydney, sought a job at the Lodge (the Prime Minister's official residence in Canberra) as housekeeper or assistant cook. This was referred to Menzies' wife, Patti, who brushed it aside dismissively with a pencilled note: 'Nobody need be <u>out</u> of a cook's job today.'[72]

The supplicatory letters received by Menzies included several from writers seeking a solution to personal problems ranging from the irritating to the desperate. Mrs Herbert was among the former category when she asked Menzies to do something about her troublesome Italian neighbours who were allegedly mistreating their lovely pet dog.[73] Others hoped the Prime Minister would answer more serious physical and emotional needs. They asked, for instance, for any old clothes which the Menzies family had to spare. This was typical of the extreme hardship frequently expressed by aged pensioners. Others needed a loan, like an Austrian immigrant who asked Menzies for £50. He was out of work, ineligible for a pension because he was only fifty-nine years old, and faced eviction from his residence in Mount Gravatt (Queensland). He begged Menzies 'don't, don't let me down' several times, underlined in red.[74] He was refused and was told that the Prime Minister received many requests for loans, but that he would only respond to residents of his own electorate or charities like the Red Cross.

Menzies' intervention was required on occasion to resolve marital disputes. One divorcee in London, for example, wanted Menzies to compel her husband in Victoria to pay her maintenance.[75] A Ballarat man wanted Menzies' help in a child custody dispute with his former wife, who had taken their nine-year-old son to live in New South Wales.[76] Menzies sensibly told him to take his solicitor's advice, but it is notable that such requests received a reply at all. More harrowing was a letter from a Croatian woman who sent in an example of her needlework and asked in vain for a job. She was suffering from extreme anxiety and perhaps great loneliness, when she wrote in German: 'I am not happy in my marriage, for my son is very badly treated and I cry every day and endure my lot with daily weeping.'[77]

One fundamental assumption of writing upwards was that ordinary people had a right to direct personal access to their superiors. Writers implicitly believed that if they could reach a higher authority in person, they would receive humane treatment and a sympathetic hearing. Writing upwards strove for an unmediated connection with the leader, and assumed it was possible. Supplicatory letters, however, had exaggerated expectations of Menzies' powers. They might be useful in obtaining a telephone connection or a letter of introduction and, very rarely, they secured a small donation. At the same time, writers assumed that Menzies possessed the ability to smooth their access to high places (especially when royalty was going to be present), to secure them employment and even resolve conjugal discord. Obiba Forson, from the Gold Coast in West Africa, wanted plenty: he sent a wish list for books, papers, two Bibles, 'your own team photo' and a bandage to cover his leg. 'If you sent all them to me,' he assured Menzies, 'I will send you some monkey skin and some interesting things.'[78] But Menzies apparently had little use for a monkey skin.

Notes

1. National Library of Australia (NLA), Menzies papers ms 4936, Box 42, folder 51, Reg Longden, 26 December 1949. All future citations from the Menzies letters refer to this collection and this call number. I normally use correspondents' real names, in the interests of transparency and to enable researchers to locate my sources.
2. Maarten Van Ginderachter, '"If Your Majesty would only send me a little money to help buy an elephant": Letters to the Belgian Royal Family (1880–1940)', in Martyn Lyons (ed.), *Ordinary Writings, Personal Narratives: Writing Practices in Nineteenth and Early Twentieth-Century Europe* (Bern: Peter Lang, 2007), pp. 69–83; Henrik Eberle (ed.), *Letters to Hitler*, English version, ed. Victoria Harris, trans. Steven Randall (Cambridge, UK: Polity, 2012); Anne Wingenter, 'Voices of sacrifice: Letters to Mussolini and ordinary writing under Fascism', in Lyons, *Ordinary Writings, Personal Narratives*, pp. 155–72; Béatrice Fraenkel, '"Répondre à tous": une enquête sur le service du courier présidentiel', in Daniel Fabre (ed.), *Par Écrit. Ethnologie des écritures quotidiennes* (Paris: Maison des Sciences de l'Homme, 1997), pp. 243–71; Jeanne Marie Laskas, *To Obama, with Love, Joy, Hate and Despair* (London: Bloomsbury Circus, 2018).
3. Fraenkel, '"Répondre à tous"', pp. 243–71; Laskas, *To Obama with Love*, pp. 65–6.
4. For another example of letters to a ruler, in this case abusive and menacing, see Renato Monteleone, *Lettere al re* (Rome: Editori Riuniti,1973), and in a factory setting, Giampolo Gallo, *'Illmo signore Direttore' … Grande industria e società a Terni fra Otto e Novecento* (Foligno: Umbra, 1983). On petitions, see Emily E. Pyle, 'Peasant strategies for obtaining state aid: A study of petitions during World War 1', *Russian history/ Histoire russe* 24:1–2 (1997), 41–64; Chiara Gamboz, *Australian Indigenous Petitions: Emergence and Negotiations of Indigenous Authorship and Writings*, unpublished Ph.D. thesis, University of New South Wales, 2012; Sami Suodenjoki, 'Whistleblowing from below: Finnish rural inhabitants' letters to the imperial power at the turn of the twentieth century', in Ann-Catrine Edlund, Lars-Erik Edlund and Susanne Haugen (eds), *Vernacular Literacies – Past, Present, Future* (Umeå: Umeå University and Royal Skyttean Society, 2014), pp. 279–92.
5. Martyn Lyons, 'Writing upwards: How the weak wrote to the powerful', *Journal of Social History*, 49:2 (winter 2015), 317–30.
6. Camillo Zadra and Gianluigi Fait, *Deferenza, Rivendicazione, Supplica: le lettere ai potenti* (Treviso: Pagus, 1992).
7. James C. Scott, *Weapons of the Weak: Everyday Forms of Peasant Resistance* (New Haven, CT: Yale University Press, 1985).
8. Box 61, folder 214, Harbord (NSW), 15 February 1954.
9. For a fuller study of this corpus, see Martyn Lyons, *Dear Prime Minister: Letters to Robert Menzies, 1949–1966* (Sydney: University of New South Wales Press, 2021).

10 Percentages include letters sent by married couples and jointly by families so they add up to more than 100.
11 Box 122, folder 702.
12 Box 43, folder 57, Rhoda Payne, 29 December 1949.
13 Box 49, folder 116, Elwood (Vic), undated March 1953.
14 Box 55, folder 162, Mary Brown, Burwood (Vic), 29 September 1954.
15 Box 42, folder 50, Charles Kennedy, Gympie (Qld), 3 April 1950.
16 On the direct channel to the top, see Martyn Lyons, 'Writing upwards: Letters to Robert Menzies, Australian Prime Minister, 1949–1966', *Journal of Epistolary Studies*, 2:1 (Fall 2020), 34–51: https://jes-ojs-utrgv.tdl.org/jes/issue/view/7, accessed 23 February 2023.
17 Box 97, folder 510, 15 December 1960.
18 Box 84, folder 401, Sister Wooly, Townsville (Qld), 22 August 1958.
19 Box 71, folder 294, Wingham (Kent), 24 May 1955.
20 Box 70, folder 285, CK Punjabi, Kandla Port (Gujarat), 11 June 1955.
21 Box 119, folder 682, Arthur D'Ombrain, Sydney, 4 February 1964.
22 Box 75, folder 333, Robert Jaya Kumar, Eluru (Andhra Pradesh), 15 April 1957.
23 Box 106, folder 577, Balamban, Cebu (Philippines), 4 November 1961.
24 Box 71, folder 295, Blackheath (Greater London), 1 February 1955.
25 Box 45, folder 76, Chullora Railway Camp (NSW), 14 June 1951.
26 Box 42, folder 54, Melbourne, 9 April 1950.
27 Box 80, folder 366, Mundaring (WA), 17 March 1958.
28 Box 42, folder 48, Toorak (Vic), 16 June 1950.
29 Box 68, folder 266, IC Kempe, Ramco (SA), 20 July 1955.
30 Box 80, folder 369, Redcliffe (Qld), 7 November 1958.
31 Box 42, folder 48, LA Houghton, undated September 1950; Box 56, folder 166, E Campbell, 27 April 1954.
32 Box 86, folder 413, South Yarra (Vic), February 1959.
33 Box 51, folder 130, East Melbourne, 25 April 1953.
34 Box 81, folder 367, Oyster Bay (NSW), 27 October 1958.
35 Box 57, folder 175, Mitcham (Vic), 25 January 1954.
36 Box 85, folder 405, George Arnoldt, Hobart, 11 January 1959; Box 86, folder 421, Miss JFD Eales, Morpeth (NSW), 1 May 1959.
37 Box 88, folder 432, Manning (WA), November 1959.
38 Box 81, folder 367, Little River (Vic), 2 April 1958.
39 Box 119, folder 678, Agnes Cleary, Kew (Vic), 7 April 1964.
40 Box 86, folder 413, South Yarra (Vic), undated February 1959.
41 Box 76, folder 334, Mrs Joan Lewis, Cardiff (Wales), 17 July 1957.
42 Box 50, folder 119, Miss E Porter, London, 5 June 1953.
43 Box 48, folder 105, 19 March 1953.
44 Box 44, folder 71, Sir Ernest Fisk, Hayes (Middlesex), 12 February 1951.
45 Box 48, folder 105, Mrs RJ McGarvie, Pomborneit (Vic), 30 September 1953.
46 Box 54, folder 143, 3 August 1953.
47 Box 71, folder 293, Scottish Secretariat, Glasgow, 21 January 1955, for example.

48 Box 42, folder 51, Florence Love, Middle Park (Vic), 11 April 1950; Box 42, folder 52, Mrs McGlashan, 16 January 1950.
49 Box 52, folder 136, Mrs MC Thomson, Northbridge (NSW), 7 October 1953.
50 Box 42, folder 50, John Fraser Kelly, 14 December 1949.
51 Box 89, folder 448, GA Robertson, Brisbane, 24 April 1959.
52 Box 50, folder 118, London, 28 June 1953.
53 Box 48, folder 105, Rev Ian McLellan, 25 June 1953.
54 Box 41, folder 42, East Malvern (Vic), 5 July 1950.
55 Box 41, folder 43, IF Heathershaw, Secretary of the Council of Elders of the Presbyterian Church of Victoria, 31 March 1950.
56 Box 56, folder 166, 1 February 1954.
57 Box 68, folder 272, 6 October 1955.
58 Box 47, folder 100, Kew Traders' Committee (Vic), 10 December 1953.
59 Box 64, folder 239, Ascot Vale (Vic), 10 August 1955.
60 Box 51, folder 134, Ashburton (Vic), undated August 1953.
61 Box 60, folder 205, Roseville (NSW), 17 May 1954.
62 Steven King, *Writing the Lives of the English Poor, 1750s–1830s* (London: McGill-Queen's University Press, 2019).
63 Van Ginderachter, ' "If Your Majesty would only send me a little money" ', p. 69.
64 Box 100, folder 528, Bob Demaine, Melbourne, 11 August 1961.
65 Box 47, folder 100, 3 June 1953.
66 Box 50, folder 124, Dorothy Rookwood, Finsbury Park, 14 June 1953.
67 Box 51, folder 130, Mrs Sydney Smith, London, 9 June 1953. England won by eight wickets.
68 Box 63, folder 229, Betty Amer, Romford (Essex), 23 July 1953.
69 Box 49, folder 113, Mrs F Norris, Totnes (Devon), date unknown 1953.
70 Box 48, folder 107, Panania (NSW), 30 November 1953.
71 Box 51, folder 131, Wendy Solling, Maitland (NSW), 18 February 1953.
72 Box 42, folder 51, 10 April 1950.
73 Box 75, folder 328, Mrs H Herbert, North Carlton (Vic), 5 November 1957.
74 Box 51, folder 131, Waldemar Sommer, 26 August 1953.
75 Box 52, folder 137, PG Tolley, London, undated June 1953.
76 Box 47, folder 98, Owen Johnston, 29 October 1953.
77 Box 62, folder 221, Anka Popovich, Fairfield (NSW), undated June 1954.
78 Box 58, folder 185, 8 March 1954.

Select bibliography

Acín Fanlo, José Luis, Elena Aquilué Pérez and Rosa Abadía Abadías, *Los grabados de la torre de la cárcel de Broto* (Broto: Ayuntamiento, 2005).
Adams, William Edwin, *Memoirs of a Social Atom*, 2 vols (London: Hutchinson, 1903).
Agutter, Karen, 'Exploring the migrant experience through an examination of letters to *The New Australian*', in Catherine Dewhirst and Paul Scully (eds), *The Transnational Voices of Australia's Migrant and Minority Press* (London: Palgrave Macmillan, 2020), pp. 151–67.
Ahnert, Ruth, 'Writing in the Tower of London during the Reformation, circa 1530–1558', *Huntington Library Quarterly*, 72:2 (2009), 168–92.
Algarra Pardo, Víctor Manuel and Paloma Berrocal Ruiz, *Los grafitis históricos del castel de Alaquàs* (Alaquàs: Ayuntamiento, 2016).
Altick, Richard D., *The English Common Reader: A Social History of the Mass Reading Public, 1800–1900* (Chicago: Chicago University Press, 1957).
Amelang, James, *The Flight of Icarus: Artisan Autobiography in Early Modern Europe* (Stanford, CA: Stanford University Press, 1998).
Artières, Philippe, *Le livre des vies coupables: Autobiographies de criminels (1896–1909)* (Paris: Albin Michel, 2000).
Artières, Philippe, *Un séminariste assassin: L'Affaire Bladier, 1905* (Paris: Centre National de la Recherche Scientifique, 2020).
Ascoli, Francesco, *La penna in mano: per una storia della cultura manoscritta in età moderna* (Florence: Leo S. Olschki, 2020).
Ashplant, T. G., 'Life writings from below in Europe', *History Workshop Journal*, 79:1 (2015), 274–89.
Auer, Anita, Daniel Schreier and Richard J. Watts (eds), *Letter Writing and Language Change* (Cambridge, UK: Cambridge University Press, 2015).
Ayres-Bennett, Wendy and John Bellamy (eds), *The Cambridge Handbook of Language Standardization* (Cambridge, UK: Cambridge University Press, 2021).
Bacconnier, Gérard, André Minet and Louis Soler (eds), *La Plume au Fusil: les poilus du Midi à travers leur correspondance* (Toulouse: Privat, 1985).
Barczyk, Ewa, 'Polish migrant memoirs and letters: Documenting the World War II diaspora', *Polish American Studies*, 77:2 (2020), 84–5.
Barthas, Louis, *Les Carnets de Guerre de Louis Barthas, Tonnelier, 1914–19* (Paris: Maspéro, 1978).
Barton, David and Mary Hamilton, *Local Literacies: Reading and Writing in One Community* (London: Routledge, 1998).
Barton, David and Nigel Hall (eds), *Letter Writing as a Social Practice* (Amsterdam: John Benjamins, 2000).

Barton, David, Mary Hamilton and Roz Ivanic (eds), *Situated Literacies* (London: Routledge, 2000).

Beverley, John, 'The margin at the centre: On *testimonio*', *Modern Fiction Studies*, 35:1 (1989), 11–28.

Borges, Marcelo and Sonia Cancian (eds), *Migrant Letters: Emotional Language, Mobile Identities, and Writing Practices in Historical Perspective* (London: Routledge, 2019).

Boudon, Jacques-Olivier, 'Sous les parquets du château de Picomtal. Les écrits post-humes d'un menuisier des Hautes-Alpes (1880–1881)', *Histoire, économie et société*, 33:1 (2014), 72–86.

Brandt, Deborah, *The Rise of Mass Writing: Redefining Mass Literacy* (Cambridge, UK: Cambridge University Press, 2015).

Brignon, Laura, *Traduire la littérature brute: le second tapuscrit de Vincenzo Rabito* (Linguistique: Université Toulouse-le-Mirail – Toulouse II, 2017).

Brown, Elaine, 'Gender, occupation, illiteracy and the urban economic environment: Leicester 1760–1890', *Urban History*, 32:2 (2004), 191–209.

Burnett, John, David Vincent and David Mayall (eds), *The Autobiography of the Working Class: An Annotated Critical Bibliography*, 2 vols (Brighton, UK: Harvester, 1984–89).

Caffarena, Fabio and Nancy Murzilli (eds), *In Guerra con le parole: il primo conflitto mondiale dalle testimonianze scritte alla memoria multimediale* (Trento: Fondazione Museo Storico di Trento, 2018).

Carpenter, Alton E. and A. Anne Eiland, *Chappie: World War II Diary of a Combat Chaplain* (Mesa, AZ: A. Anne Eiland, 2007).

Carter, Natalie and Steven King, '"I think we ought not to acknowledge them [paupers] as that encourages them to write": The administrative state, power and the Victorian pauper', *Social History*, 46:2 (2021), 117–44.

Castillo Gómez, Antonio (ed.), *La conquista del alfabeto: Escritura y clases populares* (Gijón: Trea, 2002).

Castillo Gómez, Antonio, *Entre la pluma y la pared. Una historia social de la escritura en los Siglos de Oro* (Madrid: Akal, 2006).

Castillo Gómez, Antonio, '"Être non seulement libellé mais aussi exposé au public". Les inscriptions censurées au Siècle d'Or', in Alexandra Merle and Araceli Guillaume-Alonso (eds), *Les voies du silence dans l'Espagne des Habsbourg* (Paris: Presses universitaires de Paris-Sorbonne, 2013), pp. 309–28.

Castillo Gómez, Antonio, 'Secret voices: Prison graffiti in the Spanish Empire (16th–18th century)', *Quaderni Storici*, 157:1 (2018), 137–64.

'"Cher Philippe": A *Festschrift* for Philippe Lejeune', special issue of *European Journal of Life Writing*, 7 (2018).

Civale, Gianclaudio, '"Animo carcerato". Inquisizione, detenzione e graffiti a Palermo nel secolo XVII', *Mediterranea*, XIV:40 (2017), 249–94.

Coombes, B. L. (Bert), *These Poor Hands: The Autobiography of a Miner Working in South Wales* (Cardiff: University of Wales Press, 2002, first ed. 1939), with introduction by Bill Jones and Chris Williams.

Crone, Ros, 'Educating the labouring poor in nineteenth-century Suffolk', *Social History*, 43:2 (2018), 161–85.

Davies, Margaret Llewelyn (ed.), *Maternity: Letters from Working Women* (London: Virago, reprint, 1978), first published 1915.

Davies, Margaret Llewelyn (ed.), *Life as We Have Known It, by Co-operative Working Women* (London: Virago, reprint, 1982), first published 1931.

De Sutter, Bart and Maarten Van Ginderachter, 'Working-class voices from the late nineteenth century: "Propaganda pence" in a socialist paper in Ghent', *History Workshop Journal*, 69:1 (2010), 133–45.

Dekker, Rudolf, 'Jacques Presser's heritage: Ego-documents in the study of history', *Memoria y civilización*, 5 (2002), 13–37.

Dodd, William, *A Narrative of the Experience and Sufferings of William Dodd, a Factory Cripple. Written by Himself* (London: L. and G. Seeley, 1841).

Dossena, Marina, and Gabriella Del Lungo Camiciotti (eds), *Letter Writing in Late Modern Europe* (Amsterdam: John Benjamins, 2012).

Driscoll, Matthew, *The Unwashed Children of Eve: The Production, Dissemination and Reception of Popular Literature in Post-Reformation Iceland* (Enfield Lock, UK: Hisarlik Press, 1997).

Driscoll, Matthew J. and Margrét Eggertsdóttir, *Mirrors of Virtue: Manuscript and Print in Late Pre-Modern Iceland*, Bibliotheca Arnamagnaeana XLIX: Opuscula XV (Copenhagen: Museum Tusculanums, 2017).

Droste, Heiko and Kirsti Salmi-Niklander (eds), *Handwritten Newspapers: An Alternative Medium during the Early Modern and the Modern Period*, Studia Fennica Historica 26 (Helsinki: Finnish Literature Society, 2019).

Eberle, Henrik (ed.), *Letters to Hitler*, English version, ed. Victoria Harris, trans. Steven Randall (Cambridge, UK: Polity, 2012).

Eckardt, Wilhelm A. and Helmut Klingelhöfer (eds), *Bauernleben im Zeitalter des Dreißigjährigen Krieges. Die Stausebacher Chronik des Caspar Preis 1636–1667* (Marburg an der Lahn: Trauvetter and Fischer, 1998).

Edlund, Ann-Catrine, T. G. Ashplant and Anna Kuismin (eds), *Reading and Writing from Below: Exploring the Margins of Modernity* (Umeå: Royal Skyttean Society, 2016).

Eichhorn, David Max, *The GI's Rabbi: World War II Letters of David Max Eichhorn*, ed. Gregg Palmer and Mark S. Zaid, with introduction by Doris L. Bergen (Lawrence: University of Kansas Press, 2004).

Eley, Geoff, 'Labor history, social history, *Alltagsgeschichte*: Experience, culture and the politics of the everyday – a new direction for German social history', *Journal of Modern History*, 61 (June 1989), 297–343.

Eliot, Simon and Jonathan Rose (eds), *Companion to the History of the Book*, 2 vols (Oxford: Wiley-Blackwell, 2nd ed., 2019).

Elliott, Bruce, David A. Gerber and Suzanne M. Sinke (eds), *The Epistolary Practices of International Migrants* (New York: Palgrave Macmillan, 2006).

Elspaß, Stephan, *Sprachgeschichte von unten. Untersuchungen zum geschriebenen Alltagsdeutsch im 19. Jahrhundert* (Tübingen: Niemeyer, 2005).

Elspaß, Stephan, 'Private letters as a source for an alternative history of Late Modern German', in Anita Auer, Daniel Schreier and Richard J. Watts (eds), *Letter Writing and Language Change* (Cambridge, UK: Cambridge University Press, 2015), pp. 35–52.

Elspaß, Stephan and Michaela Negele (eds), *Sprachvariation und Sprachwandel in der Stadt der Frühen Neuzeit* (Heidelberg: Winter, 2011).

Elspaß, Stephan, Nils Langer, Joachim Scharloth and Wim Vandenbussche (eds), *Germanic Language Histories 'from Below' (1700–2000)* (Berlin and New York: De Gruyter, 2007).

Fabre, Daniel (ed.), *Écritures ordinaires* (Paris: P.O.L/Centre Georges Pompidou, 1993).

Fabre, Daniel (ed.), *Par écrit. Ethnologie des écritures quotidiennes* (Paris: Maison des Sciences de l'Homme, 1997).

Falke, Cassandra, *Literature by the Working Class: English Autobiographies, 1820–1848* (Amherst, NY: Cambria, 2013).

Farge, Arlette, *Instants de vie* (Paris: École des Hautes Études en Sciences Sociales, 2021).

Fitzpatrick, David, *Oceans of Consolation: Personal Accounts of Irish Migration to Australia* (Melbourne: Melbourne University Press, 1995).

Fitzpatrick, Sheila, 'Supplicants and citizens: Public letter writing in Soviet Russia in the 1930s', *Slavic Review*, 55:1 (1996), 78–105.

Fiume, Giovanna, 'Soundless screams: Graffiti and drawings in the prisons of the Holy Office in Palermo', *Journal of Early Modern History*, 21:3 (2017), 188–215.

Fiume, Giovanna, 'Justice, expiation and forgiveness in the graffiti and drawings of Palermo's secret prisons', *Quaderni storici*, 157:1 (2018), 71–108.

Fiume, Giovanna, *Del Santo Uffizio in Sicilia e delle sue carceri* (Rome: Viella, 2021).

Fleming, Juliet, *Graffiti and the Writing Arts of Early Modern England* (Philadelphia: University of Pennsylvania Press, 2001).

Frankel, Oz, 'Scenes of commission: Royal commissions of inquiry and the culture of social investigation in early Victorian Britain', *European Legacy*, 4:6 (1999), 20–41.

Frankel, Oz, *States of Inquiry: Social Investigations and Print Culture in Nineteenth-Century Britain and the United States* (Baltimore, MD: Johns Hopkins University Press, 2006).

Frondizi, Alexandre and Emmanuel Fureix (eds), 'Écrits et écritures populaires', thematic issue of *Revue d'histoire du XIXe siècle*, 65 (2022).

Gabrielle, Patrizia (ed.), 'La storia e i soggetti. La "gente comune"', *Revista de Historiografía*, 37 (2022), 8–126.

Garvey, Ellen Gruber, *Writing with Scissors: American Scrapbooks from the Civil War to the Harlem Renaissance* (New York: Oxford University Press, 2013).

Gerber, David A., 'Acts of deceiving and withholding in immigrant letters: Personal identity and self-presentation in personal correspondence', *Journal of Social History*, 39:2 (2005), 315–30.

Gerber, David A., *Authors of their Lives: The Personal Correspondence of British Immigrants to North America in the Nineteenth Century* (New York: New York University Press, 2006).

Gerber, David A., 'Moving forward and moving on: Nostalgia, significant others, and social reintegration in nineteenth-century British immigrant personal correspondence', *History of the Family*, 21:3 (2016), 291–314.

Ghizzardi, Pietro, *Mi richordo ancora* (Macerata: Quodlibet, 2016).

Gibelli, Antonio and Fabio Caffarena, 'Le lettere degli emigranti', in Piero Bevilacqua, Andreina de Clementi and Emilio Franzina (eds), *Storia dell'Emigrazione Italiana* (Rome: Donzelli, 2002), pp. 563–74.

Gimeno Blay, Francisco M. and María Luz Mandingorra Llavata, *'Los muros tienen la palabra'. Materiales para una historia de los graffiti* (Valencia: Publicacions Universitat de València, 1997).

Gittelsohn, Roland B., *Pacifist to Padre: The World War II Memoir of Chaplain Roland B. Gittelsohn, December 1941–January 1946*, ed. Donald M. Bishop (Quantico, VA: Marine Corps University Press, 2021).

González Gonzalo, Elvira and Bernat Oliver Font, *Los barcos de piedra. La arquitectura náutica balear a través de los grafitis murales. Siglos XIV–XVII* (Palma de Mallorca: Institut d'Innovació Empresarial de les Illes Balears, 2007).
Goody, Jack (ed.), *Literacy in Traditional Societies* (Cambridge, UK: Cambridge University Press, 1975).
Goody, Jack, *The Domestication of the Savage Mind* (Cambridge, UK: Cambridge University Press, 1977).
Goody, Jack, *The Logic of Writing and the Organisation of Society* (Cambridge, UK: Cambridge University Press, 1986).
Goody, Jack, *The Interface between the Written and the Oral* (Cambridge, UK: Cambridge University Press, 1987).
Graff, Harvey J., *Literacy Myths, Legacies and Lessons: New Studies on Literacy* (London and New York: Routledge, 2011).
Graheli, Shanti, 'Readers and consumers of popular print', *Quaerendo*, 51 (2021), 61–94.
Grosse, Siegfried, Martin Grimberg, Thomas Hölscher and Jörg Karweick, *'Denn das Schreiben gehört nicht zu meiner täglichen Beschäftigung'* (Bonn: Dietz, 1989).
Guichard, Charlotte, *Graffitis. Inscrire son nom à Rome (XVIe–XIXe siècle)* (Paris: Seuil, 2014).
Güntzer, Augustin, *Kleines Biechlin von meinem gantzen Leben. Die Autobiographie eines Elsässer Kanngießers aus dem 17. Jahrhundert*, ed. Fabian Brändle and Dominik Sieber (Cologne, Weimar and Vienna: Böhlau, 2002).
Guttormsson, Loftur, 'The development of popular religious literacy in the seventeenth and eighteenth centuries', *Scandinavian Journal of History*, 15:1 (1990), 7–35.
Hamilton, Mary, David Barton and Roz Ivanic (eds), *Worlds of Literacy* (London: Multilingual Matters, 1994).
Helbich, Wolfgang, Walter D. Kamphoefner and Ulrike Sommer (eds), *Briefe aus Amerika. Deutsche Auswanderer schreiben aus der Neuen Welt 1830–1930* (Munich: Beck, 1988).
Hellbeck, Jochen, '"The diaries of Fritzes and the letters of Gretchens": Personal writings from the German–Soviet war and their readers', *Kritika: Explorations in Russian and Eurasian History*, 10 (2009), 571–606.
Hernández-Campoy, Juan M. and J. Camilo Conde-Silvestre (eds), *The Handbook of Historical Sociolinguistics* (Chichester, UK: Wiley-Blackwell, 2012).
Hitchcock, Tim, 'A new history from below', *History Workshop Journal*, 57:1 (2004): 294–8.
Hilliard, Christopher, 'Producers by hand and by brain: Working-class writers and left-wing publishers in 1930s Britain', *Journal of Modern History*, 78:1 (2006), 37–64.
Houston, Robert A., *Literacy in Early Modern Europe: Culture and Education, 1500–1800* (London: Routledge, 2nd ed., 2014).
Isaac, Jessica, 'Graphing the archives of nineteenth-century amateur newspapers', *Book History*, 19 (2016), 317–48.
Jenkins, Henry with Katie Clinton, Ravi Purushotma, Alice J. Robison and Margaret Weigel, *Confronting the Challenges of Participatory Culture: Media Education for the Twenty-First Century* (Cambridge, MA: MIT Press, 2006).
Jones, Bill and Chris Williams, *B. L. Coombes* (Cardiff: University of Wales Press, 2002).

Jones, Peter and Steven King, *Navigating the Old English Poor Law: The Kirkby Lonsdale Letters, 1809–1836* (Oxford: Oxford University Press, 2020).

Jones, Peter and Steven King, *Pauper Voices, Public Opinion and Workhouse Reform in Mid-Victorian England – Bearing Witness* (Basingstoke, UK: Palgrave, 2020).

Joseph, Brian D. and Richard D. Janda (eds), *The Handbook of Historical Linguistics* (Malden, MA, and Oxford: Blackwell, 2003).

Joyce, Patrick, 'The people's English: Language and class in England 1840–1920', in Peter Burke and Roy Porter (eds), *Language, Self and Society: A Social History of Language* (Cambridge, UK: Polity, 1991), pp. 154–91.

Kertzer, Morris N., *With an H on My Dog Tag* (New York: Behrman House, 1947).

Kimball, Clyde E., *Diary of My Work Overseas* (Nashua, NH: E. E. Kimball, 1947).

King, Steven, *Writing the Lives of the English Poor, 1750s-1830s* (London: McGill-Queen's University Press, 2019).

King, Steven and Peter Jones, 'Testifying for the poor: Epistolary advocates for the poor in nineteenth-century England and Wales', *Journal of Social History*, 49:4 (2016): 784–807.

King, Steven, Paul Carter, Natalie Carter, Peter Jones and Carol Beardmore, *'In Their Own Write': A New Poor Law History from Below* (London: McGill-Queen's University Press, 2022).

Klenk, Marion, *Sprache im Kontext sozialer Lebenswelt. Eine Untersuchung zur Arbeiterschriftsprache im 19. Jahrhundert* (Tübingen: Niemeyer, 1997).

Koch, Peter and Wulf Oesterreicher, 'Language of immediacy – language of distance: orality and literacy from the perspective of language theory and linguistic history', in C. Lange, B. Weber and G. Wolf (eds), *Communicative Spaces: Variation, Contact, and Change. Papers in Honour of Ursula Schaefer* (Frankfurt am Main: Peter Lang, 2012), pp. 441–73.

Köhler, Karl-Heinz, Grita Herre and Dagmar Becke (eds), *Ludwig van Beethovens Konversationshefte*, Vol. 9 (Leipzig: Deutscher Verlag für Musik, 1989).

Kuismin, Anna and Matthew J. Driscoll (eds), *White Field, Black Seeds: Nordic Literacy Practices in the Long Nineteenth Century* (Helsinki: Finnish Literature Society, 2013).

Kula, Witold and Josephine Wtulich, *Writing Home: Immigrants in Brazil and the United States, 1890–1891* (New York: Columbia University Press, 1986).

Kumar, Arun, 'Letters of the labouring poor: The art of letter writing in colonial India', *Past and Present*, 246:1 (2020), 149–90.

Labov, William, *Principles of Linguistic Change: Vol. 1, Internal Factors* (Oxford: Oxford University Press, 1994).

Lahire, Bernard, *La Raison des plus faibles* (Lille: Presses universitaires de Lille, 1993).

Laskas, Jeanne Marie, *To Obama, with Love, Joy, Hate and Despair* (London: Bloomsbury Circus, 2018).

Lejeune, Philippe, *Le pacte autobiographique* (Paris: Seuil, 1975).

Lejeune, Philippe, *Le moi des demoiselles: enquête sur le journal de jeune fille* (Paris: Seuil, 1993).

Litoff, Judy Barrett and David C. Smith, *Since You Went Away: World War II Letters from American Women on the Home Front* (New York: Oxford University Press, 1991).

Lüdtke, Alf, 'Introduction: What is the history of everyday life and who are its practitioners?', in A. Lüdtke (ed.), *The History of Everyday Life: Reconstructing*

Historical Experiences and Ways of Life, trans. William Templer (Princeton, NJ: Princeton University Press, 1995), pp. 3–40.

Lyons, Martyn, 'La culture littéraire des travailleurs. Autobiographies ouvrières dans l'Europe du XIXe siècle', *Annales: histoire, sciences sociales*, 56:4–5 (July–October 2001), 927–46.

Lyons, Martyn (ed.), *Ordinary Writings, Personal Narratives: Writing Practices in Nineteenth and Twentieth-Century Europe* (Bern: Peter Lang, 2007).

Lyons, Martyn, *A History of Reading and Writing in the Western World* (Basingstoke, UK: Palgrave, 2010).

Lyons, Martyn, 'A new history from below? The writing culture of ordinary people in Europe', *History Australia*, 7:3 (2010), 59.1–59.9.

Lyons, Martyn, *The Writing Culture of Ordinary People in Europe, c. 1860–1920* (Cambridge, UK: Cambridge University Press, 2013).

Lyons, Martyn, 'The power of the scribe: Delegated writing in modern Europe', *European History Quarterly*, 44:2 (2014), 244–62.

Lyons, Martyn, 'Writing upwards: How the weak wrote to the powerful', *Journal of Social History*, 49:2 (2015), 317–30.

Lyons, Martyn, 'Writing upwards: Letters to Robert Menzies, Australian Prime Minister, 1949–1966', *Journal of Epistolary Studies*, 2:1 (Fall 2020), 34–51, https://jes-ojs-utrgv.tdl.org/jes/article/view/27, accessed 9 June 2023.

Lyons, Martyn, *Dear Prime Minister: Letters to Robert Menzies, 1949–1966* (Sydney: University of New South Wales Press, 2021).

Lyons, Martyn and Rita Marquilhas (eds), *Approaches to the History of Written Culture: A World Inscribed* (Cham, Switzerland: Palgrave Macmillan, 2017).

Magnússon, Sigurður Gylfi, 'Tales of the unexpected: The "textual environment", ego-documents and a nineteenth-century Icelandic love story – an approach in microhistory', *Cultural and Social History*, 12:1 (2015), 77–94.

Magnússon, Sigurður Gylfi, *Emotional Experience and Microhistory. A Life Story of a Destitute Pauper Poet in the Nineteenth Century* (London: Routledge, 2020).

Magnússon, Sigurður Gylfi and Davíð Ólafsson, 'Barefoot historians: Education in Iceland in the modern period', in Klaus-Joachim Lorenzen-Schmidt and Bjørn Poulsen (eds), *Writing Peasants: Studies on Peasant Literacy in Early Modern Northern Europe* (Odense: Landbohistorisk Selskab, 2002), pp. 175–209.

Magnússon, Sigurður Gylfi and Davíð Ólafsson, 'Minor knowledge: Microhistory, scribal communities, and the importance of institutional structures', *Quaderni Storici*, 47:2 (2012), 495–524.

Magnússon, Sigurður Gylfi and Dávíð Ólafsson, *Minor Knowledge and Microhistory. Manuscript Culture in the Nineteenth Century* (London: Routledge, 2017).

Magnússon, Sigurður Gylfi and Davíð Ólafsson, 'In the name of barefoot historians: In-between spaces within the Icelandic educational system', in Cristiano Casalini, Edward Choi and Ayenachew Woldegiyorgis (eds), *Education Beyond Europe: Models and Traditions before Modernities* (Leiden: Brill, 2021), pp. 324–44.

Marchi, Clelia, *Il tuo nome sulla neve. Gnanca na Busia* (Milan: Il Saggiatore, 2014).

Martínez Martín, Laura, *Voces de la ausencia. Las cartas privadas de los emigrantes Asturianos a América (1856–1936)* (Gijón: Trea, 2019).

McNeely, Ian, *The Emancipation of Writing: German Civil Society in the Making, 1790s–1820s* (Berkeley: University of California Press, 2003).

Moss, David (ed.), 'The story of *Terra matta*', special issue of *Journal of Modern Italian Studies*, 19:3 (2014).

Neumann, Marko, *Soldatenbriefe des 18. und 19. Jahrhunderts* (Heidelberg: Winter, 2019).
Occhipinti, Marta, 'Storia del contadino che scriveva memorie sui sacchi di carta', *La Repubblica*, 22 February 2022, p. 12.
Ólafsson, Davíð, 'Vernacular literacy practices in nineteenth-century Icelandic scribal culture', in Ann-Catrine Edlund (ed.), *Att läsa och att skriva: Två vågor av vardagligt skriftbruk i Norden 1800–2000*, Nordliga studier 3, Vardagligt skriftbrug 1 (Umeå: Umeå Universitet and Kungl. Skytteanska Samfundet, 2012), pp. 65–85.
Ozcáriz Gil, Pablo (ed.), *La memoria en la piedra. Estudios sobre grafitos históricos* (Pamplona: Gobierno de Navarra, 2012).
Penloup, Marie-Claude, *La Tentation du littéraire* (Paris: Didier, 2000).
Petrucci, Armando, *Scrittura e popolo nella Roma Barocca, 1585–1721* (Rome: Qasar, 1982).
Petrucci, Armando, *La scrittura. Ideologia e rappresentazione* (Turin: Einaudi, 1986).
Petrucci, Armando, *Public Lettering: Script, Power and Culture* (Chicago: University of Chicago Press, 1993).
Petrucci, Armando, *Writing the Dead: Death and Writing Strategies in the Western Tradition*, trans. Michael Sullivan (Stanford, CA: Stanford University Press, 1998).
Petrucci, Armando, *Scrivere Lettere: una storia plurimillenaria* (Rome: Laterza, 2008).
Pick, Richard, 'Ein Tagebuch aus der Zeit der Fremdherrschaft. Im Auszuge mitgeteilt von R. P.', *Annalen des Historischen Vereins für den Niederrhein*, 16 (1865), 127–58.
Pigeon, Stephan, 'Steal it, change it, print it: Transatlantic scissors-and-paste journalism in *Ladies' Treasury*, 1857–1895', *Journal of Victorian Culture*, 22:1 (2017), 24–39.
Plesch, Véronique, 'Graffiti and ritualization: San Sebastiano at Arborio', in Joëlle Rollo-Koster (ed.), *Medieval and Early Modern Rituals: Formalized Behavior in Europe, China and Japan* (Leiden: Brill, 2002), pp. 127–46.
Plesch, Véronique, 'Memory on the wall: Graffiti on religious wall paintings', *Journal of Medieval and Early Modern Studies*, 32:1 (2002), 167–98.
Pritchard, Violet, *English Medieval Graffiti* (Cambridge, UK: Cambridge University Press, 1967).
Pyle, Emily E., 'Peasant strategies for obtaining state aid: A study of petitions during World War I', *Russian History*, 24:1 (1997), 41–64.
Rabito, Vincenzo, *Terra Matta*, ed. Evelina Santangelo and Luca Ricci (Turin: Einaudi, 2014).
Robinson, Jennifer, *Deeper than Reason: Emotion and Its Role in Literature, Music, and Art* (Oxford: Clarendon, 2005).
Rodríguez Vázquez, Elías and Pascual Tinoco Quesnel, *Graffitis novohispanos de Tepeapulco, siglo XVI* (Mexico City: INAH, 2006).
Roggero, Marina and Maria-Novella Borghetti, 'L'Alphabétisation en Italie: une conquête feminine?', *Annales: histoire, sciences sociales*, 56:4–5 (2001), 919–24.
Rose, Jonathan, *The Intellectual Life of the British Working Classes* (New Haven, CT: Yale University Press, 2001).
Russo, Alessandra, 'Atravesando la zona de silencio: graffiti coloniales en las letrinas del convento de Actopan', in Magdalena Garrido Caballero and Gabriela Vallejo Cervantes (eds), *De la Monarquía Hispánica a la Unión Europea: relaciones internacionales, comercio e imaginarios colectivos* (Murcia: Universidad de Murcia, 2013), pp. 41–77.

Rutten, Gijsbert and Andreas Krogull, 'The observee's paradox: Theorising linguistic differences between historical ego-documents', *Neuphilologische Mitteilungen*, 122:1–2 (2021), 284–318.
Salmi-Niklander, Kirsti, *Itsekasvatusta ja kapinaa. Tutkimus Karkkilan työläisnuorten kirjoittavasta keskusteluyhteisöstä 1910- ja 1920-luvuilla* (Helsinki: Suomalaisen Kirjallisuuden Seura, 2004).
Salmi-Niklander, Kirsti, 'Manuscripts and broadsheets: Narrative genres and the communication circuit among working-class youth in early twentieth-century Finland', *Folklore*, 33 (2006), 109–26.
Salmi-Niklander, Kirsti, 'Small stories, trivial events – and strong emotions: Local event narratives in handwritten newspapers as negotiation of individual and collective experiences', in Monika Tasa, Ergo-Hart Västrik and Anu Kannike (eds), *Body, Personhood and Privacy: Perspectives on Cultural Other and Human Experience*, Approaches to Culture Theory 7 (Tartu: University of Tartu Press, 2017), pp. 163–78.
Sarti, Raffaella, 'Renaissance graffiti: The case of the Ducal Palace of Urbino', in Sandra Cavallo and Silvia Evangelisti (eds), *Domestic Institutional Interiors in Early Modern Europe* (Farnham, UK: Ashgate, 2009), pp. 51–81.
Sarti, Raffaella (ed.), *La pietra racconta. Un palazzo da leggere* (Casinina: Arte Grafiche della Torre, 2017).
Sbirziola, Antonio, *Povero, onesto e gentiluomo. Un emigrante in Australia 1954–1961* (Bologna: Il Mulino, 2012).
Schechter, Brandon M., *The Stuff of Soldiers: A History of the Red Army in World War II through Objects* (Ithaca, NY: Cornell University Press, 2019).
Schiegg, Markus and Lena Sowada, 'Script switching in nineteenth-century lower-class German handwriting', *Paedagogica Historica*, 55:6 (2019), 772–91.
Schikorsky, Isa (ed.), *'Wenn doch dies Elend ein Ende hätte'. Ein Briefwechsel aus dem Deutsch-Französischen Krieg 1870/71* (Cologne, Weimar and Vienna: Böhlau, 1999).
Scott, James C., *Weapons of the Weak: Everyday Forms of Peasant Resistance* (New Haven, CT: Yale University Press, 1985).
Sheridan, Dorothy, Brian Street and David Bloome, *Writing Ourselves: Mass-Observation and Literacy Practice* (Cresskill, NJ: Hampton Press, 2000).
Simmons, James R., Jr., (ed.), *Factory Lives: Four Nineteenth-Century Working-Class Autobiographies* (Peterborough, ON: Broadview, 2007).
Sokoll, Thomas, *Essex Pauper Letters 1731–1837* (Oxford: Oxford University Press, 2001).
Spivak, Gayatri Chakravorty, 'Can the subaltern speak?' in Cary Nelson and Lawrence Grossberg (eds), *Marxism and the Interpretation of Culture* (Chicago: University of Illinois Press, 1988), pp. 271–316.
Stanley, Liz, 'To the letter: Thomas and Znaniecki's "The polish peasant" and writing a life, sociologically', *Life Writing*, 7:2 (2010), 139–51.
Stanley, Liz, 'The scriptural economy, the Forbes figuration and the racial order: Everyday life in South Africa 1850–1930', *Sociology*, 49:5 (2015), 837–52.
Stanley, Liz, 'Settler colonialism and migrant letters: The Forbes family and letter-writing in South Africa 1850–1922', *History of the Family*, 21:3 (2016), 398–428.
Steedman, Carolyn, 'Enforced narratives: Stories of another self', in Tess Cosslett, Celia Lury and Penny Summerfield (eds), *Feminism and Autobiography: Texts, Theories, Methods* (London: Routledge, 2000), pp. 25–39.

Steffen, Joachim, Harald Thun and Rainer Zaiser (eds), *Classes populaires, scripturalité et histoire de la langue: un bilan interdisciplinaire* (Kiel: Westensee, 2018).

Stroup, Russell Cartwright, *Letters from the Pacific: A Combat Chaplain in World War II* (Columbia: University of Missouri Press, 2000).

Thomas, William Isaac and Florian Znaniecki, *The Polish Peasant in Europe and America*, 2 vols (New York: Dover, 1918 and 1958).

Timmis, Ivor, *The Discourse of Desperation: Late Eighteenth and Early Nineteenth Century Letters by Paupers, Prisoners and Rogues* (London: Routledge, 2020).

Tomkins, Alannah, 'Poor law institutions through working-class eyes: Autobiography, emotion, and family context, 1834–1914', *Journal of British Studies*, 60:2 (2021): 285–309.

Topalović, Elvira and Iris Hille, 'Perspektivierung von Wirklichkeit(en) im Hexenprozess: Geheimbriefe und Verhörprotokolle im Vergleich. Quellen, Transkriptionen, Übertragungen', historicum.net, 2007, accessed 9 June 2023.

Turunen, Risto, *Shades of Red: Evolution of the Political Language of Finnish Socialism from the Nineteenth Century until the Civil War of 1918* (Helsinki: Finnish Society for Labour History, 2021).

Van Eck, Marianne Ritsema, 'Graffiti in medieval and early modern religious spaces: Illicit or accepted practice? The case of the *sacro monte* at Varallo', *Tijdschrift voor Geschiedenis*, 131:1 (2018), 59–64.

Veronese, Angela, *Notizie della sua vita scritte da lei medesima* (Florence: Le Monnier, 1973), first published in 1826.

Vincent, David, *Bread, Knowledge and Freedom: A Study of Nineteenth-Century Working-Class Autobiography* (London: Europa, 1981).

Vincent, David, *Literacy and Popular Culture: England 1750–1914* (Cambridge, UK: Cambridge University Press, 1989).

Vincent, David, *The Rise of Mass Literacy: Reading and Writing in Modern Europe* (Cambridge, UK: Polity, 2000).

Yost, Israel A. S., *Combat Chaplain: The Personal Story of the World War II Chaplain of the Japanese American 100th Battalion* (Honolulu: University of Hawai'i Press, 2006).

Zadra, Camillo and Gianluigi Fait, *Deferenza, Rivendicazione, Supplica: le lettere ai potenti* (Treviso: Pagus, 1992).

Index

Aberdeen, Charles, worker 83, 85, 86, 93
Adams, William, Chartist 9
affective signalling 105–6, 114–16
Ahnert, Ruth, historian 32
Alaquàs, castle 22, 26, 32
Alcalá de Guadaira, castle 23
Alltagsgeschichte 122, 136n9
Altick, Richard, historian 2–3, 6
Annales school 2
archaeology 3, 14, 24
Archivio Diaristico Nazionale 7, 160, 162, 166, 167, 168, 172, 173
Artières, Phiippe, historian 6
Ascoli, Francesco, palaeographer 3
Ashley, Lord (Earl of Shaftesbury) 85, 94
Ashplant, Timothy 14, 15
Australia 8, 11, 16, 217–31
Austria 12, 65
autobiography 1, 4, 6, 7, 9, 10, 14, 48, 70, 83, 92–3, 126, 128, 159, 160, 161, 162, 164, 166, 168, 169, 170, 173
autodidacts 3, 128, 163, 173

Barcelona 7, 29, 36, 38
barefoot historians 122, 124–6, 132–5
Barnett, James, pauper 48
Barthas, Louis, cooper 7
Barthes, Roland 25
Bellver castle 34
Blincoe, Robert, millworker 83–7, 92, 93, 95
Böhme, Albert, carpenter 67
Bradford, George, pauper 55–6

Brandt, Deborah, literary scholar 121
Britain 3, 8, 9–10, 14, 23, 27, 28, 37, 45–60, 82–102, 116, 220, 221, 223, 225, 226, 227, 230
Broto military prison 26, 32
Brown, John, journalist 83, 84, 94

Carlile, Richard, publisher 83, 84, 94
Castillo Gómez, Antonio, historian 5–6, 14
censorship 16, 28, 29, 177, 195, 197, 198, 200, 201–5, 206, 207, 208, 211
child labour 83–7
Christian values 52–4, 182, 186
cinema 15, 159, 160–3, 168, 169–72, 173
clerics 25, 27, 125, 127–8, 223, 227
  US army chaplains 195–7, 203, 205–10
Coombes, Bert, miner 92–5
correspondence 2, 4, 5, 8, 9, 12, 13, 14, 15, 16, 67–8, 70–1, 72, 74, 79n31, 103–17, 126, 141, 142, 143–53, 163, 195–211, 217–31
  advocate letters 46, 50–1
  bowing letters 12
  'Dear John' letters 207
  forms of address and farewell 144, 145, 147, 150, 222
  with multiple authors 13, 48, 208
  with multiple recipients 209
  music in 15, 103–17
  pauper letters 4, 14, 15, 45–60, 68, 82, 91

correspondence (*continued*)
  rhetoric of affiliation in 219, 225–9
  rhetoric of apology in 219, 221–5
  supplication, letters of 218, 222, 229–30
  verse letters 7
Cortes Hernan 24
Covarrubias, Sebastián de 22
Cuthbertson, John, pauper 52

Davies, Margaret Llewelyn, feminist 89, 90, 91
Davies, William Josh, pauper 56
delegated writing 45, 47, 71, 149, 151, 196, 210
dialect 11–12, 15, 69, 72, 75, 167, 187
diaries *see* journals
Díaz del Castillo, Bernal 24, 30
digital humanities 16, 176, 190
divorce law 82, 87–91, 95
Dodd, William, worker 83, 85–7, 92–5

education 11, 48, 51, 121, 127, 128, 155
ego-documents 2, 3, 6, 67, 70, 128, 160, 172
  life writing as testimony 83, 85, 86, 87, 90, 94–5
Elspaß, Stephan 4, 12, 14
emigration 4, 8–9, 11, 12, 13, 14–15, 65, 68, 72, 74–5, 79n31, 103–17, 154, 172, 185, 204, 220, 223, 225
epistolary literacy 5, 12, 153, 220, 224

Fabian Women's Group 88, 89, 94
Fabre, Daniel, anthropologist 1, 6, 21
Farge, Arlette, historian 2
Finland 15–16, 176–91
First World War 7–8, 11, 12, 13, 160, 163, 170, 173, 199, 228–9
Fitzpatrick, David, historian 74
Fiume, Giovanna, historian 23, 25, 34
Fleming, Juliet, literature scholar 23, 28, 37
formulaic writing 12–13, 73, 74
Foucault, Michel 6
France 1, 6, 7, 8, 14, 26
Furet, François, historian 2

Gerber, David 14–15
Germany 8, 14, 65–77
Gibelli, Antonio, historian 172
Gimeno Blay, Francisco Miguel, palaeographer 22
Goody, Jack, anthropologist 6
Gothic script 26
graffiti 2, 4, 9, 13, 14, 21–38
  Christian symbolism in 32
Graheli, Shanti, book historian 3
grammar 11, 48, 72, 73, 74–5, 76, 149, 150
Grímsson, Sighvatur 122, 124, 125, 126, 131–3, 135
Guðmundsson, Tómas 130–1
Guichard, Charlotte, art historian, 23
Güntzer, Augustin, pewterer 67, 70

Hainhofer, Anna, widow 66
Hales, George, pauper 54
Hall, Joseph, author 28
Handcock, Benjamin, pauper 54
Hawkins, Robert, pauper 57
historical socio-linguistics 4, 12, 14, 65–77
history from below 1, 2, 7, 14, 65–6, 69–70, 71–6, 77, 161
history of the book 3, 5
history of reading 3
humanist script 26

Ibiza cathedral 30–2
Iceland 15, 121–35
Inquisition 14, 23, 25, 27, 29, 32, 34
Italy 4, 5, 7, 8, 10, 12, 14, 15, 22–3, 26, 28, 32, 36, 159–74

Jónsson, Halldór 122, 126, 127, 130–1, 135
journals 10, 24, 67, 70, 124, 126, 127, 128, 131, 164

King, Steven 14, 51, 229
Kropp, Michel Dominikus, hatter 67
Kuritus 177–86, 188–9

Lahire, Bernard, sociologist 6
Lang, Elizabeth, pauper 52
Lasinio, Carlo 22–3

Layton, Elizabeth, worker 89
Leeson, William, pauper 52–3
Left Book Club 92–3
Lejeune, Philippe 6
Lemp, Rebecca, weaver's daughter 66
Life, Mary, pauper 55
life writing *see* ego-documents
literacy 9, 16, 25–6, 45, 46, 47, 48, 49, 51, 56, 60, 61n17, 71, 117, 121, 122, 123, 125, 127, 128, 140, 160, 163, 177
  and race 141, 142, 150, 153, 155
López, Gerónimo, Jesuit priest 29
Lyons, Martyn 16, 60, 70, 199

Magnússon, Magnús H 124, 126, 135
Magnússon, Sigurður Gylfi 15
Mair, Hanns, bookbinder 66
Mairat, Paulus, weaver 66
Mallorca cathedral 27
Mannott, Catharina, farmer's wife 72
manuscript culture 3–4, 5–6, 15, 16, 122, 123, 125, 126, 127, 128, 129, 135, 176–91
Marchi, Clelia 7, 172
Martin, Joachim, carpenter 1, 11
Martínez Martín, Laura, historian 8, 13
Marxism 2, 196
Mass Observation Project 3, 6, 9–10
memory books 10–11
Menzies, Robert 11, 16, 217–31
Mitterrand, François 218
Moss, David 7, 15

new literacy studies 3, 15, 128–9
newspapers, handwritten 13, 15–16, 176–91
Nordic countries 14, 15
  see also Finland; Iceland

Obama, Barack 218
Olafsson, Davíð 15, 127
oral culture 3, 12, 45, 51, 133–5, 187, 190
  orality in the text 11, 14, 69, 70, 74
ordinary writings 1, 2, 4, 6, 9, 10–13, 14–15, 21–2, 37, 38, 46, 59, 66–8, 70, 72, 74, 75, 76, 77, 92, 103, 123, 128, 140, 142, 152, 153–5, 161

gender bias in 13, 47, 220
racial categories and 15, 154–5
rhizomatic networks of 123
unorthodox genres of 10–11, 152
see also vernacular literacy

palaeography 3, 5
  see also Petrucci, Armando
Palermo 23, 25, 26, 27, 32, 34
Parets, Miquel, tanner 7
Pearson, Hannah Berry, pauper 56–7
peasants 1, 7–8, 10, 11, 15, 121–35, 163, 172, 223
Petrucci, Armando 5, 25
poetry 58, 126, 127, 129–33, 182, 189
Poor Law 467–60, 60n2
postal services 7–8, 195, 197–200, 205
postcards 11, 199, 202, 219–20
Pouchet, Laurent, *vigneron* 8
Preis, Caspar, farmer 67, 70
Presser, Jacob 6
Price, John, pauper 52–3
prisons 6, 14, 22, 23, 25, 26, 27, 29, 30, 32, 33, 34, 36, 66
Pritchard, Violet, historian 23
punctuation 11, 15, 48, 146, 148, 149, 150, 164, 167, 224

Quatriglio, Costanza, film director 160, 169–71

Rabito, Vincenzo 4, 7, 11, 15, 159–74
Revista de historiografía 4
Ricci, Luca, archivist 166, 167
Robinson, Jennifer, philosopher 105, 114, 116
Rome 23, 28, 173
Rose, Jonathan, historian 3
Rowntree, Joseph 51
Russia *see* Soviet Union

St Miguel de Cruïlles 23
St Nicholas of Tolentino 34–6
St Sebastiano in Arborio 28–9
Salmi-Niklander, Kirsti 4, 15–16, 184, 186, 187, 188
Santangelo, Evelina, editor 166–7
Sarti, Raffaella, historian 23

Schechter, Brandon 16
Scotland 14, 46, 108, 113–15, 225, 227, 229
Scott, James C., anthropologist 219
scribes *see* delegated writing
Second World War 16, 163, 195–211, 228–9
Serventi, Eufrosina 5
Smith, Charles, pauper 58–60
soldiers 4, 7, 8, 9, 11, 12, 13, 16, 26–7, 34, 68, 72, 163, 172, 173, 195–211
  see also First World War; Second World War
South Africa 15, 140–55
Soviet Union 16, 195–211
Spain 7, 9, 11, 14, 21–38
Spanish Empire 14, 21–38
spelling 11, 48, 74, 146, 149, 150, 160, 167
Spitzer, Leo, censor 12
Spivak, Gayatri, literary theorist 10
Stanley, Liz 10, 15
Steel, Thomas 14, 15, 103–17

Tarazona, episcopal prison 25, 27
Ten Hours Bill 84, 85, 87, 94
Tepeapulco, Mexico 30
triangle letters 197, 199, 200, 201, 211

Trovador tower 26
Turunen, Risto 15–16

United States of America 16, 65, 72, 103–17, 121, 185, 190, 195–211
Urbino, ducal palace of 23

Valistaja 177–84, 186–9
Varallo, mount of 28
vernacular literacy 6, 11, 15, 121–35
Veronese, Angela 7
Victory Mail 197–9, 211
Vincent, David, historian 8
vítores 27, 30

Watson, John, pauper 49, 58
Women's Co-operative Guild 88, 89, 90, 91, 95
word separation 11, 146
workers 7, 9, 10, 14, 16, 26, 82–102, 127, 177, 182–3, 184–91, 223
  Factory Acts 82, 84
  unemployment 82, 91–4, 185
  women 87–91, 94–5, 189
workhouses 47–8, 49, 51, 52, 56, 58, 58–9
writing materials 11, 25, 28, 48, 58, 170, 171, 199, 200, 220, 224
writing upwards 16, 217–19, 223, 230

EU authorised representative for GPSR:
Easy Access System Europe, Mustamäe tee 50,
10621 Tallinn, Estonia
gpsr.requests@easproject.com

www.ingramcontent.com/pod-product-compliance
Lightning Source LLC
Chambersburg PA
CBHW052058300426
44117CB00013B/2188